Lonely Hunters

"My heart is a lonely hunter that hunts on a lonely hill"
—The Lonely Hunter,
Fiona Macleod (William Sharp), 1896

"Life," you say, "is a club . . . where they deal you only one hand and you must sit in. So even if the cards are cold and marked by the hand of fate, play up, play up like a gentleman and a sport."
—Miss Lonelyhearts, Nathaniel West, 1930

"What difference does it make? What do a few people matter—a few thousand people, black, white, good or bad? When the whole of our society is built on a foundation of black lies."
—The Heart Is a Lonely Hunter, Carson McCullers, 1940

"Will you still need me, will you still feed me, when I'm sixty-four?"
—Sgt. Pepper's Lonely Hearts Club Band, released in U.S. June 2, 1967

Lonely Hunters

An Oral History of Lesbian and Gay Southern Life, 1948–1968

James T. Sears

WestviewPress

A Division of HarperCollins*Publishers*

Published in 1997 in the United States of America by Westview Press, 5500 Central Avenue, Boulder, Colorado 80301-2877, and in the United Kingdom by Westview Press, 12 Hid's Copse Road, Cumnor Hill, Oxford OX2 9JJ

Library of Congress Cataloging-in-Publication Data
Sears, James T. (James Thomas), 1951–
  Lonely hunters: an oral history of lesbian and gay southern life, 1948–1968 / James T. Sears.
    p. cm.
  Includes bibliographical references and index.
  ISBN 0-8133-2474-2
  1. Lesbians—Southern States—History—20th Century. 2. Gay men—Southern States—History—20th century. I. Title.
HQ75.6.U52S687 1997
305.9'0664'0975—dc21   97-19782
                                                                          CIP

The paper used in this publication meets the requirements of the American National Standard for Permanence of Paper for Printed Library Materials Z39.48-1984.

10   9   8   7   6   5   4   3   2

Contents

Foreword

Jim Kepner

For American gays and lesbians, there was a vast gulf between the first and final years covered in this exciting volume. In 1948, the relatively open gay life that some found during World War II was being smothered in hetero-monogamous conformity, the national paranoia of the Cold War, and what would soon be called McCarthyism, except in the big coastal cities that many Southerners seeking anonymity had moved to. Girls might have "smashes" in school but were expected to date and marry, lest they become "old maids," fit only to teach school or be confined to an upstairs room as too ugly, unlucky, or disagreeable to find a man. Babe Didrickson, never dainty, was called a "morphodyte" because she excelled at "men's sports." Two tiny apologetic homosexual organizations in the United States that year disappeared almost without a trace. (There were several in Europe, even in Indonesia, but few of us knew of them.) A few individuals—Henry Gerber, Monwell Boyfrank, Dorr Legg, Harry Hay, Chuck Rowland, and myself—thought we should organize. Most couldn't conceive of such an idea.

Sexual Behavior in the American Male by Dr. Kinsey et al. sounded alarm bells, as did Gore Vidal's *The City and the Pillar* and Truman Capote's *Other Voices, Other Rooms*, but fewer than one in twenty homosexually inclined persons dared admit their feelings. Most literature on the subject was very negative. The press mentioned us rarely (mainly when hustlers murdered men they'd picked up) and in terms that only the worst homophobes now use. Gay bars were subject to constant police harassment and brutal raids. While a few half-openly gay teachers encouraged promising young students, as Sears describes, they were often victims of monstrous persecution—with no defenders. The vast majority lived in fear, guilt, and self-denial, and even those who were open usually believed we were sick or sinners.

En route from New York and Miami back to the West Coast at the lowest point in my life, I made my last brief visit to Galveston, little changed from my childhood days, except for a pink granite monument at the end of Broadway bearing the names of most of the boys and some girls in my high school graduating class. An old friend I ran into there with three obvious queens nearly fainted when I mentioned the word homosexual.

By 1968, our world had begun the shift that peaked in 1969 and 1970. Rock and roll, the rising counterculture, the civil rights and anti-war movements, and the Democratic Convention riot in Chicago had "the whole world watching." Three years before, I'd regretted my failure to leave my job, borrow money, and join the Selma march, as several of my friends had. National conferences of homophile organizations in Los Angeles, San Francisco, Denver, New York, Kansas City, and Chicago (Houston was proposed but canceled) had involved some forty small organizations and publications—three or four from the South. Gay militancy was rising. Some of us had begun to wear long hair, beads, and tie-dye T-shirts. The Los Angeles *Advocate* was becoming a national paper and the Metropolitan Community Church was launched. Several clashes between gay bar customers and police had previewed Stonewall. We were on the cusp of a revolution that would soon spread worldwide.

I was jealous when I began reading *Lonely Hunters*—the first published book of a project that will chronicle five generations of Southerners. The first sections here covered news I'd written about between 1954 and 1960 for *ONE Magazine* and the *Mattachine Review*—the story of Florida's great anti-gay witchhunt (my articles are being reprinted by Haworth Press as *Rough News, Daring Views*), but James Sears tells the Miami story better than I did and in greater depth. I had access to only a few clippings and disjointed reports readers sent in, a pressing monthly deadline for what was a spare-time unpaid job, a memory of two weeks in Miami, and the few Miami newspapers I could afford to buy each week on Los Angeles newsstands. Sears has dug deeper, told the stories more intimately. With only what readers sent in, I also reported other atrocities gays and lesbians suffered in Louisiana, North Carolina, and elsewhere in the South. I could rarely find newspapers from those places in the public library or on Los Angeles stands.

My longtime friend, the Reverend Flo Fleischman, was arrested in some of the Tampa and Miami raids I'd written about, which Sears covers. She has amazing tales about growing up butch in central Florida, traveling up and down the East Coast with hustling young queens, then getting into movement activism in Los Angeles from 1966 forward. Many gays and lesbians have given me widely varied accounts of gay life in that unhomogeneous area south of the Mason-Dixon line, including stories about the gay origin of the term *Dixie* and gay content of the song *Yankee Doodle Dandy*.

The South, they say, is a peculiar institution, and I used to say that east Texas, where I grew up, combined the worst of the South and the worst of the West. I spent most of my first 19 years in Galveston, a multi-ethnic but fully segregated shipping port and resort of then 55,000 people on the east end of a 30-mile sandbar facing the Gulf of Mexico. My adopted family partly resembled the peoples of Erskine Caldwell, William Faulkner, and Tennessee Williams, but these were writers I did not know until later. (In the city library, I was cruised by a man named William Faulkner, but not *that* William Faulkner, as he pretended to be.) I lived half my childhood in a fantasy world, between the Bible, Buck Rogers, Little Orphan Annie, tales of pirate Jean LaFitte, who'd built Galveston's first whorehouse and was said to have buried his treasure there, and the almost homoerotic novels of Horatio Alger Junior, which my favorite aunt sent each Christmas and birthday for my moral edification. The elegant old mansions on Broadway and the poorer section where I lived, beyond the African-American neighborhood, were sandwiched between the lusty commerce of Galveston Bay and the long, sandy beach, with the great seawall protecting the city from destructive autumnal hurricanes. After I finished high school, I was cruised a few times on that seawall, before I had any idea how to respond.

My father lost his job again just before I was about to start at Austin College at Sherman, Texas. At summer camp in Kerrville, I'd been converted to pacifism by a ministerial student from that small Presbyterian college. Years later, I heard that Jack, like half the students there, had been gay. I also was told that during the 1920s and 1930s, Galveston was one of the gayest cities in the country. I wish I'd known that at the time—but I wouldn't have been ready for it.

As a gay activist, writer, and teacher for the last 44 years, I've disliked the assumption that gay life and the gay movement are strictly bicoastal. During the 1950s, those of us active in the movement in Los Angeles, San Francisco, and New York did tend to believe that gays and lesbians didn't stay in what we called the hinterlands. In 1956 we began classes in gay studies at ONE Institute. "Homophile studies," the term we then used, did not have an apologetic slant that some have claimed. The term, used in Europe since early in this century, placed the emphasis on same-gender love rather than simply sexual activity—without trying to sweep sex under the rug. We worked hard to broaden our perspective from the bicoastal chauvinism that's still too common. We got letters from readers in Nashville, Midland, Memphis, and Baton Rouge who thought they were the only ones in town—and others describing wild gay parties. But incredible changes in Southern gay life were starting. Scholars such as James Sears are now filling in our history for regions that have been largely overlooked.

I find one important area missing in *Lonely Hunters*—though planned for inclusion in Sears's future work. The South has properly been classed as part of the Bible Belt, and religion has I think been more important, positively or negatively, to Southern gays than to those from other regions. Aside from the many gays who have felt rejected by, and in turn have rejected, the churches, at least half of gay life in the South certainly has been and is in the churches, as much as in gay bars. Every major city has long had at least one Episcopal or Catholic church and an African-American church or two that were unofficially called "the queen's church," drawing gays and lesbians who were never deep in hiding. The first meeting I know of to challenge police persecution of homosexuals was in a Miami Unitarian church in 1952. While many gays turned their backs on the churches because of homophobia, yet even in homophobic churches there are gays in the pews, the choir, and the pulpit who somehow find ways, positive or not, to resolve their religious and sexual urges.

Like many gay movement pioneers, I carried from my Texas childhood a commitment to justice for African-Americans and Latinos (a recent term) as well as for sissies and tomboys. I marched for African-American civil rights before gay marches seemed likely in this century. I wrote in July 1960 about the need for developing a gay vote. In the late 1960s, in the North American Conferences of Homophile Organizations, we Westerners, joined by some Southerners, pushed a broader view of gay goals; for example, advocating homophile education, the developing of community institutions, and the enriching of our culture, rather than focusing only on law reform and litigation, important as those are.

With far too much of published U.S. gay history still focused on three pivotal cities, I feel sure that we will soon see rich gay histories from many individual and unique Southern cities and regions, from Natchez to Mobile (which carried Mardi Gras to New Orleans), Austin (a center of early gay liberation), Corpus Christi, both Charlestons, Pensacola (from super-homophobic to a virtual gay resort), down to the hidden chronicles of many small towns and rural areas. Sears has made invaluable contributions to the job of finding psychological roots for Southern gays, claiming our part in Southern traditions that are not purely heterosexual. As our movement expands and diversifies worldwide, making ever new gains and facing ever new crises, we need to understand and honor those multicultural heritages that have fed the world-encircling river of gay life.

Acknowledgments

FIRST AND FOREMOST I THANK all those who consented to be interviewed for this project, particularly those who consented to taped interviews, allowing them to be permanently archived in my collection of papers housed at the Special Collections Library of Duke University. Additionally, I am indebted to Jim Kepner and Barbara Gittings, both gay activist veterans during the era covered here, for their thoughtful comments in the Foreword and Afterword. I also want to thank Gordon Massman, who as senior editor at Westview demonstrated the vision and commitment to secure the contract for this book, Jill Rothenberg, who ably shepherded the book into the production process, and John J. Guardiano for his careful copyediting. I also want to acknowledge Walter Williams, who arranged for my appointment to the University of Southern California during the fall of 1994, which allowed me time and access to resources in launching this project.

Thanks are also due to the following libraries for the use of their facilities: International Lesbian and Gay Archives, West Hollywood, California; New York Public Library, Manuscript Division; Lesbian Herstory Archives, New York City; Special Collections Library of Duke University; Florida State Archives, Tallahassee; University of North Carolina Oral History Program, Chapel Hill; Stonewall Library, Ft. Lauderdale, Florida; Metropolitan Community Church Archives and Library, Houston, Texas.

Additionally, I would like to thank particularly Ginny Daly at Duke University, John O'Brien and Pat Allen of the International Lesbian and Gay Archives, and Tina Murray of the Florida State Archives.

I gratefully acknowledge the following persons or organizations for granting permission to use photographs included in this volume: Florida State Archives; Merril Mushroom; Jack Nichols; the Special Collections Library of Duke University; Dawn Langley Simmons; and Sue Sponnoble. Also, I acknowledge the following for permission to quote from previously published or archival material: Julia Penelope Stanley; Southern Historical Collection, Library of the University of North Carolina, Chapel Hill; Dawn Langley Simmons; Jack Nichols; and Merril Mushroom.

A number of students worked as paid research assistants on this project: Patrick Barrett, Bill Briggman, Gabriel Chang, Mark Grant, Bill Evans, and

Ian Palmquist. Other persons who provided resources or suggestions to this volume are Ed Fojo, Catherine Nicholson, J. Dan Marshall, Sheila Morris, Jack Nichols, Judy Sullivan, Sue Sponnoble, and, of course, Bob Williamson.

James T. Sears
Christmas, 1996
Key West, Florida

Introduction

WE COME TO KNOW OUR PLACE within the world through the stories we hear and retell. Our images of lesbians and gay men are shaped by stories learned from school, family, and community. These communal stories develop and become authorized versions of how lives were lived and parables on how we should live our lives. Documenting, writing, and reading narratives of *our* communities provide lesbians and gay men with a collection of sacred, communal stories that for too long have been lost or devalued in the larger canon of heterosexist history—presented to us as fact.

During the past dozen years, an impressive volume of gay and lesbian history has emerged. These groundbreaking works have provided new insights about the construction of sexual identity, illustrated novel approaches in historiography and oral history, chronicled a long-forgotten history of a queer nation as it struggled for visibility, respect, and equality, and forged a culture against the onslaught of homophobia and heterosexism.[1]

Regrettably, gay history, like the movement itself, has had a bicoastal bias. If you were to rely on the many books found in lesbian and gay bookstores, you would assume that the South was irrelevant to the contemporary lesbian and gay movement. Even in the post-Stonewall histories, Southerners have been marginalized; the ways in which we and past generations have authored our lives have been ignored. While we can read about the emergence of the homophile movement in a southern California living room or its radicalization at a Greenwich Village bar, the pivotal roles of Southerners in these and other events are untold stories.[2]

This book documents Southern gay history and culture during the Cold War/pre-Stonewall era. Most of the people who narrate their stories were born between 1932 and 1945: between the inauguration and death of Franklin D. Roosevelt, between the discovery of the neutron and the detonation of the first nuclear bomb, between Amelia Earhart's first solo flight across the Atlantic and the election of the first woman U.S. senator, between the publications of Erskine Caldwell's *Tobacco Road* and Tennessee Williams's *The Glass Menagerie*.

This book may require you to bracket taken-for-granted understandings about the South or gay men and lesbians. Avoiding presentism, I wish neither to "out" the rich and famous nor to award the gay label to people lacking such an identity. Here I seek neither to glorify the Stars and Bars

I

nor to demonize Dixie. This book, like my earlier work, *Growing Up Gay in the South*, speaks through a cacophony of Southern voices: Richard Inman, a soldier of fortune turned taxi driver challenging the homophobia and ignorance of heterosexuals as well as apathy and timidity among homosexuals; Merril Mushroom, a quiet Jewish girl turned rowdy lesbian; Quinton Baker, a tactical African-American leader of the North Carolina civil rights movement; Rose, an "old school" lesbian who came of age at a time when little division existed between gay men and women and the "L" word was disdained; Arlen, a deeply closeted senior citizen whose memories of his daunting encounter with Charley Johns of the Florida Legislative Investigation Committee have long shaped his political outlook; Dawn Langley Simmons, a transsexual who pushed the boundaries of race, class, and gender in Tidewater society; Jack Nichols, a wide-eyed poet-anarchist who was in the vanguard of the East Coast homophile movement.

During the homophile era,[3] lesbian and gay Southerners began to transform themselves as well as the South after what oral historian Studs Terkel has called "the good war." Men and women were anxious to return to the normalcy of prewar life: marriage and families; movies and malt shops; factory worker and homemaker; the family automobile and nylon hose. Although in hindsight such a view may appear hopelessly romantic, it was the zeitgeist of postwar America. The "good war," though, had already sown the seeds of transformation in Southern society. Men and women stepped onto the foreign shores of Normandy and Wake Island or the Charleston Naval Yards and Birmingham Steel. After V-E and V-J Days, women dutifully returned from the factory floor to the kitchen and to their role as caregiver while men reoccupied those jobs, resuming their task as wage earner.

The economic independence experienced by blue-jeaned women on the line and the cultural diversity experienced by male-bonded men in uniform could not be so easily forgotten. Some women and men never returned to their homes—homosexual Southerners discharged into the ports of San Francisco and New York City, working-class women relieved from their factory jobs but remaining in the workforce, African-Americans refusing to accept the indignities of second-class status after fighting against fascism—and many who did return would soon find that both they and their communities were already undergoing change.

With the United States unchallenged as a military and industrial superpower, the world saved from totalitarianism, and the benevolence of Uncle Sam in lavishing federal benefits on its millions of stalwart soldiers, postwar Americans—at least the European-American middle and upper class—saw a future of social tranquillity and economic promise in a land insulated from the factionalism that had destroyed Europe: Norman Rockwell illustrations on covers of the *Saturday Evening Post* and the publication of Benjamin Spock's *Baby and Child Care*; the comforting music of Big Band leaders and crooning singers like Frank Sinatra; David Lean's film *Great Expectations* and William Wyler's *The Best Years of Our Lives;* as well as the technological innovations of xerography, the transistor, and the long-playing record.

In the postwar South, most families still lived in small communities or in rural areas. Main Street was lined with mom-and-pop businesses: the barbershop and beauty salon, the bank and bakery, the grocery and granary. In communities crossed by Confederate Avenue, Jefferson Davis Boulevard, and Calhoun Street, social as well as geographic divisions existed. Most towns and cities had their "wrong side of the tracks," variously populated by the working poor and people of color. Each person understood her or his role, largely invisible in everyday social life, defined against the taken-for-granted symbols and rituals of Southern life: the flag and the Bible, Confederate Memorial Day ceremonies and barbecues, Southern Baptist and Colored Methodist Episcopal steeples, azalea festivals and Little Miss pageants, the courthouse square and the county fair, "colored" and "white" facilities.

Ephemeral mainstream culture was found in innocuous pop music like "Davy Crockett" and "The Chipmunk Song," the nostalgic plays of Rodgers and Hammerstein or Lerner and Loewe, escapist pulp and science fiction, and short-lived fads such as ponytails and panty raids, the samba and cha-cha, hot rods and hula hoops. Perhaps these reflect a desire of the postwar generation to escape from the hard decisions and decisive actions confronted by the elected—support the *Brown* ruling or endorse White Citizens' Councils—or the electorate—support the Dixiecrats or challenge the Klan.

For Southerners born between the Great Depression and World War II, the Cold War and the civil rights movement were their generational anvils. Aliens—be they from Mars or Moscow, Washington or Fire Island—were poised ready to invade the South. There was the revival of the Fighting South as Fidel Castro assumed power ninety miles off the Southern shores, Strom Thurmond led the segregationist charge of the Dixiecrats, and a fellow senator, Harry Byrd, revived the pre–Civil War doctrine of nullification. The "New South" reemerged, too, in a quest for measured racial progress with the moderating voices of the *Atlanta Constitution*, Florida Governor LeRoy Collins, and the Reverend Martin Luther King Sr. This was an era ending in fear, uncertainty, ennui, and misanthropy.

In the span of a generation, however, Southern society and Southerners' self-image would alter as people clinging to small-town certainties felt assaulted by a revolution in politics, popular culture, technology—and sexuality. This generation witnessed the widespread use of air conditioning, fast-food dining, and interstate highway travel abridging Southern summer idleness, down-home cooking, and distant relatives. The defining icon of this generation's popular culture, rock and roll—an irritant to many older Southerners—grew from Delta blues, country, and Caribbean music, producing rock and roll innovators like Jerry Lee Lewis, James Brown, the Everly Brothers, Fats Domino, Buddy Holly—and Elvis. By 1968 the transformation of the South and its image of itself was nearly complete. George Wallace's American Independent Party captured four of the five Deep Southern states along with Arkansas, and the rest of the South (except Texas) voted Republican.

Insular and inward-looking in their thinking, homosexual Southerners would also undergo a change that would only become obvious a generation later. Yet the underlying stress of a queer Southern life was already apparent to the homosexual citizen-artist. Homosexual muses James Baldwin, Ralph Ellison, Jack Kerouac, Lorraine Hansberry, and Allen Ginsberg were among the lone voices crying outside in the cultural wilderness. They were joined by Southerners like Truman Capote, Carson McCullers, and Tennessee Williams.

These artists' rendering of sexual and moral ambivalence, though, was in odd juxtaposition to the black-and-white television world. There were big game shows like *Tic Tac Dough* and *The $64,000 Question,* in which anyone could be transfigured into someone by separating right from wrong responses (with a little help from the show's producer). As compulsory heterosexuality began in earnest, the Anderson, Cleaver, and Nelson homes became standard cultural fare. As uniformed officers and detectives enforced discriminatory laws against homosexuals amid growing charges of police corruption, posses deputized by the incorruptible Wyatt Earp and Matt Dillon banished villains. And amid growing racial tension and confrontation, the peculiar all-white Southern communities of Mayberry and Petticoat Junction sprouted across the television dial.

These two gay decades began with the groundbreaking sexual studies of Alfred Kinsey, extended through the pioneering research work of psychologist Evelyn Hooker, and culminated with the publication of Vance Packard's *The Sexual Wilderness.* They bridge the pulp novels of Ann Bannon with Village sit-ins. Reading *Lonely Hunters,* you will dance on the 22nd Street Beach, suffer at the hands of faceless accusers and white angered mobs, descend into the netherworld of hustlers and murderers, learn about corrupt politicians and covert operatives, and experience the transformation from infatuation to love, from man into woman, and from childhood through old age. In the process, you will come to know pugsy Merril, adventuresome Jack, shy Rose, articulate Quinton, terrified Arlen, troubled Dawn, and covert Richard.

Southern Mindscape

In reading these life stories you will enter states of mind as well as the "mind of the South." These appear against the tokens, places, and events encrusted in the Southern cultural bedrock: gumbo, mint juleps, and okra; the *Dred Scott* decision, the Scopes trial, and the Scottsboro Boys' imprisonment; belles and bubbas, Georgia crackers, and Big House mammies; demagogic politicians and devil-haunted preachers; *God's Little Acre* and *Tobacco Road;* football and stock cars, kudzu and azaleas, root doctors and conjurers; Yoknapatawpha, Harden, and Hazzard Counties; Uncle Remus and Johnny Reb, We Shall Overcome, and Dixie.

The mind of the South is also evident in Southern gay or bisexual archetypes: the tomboyish Molly in *Rubyfruit Jungle,* the timid Celie in *The Color Purple,* the Amazonian Miss Amelia in *The Ballad of the Sad Café,* the deaf-mute John Singer in *The Heart Is a Lonely Hunter,* and the heroic Idgie in *Fried Green Tomatoes.* There is also the passive mutilated Ollie in *One Arm,* the onetime high school football hero, Brick, in *Cat on a Hot Tin Roof,* and the distant intellectual Miguel Chico in *The Rain God.*

Mythmaking also mirrors the Southern mindscape. Scarred by war, pestilence, and poverty, defined by Reconstruction and desegregation, Southern mythology has long been intertwined with Southern history: the Cavalier legacy, the Fighting South, the Lost Cause, the Nativist South, the New South, the Benighted South. The Southerners' distinctive view and others' toward Southerners extends far back into history. The Cavalier Legacy of the Old South, for example, emerged during the second and third decades of the nineteenth century. As great debates raged over permitting slavery in new states, the federal government's power to impose tariffs, and Nat Turner's slave rebellion, the oratory and philosophy of John C. Calhoun saturated the South. Championing states' rights and defending the "peculiar institution" of slavery, Calhoun celebrated a new Southern consciousness. With the advent of the War for Southern Independence and the enduring burden of Reconstruction, this legacy was seared onto the psyche of future Southern generations.

Proud of the South's ideals and customs, many white Southerners today consider themselves Confederate nationals first and Southerners second. Ours is a collective memory of an idyllic past captured in Gothic architecture, mythic history, and romance literature: the founding of Jamestown and Charles Town, the firing at Fort Sumter and the defense of the Alamo, and the writings of Mark Twain, William Faulkner, and Thomas Wolfe. Ours is a land of plantations turned corporate farms under siege for most of remembered history: Cornwallis, yellow fever, abolitionists, hurricanes, Sherman's army, carpetbaggers, the boll weevil, White Citizens' Councils, pirates, daylight savings time. Our cultural geography includes beauty pageants, debutante balls, and drag shows; Confederate monuments, museums, and widows; Burma Shave and Jesus Saves signs; and Southern Baptist fortresses guarding against the isms: multiculturalism, ecumenicalism, communism, secular humanism. . . .

But there is also the less celebrated Southern history witnessed in the family albums and chiseled in the black, brown, and red faces of its minority populations. Ours is a history of struggle, defeat, and celebration: the African slave trade and the Trail of Tears; the flight from Havana and the march from Selma; lynchings and broken treaties, freedom riders and migrant workers; Denmark Vesey and Robert Smalls, Sequoyah and Sojourner Truth; the reservations of the Cherokee, Seminole, and Choctaw, the ghettos of the inner cities, the barrios of the Southwest; the Afro-Caribbean rhythms of salsa, the syncopation of ragtime, the poetic harmonies of the blues, and the black and Creole-influenced Dixieland jazz. Our cultural geography includes "colored" and "white" signs hung near water fountains; Charleston ironwork and Tuskegee architecture; Memphis's Beale Street and Atlanta's "Sweet Auburn" Avenue.

These distinctive images of the South are well captured on film. Portraits of Southern blacks figure in the *Song of the South* to *Mandingo* and non-planter whites in *Showboat* and *Huckleberry Finn*. There is also the Nativist South, with its distrust of modernism, unionism, and urbanism, aptly captured in *Norma Rae* and *Inherit the Wind*. Images of the Benighted South and its social class and racial disharmony flicker in cinematic moments of *Birth of a Nation, Roots,* and *Cool Hand Luke* and images of the Cavalier South in *The Fighting Coward* and *Gone with the Wind*.

Out of the Shadows

Like the concept of the South, homosexuality evokes multiple images. We cannot talk about "gay men and lesbians" in a cultural and historical vacuum. As historians, anthropologists, and sociologists have documented, every society includes persons who engage in same-sex behavior. How that behavior is viewed by the larger society and by those who engage in it varies widely: the Greeks of the classic age who freely practiced intergenerational sex and those workers in modern Brazil who quietly engage in "solidarity sex"; the Afro-American religions where spirit possession and same-sex relationships coexist and the elevation of women and men with "two spirits" to shamanesque positions; the practice of same-sex marriages such as in West African Dahomey or the tantamount admission of such in "Boston marriages"; the normative classification of the specific sexual positions leading to sexual binaries such as straight/gay, butch/femme, active/passive.[4]

The homosexual concept, like the South, also is fraught with ambiguity and contention. How could one be "gay" or "homosexual" before such concepts were invented? Clearly, the language to describe those who love in a manner "that dare not speak its name" has evolved: Sodomite, urning, invert, homophile, fairy, uranian, pervert, homosexual, bull-dagger, dyke, faggot, queer, gay. This evolution attests to changes in how others view the act of loving the same sex: sinful behavior, psychological deformation, criminal activity. It is also a testament to how we view ourselves: from uranian romanticism of the nineteenth century to homophile assimilationism in the 1950s, from identity politics of "gay power" to its deconstruction with "queer studies."

Shadowy sexual relations and elastic gender behaviors, of course, are Southern hallmarks. There are many stories of same-sex relationships or gender crossing. Women disguised themselves as men in order to soldier, and male Confederate prisoners of war dressed for "prison balls." In his 1888 memoirs, Philip Sheridan recalls two "Amazon soldiers" in Tennessee—one a teamster in the wagon-train division and the other a cavalry private who developed "an intimacy"; only through a drunken encounter with "apple jack" were they exposed. There was also Annie Hindle, the first male impersonator of the American stage, who performed at Broome's Variety Theater in Memphis immediately after the War of Northern Aggression. The object of many "mash" notes from female admirers, Hindle married another woman, Annie Ryan, escorted by Gilbert Saroney, a female impersonator.[5]

There are also noted examples of same-sex relationships between gentlemen. There was the wealthy planter turned U.S. senator, William Rufus DeVane King, who served as Franklin Pierce's vice president—and James Buchanan's longtime companion; the presumed relationship between John Laurens, a South Carolina legislator, with Alexander Hamilton; and, of course, correspondence chronicling the South Carolina college sexual relationship between "withering bedfellows" James Hammond (who later served as governor, congressman, and senator) and Thomas Jefferson Withers, one of the founders of the Confederacy.[6] The sexual politics of intrigue was evident in the vice president of the Confederacy, Alexander H. Stephens, a former Georgia congressman and governor, who, "lacking the virility of other men," later found consolation in his sponsorship of nearly a hundred men through college.[7] There are also less celebrated cases of the poor and minorities who languished in prisons or asylums for "crimes against nature" and the 1909 Kentucky trial of two African-Americans whose charges for engaging in oral sex were dismissed by a frustrated judge who could find no statute for conviction—a problem quickly remedied by state legislators.[8]

In future work I plan to present diverse narratives spanning the "gay nineties" of Gilbert and Sullivan, cold cereals, and Vogue to the millennia-cusped nineties of cloning, Andrew Lloyd Weber, and thrash metal. Some of the people whose stories are told lived in the sprawling New South cities of Houston, Atlanta, and Miami, others in the Old South towns of Charleston, New Orleans, and Durham. Through the century, too, some of the narrators enjoyed the surface tranquillity of the small towns bordering the bayous, sandy banks, and river mouths of the Coastal Plains, blanketing the mountains of the Great Smokies, the Blue Ridge, and the Ozarks, or dotting the hill country and grassy prairies of Texas, where Southern, Western, and Mexican cultures meet. These narratives portray the lives of lesbian and gay Southerners against the panorama of Southern and gay twentieth-century history and culture. These narrators also document the sometimes changing though never invisible markers of skin color, social class, and gender as they intimate changed sexual identities across five Southern generations.

Through the eyes, voices, and memories of these Southern generations, you will witness an evolving understanding of sexuality and sexual identity. In the first generation you will encounter Laura Bragg, the first female director of an American scientific museum and a leader in the Charleston literary renaissance, who enjoyed romantic friendships with women. During the teens and twenties she mentored young artists and helped to establish a literary salon that included DuBose Heyward, Beatrice Ravenel, Hervey Allen, and Josephine Pickney. She also greeted luminary visitors such as Sarah Bernhardt, Tallulah Bankhead, Gertrude Stein, Edna St. Vincent Millay, and Vita Sackville-West, and she displayed a lifelong special affection for Miss Helen McCormack and short-lived friendships with Belle Heyward and the enigmatic homosexual artist, Edward I.R. Jennings.

Among the second Southern generation you will learn of the innocent days of "chumming" and "smashes" as well as the college-girl crushes experienced by North Carolina feminist Catherine Nicholson during the Great Depression. You also will read from the World War II correspondence of John and Edwin, whose forty-years-plus relationship includes Edwin's lifelong friendship with Carson McCullers and John's onetime Washington roommates, "Jeb and Dash."

In this book, Merril, Rose, and Jack narrate distinctive life histories during the postwar era when bar harassment and fear of exposure crossed with parties at which songs and camp filled the ocean air. Here you will also experience the terror and intrigue of McCarthyism as Penny, Arlen, and Susan face surreptitious surveillance, unnamed informants, intense interrogation. This volume also chronicles the twin struggles for freedom and justice among African-Americans sometimes allied with white homosexual Southerners.

Emerging from the countercultural, antiwar, women's rights, and civil rights movements, the fourth generation highlights 1970s Southern activists who helped to transform the homophile movement into gay power: Southern émigrés channeled their energies into the founding of the first nationwide weekly for homosexuals, *Gay*, and the lesbian-feminist publication, *The Furies*, as well as the formation of the Los Angeles Gay and Lesbian Community Center and the Metropolitan Community Church. Others chose to remain in or return to the South: RFD and the Radical Faeries, which settled at Tennessee's Short Mountain; Integrity, which was established by a Southern gentleman who dared cross racial boundaries that others trespassed only in the steamy stillness of the night; lesbians and gay men who exercised unparalleled Texan political muscle; women who amplified their voices through the publishing efforts of *Sinister Wisdom* and *Feminary;* and the oppositional activism spawned by the infamous Save Our Children campaign of Anita Bryant.

Finally, GenXers are bracketed by the discovery of the human immunodeficiency virus (HIV) and the *Hardwick v. Bowers* decision and the steel-like determination at Camp Sister Spirit and *The Real World.* This generation is challenging the old order on its own terms: the courage and conviction of AIDS activist Pedro Zamora; the "gay-straight" North Carolina high school group, the Enloe Six; an emerging third wave of gay liberated cities with charming façades and deep-seated homophobia; a cadre of Southern lawyers and activists effectively challenging long-standing sodomy statutes; and an emerging group of gay Southern entrepreneurs confronting the old order in cyberspace.

As you read across these generations of queer Southern life, I suggest two questions for your consideration. Without the South, could the modern homosexual movement, as we know it, exist? How are sexual attitudes and identities related to regional cultures, generational personalities, and individual histories?

Traveling Across Time

Political scientists and historians interested in cultural and social change have defined *social* generations as groups of people who travel together through time and share a unique perspective that shapes their cultural understanding and civic role.[9] Unlike *biological* generations, which proceed from parent to child, social generations evince what sociologist Karl Mannheim termed *mentanite*—a particular view of social reality reflected in a generation's unique personality and shared identity. These generational personalities, or to borrow a phrase from the Spanish intellectual José Ortega y Gasset, "pulsations of historical energy," are evident in the "transcendental generation" of Walt Whitman, the "lost generation" of Djuna Barnes, and the "beat generation" of Allen Ginsberg. Each generation's personality is forged on the anvil of a coming-of-age social event (e.g., abolitionism, World War I, the Great Depression) and, as Ortega y Gasset observed, it is this "small minority of minds in the vanguard, alert souls who glimpse untouched areas in the distance" who serve as "the pivot responsible for the movements of historical evolution."[10]

Since the founding of Jamestown, there have been seventeen "gay" generations of Southerners.[11] Supported by rice, indigo, tobacco, and cotton, the South was "settled" by British aristocratic planters and merchants, Scotch-Irish farmers, Spanish missionaries, Cajun refugees, Caribbean immigrants, and African and West Indian slaves. Among these immigrants were our homosexual ancestors who participated in and contributed to the Southern legacy. In the arts, our ancestors' bequests range from the musical compositions of W. Grant Still (the first African-American to lead a major symphony orchestra) to the plays of Tennessee Williams, the stories of Carson McCullers, and the blues of Bessie Smith. Other contributions include antilynching, suffragette, and civil rights activists like Lillian Smith, Ellen Glasgow, and Angelina and Sarah Grimké. Our ancestral presence also extends onto the bloody battlefield, inside the corporate boardroom, within the crowded classroom, and in the smoke-filled courthouse. We also must acknowledge the complicity or complacency of some of our less illustrious ancestors who squandered or abused natural and social resources as well as those who profited by waving the bloody shirt or offering Mr. Jim Crow a helping hand.

Across the five Southern generations of this century are distinct generational personalities and individual histories that become most apparent in contrast to one another. Alice Mitchell's turn-of-the-century trial for the murder of her lover, Freda Ward, and the Texas publication of the novel *Norma Trist* as well as a southern folk ballad[12] based on that trial, stand in stark contrast to the coming-of-age novel *Rubyfruit Jungle*, the radical pamphlet "A Gay Manifesto," and the quarterly magazine *Sinister Wisdom* from this century's fourth generation of Southerners. Similarly, leaders of the homophile movement such as Jack Nichols, gay personalities such as Jackie Jackson, and popular culture such as that reflected in *The Boys in the Band* of the third generation appear remarkably staid when compared with Pedro of *The Real World,* the Cracker Barrel protesters, or the entrepreneurial cyberspace founder Bill Pinyon of badpuppy.com.

Several generations, of course, meet at the juncture of any given era. Some homosexual Southerners are in childhood or adolescence, others are enjoying the freedom of early adulthood or the responsibilities of midlife, and a few are tending to their golden years. Consequently, each volume tells stories of different generations who live through a common era. Their stories reflect similarities and differences in attitudes and behaviors, visions and fears, struggles and triumphs.[13] This volume captures the voices of a distinguished professor, eighty-eight-year-old Arlen Davies, dismissed from the university in 1959 for being homosexual, and that of lesbian lawyer Rose Levinson, now approaching retirement and reconsidering her long lesbian silence. These narrators stand in sharp contrast to the focused energies of movement activists Jack Nichols and Pat Cusick, the youthful transgressions of Julia Penelope and Merril Mushroom, and the tactical keenness of Richard Inman and Quinton Baker—all born a generation or two later.

Of course, in a culture in which social class, gender, sexuality, and race matter, differences also exist among individuals who are born within the span of a decade or two.[14] In our era, these differences appear in the disruptive protests of Atlanta's ACT UP (AIDS Coalition to Unleash Power) and the quiet lobbying efforts of the North Carolina Log Cabin Republicans. In this book these differences are reflected in the priority of liberation struggles distancing Pat from Jack and those separating lonely hunters like Richard and Quinton from lonely hearts like Dawn and Arlen.

In the brief span of five generations, we have gone from the love that dare not speak its name to Queer Nation, from *Norma Trist* to *Front Runner*, from "physique" magazines to Calvin Klein ads, from tearooms to cyberspace, from *Better Angel* to *Angels in America*, from "gay is good" to "silence equals death." Through diaries and letters, newspaper headlines and television documentaries, personal reminiscences and soulful reflections, this book begins your journey across a century of the Southern gay experience. As you continue to read from one volume to the next, you will come across familiar faces and meet new characters, visit different cities and view changed landscapes. Across them you will find people who conform to Southern gay icons—the gentleman town queer, the white-trash tomboy—and those who don't—the sleuthing gay patriot, the Jewish lesbian activist—all described against the panorama of Southern culture and gay history.[15]

I

Purging Perverts in Paradise

The 22nd Street Beach, Coupon-Clippers, and the Tongueston Trio

THE MONDAY EVENING FLIGHT FROM BOSTON to Miami was uneventful for Eastern Airlines steward William T. Simpson. Despite the heavy promotion of the summer air-hotel package, the aircraft was hardly full and his duties were light. As the twenty-seven-year-old served passengers, he was buoyed by after-work thoughts: Leon & Eddies, the Onyx Room, Biscayne Boulevard. Passing down the aisle, he caught a glimpse of the *Miami Herald*'s headlines for August 2, 1954: "New Attack in Asia Means War, U.S. Says"; "Good News: Food Prices About to Dip"; "'Bill of Particulars' Bolsters Move to Censure McCarthy."

Walking off the plane in the sultry evening air, he hurried toward the airport's parking area humming "Life Is But a Dream." "Plans for tonight?" asked stewardess Dorothy Hoover as he passed. Bill quipped in his Kentucky drawl: "I got an important date. Can't be late!"

Bill had shared a downtown house since April with another bachelor, Jim Perry, also an Eastern Airlines steward. Occasionally "the boys" would throw dinner parties for stewards and stewardesses, but there was "no carousing around." Bill was driven home from the 8:55 P.M. flight by fellow steward Harold Schaffer. Although Schaffer now lived around the corner from Bill, they had roomed together for two years in Coral Gables. Schaffer found Bill's mood to be "jovial" as the two talked about cars during their fifteen-minute ride downtown.

After borrowing a key from his landlady, who knew him as a "nice quiet boy," Bill showered, changed clothes, and then left around ten. As he pulled his yellow 1950 Chevrolet convertible onto the city streets, his thoughts floated freely. How long ago was it when he spotted that advertisement in the Louisville newspaper's travel section sponsored by the Miami tourist bureau advertising hotel discounts for "unattached males" to better "balance" the male-female vacationer ratio? On a lark, he visited Miami. Upon his return, he quit his trainee's position at Standard Oil and joined Eastern Airlines in 1951. His "visit" to Miami was now in its third year.

Cruising down Biscayne Boulevard, Bill tuned to WQAM. The voice of Johnny Mathis crooned over the AM airs as the bay breeze caught Bill's hair. Passing Leon & Eddies, a gay bar located near Biscayne and Ninth, he spotted a teenager with a thumb out on the corner of 23rd Street. Circling around the block, Bill caught a second—and longer—glimpse of the young man: thin, muscular, wavy blond hair, long pants (a tight ass), and a plaid shirt. He pulled up to the curb about a half a block down and tilted his head in the boy's direction.

"Need a lift?"

"Sure!" Nineteen-year-old Charles Lawrence jogged to the car.

As they moved away from the curb, the hitchhiker and the bachelor began their courtship of conversation. Meanwhile, a green '47 Chevy coupe lumbered around the corner onto Biscayne Boulevard, following the convertible at a discreet distance.

Bill began. "Where're you headin'?"

"Nowhere particular."

"Oh?" Bill's brownish eyes slowly caressed the young man's dimpled face and muscular chest. They missed the recently purchased Beretta lodged in his left boot. "Well, I'm just driving around myself. I have a date later tonight. How about a Coke?"

As the twosome pulled away from the drive-in, their conversation moved to fishing. Charlie turned to Bill. "So what are you into? Maybe we can check out some fishing spots around Arch Creek."

Bill headed north along U.S. 1 to a deserted rutted road near Arch Creek known as "Lovers' Lane."

By the mid-1950s these deserted areas were rapidly disappearing. Miami was developed in the 1890s, largely through the efforts of Henry Morrison Flagler, a financier and cofounder of Standard Oil. He extended his East Coast Railroad from Jacksonville southward, built the Royal Palm Hotel, and dredged the harbor.

At the height of its land and construction boom in the mid-1920s, one acre of Miami property was priced higher than the entire city had been in 1917. Paper profits climbed astronomically as "binder boys" sold property for a mere 10 percent down payment. During that same five-year period, the

Miami Police Department jumped from 40 officers to more than 350 as Police Chief H. Leslie Quigg recruited Georgia cracker plowhands. In 1926 buyers began to default on their payments, and, coupled with a devastating hurricane in September, the boom collapsed: Land that sold for $600,000 at the beginning of 1926 could be bought at the end of the year for $600.

Despite the economic slowdown, scores of Art Deco buildings were erected during the 1920s and 1930s. Gambling and prostitution became widespread in Miami and Miami Beach. Al Capone (later to be followed by Meyer Lansky) moved to south Florida, joining its Bahamian rumrunners and running speakeasies, protection rackets, political bribery, prostitution and juke joints, wire services, and slot machines. A generation later, little had changed.

As Bill's left hand edged beneath Charlie's shirt, the other fiddled with the young man's trouser zipper. The sound of waves crashed in the background.

Twenty-year-old Lewis Killen turned the ignition off as his Chevy coupe rolled down a bit farther along the rutted road. He stopped the car. Grabbing a .38 caliber revolver, he stealthily moved from gravel pile to gravel pile. As he crept toward the yellow convertible, Charlie's harsh voice cracked over the waves. "Give me your money!"

Bill was in shock. He had heard of beatings and robberies at Bayfront Park. Last year a man was murdered by a marine and a sailor whom he had picked up at a "notorious homosexual hangout." These nineteen-year-old servicemen had been drinking throughout the day. "Defending their honor," they bludgeoned the man and tossed him into the bay to drown. But that happened to other people, people who weren't careful, people who weren't like him. . . .

Bill awkwardly passed Charlie twenty-five dollars. "Don't waste my time! Empty your pockets. Give me your watch, your car keys, and that faggoty silver cigarette case in the glove compartment."

As Bill reached into the glove compartment, Charlie slammed it. Writhing in pain, Bill looked up at the dimpled-faced adolescent now holding a Beretta and standing outside the convertible. "Get out, faggot."

Twenty-five feet away, Lewis saw the white flash of gunfire as it pierced the darkness. The splash of car keys followed the sound of gunshot.

"Let's split," Charlie instructed as he walked swiftly past Lewis. "We got what we came for."

Moans rose through the night air. The pain was wrenching, but Bill summoned his strength to pursue his attacker.

"Head toward 151st Street," Charlie directed. He carefully wrapped his weapon as Lewis raced the engine.

Bill momentarily lost consciousness. Awakened to the distant shouts of his assailants and a Chevy coupe speeding away, he peered into the depth of the night sky. The stars began to dim. Everything went black.

After driving about a mile along the starlit bay, Charlie stopped to bury his weapon on the shore. "I'll come back and get this when the heat's off." Around midnight, a couple walking along Lover's Lane looked down to see by the moonlight scarlet-colored sand and a contorted body nearby: the head gashed, the right index finger split, ribs shattered by gunshot, clenched hands filled with loose sand and dirt. A deputy sheriff called to the scene found William Simpson's body about 500 feet from his convertible and a .22 caliber casing on the car's bloodstained carpet.

Incarceration and Consolidation

The Sheriff's Department's investigation quickly determined that the victim was a "homosexual" living in an "organized colony" of "500 deviates presided over by a wealthy, socially prominent man."[1] After a series of newspaper stories, "hundreds of tips," and the questioning of several suspects who fit the criminal profile, North Miami police used "dogged police work" to trace the Beretta automatic pistol after tests determined that it was the murder weapon. Six days after the murder, detectives questioned and then arrested two Tech High School graduates: nineteen-year-old Charles W. Lawrence, a Bell Telephone stockroom worker, and Richard Lewis Killen, a onetime supermarket bag boy. According to police, Simpson had been caught in a hitchhiking scam where "adolescent delinquents" thumbed down homosexuals, often submitting to sex before robbing their victimizer.

The number of robberies and murders had risen along with the tenfold increase in population since the 1920s. In 1954 the county's population was nearly 600,000 (within six years it would spiral to nearly one million). Unlike other Southern cities, however, Miami failed to expand its area through annexation.

"Greater Miami" was twenty-six quarreling municipalities. These included Miami Beach, with its "Millionaires' Row" along Collins Avenue, the designer communities of Miami Shores, surrounded by poorer cities, and Coral Gables, hugging the south Bay. The county's second largest city, Hialeah, was a working-class community of cheap bungalows and trailer parks under the influence of political bosses whose racetrack and zero property tax attracted heavy industry and workers. Thirty miles to the south was rapidly growing Homestead, with its new huge Strategic Air Command base.

Overlap and duplication were as rampant as lust for political power and easy money. Twenty municipal police departments protected the metro area along with the sheriff (who employed fourteen investigators for county vice operations and robberies and another six for homicides). Then there were state law enforcement agencies such as the State Beverage Department, which had only three plainclothes enforcement officers to "watch" the area's 6,500 bars and nightclubs.

Political loyalties, forged on the basis of personal relationships, seldom extended beyond municipal boundaries. With few exceptions, such as the 1930s era of "Little Tammany," when Miami was controlled by Daniel Mahoney, publisher of the *Miami News,* and Senator Ernest Graham, or the 1940s, when Commissioner Charles Crandon, owner of a wholesale drug company, cast a wide political shadow over the county, municipal politics was a free-for-all. By the mid-1940s, unable to fill "Big Daddy" Crandon's shoes, I. D. MacVicar, the new head of the five-man Board of County Commissioners, quickly ran afoul of the *Herald.*

In 1945 John Pennekamp of the *Miami Herald* successfully pushed for the consolidation of the county's ten school districts. Buoyed by this success, he launched a campaign for county consolidation in his influential column, "Behind the Front Page." By September 1953 Pennekamp had moved into the local political vacuum. The *Herald* began its relentless pounding of the County Commission for its secretive meetings, unanimous voting patterns, questionable awarding of contracts, and related Port Authority scandals. In the midst of these unfolding stories and rising circulation, the *Herald* crusaded for municipal county consolidation that would abolish the city of Miami and radically restructure county government. Three years later, all five incumbent commissioners were swept out of office, and the voters approved a more moderate form of metropolitan government the following year.

Throughout the 1950s local politicians and community leaders were locked in this bitter struggle over consolidation. Those opposed included almost every county and municipal official and employee, most of the municipal Chambers of Commerce, and some local newspapers. Miami Beach, which contributed a disproportionate share of the area's tax base and had considered forming its own county (Miami Beach enforcement wanted more control over its vice operations and income from graft rather than sharing it with the Sheriff's Department), opposed consolidation. So did Hialeah, whose longtime mayor, Henry Milander, feared loss of influence.

Supporters of county consolidation (the Metro-Dade plan) were led by Miami's reform-minded Jewish mayor, Abe Aronovitz, who was well aware of the city's declining industrial and commercial base and its dwindling proportion of county population. Other supporters included the Dade delegation to the Florida legislature, the Miami-Dade Chamber of Commerce, and the two major newspapers.

In the midst of this feudal battle among municipalities, local officeholders, and the newspapers, Richard Lewis Killen and Charles W. Lawrence awaited trial. At the murder scene with investigators, Lewis nonchalantly tossed rocks into a nearby lagoon as Charlie relayed his version of events.

Freely admitting to the murder of Simpson, he claimed "self-defense" against "improper advances." With boyhood innocence, Charlie claimed: "We didn't mean to hurt him. But we had to protect ourselves."[2]

The arrests and upcoming trial attracted newspapers' attention throughout the fall. The youths—and even their families—appeared more and more as victims than as a robbery duo on trial for first-degree murder. Charlie's working-class parents, who lived in a "pleasant white tree-shaded bungalow" near 131st Street, were too devastated to speak publicly. Donna, Lewis's tearful bride, sold her car, which lacked only two more installments, in order to hire Lewis's lawyer (the car payments had been made from money earned by the boys' "partyin' with homosexuals"). A pregnant Donna vowed: "I won't desert him. . . . He still just looks like my honey."[3]

As the duo neared their day in court, a *Herald* reporter wrote, "The trial in addition to showing the guilt or innocence of the youthful pair may well turn into an exposé of Miami area perversion."[4] Stories about sexual perversion crowded the headlines: "5,000 Here Perverts, Police Say"; "Warning for Miami: How L.A. Handles Its 150,000 Perverts"; "Clean This Place Up!" "Ordinance Would Kill Pervert Bars' Permits"; "Stiff Laws Urged on Perversion"; "Hypnotist Offers to Help Deviates."[5] Donna Killen, the petite teen bride with auburn hair, moaned to a reporter, "Why don't they clean this place up? . . . You can ask any kid from any school and they'll tell you if you want money, just go down to Bayfront Park. . . . " Living in a cramped kitchenette apartment, the bride of four months lamented: "Louie always read his Bible. Louie didn't plan it. He was only in on Charlie's racket that one time."[6]

In court a witness contradicted Killen's police statement, swearing that he saw Lawrence frequently hitchhiking in the area, with a green Chevy trailing those unsuspecting motorists who picked him up. At the trial, a sheriff's deputy testified that at the time of his arrest Lewis admitted that "the two youths had been 'robbin'' and rollin' perverts' for approximately five months."[7]

Following the three-day trial, which climaxed with tearful testimonies from each boy, a twelve-man jury deliberated four hours on a November Sunday morning before settling on a verdict of manslaughter. Questioning members of the jury, a *Herald* reporter concluded that the "principal reasons for the lesser verdicts . . . were the alleged homosexuality of Simpson and the state's failure to prove premeditation." Quoting one juror who had held out for a second-degree murder conviction, the reporter wrote: "The youths' accusations of homosexuality against Simpson 'made a big difference' in the jury's thinking."[8]

On Wednesday, November 10, the two were sentenced by Circuit Judge Grady Crawford to twenty years in prison. In pronouncing sentence, the judge took the unusual step of announcing that "the record of the trial was such that it would support a first-degree murder conviction."[9]

Patronage and Politics, Perversion and Corruption

A year before the witch-hunt in Idaho against the "boys from Boise,"[10] the *Miami Daily News* launched a series of articles and investigative reports on the "homosexual menace," placing heavy blame on the inability or unwillingness of various law enforcement agencies to eradicate it. Roused by the Hearst-like reporting of the *Daily News*, the city's competing morning newspaper, the Knight-owned *Miami Herald*, printed related, though more restrained stories charging that the "shoulder-shrugging by police is the cause of Miami's reputation as a comfortable haven for homosexuals."[11] Headlines blazed across the two dailies: "$200,000 Outlay Urged for Center to Treat Deviates"; "Police to Harass Pervert Hangouts"; "Johns Names Aide to Fight Perverts."

Local politicians with ambitions for higher office or hopes of discrediting opponents in the Metro-Dade battle quickly initiated a highly publicized crackdown. The full force of federal, state, county, and municipal power was unleashed. Police vigorously enforced vagrancy laws, fined owners of "homosexual hangouts," and arrested "femmics" (female impersonators); judges committed "sexual psychopaths" to the State Mental Hospital at Chattahoochee and sentenced homosexual felons to stiff prison sentences; politicians conducted hearings, drafted new ordinances and legislation, and criticized opponents for being soft on deviates.

Like most Southerners, many Miamians were concerned with communism, integration, corruption—and perversion. In 1954 the army television hearings led by Senator Joseph McCarthy were in the news, as was the Supreme Court's groundbreaking decision declaring an end to "separate but equal" education, to be implemented with all "deliberate speed." Southerners—already in a frenzy over McCarthy's allegations of communists in government, the Warren Court's judicial activism, and the political stirrings of the National Association for the Advancement of Colored People (NAACP) and the Congress of Racial Equality (CORE)—voiced their support for the purge of communists, Negroes, and homosexuals or simply remained silent.

Though the Florida Ku Klux Klan, active since the 1920s, never assumed the powerful role it did in other Southern states, Miami was very much a part of the Old South: segregated schools and separate drinking fountains, lynchings and bombings. Blacks sat at the rear of Miami buses; beaches, parks, and sporting events were strictly segregated; and there was only token integration of public schools. Many beach hotels and restaurants integrated only during large conventions. Lena Horne, for example, who played frequently at the Clover Club on Biscayne Boulevard, found no accommodations at nearby whites-only hotels. Compared to other parts of the South, however, Miami African-Americans had a higher standard of living and could register and vote without difficulty—although less than one-fifth were registered, and their vote constituted only 6 percent of the electorate. Though Florida entered the Union as a "slave state," south of its cotton-growing counties, such as Leon, Jackson, and Gadsden, Northern sentiments ran strong. Absent a dominant planter class, state politics was largely a free-for-all. This was an era of powerful county officials, demagogic state politicians, "pork-chop" appointments, and gutter-level politics between individual personalities. Candidates who were to meet with success in their quest for state office had to appeal to Dade County, which had one-fifth of the state's voting population. If elected, however, they would have to deal with a "pork-chop" legislature dominated by rural counties (e.g., 15 percent of the state's voters elected the majority of the legislature, because of inequities wherein a house member in a rural county such as Glades represented 2,200 voters, whereas a member in Dade represented 165,000). Further, although the governor could not succeed himself, six members of the elected cabinet could and often did hold successive terms extending over twenty or thirty years, with their tenure terminated by divine, not electoral, intervention. The patronage power of these political barons was felt throughout the state.

In May 1954, acting Governor Charley E. Johns, a former railroad conductor from the rural town of Starke and leader of the dominant group of "pork-chop" state senators, won a hard-fought three-way Democratic primary race. In those days winning the Democratic primary was tantamount to winning the election. However, Johns failed to receive a majority. In a runoff primary election he went head-to-head with reform-minded Senator LeRoy Collins. Already known as the "voice of the New South," Collins won in part because of strong support from the voters of Dade County.

At the time of the Simpson murder and the subsequent purge of perverts, Johns was in the midst of a political battle to adopt county-unit voting, giving each the same weight—effectively disenfranchising urban-based counties like Dade. Under such a plan Johns would have won the spring primary. Decrying the "gambling and vice in certain counties," Johns used the Simpson murder and its aftermath of queer baiting as an opportunity to undermine his opponents.[12]

The system of patronage and politics within county and municipal governments was similar to that at the state level. There was little party control, all elected officials ran as Democrats, often serving many years in office, and the spoils system controlled government jobs and contracts. Mayoral candidate Abe Aronovitz, a cantankerous former Jacksonville lawyer with a reputation for integrity and honesty, promised to bring an end to the era of grafting politicians and corrupt practices. To win office, however, he needed the support, first and foremost, of the *Herald*, then of the *Daily News*, and finally of business and professional leaders. He assumed the mayorship in 1953 and was quickly locked in a corruption battle against powerful local politicians such as Sheriff Tom Kelly and Police Chief Walter E. Headley Jr.

The Simpson murder and the newspaper headlines that followed, disclosing Miami as a deviate Disneyland of juke joints, drag queens, and cruising grounds, presented the opportunity to link perversion and corruption to the powerful police chief. Following one city commission meeting, Commissioner Randall Christmas reported "rumors" of payoffs to police by homosexuals and operators of downtown spots catering to them, and another city commissioner, H. Leslie Quigg (a former Miami police chief), warned, "We are just opening the gates to these people when national magazines carry stories that Miami has a lenient policy toward them."[13]

The mayor put both the city manager and the police chief on notice. Vacillating, City Manager Arthur Evans (who had been vacationing in Canada at the time of the Simpson murder) pledged to "throw the book at these places." The city commission gave its police sweeping power to "arrest and re-arrest operators" of gay bars and nightclubs for "every violation police can find."[14]

Before Chief Headley could return from his Labor Day vacation in Tennessee, Evans phoned him to finalize arrangements for the purge. Headley had long "tolerated" a few gay bars where deviates could be "watched."[15] Aronovitz accused him of promulgating a policy that was an "open invitation for perverts to come to Miami. . . . We cannot become known as a place filled with perverts, crackpots and lewd characters. . . . If the chief can't do it, we ought to get a new chief."[16]

Upon his return, Headley issued a public statement in response to the mayor's criticisms:

> Before the war, we had some trouble with perverts in Bayfront Park, but during and immediately after the war . . . I thought all the homosexuals in the country had decided to move down here. . . . We began arresting them and charging them with vagrancy, but we couldn't make the charge stick, because they had good jobs. We finally decided it was better to allow them to congregate in a few places where they were tolerated. It was about the same as localizing an infection.[17]

Headley also issued a veiled warning. Should the mayor and the city commission demand that he run "all the homosexuals out of town, members of some of the best families would lead the parade"—including those at City Hall.[18] Allegations that leading political and business leaders in the greater Miami community either engaged in clandestine homosexual conduct or had family members or close friends who were homosexual were also leveled in a locally published pamphlet: "The Miami vice sleuths have been checking—oh so discreetly!—among Florida State University [FSU] grads who form a politically and economically powerful segment of local life. This requires infinitely greater discretion than chasing out the drifters who wafted into town from L.A. and from Fire Island. . . . With the locals a mistake could cost any plainclothesman his promotion."[19]

The Purge of 1954

Chief Headley promptly formed a special squad—known variously within the department as the "Powder Puff Brigade" and the "Fruit Pickers"—to work the lunchrooms and coffee shops like Neal's, the hotel bars and clubs like the Charles Hotel and El Morocco, and cruising areas such as Bayfront and Simpson Parks, the Greyhound bus station, and Burdine's Department Store. Beginning September 2, 1954, a dozen or so bars, ranging from Leon & Eddies to the Club Echo, were raided nightly—sometimes twice a night. Because of the immense prepublicity, of course, the raids yielded few arrests, as many bars closed or, like the parks, were deserted: One bartender was arrested for a "noisy jukebox," two for serving an underage marine, another for serving a "drunk"; four arrests for vagrancy were made at Bayfront Park.

Other local law enforcement agencies also participated in the "purge." The officers of Dade County Sheriff Kelly and Miami Beach Police Chief Romeo Shepard raided bars, swarmed parks, and plucked suspicious swimmers from the 22nd Street public beach.[20] On Friday, August 13, Shepard's beach raid was "executed with all the advance planning and secrecy of an amphibious landing." Thirty-five "men who act like girls" were questioned; six were charged with disorderly conduct for failing to give a "good account of their reasons for being in Miami Beach." According to Shepard, some of these men sported "bikini" swimsuits that were "little more than a strip of cloth fore and aft" ranging from "shocking pink, and daring cerise to a leopard skin pattern."[21]

That same evening eleven four-man squads of Sheriff Kelly's deputies, armed with "accurately drawn floor plans," orchestrated midnight bar raids "to show perverts they can't set up housekeeping in Dade County."[22] Of the fifty-three patrons interrogated, nineteen, including a "fighting bar maid," were taken to County Jail, booked, examined by a health officer for venereal disease, and interviewed by a psychiatrist. All but two were released the following Monday, each on $500 bail.

Arrest and harassment extended also to lesbians as well as to people of color. During that first week of September, for example, at one bar six women were arrested, questioned, and then released. In the adjacent county of Broward during the same month, two men—one black, one white—were sentenced by Criminal Court Judge William T. Kennedy. In separate incidents, both had admitted to engaging in "unnatural sex acts." The white man was tried and convicted on a vagrancy charge by "reason of being a lewd and lascivious person" and sentenced to thirty days in county jail. The African-American, described by the solicitor as an "animal," was sentenced to fifteen years in the state prison.[23]

Justice for those with privileged backgrounds was different. For those who could afford legal representation (before the landmark 1963 Supreme Court case, *Gideon v. Wainwright,* which originated in Florida, provided such a guarantee for all offenses), the charges against them were often reduced or dismissed and their sentences lightened. In one morals case a prominent man hired a sitting city judge and a former assistant county solicitor to represent him. The head of the vice squad, John Sorenson, voiced his frustration: "We've arrested people in all walks of life; doctors, lawyers . . . and once an important judge. . . . He was whitewashed through the grand jury, and this man now is back in his social circle. He's back in his church, reading the Scriptures every Sunday from the pulpit. *And we know he's a homosexual!* . . . "[24]

In the mayor's heavily publicized effort to "break up the more brazen of the sex deviates' hangouts," new city ordinances multiplied. One made it a misdemeanor for any bar knowingly to allow two or more "perverts to congregate at one time" or to serve homosexuals alcohol, thus permitting the State Beverage Department to revoke the bar's liquor license. These ordinances were coupled with previous ones, such as the prohibition of men dressing in women's attire ("femmics"), and gave wide latitude to the enforcement of the more than two dozen vagrancy laws. The Dade County legislative group also drafted state legislation to toughen the crimes-against-nature statute, extending imprisonment to twenty years and confining "sexual psychopaths" to the State Mental Hospital at Chattahoochee.

Political support for the Miami cleanup was also forthcoming from Tallahassee. George A. Brautigam, elected state attorney in 1952 with dreams of becoming governor, pledged cooperation: "We are going to use every constitutional means at our disposal to rid the city of these people." His determination to ferret out queers was equal to his dedicated efforts to uncover Reds a few years earlier. Then, as the congressional army-McCarthy hearings neared their climax, Brautigam led a Miami witch-hunt summoning 138 witnesses—135 of them Jewish. In a process that showed little apparent concern for the Constitution, those pleading the Fifth Amendment were jailed without bail.

Acting Governor Johns, who assumed the post when the popular and youthful Dan McCarty died in office, became directly involved as well. On September 7, 1954, Johns named Miami attorney Morey Raymen (who was also a member of the boxing commission) to "coordinate Miami's campaign against perverts," helping, as he wrote in an open letter to the mayor, "to clean up this situation . . . and assist your office in the eradication and control of sex deviates."[25] Raymen, though, articulated a more cautious tone: "Embarrassing questions asked of law-abiding citizens could give the city a bad name and false arrests could lead to expensive court actions."[26]

Johns further directed the Crime Commission of Greater Miami, under the direction of Daniel P. Sullivan, to investigate corruption, perversion, and gambling. Seven years earlier the "secret six" (the two newspaper publishers and the presidents of several leading businesses) had hired Sullivan to investigate "America's winter crime capital." A year later he became the Crime Commission's first director. Sullivan's position on homosexuality was widely known. In 1953 he publicly pronounced that "Greater Miami had become a gathering place for sex degenerates," making a connection "between the open operation of such bars and nightclubs with reported cases of child molestation."[27]

The purge of 1954, then, was not a simple manifestation of homophobia but part of the larger political milieu in which the homosexual became a convenient whipping boy for aspiring politicians and corrupt officials as well as useful political fodder for proponents of municipal consolidation. The purge, however, marked a turning point in Miami's history of general tolerance of drag queens and its benign neglect of homosexuals. Throughout the 1940s, for example, the famous Jewel Box Revue had featured Miamian Jackie Jackson in its female impersonator shows sprinkled with comedy acts and chorus boys. Years later Jackson recalled: "The bar [which was originally opened at the Embassy Hotel in 1938] was gay, but the club, which was a separate room, was strictly, strictly straight. It was a beautiful room, with a 1,600-pound chandelier hanging overhead. . . . There'd always be many bigshots in the audience, and every opening night, Danny and Doc (the owners) would have all the local commissioners ringside. Danny used to bring them upstairs after the show to meet us."[28] Jackson, in fact, performed at the 1948 Policeman's Ball, receiving a police escort accompanied by sirens. But, then "everything blew up. . . . "

With the election of reformers to the County Commission in 1955 and the passage of the metropolitan government plan the following year, the fears among old-timers like Sheriff Kelly and Chief Headley and the goals of the mayor and newspaper editors were realized. The new Metro county manager and commissioners soon bypassed Kelly and Headley by establishing a Public Safety Department and transferring all law enforcement duties and powers to it. The county manager then announced the appointment of Daniel Sullivan as the new public safety director.[29]

The purge of 1954 also played as important a role in the fledgling homophile movement as in the lives of individual lesbian and gay Southerners. The editors of ONE magazine, which had been excoriated by politicians and the press, understood the nationwide importance of this highly publicized crackdown. These events proved to be the cutting teeth for the emerging movement. Years later Jim Kepner, who wrote *ONE*'s "Tangents" column, observed:

> These were really formative events in our consciousness of how to deal with this subject politically. Since then, of course, our movement has made many of its greatest advances on reactions to attacks. But we learned from events in Miami. The Miami ordeal pushed us towards greater militancy. It pushed us towards the idea that the chief purpose of *ONE* was to confront situations like that, to publicize them, and to demand justice.
>
> At that time, a lot of the attitude in the Mattachine Society was that you don't demand. You ask people to help you. We pushed the idea of demanding—demanding rather stridently. The Miami purge brought out for me several questions. For example, "Do homosexuals have the right to gather in bars that are publicly licensed places and still have a degree of privacy?"

Meanwhile, with bond denied Charles Lawrence and Lewis Killen, the Florida Supreme Court overruled Judge Crawford, granting their insolvency affidavits and ordering that their appeals for the manslaughter conviction be made at the state's expense. Within a year their appeals had been denied as they continued to serve their prison sentences.

William T. Simpson was buried in Louisville, the home of his uncle, with whom he had lived after his return from the army.

Rose, Merril, and Jim

In the midst of these media-whipped, politically motivated, and government-led efforts to purge perverts from city life, a new generation of homosexual Southerners, like Jim Patterson and Merril Mushroom, were nearing adulthood; Rose Levinson had just crossed over that threshold.

In 1950 Rose Levinson moved to Miami—the city that postmarked its outgoing mail "The Closest Thing to Paradise We Know"—to begin college. Although she had been raised in New York City, her family visited Miami every winter season. Some relatives already had moved south. "When I was eight years old I decided I was going to move down here as soon as I grew up. So when I came, I never left."

History is full of ironies. Developers, like Indianapolis Speedway founder Carl Fisher, had built Miami Beach as a gentile alternative to the "Jew-ridden" Atlantic City. On the southern tip of Miami Beach, however, the Lummus brothers, developers with less personal capital, had welcomed Jewish money, resulting in the first Jewish-American settlements south of Fifth Street. Following the land bust of 1926, local realty agents were more willing to sell properties in other parts of Miami Beach. As the Depression ended, there was a small but vibrant community of 5,000 Jewish-Americans networked by two synagogues, delicatessens, and a private Hebrew school.

Anti-Semitism, though, was still prevalent. Many beach hotel brochures in the 1930s included a warning that accommodations were reserved for "Christian Gentiles." Although large hotels like the Floridian, the Fleetwood, and the Wofford had no such restrictions, some hoteliers were less tactful, with "No Jews" warnings placed at registration desks or outside signs reading: "Every Room with a View Without a Jew," "Oceanview, No Jew," and—at the gatepost of a 43rd Street apartment hotel—"Gentiles Only. No Dogs."

At the time of Pearl Harbor, 40 percent of American Jews, including the Levinsons, lived in New York City, and many others were scattered in cities like Chicago, Boston, Cleveland, and Philadelphia. Following the war, Los Angeles and Miami were the major destinations for Jewish migration. The year Rose moved, about 650 Jews were migrating each month to Miami, and the Jewish population had already increased sevenfold. By 1955 there were nearly 100,000 Jewish residents in the Miami area. Unlike many of the white Southern and rural emigrants to Dade County, most of these newcomers, like Rose, came from large metropolitan areas in the Northeast, helping to distinguish Miami Beach for its relative liberalism.

"When I came down at seventeen, I knew I was gay—that was the *only* word we used. 'Lesbian'"—pausing as to clear her throat—"was such a clinical word." Leaving her New York girlfriend of three years, Rose bumped into Laura on one of the first days of the University of Miami semester. The couple soon agreed to share an apartment along with two heterosexual women who were aware of their relationship. Rose explored Miami's bar scene with Laura.

A petite girl with short brown hair combed back into a "duck's ass" (DA), Rose, like most "butches," wore pants on their bar visits, and Laura, the "femme," a skirt with a blouse. Though only eighteen, Rose gained easy admittance with a doctored driver's license and a knowing wink from the bartender: "At Collins Avenue and 15th Street was the Charles Hotel bar. This was a girls' bar. Although you would see a gay man coming in and out, these were often the more flamboyant ones. The gay guys I knew from school wouldn't go to these bars; these weren't fun for them. The problem for me was there were too many butches." Rose remembers occasional police bar raids before the 1954 purge.

> Sometimes they raided two or three bars a night. There was the Pan American bar, a second-floor "private club" on northwest First Street in downtown Miami. In the spring of 1951 Laura and I had become friendly with an artist and a hairdresser. These two gay men suggested that we and a couple of other friends go out for the evening. That seemed really great! But our apartment had a weekend curfew of eleven-thirty for girls. So "Uncle Doug" signed out for me.
> When we arrived we walked up the stairs. One of the boys knocked on the door. It opened. Everyone was lined up with the men separated from the

women. The place was filled with police! I had just turned eighteen and so I quickly grabbed ahold of my "Uncle Doug." The officers told us to stand against the wall. There were eight girls in that bar, one of whom was the daughter of a high Dade County official.

We stood there as the police questioned everyone. Since we had just walked in, they weren't going to charge us with drinking but with "vagrancy." Under the vagrancy law if you didn't have at least $100 in your pocket (this would be like walking around with a thousand dollars today!), they could pick you up and hold you for seventy-two hours without allowing you to make a telephone call.

The paddy wagon arrived. We were put inside and brought to the jailhouse. On the twenty-fourth floor Laura and I were separated and put into interrogation rooms: "What were you doing at the Pan American bar?" "Why were you there?" They told me they hadn't decided yet if they were going to report this to the university. I knew I was in deep trouble if they did; I would be expelled. After several hours they let us out without charging us.

After her visit to jail, Rose just "kept my eyes open more. You wanted to be sure that the bar was paying off the police. I paid more attention to where I was going, to know the bar owners, and to trust the women who ran these bars. These bars, I think, were not owned by individuals (or at least not by any legitimate individual) but by the Mafia."

Jim Patterson is three years younger than Rose. In 1935 Jim's mother traveled to her mother's home in Brunswick, Georgia, not far from the Sea Islands and from Sidney Lanier's "Marshes of Glenn." After Jim was born, they returned to their Miami home. He remembers going with his family to the 22nd Street Beach during the war. "Oddly enough, my parents were the first to take me to what turned out to be my first gay beach! Dad had a laundry route and worked on the beach. I returned there often in high school, hanging out at the snack bar near the pavilion and looking at the good-looking men and women."

Active in student council and drama at Miami Jackson High, Jim did not know that he was gay. He dated, double-dated, went steady, and did lots of "heavy petting. . . . But it wasn't an era where there was a lot of sex going on among boys and girls." Jim was known for his skill as a debater. He won the state championship in his junior year, placed in the upper quarter of those attending the national debate tournament in Boston that summer, and attended Northwestern University's High School Debate Institute. Finishing first there, he was offered a scholarship at Northwestern.

As Jim entered his high school senior year, across the causeway Merril Mushroom was beginning her first year at Miami Beach High School, where Jewish families had replaced the gentile families of a decade earlier. Jewish students often socialized among themselves in a patio area know as "LJ" (Little Jerusalem). Most of the teachers, though, were gentile, and the influence of Christianity pervaded the high school as it did other schools in the county: a required five minutes of daily Bible reading (generally from the New Testament), and Christmas and Easter celebrations.

Not fitting into the "popular set," Merril turned the collar of her blouses up to be "real cat," wore tights, smoked, and hid her brunette eyes behind sunglasses. At school she hung out with the motorcycle group, for whom James Dean was "the be-all and end-all," and with the Girls' Athletic Association (GAA) composed of "sporty girls" with a strong undercurrent of lesbianism. She reminisces:

> I was hanging around the gay girls and guys a good bit of the time, maintaining I was "straight." We didn't use the "L word" back then; it was one of the dirty words. At Beach High, there were the sporty PE lesbians who hung together. There was also a flamboyant student, Eddie, a drag queen who was very popular; a lot of kids who were coming out followed his lead. There was an undertone of being "cool" at the school, which meant not getting too academic or condemning those things that were real outrageous—being gay was certainly outrageous. Some of the kids even went to the 22nd Street Beach!
>
> At high school, you had to be either butch or femme. The role models we had for coupling were male/female heterosexual images with no alternative lesbian and gay role models. At first, I wasn't sure, so I became a "ki-ki"—meaning you could be either. But some of us thought in our hearts that anyone who was ki-ki, like my friends Dotty and Joan, was *really* either butch or femme. The advantage of being ki-ki was that you could go with someone who was either.
>
> I soon rejected that, though. It didn't feel right. Being a femme equated too much to being a girl: weak, lacking privilege, and unable to do what you want. The destiny of being a wife, a mother, a teacher, a servant to a man never appealed to me. Who the hell wanted to do that? By being butch I could swagger and strut; I could be abrupt and assertive. I wore my hair in a DA with a flattop. When I went to school I combed it into a brush-up so it looked vaguely feminine. I also wore men's clothes—since I was big, they fit me better than women's clothes.
>
> I read the *Well of Loneliness*. Of course, *The Ladder* had just gotten started. But that was really not accessible to us because we were just kids. Most of us didn't know how to get a copy of the magazine even if we would have had the courage to do so. But we knew the names: Daughters of Bilitis, Del and Phyllis. This kind of stuff was the height of radical. We were all so closeted and it was so illegal to be queer. You could be put in jail, put in mental hospitals!

Jim Patterson, eschewing Northwestern, went off to the University of Florida in Gainesville in the fall of 1953. College had a profound impact on the young Patterson. During his first year he dated girls, contemplated marriage, and experienced sexual intimacy with a sorority girl. He soon realized, though, that heterosexuality was not his lot in life. "This was the first time, at a conscious level, I knew that I clearly preferred men." Pledging Delta Tau Delta fraternity, he recalled:

I knew I had a great deal in "common" with them—two or three of the fellows who rushed me were gay! They became open with me—surprisingly so, when you think about the times. By trading our secret there was a bond that grew among us. We became very close, personal friends; I've kept up with them all through the years. We often talked about the difficulties in being homosexual. Clearly one led a double life, a secret life which at the age of twenty-two seemed quite exciting.

Jim Patterson remembers reading Gore Vidal's *The City and the Pillar,* in which Jim Willard, a rugged Virginia youth, first finds love on a camping trip with his high school buddy, Bob. Joining and then deserting the navy, Willard journeys to Hollywood and then to New York in his search for his onetime lover. Finally he runs into Bob and then strangles him in a seedy hotel (in the original version, Willard rapes him). First published in 1948, it "was exactly like all of the other literature. If you're gay, you're bound to lead a miserable life that ends in suicide." Despite its hapless ending and the failure of any gay men to find fulfillment, Vidal's virile portraits attracted young Patterson. While Merril worshipped James Dean, Jim thought that Montgomery Clift—the most promising of the postwar actors, earning an Oscar for his 1953 performance in *From Here to Eternity*—was sexy. "There also was lots of talk that popular figures like Clift and Johnny Mathis were 'probably' gay."

Through his fraternity group, Jim met a charismatic professor who was gay and "took a great deal of interest in me—and that interest was not sexual." Professor Arlen Davies fit neither the failed nor the effeminate homosexual image. Davies encouraged Jim to pursue graduate study and introduced him to the world of culture, ideas, and men. Davies was one of the humanities lecturers for the common core of liberal arts courses that all students took during their undergraduate career. "I remember to this day his lecture on the Greek temples and another about the opera *Il trovatore.* After that lecture I felt I could and should go to the opera!" Now a drama professor, Patterson further recollected: "My roommates, Jack and Fred, and I were very close. We had dinner at Professor Davies's house regularly—which was very uncommon even in those days. There were always a few students and a couple of professors—they weren't sex orgies!—for a pleasant evening of fellowship where we talked about all sorts of things: the university, current events, the arts."

The Courts of Justice and Public Opinion

While Patterson was in Gainesville, the *Miami Daily News* returned to pervert bashing in February 1956 with a series of articles entitled "Profits in Perversion." The lead story's headline read: "Lasting War on Perverts Pledged in 1954 'Purge'—What Law Enforcers Said." Above the story was a cropped photograph featuring bar signs for Club Echo and Club Benni. The caption read: "Reporter was approached at these spots. Perverts hang out at many other nightclubs here."

In the first of the exposé stories, reporters Bob Hardin and Dom Bonafede penned: "A three-week survey by the *Daily News* showed that the pervert colony is flocking back in the same places raided consistently during the 'purge' of 1954." After listing the names and addresses of seven bars, the story continued, "The Circus Bar employs as bartenders and entertainers men who wear lipstick [and] rouge. . . . " As journalist voyeurs, they recounted a sickening series of failed pickup attempts at Miami Beach's Circus Bar: "Two of the employees made approaches while a Miami *News* reporter and photographer were sitting at the bar." And at Miami's El Carol, "packed three deep from the bar, the reporter was approached each time." Undeterred by such advances, they journeyed farther into the center of Miami's seamy sexual underworld: "At the Samba Bar, a wavy-haired, bleached blond male moved alongside the reporter and bought a drink. He introduced another male as 'mother,' and his friends made other suggestive remarks. A thin, balding man who had seen the reporter at other places moved into a booth at the Carnival Bar asking 'Haven't I seen you some place before?' He became annoyed when a suspected deviate tried to sit down, and said 'I saw him first.' " [30]

In the second installment of the series, "Deviate Hangouts' Owners Prosper," the two reporters described the "lucrative business" of Miami's "pansy palaces." Listing the names of the bar owners, their home addresses, and their police records, they quoted "law enforcement bigwigs" who proclaimed no increase in the "resurgence of homosexuals." Such statements, the skeptical reporters concluded, were "in direct variance with lower-ranking officers who admit to a fresh wave of perverts."

The next day, this reporting duo chided police and described the ineffectiveness of current laws against homosexuals. An article featuring full pictures of the tavern owners' homes led off with the provocative statement: "It's no secret that Greater Miami's 'queer haunts' are operating wide open. But, the police lament, there is not much they can do about it. . . . This is in the face of 180 sex offense cases involving juveniles in Miami . . . [including] homosexualism and child molestation. . . . " [31]

Another crackdown followed the exposé. In one follow-up story, the *Daily News*, using language reminiscent of a sporting event, described a "four-day pervert roundup" as "the first in Miami this season." In one case, Miami Beach police found a man bleeding from a leg cut by a broken bottle. They arrested him after he disclosed his homosexuality. Charged with "disorderly conduct," the man was first taken to Mount Sinai Hospital (opened in 1949 by the Jewish community with a pledge to treat all persons regardless of race, color, or creed) for fifteen stitches and then to jail to await trial. In another raid on the 22nd Street Beach, forty-one people were arrested, most on charges of "failing to give a satisfactory account." Elaine Nikels, a vacationing Californian and heterosexual social worker, "shouted objections" to the raid. She was promptly incarcerated for "resisting arrest." Fearing she might "have caused a riot," police suspended her thirty-day jail sentence on the condition that she leave Dade County immediately. Others convicted received fines up to $150 or thirty-day jail sentences.

The *Daily News* sprinkled its "Profits of Perversion" series with stories on the homosexual menace. The following month, the infamous 22nd Street Beach "hangout for as many as 100 deviates at a time" became the subject of an editorial entitled "For Better Policy on Sex Perverts." Readers were dutifully informed: "Psychiatrists call homosexuality a social disease. In another sense, it is a communicable disease, as the psychiatrists generally agree that early exposure to homosexualism breeds perversion." Two other stories featured comments from a prominent judge and an anonymous psychiatrist. According to the doctor:

> Many people are struggling with homosexualism, or some other form of perversion; they can go either way. These pervert hangouts balance the scales against them. . . . The open exhibitions may actually throw them into a panic or lead them into that type of life. . . . The only hope for a cure that a homosexual has is within the medical profession. The less the law has to do with him the better he is. . . . [It] is a hard, unhappy life; most of them, consciously or unconsciously, wish they were not what they are.[32]

Dade County Judge Ben C. Willard handled most of the "pervert" cases, as he had since assuming the bench in the 1930s. In compliance with the 1955 Chattahoochee criminal sexual psychopath law, he routinely appointed psychiatrists—at $100 a case—to examine those so charged. But in exasperation Willard noted that "I have never thoroughly understood it; everyone I talk to about it construes it differently. . . . No doctor has been able to define a sexual psychopathic person for me." He recommended: "If these perverts are going to have a colony, they ought to have it in a country where it isn't against the law."[33]

The ambiguity in the law, however, did not overshadow Judge Willard's belief in the criminal seriousness of such behavior. In one case in which a Coral Gables builder had engaged in consensual sex with another man and had been observed by police gazing on with field glasses, Willard issued a three-year prison sentence. A year later the judge remanded a sixteen-year-old "confirmed homosexual" and "wrecked human being" to the state prison for fifteen years for "molesting" other boys his age. A week earlier he had imposed a suspended sentence on a seventy-three-year-old man who had admitted to molesting three young girls on six occasions. Judge Willard ordered him to move to another neighborhood within two months.

As these events transpired, a thirty-eight-year-old dramatics teacher at North Miami High School opened the jets of his gas stove and placed wet towels over his apartment door cracks. His suicide note described an "unhappy" life. Front-page headlines also blazed startling news: "Rev. Ed Wall Must Stand Trial" on three counts of "crime against nature" involving a fifteen-year-old hustler. He was later acquitted in a well-publicized jury trial.

Nineteen fifty-six also marked the appointment by the Florida state legislature of a special seven-member "legislative investigative committee" targeting freedom riders, communists, and homosexuals. Using surveillance, informers, entrapment, hotel room interrogations, and blackmail, the Johns Committee (nicknamed as such for the former acting governor, now returned as a senator, spearheading the effort), began its eight-year campaign, wrecking careers and destroying families.

Rose: Responsibility and Representation

During this era of bar raids and beach arrests, tabloid exposés and sordid headlines, harsh and lenient sentences, shakedowns and robberies, suicides and murders, there was a sense of "normality" within the lesbian and gay Greater Miami community. *Tea and Sympathy*, starring Linda Darnell, was playing to rave reviews at the Coconut Grove Playhouse; Leonard Sillman released the popular musical revue *New Faces of 1956* that included female impersonator T. C. Jones; Merril Mushroom had just "come out" to her high school friends; Jim Patterson was getting ready for graduate study at the University of Michigan; and Rose Levinson, in the midst of a four-year relationship, was attending law school.

As an undergraduate student, Rose was fond of Miami's gay beach:

> The 21st Street beachside was straight, and 22nd gay. We would dance on the "pavilion"—if that's what you want to call it. Now, this was a dumpy place! Think of an open store. Around the walls of that store was a counter to order hot dogs, hamburgers, and beer, with tables and chairs. We would go there on the weekend around eleven o'clock, with everyone bringing blankets to put on the sand. There were a lot more men there than women; most of us were in our twenties and early thirties.

Later as a busy law student, she visited the beach less often, generally accompanied by her partner, who had several children, and a heterosexual woman. Most of these excursions were uneventful, except in the early spring of 1956:

> We were sitting on the beach playing in the water and watching the kids. A policeman walked over to where my straight friend and I were sitting to announce that we were under arrest. "Why are we under arrest?" she demanded. My friend was not as shy as I—she felt no guilt since she wasn't gay. "Shut

up," he yelled. We were taken to the Miami Beach police station, charged with vagrancy, and released a couple of hours later.

Rose sought the help of a lawyer for whom she was clerking. Asked why she had visited such a notorious area, Rose simply replied that she didn't see anything wrong with it. "In those days, no one ever, *ever* admitted they were gay. I certainly was not going to sacrifice my social life. I didn't think that would be necessary. I always felt there was nothing wrong with living two lives." Rose portrays her traumatic courtroom experience:

A hearing date was set for the arraignment in which I had to go and plead either guilty or not guilty. If you plead guilty, you would be sentenced then. If you plead not guilty, the hearing could take place at that time or it could be bound over for another date. My boss was to meet me at the Miami Beach Court House. He never showed up! But what the court did—and what it *always* did (although I didn't know it at the time)—was, once the case was called up, with my name echoing throughout the room, the judge would look at the charge and then dismiss the action. That was how they harassed everyone. From that time on, I must tell you, my social life changed considerably!

As Rose prepared for the bar exam, a routine FBI investigation revealed her arrest record:

I was called downtown and went into an office building to meet with two representatives from the FBI. I had to do some *real* talking. After they got over their initial embarrassment, they had the nerve to ask the Big L question: "Are you a lesbian?" Of course, I was "shocked" that they had asked such a thing. Remember, in an era when sex was such a secret, it was a shock to hear of homosexual activities. People were really frightened. They believed homosexuality was a disease that you could catch.

There was *never* any doubt in my mind as to what I would say. Had I admitted to being a lesbian I would have never been allowed to take the bar exam.

When she began the practice of law, she no longer frequented the bars.

I didn't want to go anyplace that was public, because I might be seen or recognized. I avoided any mixed (gay and straight) groups. There was the wonderful Candlelight Restaurant in the Grove. Rarely were straight people there. But if I thought there was going to be a mixture of people, I wouldn't go.

As her law practice prospered, she represented many gay clients "who were arrested in department stores, bus stations, city parks—and even the Court House. These fellows were often charged with lewd and lascivious behavior—a more serious crime than vagrancy but not as serious as the crime against nature." Her strategy was as straightforward as it was successful:

It was simple to get them off unless this was a really serious charge involving a minor. You asked the court to withhold adjudication, promising the man would go to a psychiatrist. As soon as you used the magical word "psychiatrist," the judge would put a big smile on his face and lower his gavel: "Six months and report back." You thanked the judge and walked out with your client. The client might see somebody once or twice and that was it.

But there were a couple of guys who kept getting caught. They wouldn't stop! I would charge between $350 and $400. So it was a big deal. I remember talking to a very good friend of mine. "I don't know what's going on here. How are we going to stop these guys?" He suggested that I raise my fee. So I did. It rose to $1,500—not to make money from these men, but to stop them!

I remember another very good client. He liked straight strangers and couldn't stay away from men's rooms. There was one at the Coral Gables bus station that *everyone* knew was heavily surveilled. There were even signs up saying "THIS AREA IS BEING SURVEILLED 24 HOURS A DAY." The police would go into a crawl space above the rest room area where they could peek through a hole. As soon as the action began one of the cops would sneak out of the crawl hole and arrest the men. These men would be so scared they would immediately talk.

I also knew of several guys who would pick up navy men. These young fellows would come up to spend the day in the "big city." They would hitch back that night. Some men would cruise U.S. 1. That was another big problem.

Of course, there were no sentencing guidelines back then. One man was sentenced to ten or fifteen years for having sex with a minor. We all thought this was unbelievable, because the punishment was far beyond the crime: The "boy" was around seventeen and consenting. Then there was the case of two underage boys having sex together, and another where two men were caught at a sexual encounter in a beach area which was sort of in the woods. They were all whisked off to prison.

In one sense, it was a scary time. Although you didn't think of yourself as being a victim unless you were careless, in another sense, we were all victims. There was such an utter sadness about it all.

Merril: The Manor and Merriment

Coming out just before her high school graduation in the spring of 1958, Merril, like Rose, was aware of the risks associated with being gay but felt little personal vulnerability. "We were just kids. We didn't have jobs to lose. We didn't have families to support. And, of course, when you're a teenager you're immortal; nothing is going to ever happen to *you*."

Merril formed relationships with other lesbians, some of whom became short-term lovers but remained longtime friends.

> Penny was my first love, and she brought me out well, carefully teaching me the rules, roles, and lingo of the gay subculture. I learned how to "read" another gay person and also reveal myself through an intricate language of sig-

nals and subtleties and how to camp and carry on. I learned to use conversational gay slang terms and to sprinkle my conversation liberally with gay innuendo. My lesbian friends and I practiced developing masculine movements, aping and emulating the men we professed to despise. To be a man meant to be strong and to have power. The best we could do as women was to be like men, since we had not yet learned of women strength and women power.

The lesbians and gay men I hung out with were really close. Some bars were primarily men's bars and others primarily women's, but there was a lot of crossing over, and the bars were pretty mixed. We partied together; we went to the beach together; we danced together; we "fronted" for each other if someone needed a date for work or family.

Now the people in their thirties, forties, fifties, and sixties were cordial and friendly when we were out. But they primarily stayed away from us. It was very dangerous—not so much for us but for the adults who befriended us in any way. For them, in addition to being busted for being homosexual, they could also be booked for "contributing to the delinquency of a minor"—a very, very serious charge.

It was difficult to be an underage dyke back then. If you didn't have phony proof of age, there weren't many places to go. If you had the three required pieces documenting that you were twenty-one, those who owned or tended the bar would let us inside. But if they anticipated any problems, they wouldn't.

There were a handful of older men who lived in a small apartment complex known as the Manor—we called it the Sex Manor. They would let some of the underage kids use their apartments for trysting. Back then there was no place for a gay kid to go where you could be yourself. It was especially difficult to find a place to make love when you're both in high school and living with your parents. So some of the people who lived at the Manor would give a couple the use of their bed for a few hours. This was very brave of them, because adults involved in any way with underage kids could get busted, especially if the kid was an undercover cop.

Even meeting a woman in a bar could be dangerous. Back then there were "teases"—a straight woman who liked to get a lesbian to make a pass at her and then say, "Oh! I don't do that. I'm straight." For those who were really straight, it was an ego trip: "I may have to submit to men but I can put down lesbians." For those with lesbian tendencies it was kind of a double ego trip: "I'm better than you, because I have sex with men. I am found attractive by other women, but I'm *really* heterosexual." These women would appear in lesbian bars, befriend a lesbian, and go on dates with us. When the lesbian finally made the sexual pass, she would be slapped down. It was not only worrisome because of the rejection, the humiliation, and the degradation but because of the undercurrent of danger: What if she turns me in? There was always this fear of disclosure and arrest, which brought further humiliation and sometimes actually incarceration or loss of a job.

There also was the Coconut Grove set: the older, arty, rich, chi-chi set. They didn't mix with the rest of us. We weren't invited to their house or yacht parties. If one of the parties at a private home was raided, of course, everyone would go to jail. It would be horrendous for them. There was a middle-aged "bisexual" woman who was very wealthy and had phenomenal parties attended by other wealthy persons, professionals, show people, and some gangsters. I knew her. She explained to me once how she wished she could include us in her parties but "it's just too dangerous."

The Miami gay setting, according to Merril, was bounded by race, age, and social class:

Although there were a few professional-type people in the bars, it would be unusual to see teachers, social workers, or nurses. They had too much to lose if they were found out. Generally, folks who hung out at the bars were working-class people, students, those who owned their business or who were simply too wealthy to care. In Liberty City there was also the Sir John Club—a black rock 'n roll club where some of the gay kids would go.
    But there was no mixing between the two races on the beach or in the bars. There was some gay overlap, though, between the Anglo and Cuban cultures which was very vivacious and ostentatious. And although there was still a tremendous amount of anti-Semitism in the Miami community, the Jews and gentiles mixed pretty well within the gay scene. But I was mainly a queer who just happened to be Jewish.

By the late 1950s, Miami Beach, the county's most liberal community, included an estimated 80,000 American Jews. There were kosher restaurants and shops; orthodox and progressive Jews gathered in Flamingo Park; the public beach at 14th Street was known as "bagel beach"; and Jewish-Americans held municipal and county offices. There was, though, a "five o'clock shadow," when contact between Jew and gentile ended. Jewish-Americans were not allowed membership to prestigious clubs like the Surf and Riveria Country Clubs, and some communities, like Bal Harbour and Sunset Island, included restricted covenants (declared by the Supreme Court as unenforceable in 1948 but still widely observed).
    South Florida, then, was not immune to the bigotry, racism, and hatred that characterized much of the South and the nation in the 1950s. Despite the exposure of Nazi death camp atrocities such as Auschwitz and Dachau, anti-Semitism was far from dead in postwar America. It was further spurred by the 1953 execution of Ethel and Julius Rosenberg, convicted of espionage.
    Recalling the climate of intolerance during this era, Rose observed: "Anything Southerners could hate, they did. Blacks were not allowed on Miami Beach after dark. There was tremendous anti-Semitism. Many hotels and bars were restricted. If you had a Jewish name, you wouldn't be accepted into the hotel." There were plenty of "Gentile Only" hotels: Even Arthur Godfrey's swank hotel, the Kenilworth, was "restricted"—a euphemism for "no Jews allowed."

Immediately after the war, a group of Jewish veterans, wearing their service uniforms, began a direct assault on these restrictions by visiting each business and discussing the need to rid Miami Beach of anti-Semitism in a world just rid of Hitler. Most of the offending signs quietly disappeared. In 1949 a Miami Beach ordinance, eventually approved by the state legislature, banned signs and advertisements that publicized discrimination on the basis of religion or creed as well as race. The influence of the Miami Jewish community, though it did not eliminate discrimination, made Miami Beach more friendly to the growing Jewish population. By 1953, for example, the Anti-Defamation League found that while more than one-half of the tourist hotels in Florida discriminated against Jews, only one in five discriminated in Miami Beach.

In a time of rising racial tensions, the influence and actions of the Jewish community influenced racial politics in the city, creating its own backlash. Jews, like blacks and gays, were subjected to intimidation, discrimination, and harassment. In the spring of 1951, the Ku Klux Klan dynamited an uncompleted section of the Northside Jewish Center. Dynamite was discovered the following fall at the Miami Hebrew School, and there was another attempted bombing at the Coral Gables Jewish Center a week later. In 1958 the Orthodox Temple Beth El, Miami's oldest synagogue, was damaged by a dynamite explosion.

African-Americans, however, bore the brunt of Southern racism. Segregated across the causeway in the northwest corner of Miami near the railroad tracks, most lived in a community known as "Colored Town" (renamed Overtown). Those who did not live here resided in "Liberty City," the site of the first housing project in the southeastern United States. "Liberty Square" had been constructed in 1937 by the Public Works Administration after a series of *Miami Herald* exposés on the poor living conditions in Overtown but also as a result of the white desire for the Negro population to move farther away. But any black family who considered moving outside these "free" areas—even in the 1950s—was greeted with dynamite blasts.

Like most postwar Southern cities, Miami prided itself on its "progressive relations" with its Negro population. In 1944 the city opened its police force to blacks, but training was hidden from the public for fear of a "backlash." By the early 1950s the first black had served on a jury, and an African-American judge had been appointed for the Negro districts. Monday was designated by the county as the day for "coloreds" to use the public golf course. Discrimination was the norm, except during conventions, such as in 1956 when the Colored Methodist Episcopal Church brought 15,000 black conventioneers to Miami Beach, finding accommodations largely through the efforts of the Jewish hotel community.

That same year Maggie Gorman, a maid, refused to sit at the rear of the city bus. Negro conservatives viewed such actions as quite radical given that it had been just a few years earlier that blacks were permitted even to ride in the same bus with whites. The community's only black newspaper, the *Miami Times*, launched by black millionaire David Dorsey, took a conservative racial stance. Accommodation not confrontation, separation not assimilation were the watchwords. But Gorman, supported by her minister, persevered. Assisted by the NAACP, she sued the city and two years later won the right to sit in the front of the bus.

Despite Miami's social class, racial, and religious divisions, Merril recognized her common bond with other women. Despite the difficulties of the times, Merril focused on bars not bombings, fun not fear. "From the high-class call girls to the diaper truck driving diesel dykes, from the wealthy property owners to the high school and college girls, from the professional lady to the lady wrestler, we were essentially all the same under the skin— we all could be, and many of us were, socially persecuted and criminally prosecuted."

The bars—ranging from the most seedy to the classiest—were Merril's principal haunts. Four decades later, pouring another glass of herbal iced tea in the living room, her streaks of gray hair glistened as the afternoon sunshine streamed through the windows of her Tennessee farmhouse. She called to mind those youthful times:

In the 22nd Street Beach area there were a number of bars. On Alton Road there was the Hi Room, primarily a women's bar. The Hi Room adjoined the Red Carpet much in the same way that the Coral Bar adjoined the Onyx Room—like the lesbian auxiliary of the faggot contingent. I remember my first visit to the bar. I was terrified. I was all dressed up, with my hair combed back, looking real butch. I kept walking past the bar's entrance, up and down the street. I just knew my phony proof of age wouldn't work and that I would be thrown out, or Mom would be driving down the street and see me walking inside. I finally went home.

The next time, after walking back and forth for awhile, I pushed the door open. Behind the bar was Mikki Marr. She was every dyke's dream of a drag butch. Mikki was tall and broad-shouldered, wearing black pants and a white dress shirt. Her short dark hair was combed back in a DA. Her skin was pale and her eyebrows were dark. She had these great cheekbones and a fine strong jawline with a sensitive mouth and chin.

The Hi Room was dark, with a velvety look, immaculate and cool. The air conditioning lifted up every hair on my arms. It was wonderful; I was in fairyland; it was my dark ice palace. Soft music played over the jukebox: Johnny Mathis, Ella Fitzgerald. I went there often after that, drinking stingers and staring at Mikki for hours.

Farther up Alton Road were other bars. There was the Onyx Room, a swank, hot touristy club featuring female impersonators like Charles Pierce and Jackie Jackson. Well ventilated with a designer stage, it was "always crowded, the bartenders were always terrific, and the male drag shows were always excellent." Mondays were open talent night, when, as Merril recounts, "the queens who were not in the regular show would get up and do their numbers. Sometimes they were wonderful; sometimes they were terrible. But their makeup was always divine and their costumes spectacular."

One day Merril and two of her friends, Connie and Penny, were talking about the Onyx Room shows and wondering why they never saw any male impersonators. Sometimes a New Yorker would come down to perform, but there never was a Southern woman doing male drag, although there were plenty of drag butches in the bar.

After rejecting various performance schemes, we decided to go on as a rock 'n roll male group. We called ourselves the Tongueston Trio. We practiced and rehearsed at Connie's apartment and got our three numbers together. It was more difficult for me, because I was still living at home and underage. I had to sneak out for rehearsals, posing as a typical fifties teenager going out to do homework and listen to records with a girlfriend. I took my schoolbooks and records—and, hidden in my book bag, my brother's loafers, borrowed with his consent, and my father's tie, borrowed without his knowledge.

Well, when the big night arrived, I gave the usual teenage story about girl-friends, homework, and records and left the house. I really wanted to say, "I'll be late tonight; I'm competing in the drag show at the Onyx. Wish me luck." I didn't dare. Meanwhile, word had gotten around that we were going to perform. Every lesbian in town must have showed up to cheer us on. The club was jammed.

The fellow who did the lighting was a friend of ours; he did an especially great job for us. We fancied up our usual duck's ass hairdos with pompadours, and we wore black pants, white shirts, black neckties, white socks, black loafers, and sunglasses. Backstage, Penny, Connie, and I paced and fidgeted, trying to keep quiet while the drag queens went through their numbers. Then they were done, and it was our spot.

"And now," we heard the emcee announce, "the Onyx Room is proud to present a brand-new act—the Tongueston Trio!" The curtain parted, and hot red and blue lights moved over us as we trotted onstage in perfect step, waving and smiling. Three separate spotlights came on each of us, merging into one big spot. All the girls in the room screamed—the faggots, too! Penny, Connie, and I bunched together, ready to start. The lights went down, all throats hushed, and out over the speakers came the opening instrumental notes of our first number, "Bad Boy," by the Jive Bombers:

> I'm just a bad boy, la-la-la-la-la-la-la-la-la-la-la-la-la-la,
> all dressed up in fancy clothes. . . .

Then we did "Why Don't You Write Me Darling?" by the Jacks and ended with "Come Go with Me" by the Del Vikings.

When we came off the stage and into the barroom people hugged us, mobbed us, bought us drinks. "You were wonderful!" they all said. Of course, we had been! Everyone went crazy over us and we won first prize.

I had to go home before my curfew. The management wanted us to come back and do our numbers again for the second show, but I couldn't. It was a real struggle just doing it that one time with my living at home, my mother's scrutiny, and being underage. I suppose if I had been independent we might have gotten it together as a regular act. I was really bummed out to be so restricted.

Adjacent to the Onyx Room and separated by a freely swinging door was the Coral Bar, a lesbian dance club. Diagonally across Alton Road was the Billy Lee's, where buffets were served and well-known entertainers like Martha Raye sometimes dropped in to chat with the drag club's owner, Billy Lee. Nearer the 22nd Street Beach was the Night Owl, frequented by heterosexuals along with gay men and lesbians. "It seemed like wherever a lesbian tended bar, we would be there despite what the original crowd was like. Sometimes the bar would gradually change over to a lesbian bar, to the delight of the owners, who would pick up a lot more business."

Merril's memories also returned to the oceanfront Cas-Bar operated by a woman named Shirley. "What a wonderful casual place. People would come up off the beach. There would also be buffets, and there was a great jukebox with lots of dancing. Inside was the 'mad, mad wall' painted black where each person who hung out there would trace around her hands and put her name inside the handprint."

The "mad, mad wall" had been inspired by the lyrics of "Night and Day," written by Cole Porter, as performed by Frances Faye in her jazzy album *Caught in the Act*. In her nightclub performance, before beginning that song she would sometimes sing, "Way Down Yonder in New Orleans," warning her listeners that she never does it "on account of the gay kids. They resent one word." Then she begins in her alto voice, horns and snare drum in the background: "There is heaven right here on earth with those beautiful queens." Abruptly, she stops singing and asks a laughing audience, "See what I mean? I never do that song, such a drag!"

Though that song does not appear in *Caught in the Act,* there is a rendition of "Night and Day," sung against the syncopated rhythm of horns, drums, cymbals, and bongos:

> *Like the tic, tic, toc of a steady clock as it stands against the wall*
> *the crazy wall,*
> *the mad, mad wall*

Pulling the album from her collection, Merril then sings the lyrics of another Frances Faye song, "Frances and Her Friends." Again the singer first warns her listeners, "This is not dirty. It's the way I say it." Merril mimes:

> *I know a guy named Joey*
> *Joey goes with Moey*
> *Moey goes with Jamie*
> *And Jamie goes with Sadie*
> *And Sadie goes with Abie*
> *And Abie goes with Davy*
> *And Davy goes with Howard*
> *And Howard goes with Charlotte*
> *And Charlotte goes with Shirley*
> *And Shirley goes with Pearly*
> *And Pearly goes with Yetta*
> *What a drag, what a drag*
> *I'm not mad*
> *I'm too hip to get mad. . . .*

Merril smiles. "That was a very popular album among us. It was a big deal that she was so blatant, so publicly open. We had so little. This was so precious."

Jim: Teaching and Trysting

Jim Patterson returned from his one year of graduate study at the University of Michigan in the fall of 1958 to teach at the newly built West Hollywood High School, north of Miami off of Highway 19. "In that era, nineteen miles was not an easy commute. It was unusual. This naturally raised some questions. But I knew that I couldn't be a teacher, a homosexual, and also live there."

Patterson remembers the Miami police as "outrageous in tracking down homosexuals. They would find out where the gay bars were and stake out the parking lot, taking notes of license plates. If they didn't raid the bar they would call you in and threaten you with publication of your name, address, and profession in the newspaper. I always parked my car far away."

During his two years at the school, Patterson did "pal around" with one of the two lesbian teachers at the school. Roberta talked with Jim about the difficulties facing homosexuals who were teaching in Florida.

> Disclosure was the great fear. During that time, I didn't know anyone who was "openly" gay. I also met a fellow in Miami who was teaching at Coral Gables High. He wouldn't even go to the bars, and he dated a woman for cover. Being a homosexual was always a sub rosa life.
>
> At the same time, I was trying to find out who I was and why I was. The only books I found weren't describing me. The newspapers painted a picture of a life that *wasn't* mine. I didn't cruise the parks or the rest rooms. I wasn't a child molester. I had a good job. But the pervasive attitude back then was that

if you wanted to change bad enough you could. But I didn't want to change. I was who I was.

While I didn't cruise the parks or the johns, the beaches were a different story. The cruising was great! We always went either to their place or mine; it was *never* public. Running into a plainclothesman was a consideration. But, boy, you could talk to someone and scope them out real quick: Does he know the scene? Does he know any of your friends? What does he do for a living? And, then, is *he* going to make the move?

I spent a lot of time with the Coconut Grove group. I was the "new young thang" of '59. We would go to the Candlelight Restaurant in the Grove for drinks and dinner on Friday or Saturday evenings or after the beach on Sunday afternoons. It had a nightclub atmosphere, often with a piano player. The restaurant had a six- or eight-foot awning lit underneath, with the words "Candlelight" along the scalloped edges. You would see it as you drove up. Around the corner was the Coconut Grove Theater, so a lot of actors would hang out at the Candlelight.

But what I remember most are the people and the conversations. It was an "in" place. I remember a number of us having a charming dinner with Tennessee Williams, who was there for a production of *Garden District*, with Diana Barrymore playing the leading role. I asked him what he thought of her performance—he just laid her low!

The linchpins of the Coconut Grove men's group were wealthy "coupon-clippers"—men who did not live on earned income. So much of what happened, you see, happened in homes. They had wonderful houses with pools and boats. The dinner parties were grand. They were not always sit-down affairs; there were also occasions for drinks and heavy hors d'oeuvres. But there were always between twelve and twenty men who had all died and gone to preppy heaven: Madras Bermuda shorts, French Izod shirts (when it really was an exclusive shirt!).

During his second year of teaching in Hollywood and living in Miami, Jim met an architect who offered him a "seasonal position"—being his "boy":

He was very clear as to what that would entail: playing bridge, enjoying dinner, having sex. I wouldn't even have to give up my teaching job. Well, I was insulted! I preferred the company of a tall, trim, charming, dark-haired man about my own age who worked in advertising for Burdine's Department Store. He had a bungalow apartment in the Grove, which we practically shared. We liked each other, enjoyed the sex—when we had it, we had a lot of it! But it was not "romantic" in that we made plans to live together.

There was a good deal of disdain among the Grove crowd for the arrests and harassment that were going on. They thought that they were above all of that. Though they trolled for all the sweet young thangs, this group really was not part of the Miami bar scene. When they would go to bars it was like a royal appearance.

While the Grove crowd spent little time in the bars, Jim Patterson, like the fictional Jim Willard, frequented bars for entertainment and sexual rendezvous. A gleam comes to Jim's eyes as he recalls his "barfly" period:

There was the Red Carpet Lounge on the beach, where Ray Bourbon entertained. Then there was the Onyx Room, where Charles Pierce, a young Miamian, was beginning his career and where Jackie Jackson performed. Frances Faye, who had that fabulous album, *Caught in the Act*, and T. C. Jones, a female impersonator, also appeared occasionally at clubs. These beach bars had a show-biz glitz. They had pinspots and little inkies over the wall and stage. There was glitter and lamé to give it a sense of "upscale." These were the show bars, not the ones you hung out in if you were looking for a date. You were there to see the act, not act.

I hung out a lot at the Red Carpet, and it was always an occasion to see Ray Bourbon perform—especially since I was dating the bartender! Ray Bourbon was about 5'9" and 220 pounds with a doyen drag persona—not unlike the British drag queen, Dame Edna, whose trademark was her rhinestone glasses. Bourbon wore evening gowns highlighting his large breasts, suggesting a décolletage when he pushed them upward. He drank through the entire act, saying things like, "You know, I really don't like the liquor. I just want the serviettes." He kept putting the cocktail napkins in his bosom, tittering: "When I get enough of them then I can go to the bathroom." I heard that joke dozens of times and laughed every time. It was a sense of celebrating who you were in a way that was liberating.

I went to the other bars in Coral Gables and south Miami to cruise, like the Stockade. These were more neighborhood bars with a jukebox playing songs of Judy Garland, Patti Page, Johnny Mathis—nothing like the disco bars of today! There was absolutely no dancing; you went there for talk and pickups. I was a pretty aggressive "barfly" back then. I'd scoop somebody up and be gone!

Lesbian Lives

In reading the news stories of bar busts, precinct bookings, and criminal convictions, one might conclude that lesbians were generally immune from this hate, harassment, and homophobia. Merril cautions against such a brash assessment:

Women were simply not reported on. Women weren't important; lesbians were invisible. After all, who cared about women anyway? There may have been an underlying belief that if they reported about lesbians then they were acknowledging lesbians—and if they acknowledged us they'd have to think about the possibility of the women they owned loving one another.

But we were harassed, we were arrested, and we were subjected to that same bullshit as the men—but not in the same numbers. At the bars, paddy wagons would pull up to the doors, police would enter the premises, alert for any sign of same-sex relating, from dancing to handholding. We paired off to appear heterosexual—"Oh, heh, heh, officer, I just came in here with my boyfriend to have a drink, I mean I had no idea. . . . " They would read the contents of wallets carefully, make lewd comments over photographs, ask personal questions. Anyone who appeared to be too much in drag was immediately hustled off to the precinct house to be physically inspected for three articles of sex-appropriate clothing as required by law. Anyone else the police chose to bust was held "on suspicion." Sometimes lesbians—drag queens, too—were beaten up or raped by the cops.

Lesbians were an easy target. I remember my friend Lynn once coming in late to the bar. She was a mess. "What happened?" we asked. "Oh, Officer so-and-so caught me again. I had to go and blow his dick. He messed me up a bit." No one got too incensed. There was *nothing* we could do, and this was *not* that unusual. No one ever considered filing a complaint! These were the police. They could do whatever they goddamned well pleased. We were queers. We just tried to keep out of other people's way. If we were harassed, well, that was just part of queer life.

Of course, the cops weren't the only ones we had to worry about back then. All it took to be put in a mental hospital was for your husband or parents to bring you in. If you were a woman, of course, you were a possession. You'd show up to the bar one night and ask, "Where's Diane?" A person would reply matter-of-factly: "Oh, she's in a mental hospital. Her mother committed her." Again, this was *not* that unusual. If you were a lesbian then you were inflicted with "homosexualism." You needed to be purged of this illness through electroshock therapy and lots of medication.

Marcia, another of Merril's friends, was "very pretty, very femme, and very arrogant. Every conceivable time they would drag her in and make someone get her out." Marcia later was involved in a motorcycle accident and only recently has begun to remember events from the 1950s. One of the most traumatic events was when she was lying awake in her jail cell one night. A strange feeling of dread came over her. She heard the sound of broken glass.

Merril reads from Marcia's writing:

I heard the crash of the broken window in the next tank—glass shattered all over the floor. I just barely saw the shadow of feet as he fell two stories below.
"Oh God, NO—Please no—EDDIE!!"
Before I looked, I knew . . . I didn't have to see.

The police station was surrounded by huge iron gates with sharp spikes on the top of each rail. Eddie's body was impaled lifeless on one of the razor-sharp points.

Reflecting on the incident years later, Merril added:

Sometimes the only escape was suicide. I never will forget that day when Eddie jumped from a window in his extreme fear and died in a hideous manner for being a queer. . . . He jumped in a panic, in a frantic attempt to escape, because he was a young Latino fairy without immigration papers who had been taken in a raid on a gay bar, arrested with scores of other lesbians and gay men. In his terror over what his future might bring when he was discovered, he brought his chance of any future at all to a stop by dying of his wounds.

Like Rose, Merril often frequented the 22nd Street Beach. Again her memories of fun are mixed with those of fear:

On the 22nd Street side was the Sea Isle Hotel and a long pavilion with a juke-box and snack bar. We would all dance to six plays for a quarter on that pavilion—it wasn't more than a pier with a roof over the snack bar and a seawall jutting out into the Atlantic where we danced: mambo, pasa doble, cha-cha-cha, fox-trot, Panama City bop, chicken, lindy, and the hully-gully. We would do mixed-gender dancing and group dancing. If you could get two guys and two girls together and dance in a foursome, you could look like you were dancing cross-gender and really not be. That was our kind of passing—doing what we really wanted to do in a way that we could get away with it.

There were some occasional brave same-gender couples fast dancing, but never slow! There was a lot of Cuban music and black music; not much of American Bandstand. Johnny Mathis, of course, was the all-time favorite as well as Frances Faye. There was also a lot of bluesy, jazzy, slow kind of music: Perry Como, Della Reese, Roy Hamilton, Ray Charles, Diana Washington, Ella Fitzgerald, Dave Brubeck.

There were also lots of plainclothes police. Normally, they had a "cop" look about them. Sometimes they were wearing swimsuits; other times cotton pants. I remember a friend giving me the elbow: "There's a cop." I looked to see an ordinary fellow with a mustache, smoking a cigarette, with one foot propped up on a bus stop bench, leaning on his knee, gazing over the beach as though he was cruising.

Now, if they caught anyone same-gender dancing, they would pop you and take you in—no questions asked. Of course, a lot of times the beach was raided anyway. Sometimes, as we lay on our towels and blankets, sat on our chairs and chaises, floated on our rafts and inner tubes, we would suddenly be assaulted by an onslaught of uniformed and plainclothes police, ordered to our feet, and marched from the beach. "With what am I being charged, officer?" "Vagrancy." Back then there were twenty-seven different counts of vagrancy and we could be put into a jail cell for hours "on suspicion."

The police hated us; they *hated* us. They were cruel, vicious, and loved nothing better than to catch a lesbian in the act and make her blow him. This was second only to catching a queen and raping him or beating him up.

Sometimes, as we ate our hot dogs and hamburgers, drank our beer and soda, we would be pulled up by police and thrust toward the street, leaving our food behind. We would be pushed all together—the dancers, the swimmers, the diners, the sunbathers—into paddy wagons that lined the road, shoved in the back, herds of half-naked bodies pressed into the vans until the space was filled and the doors, with mesh-barred windows, would be slammed and locked. Then off we would go to the local precinct house, there to be fingerprinted, booked, and thrown into a cell, with the promise of public humiliation yet to come.

Merril also remembers sitting around a living room hearing others naming names of well-placed Miamians:

These included family members of high administration officials who were secret queers. There were some big names. The talk was that some of these people were trying to put a damper on some of these investigations. The message was "stay with the peons. Don't go across the board. Keep busting the bars, keep raiding the beaches, keep prowling the parks, but don't move into the business or political communities."

Sitting poolside at her south Florida home, Rose, now in her sixties, recollects frank conversations among friends:

We used to sit around in the fifties and discuss if we thought being gay was something that was acquired or biological. Many felt so lost and so afraid.

Life was tough, especially if you were a man. You couldn't belong to a club and be yourself. It was *very* important to be married. You could *never* hold a job such as a teacher unless you had a wife and children. You simply weren't going to be accepted into the inner sanctum of the corporation or school.

It was totally different for men and women. There was one publicized case in which six women were arrested, but they were quickly let go. In none of the newspaper articles back then did they talk about lesbians. I would be surprised if there were any articles about women in the newspapers. We didn't have the same kind of problems—but we weren't doing the same things either.

A single female was far more acceptable than a bachelor; people didn't think very much of women anyway. It wasn't very important what we were or who we were with. Lesbianism wasn't as repulsive to the general public—if they knew or believed it even existed.

Women, of course, faced other problems. Very few women were financially independent or successful. And for a woman to be successful then, as now, you had to be better than a man.

Reflections from Golden Eyes

Having pride as a woman, as a Jew, as a person of color, or as a homosexual was difficult to achieve in the South. During the 1950s, in a region saturated with hate, fear, and ignorance, human beings were routinely humiliated, scorned, and persecuted by public officials, the police, the press, and the public. Yet, despite the manipulation of these minorities to skewer political opponents, to balloon meager law enforcement salaries, to increase newspaper sales, and to appease a frightened citizenry, for Rose, Merril, and Jim—now into their golden years—it was the best of times.

The youthful gay spirits of the 1950s glided Icarus-like between the glitzy world of Miami hot spots and gay gatherings and the netherworld of police shakedowns and scam artists. By luck or fate, these three—unlike William T. Simpson—matured to see the lurking dangers posed by being queer in the Sunshine State wane. However, despite—or maybe because of—the endless series of raids, the fear of exposure and entrapment, the incarcerations and commitments, there is a collective nostalgia for that time so many decades ago. This was an era of long-term friendships and relationships, dinner parties and nightclubs, camping and cruising. Through the mist of memories, they reminisce:

MERRIL: When you are dancing and having a good time, you don't think about being raided until they walk into the door. People who were really, really afraid simply didn't go out to the bars or the gay beach.

ROSE: By the early sixties it was impossible to go to bars. There were few or no gay women's bars and just a couple of men's bars, which were pretty rough. These were the days of very large evening parties. It was not unusual for us to have a party for a hundred or one hundred and fifty persons. But we always did it with a list. It wasn't a heterosexual list like John and Mary but it was Charlotte and Pearl or Howard and Joey. There were tremendous friendships.

MERRIL: You know, when people have a common oppression it binds us to one another. We formed a lot of close relationships: There was lots of loving and caring, calling to check on one another, supporting someone if things went wrong. Back then, if someone got busted, there would be twenty people down at the station ready to help put up bail. We were all family.

ROSE: There was always someone's house to go to and it was nothing to make dinner for ten or fifteen people. I was part of a group of forty or fifty people in their twenties and early thirties, evenly split between men and women. Every Saturday night the same forty people would be at the dinner party. We had a glorious time! Men wore jackets and ties; women wore cocktail dresses. These were wonderful all-gay events. Yet, if anyone would have walked into those parties, we all looked terrific!

MERRIL: There was something special about being somewhere, spotting someone else, and both knowing each other is secretly queer. In an odd sort of way it gave us a sense of power in a time where, in reality, we had very little power. Pride grew in me as a defense with each police raid, each scandalous newspaper headline, each insult from a passerby.

JIM: This was a time of great danger but also grand excitement. I lived multiple lives: high school English teacher by day, Miami barfly by night, Coconut Grove "young thang" on the weekends. I can't tell you the number of times when I went to the Stockade only to find the paddy wagon pulled up with people booked for vagrancy. The names, addresses, and employers appeared in the newspaper the following day. You know, when you are young, you think you are invincible, that it isn't going to happen to you. Isn't that one of the great things about being young? I just believed that arrests, harassment, and violence weren't going to happen to *me*.

ROSE: When the stories of the crackdowns hit the paper, it was subject to campy wit. The attitude of people always was, "It's not going to happen to *me*." You don't stop something because you might be arrested. How else are you going to live? You can't give up your social life.

JIM: But, the *Miami Herald* was delivered to my apartment every day. A week didn't go by without something about perverts and deviates. The headlines were everywhere. After you read article after article in the newspaper about bar raids, entrapment, beatings, and murders, you'd finally just say to yourself: "Get Out!"

ROSE: It was a wonderful time in life to be gay. It was a very carefree, fun time. Everyone always camped. Everyone was always laughing. We just laughed our way through the fifties and sixties. One of the big things was musical comedies. Everything was a musical comedy. There were revues like New Faces of 1952 and shows like *South Pacific, Wish You Were Here, Oklahoma,* and *Carousel.* When we would get together on the weekends, we would get pretty drunk and do all the songs. Back then I had all the lyrics to all the musical comedies memorized! A couple of the guys might get dressed up in drag and do some of the numbers. It was just so fun! I would love to go back to those times!

MERRIL: It was a fun time even with all the contradictions. I loved it! It was a terrible time to live—that's why we used the word "gay"—for irony. We put on this happy face, but beneath it all was tragedy: beatings and arrests, humiliation and harassment, sordid and silent love affairs. But on the surface we had a great time. People drank, danced, and partied. Of course there was no awareness of alcoholism, becoming codependent, or contracting AIDS.

JIM: When I began reading articles that the Johns Committee was shifting its focus from college educators to high school educators, the handwriting was on the wall. I may not have been brilliant back then but I wasn't dumb. A talented college professor I knew, Arlen Davies, had already been fired. So I said, "Fuck this!" I moved back to the University of Michigan to get my Ph.D. The Johns Committee drove me out of Florida! Maybe that was their real intention.

2

Dark Nights of the Soul

Charley Johns and
the Chicken Ranch

IT BEGAN AT THE UNIVERSITY OF FLORIDA.
In September 1958 Merril packed some clothes and a few mementos of
her halcyon adolescence in Miami and journeyed to Gainesville, escorted
by her mother. The impressions of campus life are still vivid in Merril's
memory:

> It was a culture shock for me to leave Miami Beach and to go to this very
> Southern town. The major establishment for entertainment was Humpty
> Dumpty's ice cream palace. The student body was largely gentile; there were
> only three other Jews in my dorm; there was one woman who was "open"
> about being Catholic. It was a low-cost state university attended mostly by
> bubbas and belles from small Southern towns. Most of the girls were there to
> get their MRS degree. The fraternity/sorority system was the focus of most stu-
> dents, and most of the girls in my dorm were really involved in rush. They had
> these momentous decisions about what they were going to wear and heart-
> breaks when they weren't called back. Of course, I was very disinterested in
> going sorority; I was more interested in "rushing" the gay bar scene.

The pastoral setting fit the era: two semicircular drives shaded by huge
oak trees; gothic stone and brick buildings linked by meandering pathways.
"The campus was absolutely beautiful. It was small, but when we had to
walk from one end of campus to the other it didn't seem so small. There
were a couple of ponds with alligators, and Century Tower, known as the
suicide tower."

The same month that Merril arrived on campus, members of the Board of Control met with members of the Florida Legislative Investigation Committee, chaired by Senator Charley Johns. The closed-door meeting centered on homosexual faculty, with initial evidence collected by its chief investigator, R. J. Strickland.

Earlier, Strickland had met with former governor R. H. Gore at his Ft. Lauderdale office. Strickland discussed homosexual activities at the University of Florida (UF):

> Mr. Gore stated to me, at that time, that on a previous occasion when he was a member of the Board of Control . . . that it had been called to his attention by a student . . . along with his father . . . that this student in particular had been approached by members of the faculty in regards to homosexual activity on his part. . . . Mr. Gore stated that he had sent to Dr. Wayne Reitz, who is President . . . a letter calling this situation to his attention and that on a later date he had discussed this with him. . . . [1]

Demanding "proof" before any action was taken on the occasion, the board immediately contacted President Reitz to seek his cooperation. Reitz asked only that allegations brought forth by the investigators be "airtight" cases; the University of Florida Police Department would assist Mr. Strickland in his investigation.

As Strickland set his course of action, Merril dutifully sat through her courses. As in many colleges, the undergraduate curriculum consisted of a series of required general education courses in the arts and humanities as well as the natural and social sciences. At the University of Florida a series of comprehensive courses were taught through lectures to several hundred students coupled with small discussion groups.

In addition to these "C courses," she attended classes in the honors program. Her English professor was a flamboyant man in his mid-forties with blonde hair that was receding rapidly. "He was very nelly and wore a big pinkie ring—which, of course, was a giveaway sign."

In search for intelligent homosexual life on campus, Merril longed to make a connection with Professor Jeffries.[2] She lingered after class or ambushed him along the walkway from his office to the classroom: "I started blatantly camping the way Penny had taught me: using limp wrist and butchy type mannerisms, sprinkling 'Oh mercy' and 'Mary' frequently in conversation, and just carrying on. I was excited and wanted to make a connection with him; he got very distraught. I turned him off because I was very obviously queer. He got scared. He got as far from me as he could get!"

During this first semester she also took the required course in physical education (PE), which was taught by two lesbians. "They were very, very closeted but they did show preferences for girls in their classes who were dykes." Merril continued to elect PE classes every semester just to be around them. "I particularly remember Miss Patton. She was very butchy, very gorgeous, and very self-assured. She was probably in her thirties, but to me she looked ancient." Although Miss Patton did not respond to Merril's campy language and obvious affection, unlike Professor Jeffries she was "very nonchalant."

With the exception of PE and some honors courses, Merril was "not interested in my classes. I was more interested in going out of town to the bars." When she did attend other classes, Merril was rarely attentive to the instructor or the lecture:

> When I went to class, the first thing I did was look around to see who was queer. If I spotted someone, I would try to sit near her. I'd try to catch her after class. I would try to engage her in conversation. I remember biology, which was one of these huge classes held in an auditorium with a lectern on the stage and everyone sitting quietly in chairs. There was a girl who sat two rows down from me who was beautiful and so obviously a lesbian. She would go out the other way to avoid me. People were *very* careful.

Mae West, East Texas, and North Africa

Though some of the lecturers were pedantic and out of touch with this postwar generation of students, others like Professors Sigismond Diettrich in biology, William Haines in the political science department, and Arlen Davies in music were not. Popular and highly regarded by students as well as faculty, William Haines, nicknamed "Wild Bill" by his students, was known for zestful and insightful lectures. Arlen Davies's humanities comprehensive course, C-5, integrated philosophy, music, art history, and world literature. He recalls: "I was not interested in counting commas in *Beowulf* or doing research on some obscure Italian paper. Teaching in this broad humanistic field appealed to me." Professor Davies delivered many of the art lectures as well as some of the philosophy and music lectures. Sometimes he even played the piano to illustrate a point. "If it were romantic music, I would play Bach's concerto. I also played all sorts of records. I put in some scandalous things about the composer's life—nothing homosexual, of course. I lectured about van Gogh cutting off his ear and Gauguin living in the South Pacific and contracting syphilis and cancer."

Jim Patterson, who had graduated before Merril arrived on campus, had been one of those students attracted to Davies's personality, intelligence, and style. Though not assigned to the fortyish professor's discussion group, he had been a faithful and attentive student during coursewide lectures.

> Professor Davies was a very popular teacher. Whereas some teachers would consult their notes, hem and haw, and read part of it, Davies *never* consulted notes. You got the feeling that he was telling you things that he knew and that

he believed. He was communicating these ideas in such a way that a fellow like me who was not very sophisticated could understand what there was to admire about the structure of the Parthenon or what was going on in the anvil chorus in *Il trovatore*. He was a good undergraduate teacher. He would repeat and restate ideas—all the kind of little techniques that now I know to be a sign of good communication. He was always dynamic, although he had a slight stammer. He always wore a coat, white shirt, and tie—although he didn't always keep the coat on during his lecture. He was bald with kind of a monk's fringe around the side. He wasn't a classically handsome man, but he was distinguished and compelling. His face was large with very piercing eyes—he really looked at people and he *saw* them.

Davies first noticed young Patterson when he played the role of Hotspur in *King Henry IV,* First Part. Before beginning his lecture on Greek architecture, Professor Davies, who "always accorded respect to students," praised Jim's performance as "one of the finest amateur performances I have seen in any college play." Patterson approached the dais afterward to thank him.

I was thrilled! Here you went to a lecture that seated several hundred people taking notes and all of a sudden this professor recommends to these five hundred students that they go see this production of the Florida Players because there is an unforgettable performance in it—a performance you gave! So I went down to the stage and said, "I'm Jim Patterson. I really appreciate your plugging the play and the kind things you said about me." He said something like, "Young man, you have a career in theater. Come 'round and see me some time." Well, it may as well have been Mae West!

Like many UF students of that era, Jim had little exposure to high culture or the arts. Davies, who had grown up a generation earlier in turn-of-the-century east Texas, was more fortunate. Raised in an Episcopalian middle-class family, Davies "always read, read, read. We had a great library at home." Completing his undergraduate studies in English with a minor in French, he quickly went for his master's degree in English and, after his wartime experience, pursued doctoral studies in art history at an Ivy League school.

Also unlike the young Patterson, Davies had been sexually active with boys and men from his childhood days in the Scouts and on the prairie. "I will never forget when I was thirteen and this boy wanted to fuck me in his barn. It hurt me. I was frightened and afraid. But finally I began to like it." Davies continued to have sexual experiences with men ranging from a trolley conductor to a junior ROTC major. "Eventually I was going to stop, screw girls, and get married." Davies didn't view himself as a homosexual or queer. "The word in Texas was 'fluter'—like playing the flute—and I also heard the word 'pervert.' I was neither. It was something that I was just doing then."

An octogenarian now living in the new "gay nineties," Davies has never "flaunted" his homosexual lifestyle, identified himself as a fluter, or associated with openly gay people. "I avoided people who were known to be queer. If you lived in the South you *had* to be in the closet. There was *no* choice. Now, after all these years of hiding, what good is it going to do for my family to know?"

Davies hid his homosexual escapades from his family for a lifetime and avoided having sex with a woman until he was twenty-three. He dated frequently and exchanged heterosexual bluff and banter still common among closeted Southern boys:

> I remember the first girl I dated: Marjorie. I kissed and she kissed me back, opening her mouth! I thought it was the nastiest thing I had ever done in my life; I couldn't spit enough on my way home. Later, I talked to a friend of mine and asked him if he had ever had a date with Marjorie.
> "Yeah, she's hot stuff isn't she?"
> "Yeah, sure. I kissed her last night. She opened her mouth!"
> "She did with me, too! She calls that a 'soul kiss.'"

Coming of age during the 1920s, Davies continued to deceive himself and others, justifying it as "just a stage I was going through." At seventeen, though, homosexual feelings merged with homosexual behavior:

> I was about ready to go to college when masturbating mutually with Turner and kissing him, I felt that I *loved* him—the first intimation of love and sex combined. . . . Love gave an extra dimension. . . . I also had a high school crush on two older boys, both "my types," tall, handsome, blue-eyed, and blond-headed. . . . These two crushes seemed purer and "better" without any sex at all. Maybe I thought I wanted to love unselfishly and that I wanted to be loved "for myself" alone. For the rest of my life, sex with some sort of "love" or emotional feeling was far superior to just plain sex.

The gangly Texas teen who wore knee britches and visited five-cent Saturday matinees turned into a handsome collegiate sporting a raccoon coat and visiting speakeasies. In his freshman year at college, Davies joined a fraternity of about fifty men:

> I joined the fraternity because I liked the people. We had a big, beautiful fraternity house which had been paid for by a very rich alumnus. It was a good fraternity where I had my meals and a whole lot of fun. Very few people had automobiles, but some did, and we would go out to a wonderful natural spring at the edge of town where there were lots of concerts and where only "nice" people went—meaning no blacks or Mexicans.
> Among these boys, there were five who were homosexual. I had sex with three of them and I was sure about the others—absolutely sure! But it was all *very* hush-hush. Sometimes at the big urinal upstairs we would look at each other's cock, smiling as we got hard. Since I never permanently lived in the

house, I had a tiny garage apartment where we could go. But I was always very, very careful. If I made the first smile, the other would have to smile, too. If he shook his cock, I would shake mine. It was step-by-step, always fifty-fifty. These were good ol' groups of Southern boys who would talk about the "purity of Southern womanhood" and jack off two or three times a day or fuck each other.

But I was always very careful—you *had* to be. There was an architect who had lost his job at the university because he wasn't careful. He was a wonderful teacher, but that didn't matter. I also knew some gay men in other fraternity houses. There was one frat boy who I wanted to have sex with, but my brother would come down a couple times a year and stay at the house. I didn't want him to know anything about me so I never had sex with this boy.

Davies enlisted in the army during World War II. "The war was a great catalyst; it was a dividing line. I never considered myself queer until then." Before being shipped out, Davies spent two winters and one summer in New York City:

I would pick up a copy of *Life* magazine with photographs of bloated bodies on the beach in Guna Guna. I'd think, "My God! I could be that in a month from now." So many men who had been completely in the closet would come out just a little bit. There were a lot of men who would do it for the first time—married men. It was also amazing how many Southern men were available. Given the anonymity of New York and the prospect of dying, they took their last two-week leave in the city. For many boys from the South who had masturbated with friends, this was their last opportunity. That was when many, many Southern boys found out that they were gay. It was just a wonderful time.

Eventually stationed in North Africa, Davies met a fellow army officer and Southern gentleman, Cusperd Lester. Though Lester was heterosexual, their friendship flourished: "He knew I was gay. He didn't give a damn." Following their discharge, Davies attended one Ivy League school, keeping in touch with Lester, who enrolled at another. After Lester took a position at the University of Florida, he encouraged Davies to take up academic residence.

Chicken à la King and *Aida*

In the fall of 1950, Professor Arlen C. Davies began his university teaching career, sharing a house with Lester: "Gainesville was a little, delightful, ingrown Southern town. It really was south Georgia—like Waycross or Thomasville. You'd have to make a liquor run once a month to the county line. The college was very easygoing, very pleasant, with not particularly high academic standards. All the faculty knew one another and there was a good relationship with the students."

Davies soon became active in church as well as campus activities, particularly those related to the arts and fraternities. He bought a three-bedroom cottage adorned by azaleas near Lester's home. Across the street lived a gay English professor. "Stowe always had a good car, went to Europe every summer. He didn't flaunt his wealth, but he had no financial worries." Most of Davies's friends, however, were not homosexual—or at least not openly gay. He spent a great deal of time with two married couples—one of the husbands was "highly closeted." Davies was often seen in the company of fraternity housemothers, who sometimes accompanied him as chaperones on student trips. His associations with other homosexual faculty were mainly at receptions, commencements, and the like: Nelly Professor Jeffries could be spotted at occasional university meetings, and Davies cordially greeted the assistant dean of women (a major in the army reserves living with another woman) at receptions.

Professor Davies devoted much of his free time to students. He tutored for the University Athletic Association for football players and other athletes and hosted regular dinner parties to which he invited a half dozen or so fraternity brothers. On the basis of the physical attractiveness or mental attitude of the student, a smile, or a common interest, Arlen would extend an invitation to a prospective dinner guest: "Oh, by the way, I am having some friends over Thursday night. Are you free? I am making some Italian spaghetti—a specialty of mine!"

In Southern colleges of the era, proper dress, seemly decorum, and polite conversation were the norm. "We would wear coats and ties, but it was all very informal, very pleasant, very easygoing. First we would have a glass of sherry (liquor was too expensive back then and salaries were too low) and sit around in the living room." As students sipped sherry and listened to *Aida* or *Rigoletto,* Arlen engaged them in conversation about school concerts and plays and tutored them on operatic legends and classical musicians. When it was time to dine, Davies would sit at the head of the long oak table, raising his hand and enjoining them, "Sit where you want, boys."

Among the guests at Davies's dinner parties were two regulars, Ford and Jules—joined later by their fraternity brother, Jim Patterson.

Jules and Ford were high school buddies. Ford was a musical high school star who played the piano and was a member of a jazz band. Jules was a wallflower who bloomed during his college years. Six feet tall, blond, and blue-eyed, Jules enjoyed athletics ranging from wind surfing to mountain climbing. Later he became a captain in the air force and earned an advanced degree in mathematics. Ford, though shorter and less athletic than Jules, eased into college groups with his good ol' boy personality. Davies recalls:

When Ford, Jules, and I were together we sometimes talked about being gay. We talked about people who we thought were gay or who we knew one of us had been to bed with. It was speculation based upon fact. There were very, very few gay books out at that time like *City and the Pillar*. We talked about them in a free and easy conversation. But we never talked about their dark side. We had never heard of Mattachine or *ONE*. I wouldn't have bought ONE even if I would have seen it at the store. I would have more likely picked up a men's physique magazine. All of us knew that if we would come out we would be ostracized or kicked out of college.

For most of the heterosexual men attending Davies's parties, the homosexual subtext was unrecognized; for those who were gay, the heterosexual pretext was unimportant. Here the opportunity to engage in spirited conversations and to experience music orchestrated by an enigmatic, talented, and charismatic professor was the lure. The friendships formed around the dinner table as the boys feasted on spaghetti or chicken à la king, discussed a recent production of *Fidelio*, and sipped sherry in the living room listening to Maria Callas often lasted a lifetime. Forty years later, Davies continues to hear from many of his boys, long since married, with children now attending college. "I still keep up with them. Now, they may suspect—but they sure don't know a damn thing."

For these University of Florida students, Davies ushered them into a world of high culture. For the handful who were gay, Davies escorted them into the subterranean world of homosexual culture.

History of the Johns Committee

On May 17, 1954, the United States Supreme Court issued a unanimous verdict in *Brown v. Board of Education*, outlawing "separate but equal" public schools, and twelve months later the Court would mandate desegregation "with all deliberate speed." Political leaders in Georgia, Alabama, and Mississippi advocated staunch defiance and civic militancy against the ruling; those in other Southern states, most notably Florida, evidenced greater restraint.

Although Florida was one of four states with an exclusive segregated school system, its relatively low proportion of African-American citizens, coupled with the moderating influence of south Florida's tourist industry and Northern émigrés, contributed to this reaction.[3] Most newspapers, such as the *Miami Herald* and the *Orlando Sentinel*, urged calm, and many political leaders, most notably former Governor Spessard Holland, implored "patience and moderation."

Meanwhile, in the heated Democratic gubernatorial primary between acting Governor Charley Johns and State Senator LeRoy Collins, race was an issue. Collins pledged to use all legal power to maintain segregated schools; Johns, pressed by neighboring Lake City and Gainesville legislators, informed the press that he was inclined to call a special legislative session to protect state rights. An ardent segregationist, Johns had earlier refused to commute the death sentence for Walter Irvin, one of the Groveland Boys convicted of the 1949 alleged rape of a white woman. Despite dubious testimony, falsified evidence, a host of trial errors acknowledged by the appeals courts, and requests for clemency from newspaper editors, church leaders, and even the state's prosecutor, Irvin languished on death row; later a victorious Collins commuted his sentence to life imprisonment.

Deprived of the governorship and reelected to his senate seat, Charley Johns, in the midst of the 1956 bus boycotts in Montgomery and Tallahassee, wrangled the formation of the Florida Legislative Investigation Committee to "investigate all organizations whose principles or activities include a course of conduct on the part of any person or group which would constitute violence, or a violation of the laws of the state. . . . " The seven-person special joint committee, first chaired by Representative Henry Hand, probed race relations with a relatively evenhanded investigation ranging from probes of the NAACP to the Seaboard White Citizens Council.

By 1957 civil rights activities and confrontations were erupting throughout the South. In September Little Rock's Board of Education followed through with its planned integration of Central High School. Facing a riotous white mob and the prospect of armed confrontation, Governor Orval Faubus stonewalled. President Dwight Eisenhower federalized the guardsmen of the 101st Airborne, ordering them to escort nine black adolescents through the angry crowds encircling the school. Meanwhile, a special session of the Florida legislature passed a bill, signed by Governor Collins, mandating the closure of public schools should federal troops interfere in Florida.

Charley Johns assumed the helm of the Florida Legislative Investigation Committee at this propitious time. Although legislators served only during the several months while the legislature was in session (Johns was a railroad conductor), the Committee consumed his legislative life. In the midst of a long-running battle over reapportionment that would erode the power of the pork-chop legislators, hints of scandal and threats of draconian legislation became bargaining chips in his game of political brinkmanship.

Swiftly, he refocused the Committee onto civil rights organizations and activists, communists and socialists, and antinuclear and peace groups. The NAACP, now characterized as a "communist front organization," became the principal target along with other organizations, including the Fair Play for Cuba Committee, the Progressive People's Party, Florida's Civil Liberties Union, the Greater Miami Foundation for Civil Education, and Radio Free Dixie.

Empowered to subpoena witnesses, take sworn testimony, and employ expert assistance, the Committee echoed the political rhetoric and wielded the investigative tactics of Joe McCarthy. Merril recalls, "Johns was Mc-Carthy junior. He used to wear this little button that said, 'I'm really Joe.'"

Information about civil rights activities came primarily from informants: a Negro lawyer who claimed he was enticed to join the Young Communist League and forced to collect money for the NAACP; a state legislator who clandestinely reviewed FBI files in Washington about the president of Florida State University documenting his former ties to the NAACP; a Halifax Area Council on Human Relations member who provided detailed accounts of their meetings and strategy sessions; an informant at Orlando meetings of the Southern Conference Educational Fund attending with a tape recorder hidden in her purse.[4]

The Committee, however, met unexpected resistance from Florida's NAACP, led by Rev. Theodore Gibson of Miami, Harry Moore's successor who had been a bombing victim in his north Florida home six years earlier. Challenging the Committee's constitutional authority to demand a membership list and other investigative efforts, a series of suits and petitions bridled further investigation. With Johns's eye still on the governor's mansion, he and his band of "pork-chop" vigilantes turned their attention to the homosexual and communist menace.[5]

"Bill" and the Thirsty Gator

As the walls of Southern apartheid cracked and the Cold War raged, the Red or queer college teacher and student became attractive targets—if they could be detected. As is evident from these informant reports, an important source of support for the "intergration [sic] of the races" was from those at schools and universities. Some white students engaged in civil rights sit-ins and related activities, encouraged by "radical" teachers and professors often holding leadership positions in local allied organizations. Consequently, files on University of Florida "intergrationists" were maintained along with others suspected of homosexual activities.[6] Notations on the files included an education professor "known to be a staunch intergrationist [sic] . . . looked upon by the local people as a VERY PINK character"; a professor of biology "considered by the local people one of the worst PINKS"; and a plant pathologist who, along with his wife, gave "intergrated [sic] parties in their home."[7]

Unlike the homosexual professors questioned, these civil rights activists staunchly defended their position, refusing to assist the Committee in any manner. An English instructor commented: "When freedom of ideas is controlled in a University, it is a University no longer but a propaganda machine, sadly resembling the communistic system of education." Another categorically stated: "I am not a servant of the State." When asked whether for the sake of "teaching" and "fairness" that "the other side of integration" should be presented in the classroom, the response was curt: "There is no other side."[8]

During its reign of terror against homosexuals, the Committee employed networks of paid informants, plainclothes police, private detectives, and state administrators using interrogation and entrapment, blackmail and harassment, innuendo and rumor, and threat and intimidation to flush out the homosexuals. The institutional outcome was the dismissal, suspension, expulsion, or resignation of hundreds of university professors and students, public school teachers, and administrators in Florida. Wrecked careers and failed marriages, loss of self-esteem and reputation, suicide, alcoholism, and drug abuse were some of the costs. Though one surviving Committee member, W. Cliff Herrel, blamed Chief Investigator Strickland for occasionally going "off on his own," Johns controlled the Committee, its staff, and its political agenda.

At the outset of the University of Florida probe, Strickland spoke with George Evans, the clerk of the Circuit Court for Alachua County, whose office was located at the Gainesville courthouse. According to Strickland's account:

> Mr. Evans stated to me that on a previous occasion, one night he had to return to his office to do some work . . . upon returning he had brought with him a flashlight for the purpose of going up the stairs into his office which was dark. Mr. Evans stated that upon entering the hall . . . he heard a noise which attracted his attention in the hall. . . . He immediately flashed his light on and threw the beam in the direction from which the noise came, and detected two men backed up in the corner of the hallway. These men immediately separated themselves and ran in opposite directions. One of them [a university administrator] he readily recognized . . . [and] on several occasions he has observed the above stated around the courthouse in the late afternoon and early evening. . . . [9]

The following Monday evening Officer John Tileston of the University Police Department staked out the Thirsty Gator Bar—a known "homosexual hangout." Jake Madsen, a recent UF graduate bound for graduate school at Florida State, approached the officer, who presented himself as "Bill." Bill told the unsuspecting twenty-two-year-old that he was a salesman staying over a few days in Gainesville. At Bill's suggestion, a 5:00 P.M. "date" was set for the following evening. Strickland reported that the two arrived at the Hotel Thomas around 5:20 and immediately went to Room 202:

> I waited approximately three to four minutes before entering myself. Upon so doing, I found Mr. Tileston and Mr. Madsen in a general line of conversation in the room. I identified myself to Mr. Madsen stating that we were aware of his activity as a homosexual and of his attempt to get Mr. Tileston to have homosexual relations with him the night before. . . .
> Although Mr. Madsen talked freely about his personal activity and his being a homosexual, he refused to name anyone whom he knew of being the same,

but readily admitted that there were several students and members of the faculty of the University of Florida whom he knew to be homosexuals, but stated that he was too much of a man to involve anyone else. . . . When pinned down to the finer points of these relations, he stated that any person being familiar with such type of activity could have easily observed such people hanging in and around the Courthouse. . . .

He realized . . . that it [homosexual behavior] would eventually get him into trouble or put him in such a position that would become very embarrassing, but he also stated that he did not intend to try to break such a habit, at least until such time as he became financially able to support a family or wife, and at such time that he might become married he felt that then any desire that he might have for sexual relations could be conquered by a female mate.[10]

Surveillance continued at the Thirsty Gator Bar, where a student informant reported the presence of several UF faculty members. Investigators also learned of one member of the university staff who "on numerous occasions surrounds himself with boys . . . [and] on many occasions has been observed carrying at least two or three boys around with him in his 1958 Cadillac convertible."[11]

While these provided useful leads, as did occasional stakeouts of the basement lavatory in the Florida Union Building, the second floor of the University Library, the Burger House Bar, and Mike's Newsstand, located next to the fire station, Strickland quickly determined that the most promising place was the courthouse men's room. "From talking to and observing actions going on at the Courthouse in Gainesville, it seems to be the meeting place or one of the most publically [sic] known meeting places of the homosexuals in this territory."[12] Arrangements were made to keep the "dirty, filthy, stinking place"[13] open during extended hours to entrap as many men as possible.

The routine established was for the youthful Tileston to feign being a homosexual on the lookout for easy sex. The victim would be identified and then he was seized either after his departure or after arrangements had been made for a future rendezvous. The men's room, located in the courthouse basement with an outside entrance, consisted of two toilet stalls without doors and a wooden partition between them. A hole had been cut years earlier between them. Drawings of men engaging in homosexuality, lists of meeting dates, and related graffiti were scrawled on the walls.

A diverse group of men were snared in this two-man dragnet operation, including a Presbyterian minister with three children, a twenty-seven-year-old shoe store clerk, a former patient at the State Mental Hospital at Chattahoochee, a married insurance agent, a former Jacksonville schoolteacher earning a few dollars hustling, and a truck driver who admitted to more than 200 visits. From most, the stories were the same: occasional visits for homosexual trysts; partners known only by face; busy late afternoons and early evenings. These felons-turned-informants provided specific information, often taped on a wire recorder, about university homosexuals who could be recognized "upon the type of dress, the manner in which they dress, and the conversation that is engaged in prior to making a homosexual approach."[14]

Later they would return to give sworn testimony before the Johns Committee, identifying photographs of other gay men, escorting investigators to the apartments and homes of their anonymous sexual partners, describing lurid details of their homosexual acts, providing descriptions of home furnishings and automobiles, and walking through campus or passing lecture halls to confirm identities of other sexual deviates.

Some leads into the university, of course, resulted in dead ends. In a report summarizing his efforts through mid-October 1958 Strickland wrote in his characteristic *Dragnet* style:

> Questioning of several subjects . . . revealed a considerable homosexual operation being in existence at the above stated University. . . . It was learned that three subjects who formerly worked at the Burger House as part-time bartenders and were also students at the University of Florida might have considerable information. . . . Upon contacting these subjects we were asked to give them a little time to think the proposition over in re of our request. After four days having passed, said subjects were contacted again but at that time refused to give us any information. . . . Another student at the University of Florida and a member of the SAE Fraternity was also questioned and cooperated with this Committee and will continue to do the same . . . [he] admits that on several occasions he was approached and will try to obtain the names of said persons who did same.[15]

One of those bartenders was twenty-one-year-old Devon. He later admitted to having a "blow job up here. . . . If you are out drinking and somebody tries to put it on you—well, if it strikes me right, hell, I let him do it." Devon, though, was angered by the suggestion that he, like his roommate who had bartended at the Burger House and had spoken with Strickland, was a homosexual: "I didn't have any damn sex relation with any damn male up here. . . . I told him [his roommate] right there . . . to get his damn things straight and if he thought that I had been out sucking cocks he was crazy as hell!"[16]

During the next few months, statements of fact, depositions, and files were compiled on a score of university faculty members. One such person was Kenneth Quigby, an English professor who went into the men's room around eleven o'clock on the morning of December 5, where he "began to masturbate himself in the presence of Officer Tileston." Strickland continued his report:

> After agreeing to be a receptive partner in a homosexual act . . . the officer then identified himself and asked Prof. Quigby to accompany him to the

County Jail. Upon questioning, Prof. Quigby admitted that he was a homosexual . . . [and] stated that he had been trying to correct his trouble for the past two or three years. . . . After giving him a chance to calm down, which at the beginning he was very nervous and frightened, . . . he began to cooperate in naming other people who were involved in the homosexual activity and who were faculty members of the University of Florida. [A list of "homosexual or homosexually inclined" faculty members followed.]

When Professor Quigby was asked how he felt about his condition he stated that he was very much worried about the whole thing and also stated if he was brought out into the open in the homosexual investigation that he was going to commit suicide rather than let his family and friends learn about his homosexual life. Professor Quigby agreed to cooperate with this investigation in obtaining names and dates and other information that he could gather in regards to other homosexuals both students and faculty members.[17]

Three days later, the professor called the campus police, inviting Officer Tileston to speak with him at his third-floor office. When he arrived around eleven o'clock, the distinguished professor provided another list of homosexual faculty—most of whom were members of the arts and humanities faculty. Strickland noted in his report that the professor then "attempted to get an agreement of immunity from Officer Tileston stating and asking if there would be any repercussion from his being found out as a homosexual. Officer Tileston states that Professor Quigby was advised that the investigation was entirely out of his hands. . . . "[18] Ten days later Quigby, appearing at the university police station for a voluntary deposition taken by Tileston, disclosed his suspicion that his wife "knows this is going on because last night I heard her up and down during the night until finally she took a sleeping pill and this morning she was so doped she could hardly get out of bed."[19] He went on to tell Tileston, "I think your talks with me have been a tremendous help . . . you have gone beyond the call of duty. . . . It is really a relief to talk to someone who is aware and sympathetic and knows the problem and I do want to try to overcome this and grow old gracefully and with honor and not lose everything." Tileston curtly responded, "If this is all, Ken, we will conclude this."[20]

Other faculty members caught in the courthouse sting operation expressed various levels of concern about the "repercussions." A voice instructor in his twenties "has apparently come to the conclusion, at this time, that nothing will come of this investigation. That he will not be discharged, although this investigator stated to him that this was not a matter for prosecution there has been no promises made to him. . . . "[21] A recently married operating technician at the university later confronted the Committee:

I talked to Mr. Strickland before and he said that this was to be kept quiet, but it has all come out in my job. . . . I was called in and told that there was an investigation going on, and that I was involved in it, and that I had a choice of leaving or staying. . . . They told me that the investigation would be dropped if I voluntarily left the employment of the University. . . . My immediate supervisor called me down and told me that she had been contacted and that this investigation was in process. . . . She said that the information had been passed to her that if I terminated my employment voluntarily by January 1st, the proceedings would be dropped.[22]

Scoffing at the notion that the Committee would use such underhanded tactics, Mark R. Hawes, the Committee's legal counsel and chief interrogator, told the technician: "Nobody at that university has any control over this investigation at all—I don't care who it is, including President Reitz."

Word Is Out

As Christmas break approached, Merril first learned about the Johns Committee's campus activities: "Word of mouth was that the investigation had finally come to Gainesville. When we would talk about professors, we were cautioned, 'Don't even ask if he is gay. You'll put him under suspicion.'" Meanwhile, Arlen Davies was on his annual winter trip. Near the end of his vacation he was attending a Carnegie Hall concert. "While hearing Jeanna Bartell play a Prokofiev dissonant concerto movement, I heard the Johns Committee was investigating homosexuality at the University. I was paralyzed."

By mid-January the Committee's probe had become widely known—much to the chagrin of Johns, Hawes, and Strickland. Rumors published in the *Miami News* placed the number of homosexual faculty at 150 and noted that "10 percent of the 12,000 plus student body may be infected." Although the reporter for the story observed that such rumors were "absurd," he wrote that the Board of Control and university officials were "awaiting only the evidence before they crack down on alleged homosexuals. . . . " James Love, the chairman of the board, told the press: "The sooner we get the Johns Committee report the better. . . . We wouldn't want to smear a man or woman unless we had the necessary information."[23]

As Davies enjoyed his holiday, Hawes spent most of his time preparing for the closed-door hearings that would begin on the first Monday of January. Davies had emerged in Hawes's mind as "perhaps one of the worst homosexuals out there"[24] but one who was never spotted during the courthouse sting operation. Reviewing all of the testimony, informant notes, photographs, and wire tape recordings, this UF alumnus mapped out his strategy for interrogation. Each witness would be used to corroborate evidence already amassed and to confront more hostile or less naïve witnesses; a telephone call or a visit by the local police would summon the unsuspecting witness to the Committee; those not previously "interviewed" during the courthouse sting operation, like Davies, would first be questioned by

one of the investigators before facing the Committee meeting in an adjoin-
ing room. "Voluntary" testimony would be elicited to avoid a scrutinizing
media and stonewalling lawyers.

As Davies returned from his holiday, "all the gay people were frightened
to death. Word had it that they had gotten to a notorious gay man who
worked in the music department." Folders of suspects bulged in the Committee's locked metal file cabinets. Davies now had his own blue file folder,
overflowing with hearsay and circumstantial evidence as well as sworn testimony:

> There were police provocateurs who made you think they were gay, maybe
> you would suck their cocks, and then they would turn you in. There was a fac-
> ulty member who had been at my house. We had two or three sexual encoun-
> ters. He was arrested at the courthouse's glory hole. They put the screws on
> him. Stanley Palmer was told that if he cooperated he would keep his job. He
> mentioned names, including mine. Well, I called Stanley and told him I wanted
> to talk with him. He was frightened to death. He knew that he snitched on me.
> So I picked him up and we went out in the car and talked for a couple of
> hours. I said, "You can ruin my life."
> A second man I knew, Elmer Potter, worked at an insurance office and was
> married with children. He, too, was caught. They threatened him with a long
> prison term but promised him immunity if he talked. He also mentioned my
> name. This guy had only been in my house one time. I never confronted him.
> There was no use in doing that. My God! In life, you don't have to make trou-
> ble; you get it anyway.

The testimony provided by Mr. Potter and Professor Palmer proved dam-
aging.[25] Elmer Potter had attended the University of Florida as a student
right after the war and now worked as an insurance agent. Officer Tileston
had spotted him that past November "playing with myself" in the courthouse. "He asked me if I would care to go to his hotel room and I told him
I didn't know. I asked him if it was safe, and he showed me his badge and
said to come with him."[26] Visiting the rest room rendezvous about twice a
week, Potter fingered Davies, whom he claimed to have met in the Florida
Union rest room:

> As I went in he got up and dressed. As I was sitting down there he stood there
> a minute and mentioned something about how warm it was. . . . Then he
> started playing with himself, and he asked me if I had a few minutes. I said,
> "Yes," and he suggested that we go to his house. . . . I have been to his house,
> once . . . this must have been a year ago. . . . I would say he was in his late for-
> ties, medium built, partially bald. . . . He told me he taught in the Humanities
> Department. . . . He made no bones about his name.[27]

Potter went on, in response to Hawes's questioning, to describe Davies's
blue Plymouth, the location of his home, and its interior: "There was a

stoop and on the door there was a bronze nameplate . . . with his initials. . . . There were carpets on the floor throughout the house. I would say nicely furnished but I was not impressed with the type of furniture. . . . There was one room that was a den, with books that ran from ceiling to the floor."[28]

Summoned as the first witness before the Johns Committee, twenty-eight-year-old Stanley Palmer had been a member of the music faculty for only two years. Caught in the courthouse sting operation, Palmer freely admitted to several sexual contacts among faculty, including Professor Davies. He testified that Davies had telephoned him on an October afternoon in 1956 and invited him to his home to "listen to some records, and I said, 'Surely.' . . . After talking some few minutes, he approached me for an immoral act."[29] Palmer then reported that Davies called a few weeks later with a similar invitation resulting in a similar sexual escapade. Hawes then initiated the following exchange with Palmer:

> *Since you have been here and since then, have you learned anything of Professor Davies' reputation as a homosexual on the campus out there?*
> I have overheard students talking, wondering if this were true, but I have never participated in any discussion concerning this.
> *Don't you know that he bears the reputation of being perhaps one of the worst homosexuals out there . . . ?*
> I haven't heard any students questioning this fact.
> *Isn't it true, Mr. Palmer, that you broke your association with that man because his reputation along that line was too bad for him to be associated with out there?*
> Well, when you hear talk like that—
> *Open talk?*
> Yes, then it seems that it is the logical thing not to continue such.[30]

That Wednesday afternoon, Palmer was abruptly pulled out of his private music instruction for further testimony. This time he refused to answer all questions regarding his alleged homosexual activities with students. Hawes put the screws to him. After a few minutes of Palmer's semantic dodging, an irritated Hawes interrupted: "You know that you have had homosexual contact with some students in that university out there . . . and we know that there are things that you did not tell us about when you were up here day before yesterday and yesterday, purportedly telling us all you know. . . . Give *me* the names that you do know."[31]

Admitting to homosexual relations with students, Palmer confessed, "I am so flustered now. . . . I know you think I am absolutely stupid." Hawes cut in. "No, I don't think you are stupid. I think that you think we are stupid. You came in here purportedly, telling us all you know about this thing, and you didn't tell us all you know about it, and I know you didn't!"[32]

Commanded to go into the next room and "do a little thinking" with a paper and pen in hand, Palmer returned twenty-five minutes later with a couple of first names jotted down. Following his testimony, Palmer inquired: "How about the outcome of all this investigation? Does this mean that I am going to get fired right off the bat? If I am, I should make plans."

Hawes responded plainly, "Mr. Palmer, none of us is in a position to tell you what the outcome of this thing is going to be yet. . . . The only thing I can advise you to do is to go about your daily business in a normal fashion."

Palmer persisted: "Would you advise me to look for another job or go back to school? . . . I am trying to work very hard for promotion." Faced with another noncommittal response, Palmer rambled pleadingly:

> It has done enough for me to make me realize that I have been making some pretty bad mistakes, from the standpoint of my own personal soul and self and from the standpoint of my career which I enjoy doing and which I want to do a good job with—and I am having some success in what I am doing, achieving something, and it has made me aware of my mistakes and, to use a religious term, I have repented and have made up my mind that this was the wrong thing to do. . . . [33]

His pleas fell into a void of silence; he departed in shame from the Hotel Thomas.

These were not the only people who implicated Professor Davies, however. Strickland had contacted a local wholesaler at the beginning of his investigation because of rumors about the man's son, Reeves. Meeting at the man's Gainesville warehouse, Reeves described his suspicions to the investigator, who later prepared a field report:

> Professor Davies made calls to him at his home in Gainesville trying to get him to come to his house, or to meet him someplace, which he refused to do. Then on one occasion in particular, Professor Davies invited him to his home for dinner one evening but upon inquiry, Reeves stated that he found he was to be the only guest, therefore, he refused to attend. . . . Although Reeves stated that no open approach had been made with regards to homosexual activity, that the actions and maneuvering of one Professor Davies made him believe in his opinion that said Professor wanted to induce him into such a position. . . . [34]

There was also Professor Roberts, who taught music and was an adviser to one of the men's fraternities. Declaring that his "talk" with Mr. Strickland and Officer Tileston following his apprehension in the men's room was "the greatest lesson of my life," he rattled off names of faculty members whom he had encountered performing illegal acts in Gainesville's various rest rooms. When asked about Professor Davies, however, Roberts admitted that he had never been approached by him for "homosexual contact" and had never heard of any professors or students whom Davies had approached. His disdain for and jealousy of Davies were apparent:

> I found him quite an obnoxious person. . . . I've noticed him just always call-ing all the boys "Sport" and always putting his arm around them, but never anything that you could put your hand on. . . . I couldn't stand to let him paw me, but I know the boys don't seem to mind it. They always have him at their rush parties, have him talk to their rushees. I don't know. He must have some of them buffaloed. . . . There are a lot of professors that can give a better talk. They said that he gives them a good talk. They like him. They said that he gets the men all steamed up for rushing. . . . I have seen him at receptions—that is, at the concerts, talking very obnoxiously in front of women . . . saying words like "Oh, shit!" or "Oh, crap!" . . . I have heard them [students] remark that he talks about sex an awful lot in his classes . . . it is very embarrassing to women. . . . There is definitely a sort of sexual suggestion, that he makes kind of a joke out of it.[35]

The loquacious Professor Quigby shared a similarly dour opinion of Davies, although, like Roberts, he never observed the vilified professor in any homosexual act—or in his words, evidence that Davies "may have stepped aside." Quigby described him as the "Bohemian type, very outspo-ken, and I think he is very ill-mannered." Examples of Davies's unmannerly behaviors included a social reception where he approached the server say-ing, "Honey, give me some punch." He added that Davies "likes to shock people. For instance, he will yell out something—'God bless you, honey'"— or ask "vulgar questions" like "Is sex here to stay?" Though judging Davies to be "a rather poor example to teach humanities, which is supposed to be the thing to inculcate tastes," Quigby, like others, gave testimony to Davies's outstanding teaching, knowledge in the humanities, and personal relation-ships with his students: "Mr. Davies is a very fine teacher. . . . Students fight to get in his class, and he tutors the football players. That is a required course that they have to take and he tutors them and is very successful some-how. . . . He knows Europe as well as or better than I know Florida. He knows every hotel, every pass, every portal, and everything in Europe."[36]

Davies's Trials

On a January Monday morning in 1959 a Florida state trooper knocked at Davies's cottage door. Arlen Davies, an aficionado of the opera and a lover of men, was wanted for questioning. "Well, I had a class that morning, so I was told to be there at 2:30. I knew what it was."

Davies consulted an attorney: "I paid him $300, which was a hell of a lot of money in those days—I was only making $5,700 a year. But he really did a lot for me. He never asked me if I was guilty. I was simply told: 'Deny, Deny, Deny!'"

That afternoon, Davies drove to the Hotel Thomas, located at the edge of town. This fateful encounter is seared into his memory:

> I was brought into a big room where I sat directly in front of a long table. Standing around were state troopers and a man from the sheriff's office. There were five people sitting behind the table. A man who seemed to be the prosecuting attorney brought in the people. The Committee simply handed you pages of their testimonies with much of the material already blacked out. Someone was there taking down what I said.

As standard procedure, Hawes would first inform the witness about the nature of the investigation:

> I am Mark Hawes. I am Counsel Chief Investigator for the Florida Legislative Investigation Committee. Mr. Strickland here is our chief investigator. These two men here are connected with the University police force. This gentleman here at the end of the table is Senator Charley E. Johns, from Starke; he's Chairman of the Committee. The gentleman over here in the brown suit is Senator Randolph Hodges, from Cedar Keys.
>
> We are conducting an investigation into the homosexual activities out at the campus among students and faculty, and among both of those groups of people and townspeople and others in this immediate community. We must learn the facts and see what steps, if any, can be taken effectively to curb what seems to us to be the growing, the rapidly, alarmingly growing rate of homosexuality out on that campus.
>
> Therefore, I am going to propound certain questions to you in regard to this type of activity and, as you realize, you are under oath, and I ask you to answer these questions truthfully and fully, to the best of your knowledge. We don't want to harm the school, nor do we want to harm the individuals concerned, any more than is absolutely necessary.[37]

Without counsel and uninformed of his constitutional rights, the closed-door interrogation commenced at 3:52 P.M. Hawes inserted a statement regarding the subject's "voluntary" participation:

> You realize this Committee has subpoena power. But in order to invoke that power we have to have a public hearing declared, which means the press and the public can be present, and it means all sorts of notoriety. For the protection of the University and for the people involved in this thing, we are trying to keep it on a voluntary basis, and we have asked you here on a voluntary basis to answer some questions which we have, because we wish to avoid that condition. The other people that we have talked to have agreed to do that. Are you willing, under those conditions, to answer questions for us?[38]

Nodding agreement, Davies was sworn in, and he quickly delivered a long extemporaneous statement. Beginning with a chronicle of his employment and educational history as well as his initial living arrangements with Cusperd Lester, he concluded:

I've always been rather independent in what I do and say. I think that this is a free country, and I think that one of the things we ought to do is that we ought to have more people just be themselves and stop all this business of aid and of conformity . . . so that they are afraid to say anything, afraid to be anything, afraid to do anything. I've always been the sort of fellow who spoke in plain language about things. . . .

I am sure there are a whole lot of people who don't like me. You know, everybody doesn't like you. You just can't expect everybody to like you. . . . I have a lot of friends of all types and of all kinds, and I am sure that all sorts of things are often said about me, as they are about other people. You can't expect anything else.

I know five or six years ago, when I was driving along University Avenue going to classes, I picked up some student on University Avenue and as we drove along he said, "Do you know that man over there?" I said, "Yes. He teaches in the English Department." He said, "He is a queer." I said, "Do you know him?" He said, "No, but he is a queer." I said, "He looks like it." There you are. I don't know the man too well. He is not a personal friend of mine. He has never been in my house and I've never been in his. He is married and has a couple of children, and, as far as I know, he is a very responsible man, and a reputable man, as far as I know. But I am sure that there are—you know, these people bandy about terms and say things all the time that they really don't know anything about and that they don't actually mean. I think in many instances in these days that if people don't like somebody they will call them a queer or red. . . . [39]

After Davies's soliloquy, Hawes, following his customary procedure, interjected:

I should also tell you than an act of homosexuality or homosexual contact between two males in this state is a felony, is a criminal offense for which, if you are convicted, you could be sentenced to a term of years in Raiford. I will also tell you that any man who cooperates with this Committee, then his testimony and the testimony of other people concerning him in that regard will not be turned over to any prosecuting official. Do you understand that?[40]

Hawes then came directly to the point: "Well, have you ever participated in homosexual acts?" Davies replied, "No sir, I have not." Reiterating the question and receiving the same response, Hawes then reminded the witness that he was under oath, asking him if he was aware of the penalty for perjury and informing him that "you could get up to twenty years for it." He continued, "Bearing that in mind, I'm going to ask you whether or not you have ever had homosexual relations with a man named Stanley Palmer, an instructor in the Music Department at the University of Florida?"[41] Acknowledging meeting Palmer on his arrival but denying engaging with him in sex, Davies was then asked pointedly by Hawes: "Did you on that occasion have a homosexual relationship with Mr. Palmer where, as I remember the testimony, he took your penis in his mouth and you took his in yours?" Davies uttered a simple "No." Hawes persisted, "That never happened." Unflinching, he replied, "No, sirree."[42]

Questions and denials continued:

> Have you ever had any homosexual relationship with any other professor at the University of Florida?
> I have not.
> Have you ever had any homosexual relationship with any student at the University of Florida?
> No.
> . . . Do you know any that you have seen commit any homosexual act?
> Not that I have seen.
> Do you know any that ever told you they were homosexuals?
> Yes.
> Any faculty members?
> Yes.
> Who was that?
> Professor Fullam.
> He is dead now, I believe?
> Yes. . . . [43]

Hawes then turned the interrogation to the subject matter of Davies's teaching:

> In your lectures before the classes do you ever discuss matters of sex?
> Never homosexuality, of course. Where sex does come up—and please remember that this is a University class, a Sophomore class, and we read many works where sex does play a part, as it does in all the great novels that we study, all the works of literature that we study. . . . Today in this lecture that we do on the opera *Rigoletto,* which deals, of course, with the Duke, who was a libertine, and who is trying to seduce and does seduce Gilda. Rigoletto, himself, is the jester of the Duke. It is impossible to avoid talking about it, any more than we read the novel *Of Human Bondage.* . . . [Sex] is a primary motivation in any work of art—literature, painting. . . . I've always tried to handle it honestly and frankly. Like in these lectures on art, if it is an Italian Renaissance lecture, where they have a lot of nudes . . . I've always handled it in my classroom discussions and in talks with any student on a frank and open basis, as sex is being talked about these days. It isn't "hush-hush" any more.[44]

The examiner then directed Davies's attention back to Stanley Palmer, who had admitted a homosexual encounter with the popular humanities professor. Davies again denied the accusation, and Hawes asked, "Do you know of any reason he had for saying a thing like that if it were not true?" Davies answered:

> I can't imagine why he would dislike or hate me that much. I really can't. I know that when he was in my house . . . I did not find him a person that I wanted to have a friendship with. . . . I can't understand why that sort of thing

would make him say a thing of that kind about me, unless maybe, if he were on the pan—and I don't know what you know about him—it may be that he is just clutching at somebody.[45]

After several more minutes of dodges and denials on Davies's part, Hawes stared forcefully at Davies: "Mr. Davies, you have not had sexual relationships with any of your students or with any member of the faculty?" Davies replied, "No sirree." Hawes added: "Or with anybody else, for that matter?" After admitting to a homosexual experience as a Boy Scout of thirteen, Davies went on to make another lengthy statement, which included:

> I have what I think is a very satisfying life and I am doing the things I like to do in the way I like to do them. I realize, of course, that there are a lot of things, all sorts of things, that would make a teacher undesirable—alcoholism, communism, homosexuality, having an affair with a student and having to marry her. . . . I am certainly aware of my position as a faculty member. I am sorry, perhaps, in a way, that I am not one hundred percent a conformist, perhaps, but I think it is good for the University to have all sorts and types of people. . . . I am aware of the fact that a whole lot of people don't like me. I am sorry; I wish they did, but they don't. I can understand them saying, "Hell! Here's Davies. He wears these fancy jackets," or "Here's Davies who goes to Europe every summer." . . . I can understand how there can be, maybe, a little bit of envy or jealousy. . . . I know a number of instructors who are probably not as well liked by their students as I am, and they may resent the fact that the students like me. . . . God knows, I've heard everything in Gainesville that everybody else has heard, some of which I suppose is true. . . . But, as for this casual stuff about this person or that person, I have no idea whether it is true and in many cases I don't give a damn.[46]

Continuing to deny any homosexual involvement, Davies was dismissed at two minutes before five with a warning that he would likely be recalled.

Before Davies was next summoned before the Committee, others were called forward to incriminate him further. Mr. Victor was a middle-aged employee at Wilson's Department Store who frequented the courthouse men's room and was once jailed for soliciting. He acknowledged spotting Davies (twice at the courthouse), whom he described as a "rather pompous, big man." Victor qualified himself: "I have seen him down there, but just passing through. He came in and went out again, but I certainly would not say there was anything wrong. He moved in and rushed right out, as he does most things."[47]

Victor had little affinity for Davies. Davies had visited his home on two occasions to see Taylor, Davies's former student:

> He has never been invited back and he never will be because I don't like Davies. . . . He was not made welcome when he came. . . . I said, "How are

you, Davies?" That was it. I didn't even bother to go and say good-bye to him.
. . . Davies is loud and vulgar. He irritates me. . . . If someone comes into a
room and shouts at you, when you are standing a couple of feet away from
him, brags about his possessions, about his trips to Europe, about everything
he has, when you have not particularly asked for any of that, I consider that
exceedingly bad manners and a kind of vulgarity.[48]

Later that day Taylor, who was a Davies dinner party regular and had
watched over his house while he was in Europe for the summer, testified.
Still sharing a home with Victor and another gay man, Taylor freely admitted his homosexual activity. He had just finished a year's suspension for a
sexual incident with a university janitor. Currently undergoing weekly psychiatric treatment, Taylor told Hawes, "I feel like he [the doctor] has
helped me a great deal. . . . Actually, he told me it stems from things that
happened in childhood."[49] Asked if he had had sexual relations with
Davies, he was equally forthright: "With God as my witness, he has never
approached me, never. . . . When I moved out of that place, there was a
question about the telephone bill and I think I owed him about forty dollars and he came out to get it. He had come back from Europe and he had
spent all his money there and he actually needed the money very badly."[50]

The following day a local repairman also testified to having seen Davies
occasionally in the courthouse rest room. Like the others, Mayfield never
observed Davies engaging in any sexual activity, although he gave an apt
description. "He always has a shirt and tie on, but I always noticed that he
had on that charcoal and white coat, but there is more charcoal than white
in it."[51]

At midmorning on Thursday, January 8, Professor Davies was summoned to the Manor Hotel for his third interrogation. He tried to walk a
delicate balance between acknowledging acquaintances and disclosing
names while appearing forthright and responsible. As he put it later, "In
most cases I knew these people but I hadn't had any sex with them or even
any sex talk. I tried to get out by saying it was all a damn lie. I was trying to
curry favor, stay in good, and keep my job; I was ass kissing."

After being resworn and confirming his "flat denials" regarding homosexual activity, Davies volunteered: "This week we have to hand in an approved
list of our students and when I read my list of my students, I noted the name
of that Reeves boy, who is in my class, and whom I've had coffee with, and
seen several times, and I do remember him. I did not remember him Monday.
. . . I know a great many students whose names I do not know. . . . "[52]

Hawes began:

> Now since you've been before the Committee, Mr. Davies, I want to tell
> you that we've had further sworn testimony.
> Against me?

Yes, sir. Do you desire to make any change in your testimony at all?
No, I do not, sir. . . .
If you're an innocent man, you should stand by your position, but I want you to understand fully the consequences and the position of the Committee.
Yes sir, I do.

Hawes barraged him with questions while Davies frequently interrupted.

Have you ever picked up a man in the rest room at the Student Union Building during the day time—
I never go to the Student Union Building.
Wait a minute, let me finish my question. During the day time, during a break in your classes, and take him over to your apartment in your car—to your house, not your apartment—in your car, and have a homosexual relationship with him?
No, I have not taken anybody over there at a break of class to have a homosexual relationship.
Have you ever taken anybody over there at all from the Student Union Building bathroom?
No, not from the bathroom; I have taken students to my house at various times from all sorts of places, but not from the Student Union bathroom, toilet, no.
Did you ever take any businessmen in Gainesville—
Not that I know—
—to your house at all?
I don't know very many businessmen in Gainesville anyway, sir.
Did you ever take a businessman in Gainesville to your house that you made a contact with in the bathroom at the Student Union Building—
No—
—during the day time, and have any homosexual relationship with him?
—not that I know of.
Did you do that, and later call that man's office and leave word with his secretary to contact you?
I'm sure not; don't remember anything like that.
Did you leave with his secretary your telephone number—
Sir, I've left—
—and name?
I've left my name and number, sir, with a number of Gainesville businessmen for all sorts of reasons, but I, not this, not for that reason. . . .
Have you had any businessman in Gainesville in your house at all?
Well, I suppose so, yes. I've had merchants and, as I say, collectors, people seeing me about various things. . . .
You've had no Gainesville businessmen in your home socially at all?
Well, I can't remember that I have; no, I really can't. Maybe I have had, but I can't remember.
Certainly, not that you had any homosexual relationship with?
No.

Pausing in the sprint of questions, Davies puzzled:

The thing that I can't really understand, sir, is this: That here I am at the University; I have a good reputation here, and I've had it all the other places I've ever been, and I've been all sorts of places, and so forth, and as I said before, I may be the kind of personality that a great many people may not like, but I certainly don't go with people of bad reputation or bad moral character, or riffraff of any kind, and I am puzzled, worried, concerned, and so forth, at the fact that I have been more or less—I mean, the focus of something which seems to be—you almost think would be a plot, the—or that I'm going to be the fall guy for something. . . .

Interrupting, Hawes declared: "Mr. Davies let me tell you something: This Committee is not trying to make any fall guy out of you."

Davies equivocated: "No sir, I didn't say you were, Mr. Hawes. I didn't say you were at all, but I—I mean, I can't understand, you know—I didn't imply that, I don't think you meant—I mean, that I actually said that—"

Regaining advantage, Hawes pressed:

Now you said there seems to be a plot against you?
No—well, I mean—
What do you mean by that?
Well, I mean, why I—I just wonder why I, who, seemingly, is a pretty good, decent citizen fellow although, of course, I can realize why a number of people may not have cared for me, or liked me, I just wondered why I am—I am the sort of focus of this—I don't mean from you, but from these people. . . .
What motive, what possible motive—
God knows.
—could a businessman that you've had that little contact with have—
—God knows, I can't see it.
—for giving false testimony here against you?
I can't see it, I can't see it.
Can you imagine any motive that a Gainesville businessman that you know so little—
No, I can't, I really can't, I swear. . . .
Can you imagine why a Mr. Palmer would want to make such a statement as this about you? . . . You don't have much contact with that man, do you?
I haven't—I haven't seen him, I suppose, half a dozen times, and I haven't talked to him over two or three times in over a couple of years. . . . I've seen him at the Campus Club or the Hub. This year I don't think I've—I have seen him I think, once or twice on campus. . . .
You couldn't have had enough contact with him for him to dislike you extremely, could you, to the point of making a false accusation of this kind?

Rambling, Davies sought to make his case:

Well, the only thing—the only thing, Mr. Hawes, that I could think of, was at the end of our testimony the other day, Monday, I believe, I thought that since I did know him, know who he was, and we talked and we have—our interests were only on musical subjects, that—and then, I didn't have him around. I mean, I've had some dinners—I had a supper party for a pianist who played here last year. I've had a number of other musical evenings. I had a party for a Metropolitan Opera singer when she was here. I've had some other musical people around, and I've never had him over, never even thought about him. In fact, I found him very uninteresting and just dropped him like a hot cake. I mean—just never have anything to do with him. I think that he is aware of some of my, oh, social activities, some of my travels. . . . I mean I go about, do a lot, have a good collection of phonograph records, and I entertain a lot, and so forth. Maybe he disliked me, resented my lack of interest, or invitations, and so forth, and maybe he was—if he is, as you say, an admitted homosexual—maybe he was frightened, terrified, frantic, or something and clutched on me as the . . . [53]

About an hour into his testimony, Hawes requested that Davies wait around the hotel for a few minutes. A short time later Davies was escorted back into the hotel room. "Sit down," snapped Hawes. "I want you to hear this man's testimony."

It was a rare moment during these secret hearings that accused confronted accuser. Professor Stanley Palmer entered. Confirming his visit to Davies's home in the fall of 1956, he testified: "After talking or, perhaps, a drink or a Coke or something to eat we participated in a homosexual act." Davies declined Mr. Hawes's offer to ask Palmer questions.

Hawes then turned to Palmer, asking, "Do you have any reason to tell a lie about this man?"

"I have no reason to tell a lie about anyone. I would not, ordinarily, disclose anything like this, of this nature. I respect Mr. Davies as a professor and it's my understanding that he is one of the finest professors in his area; and had I not been under sworn oath and agreed to have told the whole truth, and nothing but the truth, I would not have said anything."[54]

After dismissing the music professor, Hawes turned to Davies. "I remind you, Mr. Davies, that you remain under oath. Was what he said the truth?" The professor calmly replied, "Not concerning me." Hawes went on to ask Davies if he would care to listen to Mr. Potter, the businessman. "If you want to, it's all right with me, sir," responded Davies. Reiterating full denial, Davies was dismissed for the day.[55]

Davies worried obsessively: "Who's going to snitch on me?" "Who's going to be next?" He got some inside information from his neighbor, the gay English professor, who "could afford to hire a lawyer for $3,000, half a professor's annual salary. Stowe had an 'in' with the Committee. He knew who was going to be questioned the next day." Davies would surreptitiously meet with Stowe: "We would go out in his car or my car and park in a secluded area. Then we would walk away to talk. We were afraid that even the cars were bugged. We certainly would never say anything over the telephone. He would tell me who the Committee had examined that day."

Four decades later a pained expression appears on Davies's grimacing face as his emotions surface: "It was a fearful time. Every waking moment—fear. Fear of disgrace. Fear of losing my job. Fear of no money. It was awful. It was a horrible experience. It was all conspiratorial; at times, I felt I was in a chapter of a Dostoevsky novel."

Tactics and Semantics

During the three weeks of testimony in Gainesville, nearly fifty men came before the Johns Committee. These ranged from the sheriff, university psychiatrists, and student informants to homosexual schoolteachers, university faculty and staff members, and other gay men living in the community. Only one woman, the estranged wife of an accused professor, testified. Although a few were hesitant, all but one acceded to the Committee's demand for sworn testimony, and only two were accompanied by attorneys. Some employed tactics of memory loss, and others offered a variety of excuses for their homosexual lapses.

Along with Arlen Davies, another professor on whom the Committee had amassed substantial information was Abe McCormack. Like Davies, he appeared before the Committee for three lengthy sessions under Hawes's rapier examination. Returning for the second time, following others' sworn testimony implicating him, McCormack continued to deny all. He admitted, though, that he had had conversations with several potential witnesses about "what they accused me of." Hawes seized on McCormack's words with prosecutorial prowess:

> *Are you being accused of anything here?*
> Well, what's the hearing about then?
> *There hasn't [been] anybody in this room accuse you of anything in this room has there? We have asked you certain questions, haven't we?*
> You know, Mr. Hawes, I had better wait for my lawyer because you are a very, very smart man.
> *Has anybody accused you of anything in this room?*
> Well, there is a hearing . . . and you said that you had affidavits.
> *I told you that we had certain evidence and testimony.*
> And affidavits, yes.
> *Did I say "affidavits?" . . . or is that your impression of what I said?*
> Yes it is. This is my impression. . . .
> *We will let the record speak on whether I said anything about any signed affidavits.*
> Well, excuse me—sworn testimony.[56]

6 spaceDARK NIGHTS OF THE SOUL

After a series of questions about McCormack's contact with one of the witnesses and begrudging responses from him, the clearly frustrated professor declined to answer any further questions. Another hearing was scheduled for the following day.

Also summoned before the Committee was the male couple who owned the infamous "Chicken Ranch," named for two long, now vacant chicken houses sitting near the white-framed L-shaped house with jalousie windows and a large porch. Winslow had bought the five-acre property when he and Lowell had moved to Gainesville in 1949. Winslow had graduated from Dartmouth before World War I and had served in the Red Cross in the Philippines and China before returning to the New York theater. He eventually journeyed to Hawaii, and during World War II he entertained troops in the Pacific, where he met a badly wounded Marine, the much younger Lowell.

The seventy-year-old Winslow, who occasionally produced plays for the Gainesville Little Theater group, rambled on about his early years in the theater and in the Pacific. Hawes tried to pin the elderly man down. "We have received considerable sworn testimony that certain homosexuals among the student body and the faculty of the University of Florida have attended parties, predominantly homosexual, at your farm. . . . Now, what I want from you is what you have in your mind, facts in your mind, concerning homosexuals in this area."

The gentleman shrewdly responded:

Well, undoubtedly, of course, there are, but from my own personal contacts, as you might say, you can't prove it by me on a thousand Bibles. I—whenever we had those parties, I was too busy in the house. . . . That was years ago, before I had my stroke, but they got out of hand and that's chiefly why we stopped them. . . . People coming down there that I didn't know anything about. . . . I don't remember names; I wouldn't remember names. In fact, I couldn't tell any of you people's names; my memory doesn't retain it. I couldn't for the life of me.[57]

Denying having engaged in homosexual activity while in Florida (with the exception of one young man "who crawled in bed with me . . . and woke me out of a sound sleep"), he refused to answer whether his long-term companion was homosexual: "Whatever he is I consider that his private affair. . . . You just don't say such a thing about people!"[58]

Winslow went on to describe the legendary parties at the Chicken Ranch. Twenty or thirty carloads of people would appear, mostly uninvited friends of friends whom Lowell had invited while he was drinking at the Burger House. A handful of women attended. "'Dikes,' [sic] to use the vernacular . . . but they behaved themselves," dancing with themselves while the men danced together to gramophone music. Winslow would drink one or two highballs or old-fashioneds while Lowell guzzled beer, and the couple seldom paid any attention to goings-on in the automobiles or out in the darkness of the lawn.

The testimony from Lowell, a native Georgian, followed on the heels of Winslow's. Denying ever engaging in homosexual activity, he explained away the homosexuals crowding the ranch:

> We just had open house and I noted a lot of the crowd didn't seem according to Hoyle, but they never caused any trouble or anything; they always brought their bottles, they didn't cost us anything. Then one day the Sheriff came over to the hardware store and he first told me that he had staked out my place that night . . . he told me what kind of a crowd it was. . . . I heard them talk, but I never heard them talking homosexual. . . . Oh, they sometimes acted not according to mannish actions out there, but when they get to drinking and everything, who can tell?[59]

Lowell, too, suffered memory lapses at the Committee hearing. "Tell me a telephone number and I can tell you what it is a year from now; tell me your name, and I'll forget it in ten minutes."[60]

Later testimony from the sheriff, who had formerly been head of university security, recalled driving out with student reporters from the school newspaper, the *Alligator,* and surveilling it for several hours. When the party broke up, the sheriff trailed one of the estimated twenty-five to fifty cars, eventually stopping the driver, only to find "no trace of alcohol." Informed by the county prosecutor that he lacked legal authority to intervene, the next day he confronted Lowell: "I was not going to tolerate that sort of thing in Alachua County, that I was not aware what, legally, could be done, but I wanted to assure him of one thing, that I could do it publicly-wise that would wreck him and everybody else."[61]

Challenges and Explanations

Despite the extensive publicity and heavy-handed police techniques, few challenges to the Committee were voiced within or outside the hearing room. A few witnesses were more forceful in their insistence on legal counsel or refused to testify. Dr. Yolander answered pro forma questions regarding his name, occupation, and so forth. In response to Hawes's question regarding homosexual activity, he replied, "Before I answer that question I think I would have to consult an attorney." Hawes snapped:

> Go and contact your attorney. You are here because we have sworn testimony, already taken, that you have engaged in homosexual activities within the last two years, here in this county, with certain people connected with the University. . . . Homosexuality is a felony under the statutes of Florida, as he can advise you. It is a crime and the penalty for it is a term of years in state prison.

. . . If need be, for those people who do not cooperate with us, and who we have sworn testimony on, in order to get to the root of this thing . . . we may have to turn this information over to the State Attorney for criminal action; but for those people who cooperate with us and tell the truth, we do not intend to take any criminal action at all.

Yolander deciphered Hawes's legalese, noting that "you do not intend to take any criminal action, but if testimony were made it would be available to some other—"

"No," Hawes interrupted.

Persisting: "But if it is taken it can be given up—"

Interrupting again, Hawes asserted: "This is not a public hearing and the record we will make here is not open. It will stay in our Committee files and we will not release it."[62]

The interrogation lasted eight minutes. Within an hour Yolander returned to the hearing room accompanied by his attorney. Queried about his homosexual activity, Yolander invoked his Fifth Amendment right not to offer testimony that might incriminate him. His attorney then interjected, "We challenge the authority and the jurisdiction of this committee to pursue that line of questioning against this individual." Hawes curtly replied, "We have been challenged on that ground many times. Thank you, gentlemen."[63] This two-minute appearance marked his last before the Investigation Committee.

Only one admitted homosexual student refused to cooperate with the Committee, Caldwell Fenton. Summoned during the Committee's second week of closed hearings, Fenton declined to answer questions about sexual activities or identities of other gay men. Sent outside to reconsider his options and the failure to testify "at his own peril," Fenton returned an hour later to engage in an emotionally bludgeoning examination:

I have just been pulled over here without any counsel whatsoever.
Well, you are—you have already declined to answer a number of our questions. . . . We have honored that denial, haven't we? We haven't pressed you for an answer. . . . Do you now decline to go any further in your testimony?
No sir, I do not, but I—I—I want an extension of time in order to do it.

At that point the discussion moved off the record. The record continued with Fenton agreeing to testify, "but I make it under very strong emotional pressure. . . . The extreme urgency of having to do it now, and having to give names of all these people. . . . "

Hawes objected. "You're not going to sit here and give me any testimony, Mr. Fenton, prefacing, in the record with a statement that you are being pressured, that you are being compelled to give any statement here. Do you understand that, sir?"

The chief counsel whittled away at the youth.

I realize that, Mr. Hawes. You don't have to raise your voice. . . . This sort of thing has certainly brought—aided in bringing about the anxiety that has brought about this pressure right now.

What sort of thing?

This kind—the talk that has been going on, the alternatives which I have; the fact that I have only these few hours in which to decide whether I want to testify; that all contributes to the emotional pressure under which I will testify.

Well, you're not going to testify before this Committee under any emotional pressure at all, sir. . . .

All right, I will testify.

No sir, no sir.

All right, then I will testify unconditionally. Is that fair?

Let me tell you something, Mr. Fenton. I never have, and I don't intend to take any testimony from any witness who sits and faces me and tells me that he feels like he's being compelled to testify. . . . You're either going to testify freely and voluntarily, or you're not going to testify any further at all. Now, there ain't any 'ifs,' 'ands,' and 'buts' about that. Do you understand that, sir?

Yes.

Do you desire to testify freely and voluntarily or do you desire to exercise one of your other alternatives and walk out of here unencumbered, unhindered by any of us?

All right, I'll testify.

Is that the alternative you desire to exercise?

Yes.

Now, that's your alternative?

Yes.

You chose it; we didn't choose it for you, did we?

No.

All right, sir. Mr. Fenton who on the University of Florida faculty have you had homosexual relations with?[64]

Fenton then proceeded to name Professor Palmer as well as other homosexuals working in a nearby school system.

Another student was also wary of the Committee's authority and tactics. After a long exchange regarding his obligation to testify against himself and the necessity to provide all requested information, Lee, who now lives in New York City, freely admitted his homosexuality. He went on to observe, however: "It seems to me that I have a certain kind of responsibility to myself; I have to make some judgment about whether what I say is going to be useful or whether it's going to be—perhaps, do more harm in some other direction than it would do good to you. This is not a judgment that *you'll* make. . . . I can't just come here and tell everything I know or have heard rumored."[65]

Unlike Yolander, Fenton, and Lee, most chose a less confrontational approach. They attempted to skirt declarations of their homosexuality, or they bracketed their eventual admissions with excuses: Alistair, a graduate student, said that he frequented the men's room with sex "evidently . . . in the back of my mind." After he had witnessed some homosexual activity, it began "to prey on my mind. I guess it was more curiosity. . . . Such acts never occurred to me until I would go to the rest room and see some of the writings on the wall and pornographic pictures . . . and anybody engaged in it."[66] Hastings, the operating room technician who had been loitering on the courthouse commode for nearly a half hour before being apprehended, claimed, "My normal bowel movement requires about that length of time."[67] Mayfield, who had graduated in 1932, acknowledged that the rest room bore that reputation even then but claimed his multiple visits were the result of chronic diarrhea.[68] Another man whose wife was pregnant claimed that a physician's diagnosis of "gleet" and prescription of sex twice a week drove him to the courthouse men's room.

Departures

University life in the sleepy 1950s was quite different from campus life a decade later. Merril recalled: "When the professors were being fired I was pretty outraged by it but it wasn't at a personal level, because I didn't associate with faculty members. It wasn't until they started to purge the student body that it came home to me." Jim Patterson noted: "Nowadays if a professor, let alone a small army of professors were fired because of their sexual orientation, the whole university would be up in arms. But back in those days, 'queers shouldn't be teaching.'"

As the Johns Committee wrapped up its hearings, moving back and forth between the Manor and Thomas Hotels to keep reporters at bay, the university chapter of the American Association of University Professors (AAUP) distributed a mimeographed flyer recounting the history of the Johns Committee and announcing a meeting to discuss the Committee's extralegal procedures, the feasibility of employing counsel for staff members, and issues relating to tenure and dismissal. Reiterating "our firm hope and belief that members of the faculty will always cooperate with the administration or with properly constituted committees," the flyer underscored that "it is essential that there be no infringement upon the legal rights of any citizen, nor upon the principles of academic freedom and tenure. . . . "[69] By the time the local AAUP chapter met on January 27, the Florida Legislative Investigation Committee had already left town, hauling nearly 2,000 pages of sworn testimony, boxes of investigative field reports, compromising photographs, tape recordings, and faculty files to the state capitol.

In early April, President Reitz announced the dismissal of fourteen employees for homosexual activities. Refusing to release the Committee's report to the university, he emphasized that "there is no reason to believe that the extent of homosexual conduct at the University of Florida is unique. . . . Certainly this statement neither condones such activity nor alters our firm position in taking action whenever we develop adequate evidence."[70]

Meanwhile Arlen Davies waited. "It was a Spanish inquisition–type experience. The whole university was terrified; everyone talked about it and the ones that didn't talk about it were secretly worried that they would be next or that they would have to testify against someone else."

Never having been apprehended by law enforcement officers for engaging in homosexual activity and absent adequate evidence to merit a criminal indictment, Davies was not among the fourteen. Though he was a well-respected tenured assistant professor, he awaited word from the president following review of his file.

"Tenure didn't mean a goddamn thing. If they wanted to get rid of you they would find a way." And they did. "It ruined careers. There were firings of professors from a whole range of departments—chemistry, English, biology, political science, art"—as well as two senior administrators. One administrator was dismissed "for picking up niggah boys." Stowe "was never interrogated, his name never appeared in the newspapers. He took a leave of absence to teach at a college on Long Island then returned a couple years later to quiet retirement."[71] Professor Jeffries (the "nelly English instructor") "was never questioned or arrested, but quickly married and then divorced, later remarried, and divorced again."

A memorandum to Charley Johns from Mark Hawes assessed the aftermath:

> The President had the affidavits and information furnished by this Committee. Several other faculty members admittedly were released for this reason but it was impossible to determine . . . whether they had been recommended to some other institution for employment. A total of 16 persons on the University of Florida payroll with a rank of faculty member or above were proven to have engaged in homosexual conduct while employed at the University of Florida.[72]

Deceit, Denial, and Defiance

As the graduating class of 1959 prepared for final exams, two more dismissals raised the total to sixteen.

Sigismond Diettrich, who under Hawes's scrutiny had admitted homosexual activity but refused to reveal any other names, was the chair of the university's geography department. "I never knew when the blow would strike. I had my plan when the president would call me. . . . I acquired a lethal dosage of aspirin (the only damn thing I could lay my hands on) and I would jump out of the tower. Doesn't it all sound melodramatic?" As he trekked to the administration building on a mid-April morning, his thoughts turned to his first year of teaching on campus and first lingering in the courthouse men's room twenty-eight years earlier.

> Even now I cannot retell that short twenty minutes which finished my life. All I remember is that he started off saying, "Sig, this is a most serious and, to me, most unpleasant task," and somewhere from a cold crypt my voice came hollow and raw, "Yes, I know." . . . I slowly composed myself. I have to execute my plan. I went over to the Church and in my blind arrogance I argued with God that killing myself is a necessity and cannot be a sin. This settled, I went out to school—I had the aspirin there. I took 85 of the damned pills. . . . I climbed up and looked down onto the cold wet concrete sidewalk. I turned yellow. I could not jump. . . . I was guilty of breaking conventions. I was guilty of not measuring up to what I was supposed to have been.[73]

Arlen Davies also received a call from one of the vice president's offices asking him to come over.

> He was a nice guy. We had a very civilized discussion. We talked about Germany, the war, and art. Then he said, "This is the whole big thing." He handed me a file with a blue cover. He showed me copies of the materials the Committee had forwarded to the university, including my statements and those of my accusers. "The President has reviewed these materials and considered your situation. We are going to have to release you." He didn't use the word "fired," but he told me they were going to let me go for "gross indecency."

Sixteen faculty and staff had now resigned or been dismissed and a few others quietly retired or accepted extended, unpaid leaves of absence. Like Diettrich and Davies, some were distinguished faculty members with stellar academic and teaching credentials.[74]

Professor Roberts had "left an Associate Professorship to come to us and help build here a well rounded music program. His musicianship, teaching composition, and concertizing are highly regarded. . . . A productive teacher and an unusually versatile musician. . . . He assumes leadership in campus and community projects."

Professor Quigby "has done particularly fine and important work as a member of the staff in English and his contribution to Upper Division work has been highly regarded."

Professor Stowe "has proved himself a proficient member of our staff, an active member of national organizations, a productive scholar, and a regular participant in the cultural affairs of the community. . . . Teaching has been excellent . . . we now have to offer the course in several sections. It is one of those courses which gives our University students . . . an opportunity to continue the broadening aspects of their education."

Davies remained in Gainesville through the end of the spring semester. "I told my family that I was taking a year off because of heart trouble—

which, of course, was not true. I just lied; it was a tissue of lies. I think mother and dad both suspected something."

While his family suspected, the army knew. An army reservist for seventeen years, Major Arlen Davies was summoned "before a board—it wasn't a court-martial." Despite the appearance of character witnesses, Davies was forced to forfeit his monthly pension.

Without any income, Davies lost his house. He drifted from place to place with his possessions crowded in a 1954 Plymouth sedan that "was falling to pieces. I was frightened all of the time. I didn't have anything. . . . It was difficult: lying, wandering, borrowing, sponging. It was a hand-to-mouth existence. I borrowed $300 from Jules. He said, 'Arlen, you've had a great influence on me. You did a lot for me. Of course, I will help.' Some of my other students helped me out. Patterson lent me money to have the brakes in my car fixed."

Finding another college teaching position was a momentous obstacle. "I applied for job after job. I drove to Alabama for one job interview and had to sleep in the car." At another prospective university an administrator asked Davies why he left Florida. "Schools in Florida and the states surrounding it had heard about the Johns Committee. I said it was a witch-hunt. He was very sympathetic. But he couldn't 'take a chance' on hiring me."

As Davies lapsed into his second year of unemployment and moved from one friend's home to another, he informed his family that he was taking "a leave to travel. I didn't want to disgrace them." Suddenly fate appeared to smile. Davies was the first choice at a university for "the best job I ever had been offered in my life. The man even showed me my desk and asked, 'Could you start Monday?'" Before formally offering Davies the position, a telephone call was made to his old UF department chairperson: "The chairman had stood up for me and, in fact, had put his two sons in my classes [one of whom, according to Patterson, 'was a known homosexual in town']. He was asked, 'If we hire Professor Davies for a year, would you hire him back?' That was just a routine question. The man simply said, 'No.' If he only had told a white lie. . . . "

Five years after his dismissal from the University of Florida, with letters of recommendation in hand and an administrator choosing to believe that Davies had been caring for his bedridden father, Professor Davies returned to the classroom at a junior college. "It was a job. Honey, I would have taken a job at a high school! I had to work; I had to teach. Oh! The lies I told for survival, just survival!"

As the mid-1960s witnessed freer sexual attitudes and mores, Davies continued to lead a sexual double life and deny his Florida past. "I was constantly frightened and afraid that I would be exposed." Later, as Stonewall erupted in Greenwich Village, Davies was finally ready to put his past aside. Symbolically, he burned his blue file.

As the years passed, Southern gay events rapped at Davies's closet door: the formation of campus gay organizations at the University of Florida and Florida State University and their battle for state recognition; Dade County's adoption of a nondiscrimination ordinance and the subsequent fury of "Hurricane Anita"; the growing muscle of the Houston Gay Political Caucus, which helped to elect a reformist mayor; the growth of Southern lesbian and gay publications; the proliferation of bathhouses and bars, coastal resorts, and rural enclaves.

As a new generation, dancing to the music of Madonna and Queen, entered into Southern gay life, few remembered Charley Johns's campus tirade. Meanwhile, Jules was diagnosed as HIV-positive in California, Ford operated a co-op in New York, Jim rose to full professor in theater, and Arlen Davies quietly retired as professor emeritus. As popular music evolved from disco and punk to rave and industrial, Davies was still plagued by what-ifs: "Maybe if I had enough money, I could have fought it. Would they have been willing to hold a public hearing? How far would they have gone?" Over the decades, though, Davies's spirit has been tempered and his self-esteem strengthened:

> I am sorry this happened, of course. Oh, God! I am sorry. It was the darkest night of the soul that St. John of the Cross talked about. Those were just horrible years. I was gasping for breath, just trying to breathe and live.
>
> But any experience you have is good for you unless it crushes your spirit. I started out again at the age of forty-nine. I now live in a great city with an excellent opera company, a great ballet, and every cultural event. I have lots of friends and I own a home which I bought for a song.
>
> *Now,* if someone says now, "Arlen, didn't you get fired from the University of Florida?" I'd say: "You're damn right I was! Why the hell are you telling me that? Are you trying to hurt me? Trying to insult me? Trying to blackmail me?" You see, *now* I am in command.

3

Ferreting Out
the Lesbian Menace

The Purple Pamphlet
and the Deans of Women

IN 1947 A FISHING BOAT, the *Poor Poppy*, exploded at sea, killing all aboard. The intention of the businessman who had placed the bomb was to murder his wife in order to marry his mistress. At the last moment, the wife failed to board; the father of a pugnacious little girl about to celebrate her sixth birthday did.[1]

A few years later this small and sickly child blossomed into a butch fifth grader. "Protecting" girls, Penny sent one boy to the hospital with a broken collarbone and another with a cracked skull. Penny's unconventionality continued into adolescence. During her high school years, Penny was known for her "wild parties," where mostly gay kids would romp and dance, drink, and make out:

> My stepfather and mother went fishing down in the Keys every weekend. So we would go to my house and party. We would drive down Flagler, Miami's main street, yelling the address out. Hundreds of people would come. It was mainly gay kids, but there were a few "fag hags" who would hang around the boys and the straight men in love with lesbians. We tolerated them. We'd dance the night away—boys with boys, girls with girls—to the Panama, the chicken, the hully gully. We would get up with our hangovers the next day and go to 22nd Street Beach.
>
> Routinely the police would get a complaint. But what finally did it was when they busted up our party and found two guys out in a blanket in the

backyard. They told my mother. She started staying home and letting my step-
father go fishing while she chaperoned these wild parties.

The Hialeah senior high school class of 1958 was full of "gay kids," as
they called themselves. "We had found ourselves and we were mighty
happy." Penny hung out with a gay man "pretending to pretend to have a
front." Holling Merritt escorted her to the senior prom; she led.[2] They
walked each morning holding hands through the center of the school,
where the football players and cheerleaders congregated. "They would jeer
and catcall; we would yell back equally insulting things."

Penny dreamed of attending Barnard; its location near Greenwich Village
was not lost upon her mother. "She knew exactly where I would end up
and what I would do." Thus Penny attended the more conservative and af-
fordable Florida State University (FSU). "I was forbidden to major in PE—
given its reputation and because I was so blatant—so I majored in modern
languages."

When Julia Penelope Stanley arrived at FSU in 1958, "my reputation pre-
ceded me." Penny remembers Tallahassee as a "stereotypical small, hilly
Southern town that was very segregated." Campus life was restrictive:

> The campus was cozy, with huge oak trees and Spanish moss; it also was re-
> pressive and horrendous. It had gone coed a couple years before—*that* disap-
> pointed me.
>
> Although it was still notorious as a lesbian school, no one would have any-
> thing to do with me, because I was "indiscreet and blatant." I have always fit
> the stereotype of the bull dyke: short hair, stocky, even fat. I lived in jeans.
> Since I never made any secret of who I was, I was shut out of the lesbian net-
> work. The PE majors, wearing those hideous permanents that looked like poo-
> dle cuts, had their uniform: the A-line blue skirt, the Ship 'n Shore white
> blouse, flats, and a little handheld purse. *That* was perceived as "discretion."
>
> You couldn't go out of your dorm in shorts, so all the women had to wear
> raincoats to gym class. You couldn't smoke in public. You had to be signed in
> at the dorm by ten o'clock—eleven on weekends.
>
> It was a tragedy if you didn't get into a sorority. I didn't understand it at the
> time, because I was already moving in a very different world from most of the
> girls who were freshmen. Somebody recommended me for Phi Beta Phi, and
> one of the sisters called me inviting me to breakfast.
>
> I said, "Why are you talking to me?"
>
> "You were recommended to our sorority."
>
> "Well, hon', I'm really not interested."

As a dyke, atheist, and Leninist, Penny became friendly with several gay
men. She first met the McCullersesque Leonard in a modern language course:

> Leonard considered himself a communist. He was physically malformed—be-
> coming a hunchback—but absolutely brilliant. His dream was to emigrate to

the Soviet Union, where they paid their intellectuals well. Through him I met
Hilton and his shadow, Foster. He followed Hilton around like a puppy, and
Hilton treated Foster like dog mess. Hilton was a piss-elegant faggot. He came
from money; his father was an attorney with the legislature.

During her first semester, Penny engaged in long conversations about
Marxist theory, discussed the writings of Lenin, Trotsky, and Bakunin, and
on one occasion marched in a candlelight vigil at Florida A & M in support
of civil rights:

> Leonard and I often got into intellectual arguments. In fact, it was one argu-
> ment with him that convinced me that I probably wasn't a communist. We
> were sitting in the cafeteria and he was going on as usual about how intellectu-
> als were well treated in the Soviet Union.
>   I asked, "But I thought communism was about the working class! What is
> this about intellectuals leading the revolution?"
>   "I could care less about the working class," he said.
>   That seemed a contradiction to me and we sort of had a parting of the ways.
> After that, I drifted away from communism to become an Ayn Randian objec-
> tivist!

Before their falling out, though, Leonard and Penny often hung out on
the porch after modern language classes. Penny's roving eyes sought contact with Sybil. "She was a beatnik—shades, black leotards, turtlenecks—
and allegedly bisexual." Unsuccessful with Sybil, eventually Penny made
friends with another lesbian, Jackie: "She was a Tri-Delt and involved with
this woman, Sybil, who I thought was just really hot stuff. It shocked me
that she was in a sorority. She assured me that there were lesbians in other
sororities. Sometimes we would go to the soda shop across from campus to
just talk."

Weighing the Options

By the spring of 1959 Penny and Merril were dating and occasionally traveled by bus between Tallahassee and Gainesville to see each other. Between
visits they exchanged letters that were laced with pledges of undying affection. Sometimes Merril's letters included news of the Florida State campus,
particularly that spring when she "sent me clippings from the student paper
about professors jumping out of buildings."

This was not the first time that Penny had heard about the Johns Committee:

> All the high school teachers were terrified because of his purging of the public
> schools. But it seemed very far away from me. I did have a courageous English
> teacher who regaled us by reading Gertrude Stein's "Miss Furr and Miss
> Skeene" in our college prep English class. We loved it; we cracked up! It was

one version of the story Stein told in *QED* (originally published with the title *Things as They Are*) about a love triangle she was in before she met Alice B. Toklas.

Pausing, Penny recited some lines from Stein's 1911 story:

> They were regularly gay they learned little things that are things in being gay, they learned many little things and are things in being gay, they were gay every day, they were regular, they were gay, they were gay the same length of time every day, they were gay, they were quite regularly gay.[3]

During spring break in 1959 Merril and Penny returned to Miami, where they frequented Sex Manor. There they met two other lesbians who were sociology graduate students at FSU. The conversation soon turned to Charley Johns. "The danger was conveyed to me."

As Penny journeyed back to north Florida with Merril, "all we talked about was what was going on in Gainesville." Penny continued: "Charley Johns was going to ride this pinko-queer purge into the governor's office, even though he had a relative who was gay." Merril echoed: "Penny was really anxious. Penny was known as a lesbian; I was naïve enough to think I wasn't obvious."

Penny returned to FSU "in dread." She recollected:

> During the first week back they started pulling gay guys out of classes. Someone would appear, show a note to the professor, and the student would be asked to go with this person. We knew where they were going!
>
> What we didn't know until everything was over was that, when the Johns Committee finally hit Tallahassee, the school administrators had locked up all the files and would not open them for Charley Johns. So he went down to the Tallahassee police and got the name of the most notorious town faggot. Roger was this flaming queen. They grilled him. They got names from Roger of gay men on campus. Now Roger, who hated Hilton—as many did for being so piss-elegant—served him up first.
>
> The procedure was: "You give us five names or ten names, and we'll let you go." Of course, that was just a ruse. But when they called Hilton, he gave them names—mine was one. As far as I know, I was the only lesbian in Tallahassee that was affected by the Johns Committee. Because I was not connected to the lesbian network, that's probably what saved them.

As the list of suspected FSU homosexuals lengthened, the procedures for depositions were similar to those used in Gainesville. Unlike others who faced this interrogation, Penny was quietly summoned from her history class to the office of the Dean of Women.

> We called her Kristen. She was a dyke. Although she wouldn't have called herself that, she did have a picture of her lover on her desk. They had been together for years. Kristen was in her fifties with short salt-and-pepper hair. Very

distinguished looking, she was a handsome, slender woman of 5'8" who wore tailored suits.

She announced: "We have had a report that you are a lesbian, Penny. Now, of course, this is going to go on your permanent record. It will be stamped on the record that you are a homosexual."

I was terrified; I was in a cold sweat. I was counting on a college degree. I was a lesbian; I wasn't going to get married. No one was going to support me. Not having a college degree would have limited me to driving a diaper truck or working in a factory. Options for lesbians were *very* limited those days—at least jobs where you could wear pants!

"How it affects you," she said, "is up to you."

Dismissed from the dean's office, Penny returned to her dorm in fear. As her fate hung in the balance, she weighed her options. Word of Penny's dilemma found its way to the resident assistant on her floor, who circulated a petition among the student residents, many of whom had become fond of Penny.

Since we had to be in the dorm by ten, we had a lot of time to socialize. We used to sit up to all hours playing Whist, hearts, and spades. We smoked until our rooms were a blue haze. We talked about everything. There had been a couple of lunch-counter demonstrations in Tallahassee: Would you want to eat sitting next to a Negro? Should black people have to sit in the back of the bus? But we *never* discussed lesbianism. But these straight Florida girls from places like Winter Haven and Frostproof signed a petition protesting my expulsion.

Several days later, Penny—tired, troubled, and alone—was again summoned to the office of the Dean of Women:

She offered me some very limited choices; she didn't want to just expel me.

"If it weren't for this petition, I would have to expel you," I was told. "You will visit the school psychologist once a week to be cured. We will pick your roommate for your sophomore year—someone who isn't susceptible."

Of course, I had already picked out a roommate who was straight but simpatico; they considered her "susceptible."

"So what this means," I said finally recovering my nerve, "is that you are going to put me with someone who is going to spy on me."

"Yes."

Penny chose her only real option.

During summer school Penny became quite ill and returned home. Kristen proposed that Penny remain in Miami for a year to recover: "Well, I know the Dean of Women at the University of Miami. I think we can get you in there. They probably won't let you live in the dorm, but you can live at home. Stay there a year and I will take the 'homosexual' off your record and you can return."

With the possibility of a "clean transcript" and recovering from her illness, Penny enrolled at the University of Miami. During that fall, she ran into Hilton one Sunday afternoon at the gay beach: "Hilton had been expelled and his father was furious. He didn't or couldn't use his influence on his son's behalf. He was not in school; he couldn't get into a school. His father was paying outrageous fees to send him to a psychiatrist three times a week to 'cure' him." Penny elaborated:

> Hilton had always struck me as very nervous and what was called in those days "high-strung." He was more so when I ran into him in Miami after the Johns debacle, but also extremely apologetic for having given the Committee my name. He was also defensive, arrogant, and tried to downplay the fact that the Johns Committee, with his father's cooperation, had wrecked his life.

Meanwhile, Penny was having family problems of her own.

> I had a fight with my stepfather, who had tried to rape me a couple of times. I took money out of my savings account, moved out, and found an apartment in Coral Gables without the dean knowing it.
>
> Now, I was also involved in the theater group, which had rehearsals until all hours of the night. We were doing *Lysistrata,* a comedy by Aristophanes. I was one of the Spartan women. Two of the actors lived up in Hollywood and had eight o'clock classes. So they took to staying over and sleeping on my floor rather than making that long commute. Well, this little old lady who lived across the hall reported me to the dean.

Again summoned to the dean's office, Penny was asked: "Can't you go back home?" She shook her head and explained her dilemma. The Dean of Women called Penny's mother, who confirmed her story. The dean, in turn, found herself in a dilemma, declaring: "Well, we can't have you living in the dorm and seducing all of these women." Penny was tossed out of school after eight weeks—this time for allowing men to spend the night at her apartment.

Encounter of the First Kind

While Penny was struggling in Miami, Merril was in her sophomore year in Gainesville. Sitting in the student union as the 1959 fall term began, Merril chatted with Jamie, a gay student who also lived on campus. The two had met in a music class and soon came out to one another. Occasionally the two would go on "fake" dates. "He was so cute: big smile, beautiful teeth, freckles. He was so into his music and very nelly." On that particular day, though, Jamie looked glum:

> "They think they are finished with the professors now, so they are going to start hitting on the students." He paused. "But we aren't going to be in as

much trouble as the professors were. We will have a choice: leave or get help. What they *really* want is for us to get help."

When Jamie told me this, I got a little nervous, but again I thought it wouldn't happen to me because "nobody knows I'm queer." I really thought in my head that I could walk around campus looking like the biggest dyke in the universe, but no one would suspect I was queer. It was just the magical thinking of youth.

Unlike Penny, Merril developed a small network of lesbian friends who lived on campus. They would often drive to Tampa to visit the gay bars. There were other students whom Merril "suspected." One was a woman she and her friends referred to as "Stephen," who was in her archery class.

We didn't know her name. We called her "Stephen" among ourselves because she was obviously a lesbian and very attractive. She reminded us of the main character in *The Well of Loneliness*. We hovered around her. But whenever we would camp in front of her she seemed to not know what we were talking about and took to avoiding us. But one weekend night at a gay bar in Tampa, who should come walking in but Stephen and her girlfriend. She looked at me and turned green; I looked at them and got very excited. We sat down together to reassure them that we weren't cops. They told us: "You make us nervous. You're not discreet on campus."

Though her indiscretions were noticeable, Merril did not consider herself vulnerable to exposure or investigation. "My whole world was this very egocentric universe. I just didn't think it meant ME!"

Merril's first encounter with the Florida Legislative Investigation Committee occurred in a Tampa motel:

One weekend I went to a motel with some lesbian friends, two of whom were lovers, just to get out of the dorms. Of course, we got drunk. Well, one of the women stretched and accidentally knocked over a lamp. Picking it up, she moved the table. There was a wire that went under the rug, through the wall, and into the other room. She called us over. We looked at it and got out of there. When we asked about it later, the people supposedly in the know said, "Oh, yeah! They have the motels bugged because that's where people go to have sex and talk to each other. That's where they get a lot of their information." We also learned that the fraternity and sorority houses likewise were bugged and some of the members were informers.

Becoming an informant would not have been difficult. Merril remembers being approached during that fateful fall semester:

I was spending a lot of my weekend time at the Tampa gay bars. I had unlimited sign-out time in my dorm. I would write on my sign-out card that I was staying at a Tampa motel but would end up staying with my queer friends.

Around that time we had some burglaries in the dorms. There was an investigation to find out who was stealing. I was called in by this interrogator—he was just this young cop, but to me, at age seventeen, he seemed like an interrogator. My roommate had had some money stolen, and he was checking through everyone's sign-out cards.

"How can you afford to stay in all of these Tampa motels?" he demanded, as I stood before him.

I knew the jig was up! I had no experience in this kind of situation and didn't know what to do. I was in a frantic panic. I startled rattling off about my boyfriend in Tampa telling him I didn't want to get him or anyone else in trouble. I was underage and that fact could cause trouble for my boyfriend.

But this cop really rode me down until he had me practically hysterical: "Who is your boyfriend? Where do you stay over at? How long have you two known one another?" He rapid-fired questions at me until I couldn't remember my own lies.

Finally, I confessed through my tears. "I can't tell you with whom I really am staying. They are—homosexuals. I don't want to get them into trouble. You can't make me tell!"

As soon as that magic word "homosexual" came out of my mouth, his whole demeanor changed.

"Oh! You know people who are homosexual?"

"I know them and they let me stay at their house with my *boy*friend."

"Well. Do you know any of the homosexuals here on campus?"

"No, of course not!" I lied. "I have a *boy*friend. I don't hang out with kids around campus. I spend all of my time with my *boy*friend off campus."

Gently he said, "If these homosexuals trust you so much, maybe you can kind of get in with them for me and help us out a little?"

Now I really got scared. "What do you mean? I don't understand what you are saying." He sat me down. In a kind and confidential tone, he explained the facts of life to me. "These people are really sick. They need our help. If you really care about them, if they are truly your friends, then you'll help us reach these people so we can force them to get help. They don't know how sick they are, but we can help them—you and I, Merril. . . . "

I wanted to throw up, but I kept thinking as he was talking, "My God! He believes me. He has swallowed my boyfriend story." I told him I had to think about it and he let me go. But I thought to myself: "Maybe I was able to put one over on him. But this can't last." At the end of the semester, I got the hell out of there and transferred down to the University of Miami! I never told anyone why.

Life in the Backwater of Camelot

Against a cold wind and on freshly fallen snow, the aging general-turned-president, Dwight D. Eisenhower, and the stoic New England poet-philosopher, Robert Frost, looked on as the youngest person ever to be elected chief executive pledged his generation's determination to "pay any price, bear any burden. . . . " to defend the American way of life. The optimistic glow of a new decade, a new era, and a new generation washed over millions of black-and-white-television viewers.

Shortly after John F. Kennedy entered the White House in January 1961, a B-52 bomber crashed in the tobacco fields of North Carolina. The crash triggered five of the six safety mechanisms needed to detonate the 25-megaton atomic bomb on board. Within a hundred days, Kennedy clandestinely authorized 400 Special Forces troops to carry out "sabotage and light harassment" on behalf of the South Vietnamese. He also capitulated to the CIA-planned Cuban invasion, in which 400 perished at the Bay of Pigs when Kennedy refused to call in U.S. air cover. Meanwhile, as the NAACP chairman, Robert Weaver, assumed the highest federal post to which an African-American had ever been appointed, only 6 percent of African-Americans attended integrated schools. But for most youngsters popular culture overshadowed political intrigue: "Where the Boys Are" topped the music charts; the FDA approved the first oral contraceptive; the first Playboy Club opened its doors in Chicago, as did Le Club, the first U.S. disco.

During this time, the South was the epicenter for change and conflict. In the spring of 1961 two busloads of Freedom Riders were met with incendiary bombs, fists, and jeers in Anniston and Birmingham, Alabama. In the fall of 1962 James Meredith, protected by 123 deputy federal marshals, 316 border patrol officers, and 97 federal prison guards, became the first Negro registered at Ole Miss. Meanwhile, the world teetered on the brink of nuclear Armageddon as the United States blockaded Cuba, with heavy support from south Florida's Cuban community. In April 1963 mass demonstrations began in Birmingham, and Kennedy quashed financial aid to the Miami-based anti-Castro Cuban Revolutionary Council. In August 200,000 people gathered to march on Washington, and three months later deadly shots rang out at Dealy Plaza in Dallas, killing Kennedy. With a Texan in the White House, the Civil Rights Act of 1964 passed, banning racial discrimination in public facilities, and the Twenty-fourth Amendment to the Constitution, abolishing the poll tax, was ratified, adding thousands of blacks to Southern voter rolls. That summer thousands of Northerners descended on Mississippi for voter registration drives and freedom schools. While federal agents dredged Mississippi waters for three missing civil rights workers, Lyndon Johnson ordered the first U.S. bombs to be dropped on North Vietnam.

As Southern patriotism and racism were roused, Senator Johns broadened his investigation to include "communistic ideas," teaching offensive subjects, or using indecent literature—while the Committee intensified investigations of homosexuals.

In May 1961 a University of Tampa professor was informed that his appointment in the philosophy department would be terminated. Unlike other targets, Thomas Hardeman was not gay and had no affiliations with communists or "communist front" organizations. Active in the Association for the United Nations as a Unitarian Church minister, he had earned praise from students and faculty alike. A year earlier, though, he had the temerity to debate State Representative Tom Whitaker on the value of the World Court and the United Nations. No stranger to controversy, the professor had also exchanged pointed public letters with Sumter Lowry, a failed gubernatorial candidate. The Florida Coalition of Patriotic Societies, headed by Lowry and supported by Johns, then sent out a mimeographed open letter to the university president charging the professor with "following the Communist Party line" and urging recipients to "write and protest the influence of this man. . . . "[4] The president, in the middle of a fund-raising drive, directed the outspoken professor to "keep his mouth shut" and assured critics, "We are conservative right down the line." Declaring, "I won't be intimidated from speaking," Hardeman was dismissed.[5]

On another front, Charley Johns and his allies targeted the University of South Florida. Here the Committee focused on college texts such as John Steinbeck's *Grapes of Wrath,* J. D. Salinger's short story, "Pretty Mouth and Green My Eyes," and essays on "beat literature." The Committee submitted its report to the legislature, concluding that the university administration was "soft" on communism, obscenity, atheism, and homosexual activities. In response, the university's president decried the report as a "skillful blend of truths, half-truths, and omissions."[6]

The Johns Committee's incursion into the academic function of the university created some adverse public opinion. In order to extend the Committee's life for another two years, Johns resigned as chairman; the legislature doubled its appropriation to $155,000. However, Johns remained on the Committee and a major force behind the scenes.

The Purple Pamphlet

Increasingly disappointed by the Johns Committee's unseemly tactics and its attack on American literature and schoolteachers, both the public and the legislature began to withdraw their support. To shore up its base, justify its existence, and extend its mission, the Committee launched a campaign to introduce model penal reform into the next legislative session. On March 17, 1964, it released a pamphlet entitled *Homosexuality and Citizenship in Florida* to state officials, legislators, and the news media.

Estimating a Florida homosexual population of 60,000, the pamphlet appeared to convey a thoughtful and well-researched understanding of the homosexual. Acknowledging that "this Committee claims no corner on understanding the history or prognosis of homosexuality," the Committee offered a brief discussion of the definition and identification of the homosexual. It also presented "as complete and responsible a bibliography on the subject as we believe can be compiled," a ten-page list cluttered with 338 references by psychiatrists, mental health and sex offender specialists, and a few scattered references to popular magazine articles as well as the work of famed sex researcher Alfred Kinsey. The Committee augmented these materials with the "Biblical description of homosexuality as an 'abomination' [that] has stood well the test of time."[7]

The Introduction warned that "there is no single identifying characteristic of the homosexual. . . . Many active homosexuals are active members of their communities, apparently happily married, and rearing families, taking part in church and civic affairs, and, to outward appearance, the picture of normalcy." The report then outlined the aims of the "gay" movement, singling out ONE magazine and the *Mattachine Review* as "propaganda arms of national homosexual organizations."[8] It quoted at length arguments put forth for the equivalence of homosexual love with heterosexual love, the existence of more "stable" lesbian marriages, the presence of homosexuality in ancient cultures, the proposed legalization by the British Wolfenden Report published in 1957, and its legalization in the state of Illinois four years later.

The Committee refuted each argument, sometimes using the testimony of homosexuals themselves. For example, the report included an anonymous letter written by a Tampa lesbian who signed it "just a girl of 24":

I am giving you my side of the story. First of all, let me say that I do not feel shame for what I am. I have made a good adjustment to my way of life. I am happy as I am. I do not want to change. Many well adjusted homosexuals feel as I do, and there is nothing a psychiatrist can do. . . .

Like many others I lead a quiet and apparently a normal life. I have a well paying, responsible job, I own my own home, I am active in church and community affairs and I command the respect of those who know me. I love the woman I live with and I honor this love more than a great number of people honor the marital vows. . . . My life is not a merry-go-round of bars, wild parties, and changing partners as is often the case with homosexuals. Perhaps, I am an exception, but I do not believe so. . . .

I will grant you a point. Homosexuality is, as a total picture, a dread disease. It must be stopped from spreading rapidly. But I must protest the manner in which it is treated. . . . [We] are not all alike as criminals and when "investigated" are submitted to vulgar questioning, abuse and undignified treatment. This handling is not restricted to those who have committed a criminal act. . . . Must I be stripped of my privacy and all the pride and dignity that I enjoy as an American, simply because some element in my environment, some incident in my childhood, or some faulty parental relationship has produced an individual who chooses to love one of the same sex?[9]

Though not denying "the existence of some lasting homosexual relationships which pose no threat to society," the Committee used her words and cases from its primarily male-focused investigation to give the reader a "glimpse of the homosexual world . . . [that] underlines our conviction that homosexuals pose a problem. . . . " As the report underscored, "it is difficult to find the ennobling element" in a "well dressed teacher" frequenting a shopping center's men's room, the seduction of young boys by an "athletically-built little league coach," and boys posing for nude photos or engaged in prostitution with "the same ease at comparable cost as . . . the services of a 'high class' prostitute." Dryly observing that such scenes are neither isolated nor "the extreme of deviate behavior," the legislators concluded: "The plain fact of the matter is that a great many homosexuals have an insatiable appetite for sexual activities and find special gratification in the recruitment to their ranks of youth."[10]

The Committee starkly assessed the homosexual menace:

> There is a tendency to lump together the homosexuals who seek out youth and the child molesters. To most people the child molester seems to pose the greatest threat to society. The child molester attacks, but seldom kills or physically cripples his victim. The outlook for the victim of molestation is generally good for recovery from the mental and physical shocks involved and for the enjoyment of a normal life. The homosexual, on the other hand, prefers to reach out for the child at the time of normal sexual awakening and . . . to hook him for homosexuality.[11]

Observing that "local homosexuals trade photos like some youngsters trade bubble gum baseball cards," the Committee concluded that these youths, "entangled in the web of homosexuality," form "secret societies" with homosexual initiation rites, "'come out' by becoming full-fledged homosexuals," enter prostitution or the robbery-blackmail racket, and transmit venereal disease.[12]

The Committee then offered a series of legislative recommendations in the Homosexual Practices Control Act for Florida, including: the retention of "qualified personnel" by the State Board of Education to refute or affirm allegations of teachers' homosexuality; outpatient treatment centers for offenders on probation or parole; assurance of confidentiality for the first homosexual arrest (it could be waived by the judge upon the person's conviction or guilty plea); a central record depository, open to the public, of homosexual arrests and convictions; and the reclassification of the second homosexual offense as a felony.

Had the Committee been satisfied with the weight of its arguments, then the report would have likely received public endorsement if not legislative enactment. However, in order to spur public attention and legislative action, the Committee sprinkled its text with lascivious photos. Behind the six-by-nine purple cover were full-size photographs of two nude men kissing and a teenager bound by rope wearing only a black jockstrap. Following the text was a full page of twelve postcardlike photographs of boys profiled in the nude or in their underwear "indicative of the frequent homosexual fixation on youth."[13] Finally, the report included a lurid eight-page glossary of more than one hundred "homosexual terms and deviate acts":

Chi-Chi: (Pronounced she-she) Usually a room or apartment very effeminately decorated. Lace works, drapes, etc.
Queen: Leader of a group of female [sic—should be "feminine"] homosexuals
Types of Queens: 69 Queen, Browning queen, Reaming queen, Belly-up queen, hand queen, golden-shower queen (All of the above are fairly well self-explanatory)
Sea Food: Homosexuals in the Navy
Sapphism: Titillation of the clitoris through mutual masturbation or cunnilingus practiced by females[14]

After printing 2,000 copies of this forty-four-page booklet at a cost to the taxpayer of $720 and distributing 750 copies to legislators, newspapers, and "key" people, the Committee was startled by the swift public disapproval. Known as the "purple pamphlet" because of the color of its jacket as well as its contents, it was banned by Dade County State Attorney Richard Gerstein (who had earlier banned the works of D. H. Lawrence and Henry Miller). In his words, it "would become the object of curiosity in our high schools and could well become a means of engendering homosexuality."[15] Dade Representative Earl Faircloth, who already had resigned from the Committee and was then a candidate for attorney general, stated: "It leads one to wonder—which is worse, the remedy or the disease?"[16]

Gubernatorial candidates and several major newspapers blasted the report. The *Miami Herald*, calling for the resignation of those state officials responsible, lambasted it as "state sponsored obscenity,"[17] and a lengthy editorial of the *Tampa Tribune* stated:

If a private citizen had put out this publication, he probably could be arrested for circulating obscene literature. . . . It is another product of the strange mental processes which have dominated the State Legislative Investigation Committee. . . . The fact is that the Committee, or whoever has been running it in the last three years, have shown an obsessive interest in homosexuality. Its staff has spent thousands of dollars snooping after perverts, although this is a police function. . . . [18]

Television editorials also challenged the booklet's distribution. WJXT labeled it "at best crude and tasteless," warning that "when the committee's life was extended by the last Legislature, the new committee chairman promised a much-improved approach to its investigation. The 'purple pamphlet' is disturbing evidence that very little has changed after all."[19]

Less trenchant criticism, though, was evident in a WFTV telecast in which a newsman read the station's editorial: "We don't criticize the objective of the investigation but rather the flamboyant procedures; the disregard of orderly procedures; the tactical indiscretions. The booklet in question is a serious and conscientious publication which could be of considerable value in forming and educating. . . . It would be unfortunate if bad public relations should force a clamp-down on public discussion of a sociological problem."[20]

Despite the controversy, the Committee prepared for the next legislative session under its day-to-day director, John Evans, and his investigative staff, now reduced to one person, Lawrence Rice. Only a month later, though, Evans ignited another storm in a speech he gave before the Florida Federation of Women's Clubs in Jacksonville. He warned that homosexuality was still "flourishing" at Florida educational institutions, with "allegations of homosexuality and references to 123 individuals then, and presumably now, teaching in Florida schools."[21]

In June 1964 an investigative story by Robert Sherrill, longtime capital bureau chief for the *Miami Herald,* reported that no such list (like Joe McCarthy's famous State Department list of communists) had ever existed. Noting that the Committee was under no legal obligation to discuss its operation with the public or to give an accounting of its budget, Sherrill disclosed the allocation of $10,000 for informants and a nearly equal amount for travel expenses. Most damaging were the allegations of a Miami homosexual, Richard A. Inman, that a former Johns Committee investigator, Duane Barker, had offered him "$4,000 for 'anything conclusive' I could give him on five democratic politicians."[22]

The former director of the Florida Legislative Investigation Committee, John Evans, championed the report: "There is substantial evidence to indicate that the action of the Committee in issuing this report touched off the most serious and extensive consideration of this problem ever to occur on a state-wide basis, and that it triggered a new evaluation of local procedures in communities. . . . "[23]

There was some truth to these claims of popularity. The pamphlet was a sought-after collector's item, becoming so popular that mailed requests addressed simply to "Sex Tallahassee" were received. Originally priced at twenty-five cents, the pamphlet's value quickly rose to two dollars on the open market, and an additional 10,000 copies were reprinted by Guild Book Service of Washington. Soon the "purple pamphlet" was showing up on a book dealers' list alongside trashy novels with pilfered and purloined titles like *The Hell of Loneliness* and *Carnal Matters.*

Search for the Hidden Lesbian

Sue Sponnoble enrolled at the University of Miami in 1965. Quickly she pledged a sorority and joined the school newspaper. She also met Georgia, an upper-class student who was Phi Beta Kappa and a campus leader. Their relationship was romantic, sexual, and intellectual. They exchanged silver friendship rings.

Assuming the lead in the relationship, Georgia encouraged Sue to explore her lesbianism. Later that fall semester, the couple embarked on a "special project." They investigated the university library searching for homosexual literature:

> We found *The Well of Loneliness,* which we checked out. We felt very bad for Stephen, and the book raised a lot of complicated issues for us: Why had the character been portrayed like this? Was it because the author really felt that it was wrong to be gay or was the author reflecting the reality of making your way in a society that was indifferent or hostile toward us? Why did Radclyffe Hall portray it that way if she did or didn't agree with it? Was that value judgment correct? We didn't want to be like Stephen. We didn't want to be perceived as a tragic figure; we didn't want to commit suicide. We were in love!

Eagerly devouring their treasure trove of books, they talked about a variety of issues:

> We discussed the concept of hiding. That was a topic of great discussion: Was it good to hide? Would it ever change? Why did we have to hide? We went into lots of discussion about why people persecuted gays and lesbians. We were fascinated with all of the origins and myths.
>
> You have to understand how important these discussions were to us. We were eighteen or nineteen years old, the apple of our parents' eyes, the crème de la crème—we had always been labeled "good." We felt that we shouldn't be labeled bad for discovering our sexual nature. We understood our parents weren't happy with that; we wanted to understand the origin of their homophobia.
>
> We searched through all the psychology textbooks for "lesbian" and "homosexual." The message was that homosexuality was some type of aberration. Finally, we read it enough times to close those books saying, "We don't care if this is in a textbook, it is wrong!"
>
> We also found a book that purported to be a nonfiction description of homosexual society. There were chapters about butch and femme. I would think, "Is this me? Is there something wrong with me because I don't fit in with these descriptions?"

The book, *The Homosexual in America,* described dyke, baby dyke, and diesel dyke. When Sue later visited her first gay bar, she was escorted by two older butch-looking women:

> They told me that I might encounter an older "bull dyke" who might want to dance with me, but I shouldn't do that since I was with them. We drove around the bar to make sure there were no police cars and went inside. I can clearly see the woman who looked me over at the door. She came back to our

table to ask to see my ID again and to talk with me. I had never seen a woman like that: brown slacks and a white shirt with the sleeves rolled up; a cigarette hanging out of her mouth; hair combed not in a DA, the classic butch hairstyle, but in a real man's haircut. I was fascinated. But my protectors made it clear through very aggressive body language that I was *not* available.

That night I had my first dance with a woman. It was an absolutely magical moment. A full consciousness came into my being: This is who I am. Even though I was in a seedy dump that smelled like stale beer with very little light, I saw clearly that this was my identity. It was pure, youthful, virginal happiness.

Georgia and Sue continued their search for literature with positive role models. Georgia, who had come out in high school, explained to Sue that "our voices were absent from literature. It's very sad that there is not more." They had heard about *The Ladder* and the Daughters of Bilitis. "Georgia and I tried very hard to find a copy; we didn't know how to find it! We wanted very badly to try to connect with that network, but everything was so invisible." Soon they journeyed beyond the university library.

We longed for a body of literature to read, and slowly we discovered the hidden lesbian characters. We had discussions about whether we thought that between the lines the author had intended for there to be just a hint. In the works of Emily Dickinson, Edna St. Vincent Millay, Willa Cather, and May Sarton we searched for the "hidden" lesbian, and there were two who seemed more obvious: Gertrude Stein and Sappho. We had several books of Sappho's poetry that we had given each other as gifts. Here there was no question about lesbianism, but we were interested if this was a real person. Finally we found some of the early pulp paperback books in the old Greyhound bus station: *Odd Girl Out, Women's Barrack's, Warped Desire, Sorority House.* We devoured all of those books and, of course, realized that they were a very different genre than *The Well of Loneliness.*

In her sophomore year, Sue continued to live on campus while Georgia lived with her mother. At the end of the semester, Sue had just completed her last exam after cramming in three all-nighters. Relaxing in her room that Friday afternoon, she waited for Georgia to pick her up for their well-deserved holiday. The phone rang at four o'clock. It was Dean Lois J. Duckworth, who had been the chair for campus orientation while Sue served as student chair that fall semester. "Back then there were very few women professors," Sue emphasized. "I had gone through my entire four years without ever having one! So when I had the opportunity to work at the dean's office I reveled in it. Here was a woman twenty or thirty years older, in a position of power and authority, and highly educated." The dean asked Sue to come to her office.

I told her I was getting ready to spend semester break off campus: "Dean Duckworth, I'm just exhausted. Would you mind if I made an appointment and saw you when I come back in two weeks?"

Her response was very icy. "No. You must come see me immediately."

Dean Duckworth was tall and starchy. A very severe disciplinarian, she wore her black hair cut short and bright red lipstick with never a smile.

Sue called Georgia to tell her of the slight change in plans, asking her to wait at home until she returned from the dean's office. "Take off your ring, Sue," Georgia pleaded unsuccessfully.

Sue walked the short distance to Dean Duckworth's office. As she entered the office, the secretaries were dutifully completing their tasks. Two paused, peering up from their typewriters to greet Sue. "I had to sit in the waiting room in the presence of these secretaries who had always known me because of my accomplishments on campus that were positive, not because I was involved in any discipline matter. I was absolutely fear-stricken that these women might have knowledge of precisely what Dean Duckworth was going to discipline me over."

As Sue worried about what the secretaries might or might not know and considered various concerns that the dean might bring to her, she squirmed in a chair as the minute hand slowly swept up the time. A secretary's voice pierced Sue's private world: "Dean Duckworth will see you now, Miss Sponnoble."

Sue trudged down a long narrow hallway, stopping at the slightly ajar door. She hesitated. Sitting sternly behind her oak desk, Dean Duckworth beckoned her. In the cramped office with 1950s-style furnishings, there was no escape. The dean came directly to the point:

"Well, I need to tell you that there have been extensive rumors about you and Georgia. I have heard from numerous sources that you and Georgia are lesbians. Do you know what that means?"

Feeling a combination of fear and anger, queasily Sue calculated her response hoping not to appear upset. "No. Georgia who?"

"Well, in some college settings where girls live together and don't have an opportunity to be with boys they show unnatural affection for one another. Perhaps that has happened in your case?"

"I have no idea what you are talking about."

Dean Duckworth pressed further. "Is there any chance that any affection might have occurred in your room?"

Sue continued with denials.

"Well, when things like this don't happen in girls' dormitories, they happen in girls' sororities. Sometimes these are merely phases that girls go through. Maybe you are going through such a phase?"

Sue blankly responded, "I have no idea what you are talking about."

Dean Duckworth unlocked her top desk drawer, slowly pulling out a yellowed file. "Sue, I want you to carefully examine the contents of this folder."

Opening it, Sue was startled to see newspaper articles from across the country about students expelled because of their homosexuality. Her ears reddened and blood pounded in her quickly drying throat: "I don't see what this has to do with me. I don't understand."

"We happen to know that your parents are extremely prominent. Imagine how you would feel if you brought this kind of shame on them. If you're expelled you will *never* get into any college or university again. You will *never* have a college education."

Sue was dumbfounded. The dean went on to explain that an article, like those in the folder, might well appear in Sue's hometown newspaper.

Incredulously Sue asked, "But how would such an article get up there?"

"We will place it there!"

A long silence was broken by Dean Duckworth's demand: "I want Georgia to make an appointment with me."

Sue's throat cleared as questions flowed forth: "Why is this happening to me? Why are you doing this? What am I supposed to do? What do you intend to do?"

Dean Duckworth first explained about the Johns Committee and the importance of reputation for institutions as well as individuals. "If you wish to stay here, then you must prove to us that you are *not* a homosexual. You must date men and report to me periodically on your progress."

Although Charley Johns's efforts had officially ended, his legacy lived on in the hallowed halls of academe and the offices of the Deans of Women. Even at a private university like the University of Miami, administrators—particularly those on whom suspicion might fall—were eager to ferret out homosexual students.

Sue left absolutely panic-stricken.

Georgia picked me up and we had this tear-jerking conversation: Who had turned us in? How would they have suspected? Who might have seen us? What we should do next? Can our relationship survive?

Then we got into the more philosophical aspect of it. The first issue we discussed was those in the Dean of Women's office, some of whom appeared to be lesbian! Of the entire staff of deans and assistant deans, only one was married—Lois J. Duckworth—in an era when societal mandates about remaining single still lingered. These other women in that office were in their late thirties to early sixties wearing very tailored clothes. This was a time when there were still a lot of hushed whispers about "old maids" or career women.

We posed a number of questions: If lesbians can work as deans then why can't girls go to school as lesbians? Does this mean that lesbian and gay students don't deserve college educations? We could *not* comprehend why this had happened. We could *not* understand why what we were doing was perceived as wrong.

Fake Dates and Polished Professionals

After a long bout of soul-searching, Sue and Georgia concluded that they had little alternative but to "hide and pretend." Sue began to date men, following the standard dormitory procedure of completing a sign-out card listing her date, their destination, expected time of return, contact telephone numbers, and mode of transportation. Whereas some women complained about these long-practiced methods in which the university assumed an *in loco parentis* role, Sue welcomed such documentation—and went beyond it:

> In order to impress Dean Duckworth that I was getting along well with men, not only did I date but I made up a lot of other men's names. I kept a notebook, thinking that if I needed to report back every month I'd mix up the real dates with the pretend. I memorized it so that each time I met with Dean Duckworth I could report: "I had a wonderful time with Joe at the movies and Tom at the dance."

During those meetings, the dean emphasized that Sue shouldn't have sex. "You have to make up your mind whether you are a Yes Girl or a No Girl." Sue recalls:

> I was very young and the concept of the "cover date" hadn't arrived, since we didn't know any gay men. I usually didn't date the same man twice, because they wanted to have sex; I didn't want to have sex, since I was a lesbian, but I didn't want them to call me a lesbian—which, of course, was one of the first lines a young man would use in those days—and I didn't want to be unfaithful to Georgia.

After a date, Sue had to call Georgia at a certain hour. If she was late, Georgia would get upset:

> Had I kissed him? Had he done anything "improper?" She realized that this was something that I had to do, but she did *not* like it! We really looked forward to our times together. In order to see one another more often, we arranged for Georgia's mother to be an "approved hostess" for me. She had to send a letter of invitation to the dean's office each weekend I wanted to spend off campus. Of course I wanted to be with Georgia since we were passionately in love, but I was also very concerned in not wanting to spend too many weekends together should the dean suspect. So after a long weekend with Georgia, I would quickly jot three male names in my book on Monday, Tuesday, and Wednesday. It was quite a juggling act.

As Sue continued balancing her secretive relationship with Georgia with her notebook of fake dates, she moved into leadership roles through her association with the Dean of Women's office. Her initial conversations with Georgia about suspected lesbians in the office led to connections that few other undergraduates made:

> They belonged to the National Association of Women Deans and Counselors. They would invite prominent women deans from other colleges to come to the University of Miami to participate in a special program that was being pre-

sented for women students on campus. In observing the way they interacted with the women deans who invited them, it seemed to us that there was an attraction between them—but they were trying not to make it obvious to the students. Of course Georgia and I, who were starved for professional role models of professional women, picked up on it.

These women speakers, generally in their fifties and sixties, lectured on topics such as female sexuality and discrimination against women on campus and in the workplace. Sue vividly recalls these talks:

> We were very bright and were expected to attend and ask questions. They stressed abstention of heterosexual intercourse, but they hemmed over the marriage aspect. Bright students asking pointed questions about marital status would clearly have forced them into the uncomfortable position of addressing relationships with other women. They were trying to deftly avoid that.
> They also used examples of discrimination they faced at their institutions, such as the tremendous disparity in salaries between male and female administrators. One dean was very quick to point out that she had the same responsibility as the Dean of Men, and yet her salary and influence were less. Their advice to us was strive to be the most polished, poised, and highly educated professional that you can possibly be, because the higher your level of education, the more likely you are to overcome some of these disparities.

Hide and Seek

In 1968, during her junior year, Sue had the opportunity to serve as one of two student counselors for the first group of minority students at the university participating in a Great Society program, Upward Bound. This program brought talented minority students into college during the summer at the start of their first year to work with college professors, administrators, and guidance counselors, who prepared them for college and acclimated them to campus life. "At the time, the University of Miami was virtually all white. The university worked with the Dade County school system to identify students who could not afford the tuition at the University of Miami, which was very high. The Dean of Women's office was incredibly supportive of bringing in black students and asked me to be one of the counselors."

Sue, along with another white student counselor, lived with the group of twenty female students in the dorm throughout the summer of 1968, working with them on their programs and accompanying them to many of their activities. During that summer Sue pursued some of her own coursework but found herself poorly prepared to counsel Upward Bound students:

> We had been trained in all of the procedures, but what they didn't prepare us for was a real understanding of the issues that these African-American students

were about to face. We had to deal with some of their anger and hostility toward us, which were expressed very clearly. They were very pointed in expressing their anger at me: "How can you possibly understand what I am faced with? Your father is a wealthy physician and never deprived you of anything."

Sue also faced an unexpected challenge from one particular student who was also a lesbian:

Dee was very out, and Georgia was always in my dorm room. Dee would never leave. She wanted to pin me down and admit that I, too, was a lesbian—less than a year after Dean Duckworth had tried to expel me!

I had already experienced with Georgia all of the pain, anguish, and isolation of not having positive role models. Along comes another young woman who faces the double challenge of being one of the first black female students at the University of Miami and also a lesbian. She wanted me to identify myself to her as being a lesbian.

Dee did it in a very belligerent manner. Instead of coming into my room and posing it as a question, "Are you gay, too?" she entered repeatedly making the statement: "I know you're different. I know you're gay. Your friend Georgia is here all of the time. She wouldn't be here if she wasn't gay. Why don't you just tell me? I'm different and I'm sure you are, too!"

I was put off by that kind of directness, and I was afraid to tell her I was gay. Being in the position of a counselor, I didn't want to be accused of trying to seduce her. I had no idea what Lois J. Duckworth and the Dean of Women's office would say when one of the messages they were trying to convey to all us was that we needed to reach a certain level of professionalism.

During that revolutionary year of political assassinations and race riots, student strikes and antiwar demonstrations, Sue began to better empathize with those in the Dean of Women's office whom she and Georgia had long suspected of being lesbians. "They lived in silence and denial. It was the way that their generation of lesbians survived in the job market. It was hard for them as unmarried women with Ph.D.s to get a job at all. Now, I found myself on the other generational end of this game of hide-and-seek."

As the group of African-American students made their way through the university, their impact continued to be felt. These students soon insisted on a black studies program. Sue and Georgia realized that these students were seeking "some form of academic validation from the institution and also seeking their own identity through academic studies. Here I was as a lesbian helping to mentor the first group of black students and establish their own black studies program but never thought about asking for a program for what Georgia and I had been doing on our own!"

On the brink of the lesbian and feminist revolution, women's status had changed little from a generation earlier—particularly among middle-class Southerners. Those who chose to work and not marry had few career options: nurse, social worker, librarian, teacher. By 1969 Sue found herself as part of an informal social network of about twenty-five single women, many of whom were elementary and secondary school teachers, mostly a generation or two ahead of her. "Everyone was so hidden," Sue recalled, "it was hard to find one another. There weren't women's studies groups or lesbian support groups. There was certainly no authority figure that you could go to at the university." Sue reminisced:

> We gathered these friends around us with whom we felt safe and enjoyed each other's company in private. We taught one another; it was very much of an oral tradition—the sharing of one's story.
>
> There was the great debate over the use of the word "lesbian." Back in those days it was considered by many of us to be a crude and harsh word that somehow reflected the kind of coarseness befitting the image of the mannish woman. But we didn't want to think of ourselves as being coarse, rough, and masculine. While we were aware that society labeled us "homosexual" and "queer," we certainly didn't feel comfortable with those terms. So this was a very active discussion among educated women about what our language should be; there was no agreement.

Not everyone, however, within their social group was comfortable with such discussions. One such woman was a teacher in her fifties. During World War II she had been one of several dozen female pilots—the Ninety-Niners—who towed targets for the male trainee pilots to down.

> My friend said, "Sue, this woman is a lesbian but she grew up in an era when you just didn't talk about it. So the rule is whenever we are at a party we *never* mention gay or lesbian within her earshot. We know we are at a party with all women who are all lesbians—sometimes we dance—but we don't talk about it in her presence."

Some of these older women had also been traumatized by Charley Johns:

> The parents of students in public schools were encouraged to report any "suspicious" activity. All the women I knew who were teachers had been called into the principal's office and questioned for several hours. Sometimes there were other authority figures there. Sometimes they had been yanked right out of their classes and marched down to the principal's office. They were told that they were "under suspicion" because of their marital status. Now, those women still lived in fear.

June Madness

When Sue graduated in June 1969 after four years of dating men and loving Georgia, she picked up the paper and was surprised to read about the Stonewall riots:

We weren't aware of gay activism. I had a sense that I had lived an oppressed life for the three or four years. I had a sense that that was wrong, that it shouldn't have to be like that. I had a sense that there should be a "struggle," but I wasn't sure how to form it. Reading that article with Georgia, I realized that there were other people like us. The sense of joy we felt when we read that article!

A few days later, a woman who was at Stonewall during that first night described the scene in a letter to a Southern friend:

> The cops raided a long established bar called The Stonewall on Friday night and arrested several drag queens. Everything went along fairly peacefully until they tried to arrest a dyke (stone butch), who lost her mind in the streets of the West Village—kicking, cursing, screaming, and fighting—she set the whole crowd wild—berserk! They began throwing money, then bottles. . . . At that point, the fire hoses were turned on the whole crowd and they scattered. The next day all over the Village there were marches of Gay Power—hippies joined the queers and straight places turned gay for the weekend—it was complete madness in NYC.[24]

The madness that occurred during those three June nights and the subsequent emergence of dozens of "gay liberation fronts" across college campuses were neither accidental nor instantaneous. Leaders and activists had struggled for years in the "homophile movement" for this political watershed. Southerners like Jim Kepner, Jack Nichols, Richard Inman, and Julian Hodges played pivotal roles in this generational divide known as Stonewall.

Along the path to Stonewall, many lesbian and gay activists borrowed freely from the philosophy, strategies, and tactics of the black struggle for civil rights. There, too, were homosexual Southerners in pivotal roles. These women and men participated in the freedom rides, operated freedom schools, organized pickets, marches, and sit-ins, and—like the homophile activists—were interrogated, intimidated, investigated, and incarcerated. Both groups of activists had to overcome the Southern comfort with homosexuals who knew their place in a society fractured by race, social class, and gender.

4

The Father, Son, and Holy Ghost

The City on the Hill Struggles with Civil Rights and Civilities

For many Southerners living through the sit-ins and the freedom rides, or weaned on Amos 'n Andy and *Gone with the Wind,* little thought was given to one more "colored boy" sent to prison—but Quinton Baker, like the prison camp, was different. Morganton Prison Camp was one of two desegregated prisons operated by the state of North Carolina in 1963. "The chain gang was one of those experiences you say, 'I'm glad I had it; I never want to do it again.' It was there I really learned about the struggle of what it means to be human."

Born in 1942 on the North Carolina Coastal Plain, where "attitudes and even language are a little different," Quinton was the youngest of four children born to Lillie, a light-skinned Negro and a fifteen-dollar-a-week domestic, and Hermon, a laborer who had once been convicted of assault and battery while defending his wife.

When Lillie Baker worked in white people's homes, she sometimes took young Quinton.

> I was employed at about fifty cents a day to be the "play toy" for white kids. I would go where my mother worked and I would play with them while she was doing the housework. When it came to lunchtime, they would go in and my mother would feed me on the porch or outside. I would always refer to white men and women as "sir" or "ma'am," but their kids *never* referred to my mother that way.

Growing up in the segregated South, Quinton learned early about the differing status of whites and blacks:

> It was very hard to escape the fact that as a young boy there was a certain place for blacks and another for whites. There were certain things we couldn't do, like try on clothes in a store or sit at a lunch counter. On the other hand, when you are very young you don't know that you are poor and you're not really making the connection that there is something wrong socially; this *is* the way of life. There wasn't a sense that things were really going to change.

One of Quinton's earliest memories is V-E Day, May 7, 1945: "I was with my mother and we were visiting friends in an area called Over the Hill. The bells started ringing, horns were blowing, and everyone started shouting: 'The war is over! The war is over!'" Although Quinton's father did not serve in the war because of his prison record, his presence was important in Quinton's development. "My father taught us not to be subservient to anyone. He was very defiant. My father resented the way he was treated by white people; he hated white people. A white man insulted him once, and he shot him. He also ran over the foot of a white police officer. He was not known for his docility—particularly with whites." At home, though, Quinton faced a difficult relationship with his father. "My father was very much, 'You do as I say—not as I do.' But if I was accused of something, I always felt that my side of the story should be heard. He didn't think that my side of the story mattered."

In postwar Greenville, the African-American community was composed mostly of tobacco farmers and laborers, with a sprinkling of teachers, ministers, and small shop owners. Quinton lived in a single-family home.

> There were some two-family dwellings, and behind our house were whites. You walked through certain neighborhoods noticing that the white houses were better and larger with nicer lawns.
>
> There wasn't much television, so you spent a lot of your life playing or sitting around the house talking or doing homework. The black and white kids played together until a certain age. The white kids stopped interacting with us; there was *never* a time that my parents told me to stop being with them.

Greenville was a bustling Old South town of 21,000, and its black community was tightly networked. Neighbors were kin.

> The greatest sense of growing up in the South is that you knew everyone in your neighborhood and everyone knew you. The community nurtured and protected each other—particularly the children. You were fed and also disciplined by neighbors. There was a sharing of love, but there was also a sharing of discipline. If I was doing something I was not supposed to do, the neighbors had permission to discipline me and then tell my parents—who would also discipline me.

On Sundays the Bakers would sometimes visit grandparents who lived in the more rural area. Sometimes, too, on hot summer nights, Hermon would take the whole family out for an early evening ride in his black Packard. "My father loved his car and always worked on cars. He would teach my brothers and he tried to teach me. My father had a horrible time just teaching me to drive an automobile. I finally had to give up. I couldn't learn to drive with my father."

Quinton was different. As a very young boy, he had played with his older sister and her "1,001 screaming female friends." As he matured, his brothers and sister came to calling him names:

> "You ol' sissy thang." That would be the first thing they called me. That hurt a lot.
>
> I was a very sensitive kid. You could whip me and I would be fine but, if you hurt my feelings, I would be absolutely destroyed. Well, my father would hurt my feelings and I would cry. My mother would say, "Oh, don't be like that." She was trying to brace and toughen me.
>
> My brothers shunned me, of course. One brother who was four years older than me would do things with *my* friends. A big deal during that period was if your brother was going downtown you could go along. I wouldn't get to go along, but my friend across the street would be invited to go with my brother. My sense was that I was not male enough.

Like Father, Like Son

Lillie's toughening helped her son to survive in prison. One of his dorm-mates, Jake, was "overtly gay." Quinton recalls: "In prison you get a lot of 'let's play drop the soap, and I'll come on to you.' But you only get one shower a week anyway, so you get a lot of teasing about going into the shower. I learned just to tease back."

Like Thomas, the free black Civil War soldier in the film *Glory*, Quinton also learned how to "not separate myself from less educated blacks, creating a false sense of superiority." He penned letters for several older black inmates and one young white man. After Quinton scribbled his own three letters for the week, he then wrote for the others.

> I learned a lot about people and their emotions when I had to convey their feelings to someone who they loved or cared about. Having to read, talk to, and see people, and understanding what kinds of lives they have, I began to appreciate what being human is about. I began to recognize the superficiality of some of the things we surround ourselves with and how we separate our-selves. It was an incredible beginning for me in my quest to understand about being a human being and how to put into that context my blackness and my sexual orientation.

As Quinton approached adolescence, his difference began to grate more deeply on his father. "My father knew I was different and he didn't know how to deal with it. He tried his best to make sure that I wasn't different, which resulted in our not being able to be in the same room." Often the two argued about Quinton's speech pattern. Though he was not a particularly effeminate child, "when you speak the way I speak in the South, you stand out. For a lot of people my speech pattern was feminine." Quinton continues:

> My father just could not deal with the fact that I was different: "Why do you have to be goddamn different?" He was scared to death that his baby son was going to be "funny." He didn't want me to be different. He didn't want me to have the pain and anguish of being different. But he didn't have the skills to talk with me about what was concerning him so he constantly rode me and tried to change me: "Why do you have to talk so different? Why can't you hang out with kids instead of being with adults all of the time? Why can't you act like the others?"

Quinton was also different in his career choice. Working since he was thirteen, he preferred year-round employment as a shoeshine boy and drive-in carhop over the drudgery of working as a tobacco field hand:

> In those days, you would harvest tobacco by "priming" and "trucking." The trucker is a young male who had a cart with potato sacks on sides that created a storage for the tobacco. My brothers would prime the tobacco by taking off the ripened leaves and I would be expected to truck them to the barn where the women would take it and tie them on sticks to be loaded into the barn for curing.
> I was afraid to death of a mule which, of course, was in front of the truck. The primers had one rule of thumb: If you turned over a truck, you'd better be under it! So, I'm going down these narrow roads and the truck is zigzagging. The fear of the mule comes from having to unhitch the mule from one truck and put it on an empty truck and take it out to the field.

Quinton preferred to earn money through his shoeshine business at a downtown shoe repair shop, where most customers were white. In a community that lacked any civil rights organizations and where events of the mid-1950s such as the Montgomery bus boycott were distant, working there heightened his racial awareness. "I became aware because people would say things to me that wouldn't quite make sense. 'Well, you know, Quinton, if all colored people were like you, things would be really different.'"

Differences between whites and blacks also came to his attention on sexual matters: "White guys used to sit up there and say, 'Hey, boy. You ever eat one?' I'd say, 'No.' 'Well, you ain't going to be a man until you've ate one.' Whites were much more apt to be sexual and talk about sex with black people."

When Quinton was not working at the shoe repair shop, reading books, or taking long walks, he wondered about himself. "The difficulty, for me, was growing up different—and not knowing what that meant. I was different because I was brighter; I was different because I would not just accept whatever was said to me. And I was different because of my sexual orientation."

Sexual experimentation for Quinton—as with many of his friends—was common and began early in life: "Before the ninth grade it was sexual experimentation with anybody that wanted to experiment. The emotional connection began when I really needed that buddy. Because I felt so much rejection from my brothers and my father, I was constantly pursuing male relationships; I didn't pursue female relationships. I had them already and they weren't important to me emotionally."

Quinton had a girlfriend throughout high school as well as several during elementary and junior high, but "these weren't emotional. My girlfriend and I in high school sat on opposite sides of the teacher's desk; we competed with one another." He remembers once talking with his mother about marriage. "I'm never going to get married," he quipped. She eyed him carefully, weighing her words: "You may be joking, but I believe you. You look like the type."

Although Quinton and his best buddy through ninth grade, Leroy, never engaged in sex, he found himself in high school being "used" by other boys:

> There were things that were a given, but no one talked about. Sometimes you knew, though, that if you were invited to a certain guy's house to come over after school that it had sexual implications. These were never people who were really your friends; these were the users. As people began to experiment sexually, I found myself being used by other guys and then rejected. So, then, there came this emotional attachment: buddy sex. You want to be accepted and you want to have the sex thing but you don't want to be rejected because you're "funny." What was more important to me was the friendship, the commitment, the togetherness.

Quinton, though, didn't label himself. "I certainly didn't know the word 'homosexual.' I could accept the fact that I preferred intimacy with men— maybe I thought it was just a phase—but I've never accepted a gay identity."

Growing up "different" in the South echoes other childhood memories of a quiet acceptance within Quinton's community:

> Back then, you could be funny but not ostracized. The attitude was one of quiet acceptance. They may have made fun of that person behind his back, but he was able to function in the community. The choir director at my mother's church, who was also an English teacher, was known to be funny. He was respected in our community. There also were one or two women who were rumored to be that way, but most people were much more aware of men than they were of any kind of lesbian activity.

Growing up gay in the South for Quinton's generation meant being laughed at by kids for being funny or sissy. At his high school, he remembers one "flaming" adolescent, Avery, whom he befriended:

> I didn't worry about what people said about me, since they were already saying things. You don't grow up in a black Southern high school and not do all of the things that young men are doing without being suspect. I didn't think of myself like Avery. But, on the other hand, there were qualities that I shared— he was artistic and brilliant—and I was comfortable with him, except for the flaming part.

Quinton's first knowledge of any type of sexual activities between the races came through Avery, "who was making money hand over fist." He adds:

> There was a lot of sexual activity between young black boys and white men who came in and rode through the community. Most of the blacks were walking; the whites were often driving. There were certain sections in town you could walk in—usually the area between the black and white neighborhoods. In this gray area, they would come, drive around, and park. It was like any red light district, except the johns were more aggressive. They would pay five or ten dollars. We used to say, "Segregation works except at night."

As he moved on in school, knowing he was "different, but not knowing how to deal with it," and separated from Leroy, who had to repeat the ninth grade, "I stopped being a mediocre student." His father, though, was the principal motivation. Quinton remembers the turning point in his young life. It was on a late Sunday afternoon following dinner:

> My father and I had had some major disagreement at the dinner table about the way I preferred a certain word. We were sitting on the front porch. I was in the swing; my father was sitting in the chair.
> He just looked at me and said, "You're never going to be a goddamn thing."
> I was in absolute tears. At that point, I made up my mind that I was going to make my father proud of me. It was the ultimate kind of rejection that thrust me into a lot of areas. My whole academic career changed. My grades went up and I became the spokesman for the school. *Everywhere* my father turned, my name was before him. But it didn't matter. I was still different.

Beginning in his junior year, Quinton cast a long shadow over school and home. Elected to six different offices, including student body president, his gifts for organizing and motivating were recognized. "The principal gave me the run of the school. There were a number of students who didn't like me, but they would do activities I asked."

Quinton, like his father, steadfastly stood for his beliefs. "Defiance was bred into me." He demanded respect: "The strongest influence on me was probably my parents and their insistence that we, as children, respect ourselves, and therefore we would demand respect from everybody else. . . . My parents instilled in us a sense of our own importance, our dignity. But everything I saw violated my concept of what I was as a person."

A delivery boy, for instance, would come to the house to bring flowers for his mother. Asking for her by her first name, Quinton retorted: "She doesn't live here." Confused, the white youth persisted. Quinton erupted: "Why is it that you feel free to use my mother's first name? *You* don't know her." On another occasion when Quinton was working at the tobacco factory, a supervisor instructed him to call a white boy a year or so older "Mister." He waited until the boy was a distance away and then shouted: "Hey, John!"

Coupled to these racial slights were the community's Jim Crow laws. Complacently accepted, they had little personal meaning or impact: "I had either got around them or they had no emotional appeal to me. I knew nothing about living in a hotel or going out to restaurants, so those didn't have any appeal to me. And we had a black theater, which, for me, was good in that I got to know the projectionist and the owner as well as to work at the theater."

At Quinton's all-black high school, the emphasis was on individual accomplishment, not social change. The hidden curriculum held that blacks deserved equality by virtue of their achievements—a cornerstone of the philosophy of influential educator Booker T. Washington. "I remember the *Brown* decision. It captured my imagination. But in high school my teachers were much more conscious about making us aware of black people who had accomplished great things, like Ralph Bunche and Marian Anderson. They were less aware about changing the society. We were encouraged to study. We were nurtured. We were encouraged to become somebody."

However, Quinton's racial complacency and the school's political accommodationism collided with his sense of racial injustice and inbred defiance when Fred Waring and his Pennsylvanians visited Greenville's East Carolina College in 1959. He approached his school's glee club director about getting tickets. "She told me that it was not possible to go. The school was segregated; the only black people who were there were those who worked there." He persisted, trying for weeks to receive permission from the college. His persistence was of no avail.

> I was furious! There had been no other event that was segregated that I had wanted to attend. This was the *first* time that I really wanted to go someplace and couldn't do it. It wasn't an incident like going downtown, where you knew you couldn't go to the lunch counters—I didn't have a desire to go to the lunch counters and my family didn't eat in restaurants. This connected with what I *wanted* to do; I couldn't do it.
>
> This was the first time that it became clear to me that there were unwarranted, unnecessary restrictions on my life because of my color. This incident loomed large in my head. I began to pay more attention, to read more, to see more what was happening and becoming more aware of patterns of segregation.

Lunch at the Five and Dime

During his senior year, Quinton heard of a spontaneous sit-in held by four college students at a Woolworth's lunch counter in downtown Greensboro. One late Monday afternoon on February 1, 1960, four African-American freshmen from the Agricultural and Technical College (A & T) walked to the all-white counter to order coffee. "I'm sorry. We don't serve Negroes here," responded the waitress. Ezell Blair Jr. persisted. "I beg to disagree with you. You just finished serving me at a counter only two feet away from here." Looking over to the far end of the stand-up counter, she replied: "Negroes eat at the other end." After a few more exchanges, the waitress left to notify the manager. A black woman who worked at the steam table came up to the four asking them to move. When they refused, she walked away in frustration, muttering: "You're acting stupid, ignorant! That's why we can't get anywhere today."[1]

The next morning, twenty-seven A & T students along with several newspaper reporters crowded the all-white counter. "We are prepared to keep coming for two years if we have to," one protester proclaimed. Quickly the word spread, as white counterdemonstrators came to heckle or reserve stools for white customers, and as members of the established Negro and white communities wrestled with the growing number of protesters crowding the Woolworth's and Kress five-and-dime stores.

Within a week, the "sit-in movement" had spread to other North Carolina communities that had Negro colleges: Winston-Salem; Durham; Raleigh; Elizabeth City; High Point. Within two weeks, as the Greensboro students agreed to a truce for negotiations, nonviolent lunch counter sit-ins spread from Nashville, Tennessee, to Tallahassee, Florida. By the end of March, sixty-eight cities in thirteen Southern states reported sit-ins, including a wade-in at the all-white swimming pool in Biloxi, Mississippi, a read-in at the library in St. Petersburg, Florida, and a host of kneel-ins at all-white churches.

As hundreds of students across the South were jailed, Southern legislators feverishly worked to enact punitive laws against this civil rights activity. Though violence remained at relatively low levels in Greensboro, Orangeburg city officials turned power hoses against 350 South Carolina State student demonstrators. Those not hospitalized were herded into an open-air stockade in forty degree weather. In Tallahassee tear gas was used, and in the Alabama cities of Bessemer and Montgomery, angry whites took their revenge using baseball bats or iron pipes.

Unlike the earlier Montgomery and Tallahassee bus boycotts, the student-led grassroots sit-ins signaled a new era in the struggle for civil rights. These protests required little logistical or advanced organizing and were carried out without charismatic leaders or the initial support of black civil rights organizations or white Southern liberals. The student sit-ins represented a turning point in the movement. White consciousness regarding the "Negro problem" was heightened, and black conservative leadership wedded to Southern white paternalism or liberalism was challenged. The longtime activist Bayard Rustin acidly observed: "What the student movement has done is to have broken the back of professional Uncle Tomism."[2]

In mid-April students from across the South gathered at Shaw University in Raleigh to coordinate efforts and share ideas. At this three-day event, organized by Ella Baker, Martin Luther King Jr. addressed the vanguard of civil rights activists, urging them to form student organizations and to remain in jail without bond. As a result the Student Nonviolent Coordinating Committee (SNCC) emerged and older groups—particularly the Congress of Racial Equality (CORE), organized in 1942 by James Farmer—placed greater emphasis on student organizing.

As Quinton accepted his high school diploma at C. M. Eppes Auditorium in May 1960, a handful of businesses in cities such as Winston-Salem and Nashville voluntarily integrated their lunch counters (Greensboro's lunch counters integrated three weeks after the Fourth of July). Within a year, businesses in 126 Southern cities had integrated their public eating facilities; no city, though, had ended segregation of all public accommodations.

Carefully following the events from Greenville, Quinton eagerly anticipated joining the Negro college students' efforts in Durham led by another Greenville native, Lacey Streeter. "By the time I got to college I was so ready and prepared that it became almost more important to me than the academic work. It was the force."

Judge Mallard's Courtroom

Sitting in the dormitory cell at Morganton, Quinton had access to few books and seldom enjoyed watching the summer reruns of last season's television favorites like *The Fugitive* and *Andy Griffith*. Even the World Series, pitting the New York Yankees against the Los Angeles Dodgers, had little appeal. When not bantering with cellmates or writing letters for fellow inmates, Quinton spent time in soulful solitude—occasionally interrupted by visits from a handful of Durham and Chapel Hill friends and fellow activists. Even Jim Crow showed its face, as prison officials and visitors confronted a system in which one Sunday afternoon was set aside for whites and another for "the colored and Indians."

Sometimes Quinton's thoughts turned to the halcyon days of the Durham and Chapel Hill freedom movements, in which his organizational skills had become legendary. As the NAACP state youth president and an NAACP Commando, he had organized business boycotts, restaurant sit-ins, church rallies, and street demonstrations. Knowledgeable in nonviolent tactics and self-educated in the Gandhian philosophy of love and satyagraha, he shared these skills and ideas with restless high school and college youths willing to place themselves in physical peril to end racial discrimination. Stirred by the social evil of segregation, he also welcomed the Whitmanesque comradeship he found in the movement—most important, his deep friendships with Pat and John, now fellow inmates.

These three—along with a handful of others—were given prison sentences of one to three years by Orange County Superior Court Judge Raymond B. Mallard, a gray-haired gentleman with wire-rimmed spectacles and a tired face. Wearing suits and ties on an April morning in 1964, the defendants took some glee in seeing that the four rest room plaques on the heavily varnished doors long designating white and colored had been removed. Thirty years later, a bit heavier and with graying hair, Quinton's encounter with American justice is engraved in his memory:

> Judge Mallard was a short and very angry man: We had created havoc in Southern Paradise—and we had *no* right to do that. He punished us before we were tried and afterward. He treated us in court with contempt, demanding that we appear at 8:30 in the morning. We were not allowed to read or to talk. We had to just sit there and watch whatever was going on. If one of us tried to read something, he would stop the courtroom proceedings and threaten contempt. He refused to give any kind of calendar. He knew we were students; this was part of his punishment.
>
> He also was convinced that everyone was a Northerner—including me. He made it clear that "no Southern boy would do what you did." In his Southern nasal twang, he said, "It is more than passing strange that these people are from Ohio, Connecticut, and other places."
>
> When he targeted the three of us, I knew that I was in for it. I was the only African-American that got an active sentence. He figured this brazened little nigger needed to get some lessons learned. In my case, he asked the solicitor, "Is he a leader?" "Your Honor, if this was a Western you would call him Ramrod!"

Legacies and Learnings

Pat Cusick's earlier life experiences could not have been more different from those of Quinton Baker's childhood. His first eight years were spent at his grandmother's Victorian mansion. Smothered in Confederate lore and Southern virtues,

> I grew up in a very segregationist background. The family put great store on ancestors and family history. We didn't have any money, so maybe that is one reason why my mother took great pride in family. Her grandmother was a member of the Lewis family. One great-great uncle, Colonel Fielding Lewis, married George Washington's sister; another was Meriwether Lewis, who traipsed the Northwest with Clark. My great-grandfather—William Perry

Hollingworth—was a distinguished major in the Nineteenth Alabama Infantry, fighting in Shiloh, Vicksburg, Chickamauga. He was also the largest slave owner in north Alabama. He and his brother owned about a hundred slaves, who worked on the bank of the Coosa River that flows through Gadsden—where I was born. His portrait, wearing his Confederate officer's uniform, always hung over the fireplace with the Stars and Bars flag draped over it and his gun resting on the mantle. That was the lore within which I was raised.

After the Lost Cause, Major Hollingworth worked for other farmers to buy farm equipment; within two years he had made a million dollars in his mercantile business. He also formed the first Alabama Ku Klux Klan. When he died in 1878, seven years after Gadsden was incorporated, he left a fortune of $750,000.

The legacy left to Pat's grandmother, though, was more than money. Pat recalls his first cousin, who was attending the U.S. Naval Academy in Annapolis, visiting in 1936. Grandmother Standifer met him at the door of her twenty-nine-room home: "It is wonderful that you are home for Christmas. You can come in, but no blue uniform will *ever* cross this threshold!" Pat's mother, Katie, held equally strong beliefs. She once remarked to young Pat that "there is only one instance where people have the right to take the law into their own hands—when a Negro rapes a white woman."

In the spring of 1931, the year Pat was born and a year after the formation of the Association of Southern Women for the Prevention of Lynching, nine black men—the youngest of whom was thirteen—were arrested in nearby Scottsboro and charged with the rape of two white women on a freight train. For a while they were held in the Gadsden jail. The case drew worldwide attention as they were initially convicted and sentenced to death. Granted a new trial by the U.S. Supreme Court two years later, after one of the two women recanted, the men were sentenced to long prison terms.

Pat also remembers another alleged rape of a white woman by an African-American soldier stationed at Camp Sibert in Gadsden during the 1940s:

> There was about a week of searching and rumors. It was a furtive atmosphere with huddled adult conversations and younger children asking older ones the meaning of "rape." They arrested a soldier who supposedly had blood beneath his fingernails. They were taking him to the nearby town of Anniston "to ensure his safety." But on the way over he supposedly bolted from the car and ran across the field. They shot him.

Unbeknownst to young Pat, there also was the shadow heritage of Grandfather Standifer's family. They were mountain Republicans. "My grandfather's father actually rode through north Alabama urging people *not* to secede before the Montgomery Secessionist Convention. He fed Union troops, helped slaves escape, and was a well-educated attorney. Naturally, after the war he was made a judge by the forces of occupation." Recently Pat discovered that Grandfather Standifer had been a socialist and an ardent supporter of Eugene V. Debs. In 1912 he was a leading member of the "Black and Tans," a progressive faction of the Republican Party composed of blacks and whites.

The marriage of Pat's parents further contributed to his mixed family lineage. Pat's father, Frank, an Irishman from the Northern steel mills, prided himself on a day's work for a dollar's wage. "He was a very quiet man. He taught me not to trust a man without calluses on his hands—180 degrees different from the view on my mother's side."

When Pat's grandmother died in 1938 the family moved to a smaller wooden house on a shaded Gadsden street. Pat's childhood was much like that depicted in the fictional setting of Harper Lee's *To Kill a Mockingbird*. In that "tired old town . . . there was nowhere to go, nothing to buy and no money to buy it with, nothing to see outside the boundaries of Maycomb County."[3]

There weren't many "colored" and "white" signs in Gadsden. Pat remembers one Jim Crow sign in his local parish church, St. James, where the last three pews were "Reserved for Colored." There wasn't even a Jim Crow balcony at the movie house. As in Maycomb, in Gadsden everyone knew their place. "From the earliest days sitting on my mother's knee, I was taught that there were three classes of people: folks like us, darkies, and poor white trash. In some ways people might think it was deadly. I didn't think so. It was just the way it was."

Race and social class contoured Pat's small-town Southern life as it did for Harper Lee's character Scout growing up in Depression-era Maycomb.

> Behind white houses in some sections of Gadsden there was an alley with dilapidated homes of black families who originally had been servants of the white families. Across our street was St. John's Alley. The kids from there and my side of the street played football together until I was about eleven. Sometimes we played in my front yard or in the yards of houses in the alley.
>
> The mother of my best black friend, Willie, did white folks' laundry, including my family's clothes. I was fascinated by the large black cast-iron kettle in the backyard, constantly steaming over a wood fire, with a large, smooth wooden paddle to stir the clothes and the singular smell of wood smoke mingled with lye soap. I often took naps with Willie in his house on a large bed with a colorful quilt.
>
> Finally, Mother sat me down telling me that I was getting older and it was time to do other things than play with the alley kids. I got the message, but I always had to be polite. I never was allowed to say "nigger" or "nigra," lest I get a whipping.

For most white Southerners whose surnames bear a quiet dignity, the antebellum relationships—what Southern writer and activist Lillian Smith astutely described as "ghost relationships"—between blacks and whites "still haunt the southern mind."[4] Pat was watched over by a Negro, Janie, who took him for long afternoon walks. "Not known to my mother, she brought me down to the black part of town on Tuscaloosa Avenue." His memory holds a collage of impressions: a Royal Crown Cola sign; women in the beauty parlor with curling irons; strange smells of hair preparations. There was also one Negro family on the other side of town whom Pat's family annually visited to deliver Christmas gifts. "They were the descendants of the slaves from Great-Grandfather Hollingworth's plantation."

"Certain incidents sometimes just pierce through our consciousness," Pat observed as he recalled another incident that is "so etched in memory that I can still almost smell the freshly cut grass, feel the warm sunshine through the shade trees, and the lines on the gray concrete sidewalk on which I was standing." Hanging out with several of his white friends, Pat remembers spotting a black boy riding a bicycle toward them on the sidewalk:

> One of my friends started taunting him with the N-word and picked up some rocks to throw at his spokes. It was a small sidewalk, so we expected him either to ride through real fast or run away. But what the boy did was to stop the bike right in front of us: "You white motherfuckers." He gave us a real tongue-lashing. I was ashamed and shocked. This was the first time I had ever seen a black person stand up to any white.

As he grew up during World War II, Pat's favorite pastime—next to football—was "shooting Japs and Nazis. Our favorite enemy was the Japanese. We considered them worse than the Germans, who were not as 'sneaky' and 'treacherous.'" He was forbidden, though, to play near the movie house and warned by his mother never to go into the manager's office. "I asked her why. 'He has the habit of inviting little boys into his office. It is not very nice.'"

Though not yet making any sexual connection, Pat began to recognize feelings stirring within himself that he knew were sinful. Suddenly he became curious about books and magazines. "I found the books on statuary at our house. The male statues of Michelangelo were fascinating. I wasn't sure what it all meant, but I knew I was attracted to them." Paging through a 1942 *Life* magazine, he eyed photographs of soldiers in the South Pacific during their recreational time. Several featured them swimming in the nude. "I was *really* turned on; I had my first masturbation experience. But I knew that my feelings and erections were wrong."

His mother came into some money with the sale of her mother's mansion after the war. She invested it in Pat's education. At fourteen, Pat was sent to Cullman—about sixty miles from home—to attend boarding school at St. Bernard Abbey. About 150 boys shared the Benedictine facility. Although he saw the word "queer" for the first time written in the bathroom, he never knew a gay student. When he took dormitory showers, though, he took a particular fondness in scanning the football players. "I started suspecting, but I didn't know what this thing was. I thought I was the only boy in the world like this."

Pat attended dances held between St. Bernard and nearby Sacred Heart, a girl's school operated by the Benedictine nuns. Although he "didn't like dates," in his junior year he courted a blond drum majorette at Gadsden High—a convenient sixty miles distant. "We would meet and drink Coca-Cola and swap chewing gum as we kissed." Soon he graduated to double-dating and fooling around in the backseat of the car. "There was a lot of pressure to 'make out.' But I was very uncomfortable."

In his senior year Pat developed a "crush" on a Georgia sophomore, Bob, who played junior varsity basketball. Pat's close friends were his age and were aghast that he was "chumming" with a younger boy. One day the twosome defied Abbey rules, hiking three miles out to "the Cliffs" to journey down to Four Mile Creek. After they swam in the nude, they scrambled onto the huge granite stones. Stretching out, their bronzed bodies glistened in the noonday sun. As Bob's muscles twitched, Pat studied his friend's tan line, muscled biceps, and the thin line of blond hair trailing off near his naval. Both noticed the erection of the other. "We touched one another. I went to confession the next week."

At St. Bernard, though, Pat spent more time exploring his racial feelings. As some priests lectured about the evils of segregation, they met stiff resistance from this great-grandson of a slave owner and founder of an Alabama klavern: "I was one of the leading arguers against integration. I believed in separate but equal; black folks should be treated better, but they should be separate."

During midsummer 1948 Pat was "glued" to the radio listening to the Democratic Convention in Philadelphia. He was appalled when the party narrowly approved a civil rights plank on the convention floor, sponsored by the youthful liberal mayor of Minneapolis. After the adoption of the plank, there was a walkout of Mississippi and Alabama delegates (which included Birmingham's police safety commissioner, Bull Connor). The Southerners later convened in Birmingham to organize the States' Rights party, selecting Senator Strom Thurmond of South Carolina as its presidential candidate and Mississippi Governor Fielding L. Wright as his running mate. "Strom Thurmond was my hero; Hubert Humphrey was the villain. When they played Dixie and marched out, I was thrilled."

The fall presidential campaign unfolded with President Harry Truman running against the heavily favored Thomas Dewey, the ardent segregationist Thurmond of the renegade Dixiecrats, and the one-world progressive Henry Wallace. Pat learned that Wallace was to visit Gadsden in his campaign swing through the South. "He had an integrated entourage! I heard that there were 'niggers' with him. That was enough to draw a crowd to the Etowah County Courthouse. It was a mob scene. They couldn't get out of the car. There were epithets and hollering. I was embarrassed for my fellow townspeople. It *wasn't* a Southernly reception."

During Pat's senior year he found it more and more difficult to defend his segregationist position, but his sense of family honor and childhood upbringing weighed heavily on him. In his childhood his mother had compelled Pat to memorize the poetry of the Confederacy. Now a Boston community activist in the poverty-ridden inner city, Pat still remembers the slim volume of poems penned by the poet-priest of the Confederacy, Alabaman Abram J. Ryan. His voice, now roughened from years of rallies and confrontations, embellished the final stanza from "The Conquered Banner":

> *Furl that Banner, softly, slowly!*
> *Treat it gently—it is holy—*
> *For it droops above the dead.*
> *Touch it not—unfold it never,*
> *Let it droop there, furled forever,*
> *For its people's hopes are dead!*[5]

Four years at St. Bernard had tempered Pat's segregationist attitudes if not chastened his sexual feelings. "I had eaten at Willie's home. I shared the same cup as Willie and the same glass as Janie. I had eaten food prepared by black folks all of my life. Why, then, should there be separate water fountains, separate bathrooms, separate eating facilities? The inconsistency didn't make sense."

As Pat readied to graduate with the class of 1949 and as his racist attitudes softened, the groundbreaking book *Killers of the Dream* was published. Lillian Smith, who along with her longtime companion Paula Snelling[6] had published the progressive *South Today,* aptly captured the lessons in growing up white:

It began so long ago, not only in the history books but in our own childhood. We southerners learned our first three lessons too well. . . . We were taught . . . to love God, to love our white skin, and to believe in the sanctity of both. . . . By the time we were five years old we had learned, without hearing the words, that masturbation is wrong and segregation is right, and each had become a dread taboo that must never be broken. . . . As the years passed . . . parts of your body are segregated areas which you must stay away from and keep others away from. These areas you touch only when necessary. In other words, you cannot freely associate with them any more than you can associate freely with colored children. . . . Now, on the other hand, though your body is a thing of shame and mystery, and curiosity about it is not good, your skin is your consolation, your glory, and the source of your strength and pride. . . . Not only Negroes but everything dark, dangerous, evil must be pushed to the rim of one's life. . . . Each lesson thus was linked on to the other, drawing strength from it. Indeed, the relentless interlocking of these learnings grows more and more clear as one traces the paths and bypaths circling through a southern childhood. Forbidden sex play . . . forbidden dreams . . . forbidden relations . . . restlessness . . . resentment . . . guilt . . . emptiness. . . . [7]

Royal Ice Cream

When Quinton graduated from high school with honors, he was determined to excel beyond his father's lowly expectations. Accepting a local scholarship to attend one of the few liberal arts colleges available to a poor, black youth from the rural South, he entered North Carolina College (NCC) in September 1960.

Durham was much as it had been two generations earlier, dubbed by the noted sociologist E. Franklin Frazier as "the capital of the black bourgeoisie . . . with its fine homes, exquisite churches, and middle-class respectability."[8] The city boasted business enterprises ranging from the North Carolina Mutual Life Insurance Company to the Mechanics and Farmers Bank. These enterprises had grown out of the pioneering efforts of men with little experience in business but who were inspired by the self-improvement gospel promulgated by Negro leaders, most notably Booker T. Washington.[9] Men like C. C. Spaulding—successor to the ambitious founder of Mutual Insurance, John Merrick, who started out as a barber—pursued commercial ventures while others such as Mutual's cofounder James Shepard established NCC to train blacks for the practical arts. These men, like most of Quinton's high school teachers, accepted segregation as a way of life, supporting Booker T. Washington's famous 1895 dictum: "In all things that are purely social we can be separate as the fingers."[10]

Individual economic advancement and personal achievements—in W.E.B. Du Bois's phrase, "the evils of Get and Grab"—had substantially improved the social and political conditions of the majority of blacks since the publication of his masterful work, *The Souls of Black Folk,* two generations earlier. However, the Talented Tenth, described by Du Bois as "youth in the land capable by character and talent to receive that higher training, the end of which is culture,"[11] had largely been content with developing parallel black institutions such as churches, hospitals, schools, and businesses at the expense of social and economic integration with the white community.

Though scions of these black "artisan businessmen and property owners" developed a greater commercial consciousness, they also counseled "a silent submission to civic inferiority such as is bound to sap the manhood of any race in the long run,"[12] and "they still conformed to the tradition of the gentleman which lingered and shaped their morals and manners."[13] A grandson of C. C. Spaulding, who had founded the Durham Committee on Negro Affairs, was a member of Quinton's NCC class of 1964.

> Asa T. Spaulding Jr. was the president of my class at North Carolina College. I can remember the days when I was standing before my class prodding, cajoling, and begging to get massive student support, he would come on after me and go right into the class business. Here was the one black person in this city who could afford to take any position that he wanted . . . taking no position at all.

Motivated by the need to right social injustice and buoyed by the recent lunch counter activism, Quinton sought out the NAACP, founded in 1910 by Du Bois. The college chapter at NCC was headed by Lacey Streeter. Seven months after Streeter had led the Durham sit-in movement, Woolworth's department store and a handful of other businesses had been desegregated. "There were still problems of black people being hired in department stores, trying on clothes, and general problems of segregation. . . . A black woman could not try on a dress, and if she took it home she could not bring it back even though it didn't fit."

Streeter introduced Quinton to Floyd McKissick, the first African-American to enter a previously all-white North Carolina public school and later to earn a law degree from the University of North Carolina. At the time that Quinton entered college, McKissick was the adviser for the youth conference of the state chapter of the NAACP as well as the city youth chapter. "For a lot of us the immediacy of the issue was what was happening where we were. Dr. King didn't have the stature in the movement that he eventually grew to have; he was just another leader. For us, Floyd McKissick and James Farmer had greater impact. McKissick was right here. He was our attorney, our counselor, our guide before he gained national prominence."

Quinton quickly emerged as "an arrogant young hotshot college student. My first semester I was in the NAACP and I was demonstrating. I didn't stop for the four years I was there!"

Both the campus and city youth groups, comprising no more than forty committed individuals, worked closely together. "During the periods in which the students were not involved on a massive level, there was a group of us who were *committed* to it. . . . The thousand people that we brought out were not dedicated, committed people to the movement. They believed in it, but they couldn't devote their entire existence to this."

At McKissick's cramped upstairs law office, strategy sessions were held around a large wooden conference table, sometimes lasting from eleven in the morning until an hour before the scheduled demonstration. A decision was soon made to boycott particular businesses.

> We had gotten most of the lunch counters desegregated. Then we started Easter boycotts in '61 and '62. I remember the lists that we passed out. Every

week or other week a new list would come out saying "Don't buy at this store" or "Buy at this store. . . ." We would have a picket line in front of the store and then there would be one or two of us near the store handing out Don't Buy lists. Some of the lists would have cartoons on them—a caricature of the manager or a salesperson.

Quinton also remembers picketing particular businesses. One of their first activities was picketing Royal Ice Cream. "This was an ice cream shop located in a predominantly black area of Durham not far from McKissick's house that would not allow blacks to sit down and eat their ice cream." At the end of every night's demonstration, as the manger of the ice cream shop readied to close, the picketers would sing:

> Ain't no use in hanging 'round
> Royal Ice Cream has closed down
> Shut out the lights and lock the doors
> We'll be back to picket more

The group also picketed the Carolina Theater, where Negroes could only go to the third balcony. There, night after night, winter into summer, he walked the picket line adjacent to City Hall.

As Quinton rose from student picketer to president of the campus NAACP, tactical changes occurred:

When we started picketing in '60—and even with the sit-ins—everybody wore a shirt, tie, and suit or heels, stockings, and their Sunday dress. I didn't care how hot it was outside; we were dressed to kill. We wanted to prove that we were human; we were clean. We were trying to counter the stereotypes. You also didn't eat on the picket line or anything that was in any way to suggest that you were contributing to the stereotype. This continued until late '62, when we started getting more casual.

While their dress was becoming more casual, their strategy of desegregating through picketing became less certain:

In the '61–'62 period there was nothing big or massive, just a continual drive to desegregate the town—nothing glamorous, no newspapers. After we saw we weren't going to desegregate the movies this way a decision was reached . . . to massively attack everything—the whole city. A good time to do it was when we were having a new mayor coming in. . . . What we did to get up to that point was to go on our respective campuses and start smaller marches, smaller rallies . . . and plan for the day we were going to have bigger rallies and put everybody in jail.

A Circle of Friends

North Carolina College restricted the off-campus social activities of its 2,500 students. All the men lived in Chidley Hall dormitory, with the first-

year students housed on the fourth floor. As in high school, Quinton assumed campus leadership positions. Unlike in high school, there were more
students like himself. Quinton describes his special circle of friends:

> You found like-minded people by the way people looked at you and the things
> people said. We were less athletic and more intellectually oriented, so the circle
> actually developed around these common interests. We talked about a lot of
> literature, and sometimes it was just "dishing" other people.
>
> There were also a couple of students who were flaming and very effemi-
> nate—the people whom most of us avoided. What was very strong at North
> Carolina College—and at many black institutions in the sixties—was verbal
> karate. You developed these skills around both gossipy conversations as well
> as intellectual topics. If you weren't prepared, you'd be annihilated in a very
> short period of time. These guys were *very* good; they had no fear.
>
> I remember in the dining hall once, there was this huge football player,
> Elmer. One of these gay men, David—an eloquent queen with a tie flipped over
> his shoulder as he swished along—came into the dining hall. There was a long
> line of students wrapped around the dining hall, since everyone ate at the same
> time. Elmer said something about screwing him. David just turned around and
> said as loud as he could: "Before I'd have you I'd fill a Pepsi-Cola bottle with
> hot water and sit on it." He then sashayed on.

Quinton's circle of four or five gay classmates talked about their various
experiences during their year of discovery. One of his roommates fell in
love with a young man. Going to extreme lengths to look masculine, he
even bought a pair of heavy wing tip shoes. But unlike in today's campus
climate, "there didn't seem to be the tension that is there now within the
African-American community. Back then, people may have said 'Well, he's
funny.' But the hostility wasn't there. There might have been some comments about gay people on campus, but there was a level of acceptance. A
lot of student leaders and activists were often gay men—gay women were
really very secretive; we didn't know them."

During college, Quinton read everything written by James Baldwin, including *Giovanni's Room*. Published in 1956, Baldwin's groundbreaking
novel followed David, a blond American wandering through Europe with
his girlfriend. When the two separate, he engages in a six-month affair with
Giovanni, a virile Italian who tends bar at a popular gay spot. Though penning the obligatory demise with its deceit, despondency, and death—and
setting it in another country—the acclaimed author of *Go Tell It on the
Mountain* offered readers a rare glimpse of homosexual feelings.

Homosexuality, though, did not occupy a lot of Quinton's time:

> I was much more into the civil rights movement and learning more about the
> NAACP. In the circle of friends that I had at North Carolina College, race and
> sex were connected—but the issue was really civil rights. I'm not sure we dealt
> with being gay in any emotional or intellectual way, except to accept the fact

that that was who we were. And since we had our own support system, we didn't feel as isolated.

In some ways, I never tied the two issues—race and sexuality—together. Race during the time of segregation was about my right to have a fulfilled existence, to have a life that was not restricted. The sexual issue was about trying to understand what these feelings meant and how they fit into the context of human emotions.

Journeying Through the Belly of the Beast

Two weeks before the inauguration of John F. Kennedy, the U.S. Supreme Court outlawed segregation in terminals for interstate train and bus passengers. Thirteen years earlier, in the groundbreaking decision of *Morgan v. Virginia,* the Court had banished segregation on interstate trains and buses.

On April 13, 1947, sixteen interracial civil rights activists embarked upon a two-week "journey of reconciliation," traveling to fifteen upper South cities. The "freedom riders" tested compliance by having black activists sit in the front of the bus while their white compatriots walked to the rear. Among the riders was Bayard Rustin. On their fifth day, as the group boarded a Trailways bus from Chapel Hill to Greensboro, the driver asked the blacks to move to the back of the bus. When they refused, they were arrested for disorderly conduct.

Rev. Charlie Jones, the longtime white pastor of the Community Church in Chapel Hill, received an urgent phone call: Some taxicab drivers working the bus terminal were now outside the police station armed with clubs and stones awaiting the release of the freedom riders. Hurrying to the station, he placed bond and drove the four to his home—pursued by two taxis. Rustin continues: "The two cabs pulled up at the curb. Men jumped out, two of them with sticks for weapons; others picked up sizable rocks. They started toward the house, but were called back by one of their number. In a few moments the phone rang, and an anonymous voice said to Jones, 'Get those damn niggers out of town or we'll burn your house down.'"[14] Jones hastily drove the freedom riders to Greensboro. Rustin and the others would return that summer to face trial in nearby Hillsborough.

A dozen years later a new generation of youthful activists prepared to test Kennedy's willingness to enforce the Court ruling. Seven blacks and six whites were carefully selected to retrace the old freedom ride route. This time, though, they planned to travel into the belly of the Deep South, ending in New Orleans—a symbol of Gandhi's march to the sea. This time, however, blacks would enter the white waiting room as whites entered the black one. In the process, they hoped to stir public awareness and buoy the spirit of Southern blacks like Quinton Baker: "The freedom riders had an impact on me in meeting the people and being involved with them as they came through. Anytime anyone joined us or did something that supported our efforts and encouraged us to go forward, it was important."

After the freedom riders crossed into South Carolina, violence erupted as whites beat several riders departing from the Rock Hill terminal. Refusing to press charges, the group traveled south. On reaching Atlanta, they began the second and more perilous part of their journey. One Greyhound and one Trailways bus headed out for Birmingham on May 14. When the Greyhound bus arrived in Anniston an angry mob, clutching pistols, knives, chains, and clubs, greeted the riders. Electing not to enter the terminal, the driver made a speedy exit as the bus tires were slashed. Near the outskirts of town, the bus broke down and was quickly overtaken by trailing whites. Blocking the door, one white youth tossed a firebomb through the window. Several police looked on approvingly. As the flames spread rapidly and black smoke bellowed from the disabled vehicle, the freedom riders jumped through windows. The bus exploded. Photographs of its charred remains appeared on front pages of major American newspapers the next day.

The incident at Anniston and the bloody Sunday Mother's Day beatings at the Trailways terminal in Birmingham (the city's public safety commissioner, Bull Connor, dismissed any responsibility, claiming that all of his officers were visiting their mothers) surprised many Americans, including the youthful attorney general, Robert Kennedy. "None of those violent acts surprised us," Quinton countered. "I have never been surprised by any of the violence in the South."

Journey to Hope Chapel

Unlike Quinton, when Pat Cusick graduated from high school in 1949 he was not "fired up" about race relations—just concerned. Three years after the death of his father, his mother married another Catholic and the family moved to Rome—Georgia. There Pat worked at a department store until the start of the Korean War.

A year earlier President Truman had taken the bold step of integrating the armed services.[15] Stationed at Tempelhof Air Force Base in West Germany, Pat was psychologically as well as physically removed from the South. He worked as a control tower operator, and his supervisor was not only an African-American but also "brighter than I was." Although they became friends, Pat often wondered what would happen should his black friends choose to visit him in his native land: "I certainly wouldn't have been bold enough to challenge the seating arrangement on the bus, but on the other hand, how could I not do it?"

Although all of the gay bars were off-limits, Pat visited one with his secretly admired buddy. "I got so turned off because it was so heavily gay. There were aging lesbians singing in French. The waiter had rouge and lipstick; he came on to us so strongly. It confused me. 'Does this mean if I'm like this, I have to behave like them?' It wasn't a very good experience."

The danger of bar visits and same-sex affections was impressed on twenty-one-year-old Pat as a captain from Wiesbaden, caught with a sergeant from Berlin, was summarily court-marshaled. There was also that boyish soldier working in the decoding operations who frequented the Berlin gay bars. He had been exposed after getting "married" and honeymooning with his male companion on the Isle of Capri.

Honorably discharged in 1953, Pat returned to Georgia for laboratory work at Rome's new General Electric plant. During the next three years, he remained in the closet both politically and sexually. "In May of '54, when *Brown v. Board of Education* was announced, it hit like a bombshell. Every day at coffee break that's all the assistant engineers talked about—for months and months. I was too timid even to argue with my colleagues who were buying guns and promising to kill black folks before they would let their children go to an integrated school."

Though the *Brown* decision and the Montgomery bus boycott a year later aroused white Southern passions, typically little attention was paid to the "Negro problem." One exception was Lillian Smith. In a letter to the editor of the *New York Times*—the supposedly liberal *Atlanta Constitution* had refused publication—she hailed the 1954 Supreme Court decision as "every child's Magna Carta." She went on to proclaim that no "artificial barriers" such as laws can be condoned in separating children because of either color or disability, concluding that "it will be an ordeal only if our attitude makes it one."[16]

Eager to escape hardened red clay Georgian attitudes, Pat entered another Benedictine school—Belmont Abbey College, about eight miles from Charlotte. Receiving money from the GI Bill and working nights at a local bank, "the world of learning was opened to me." Majoring in chemistry, he spent little time socializing and "assiduously avoided" the only gay bar in town.

While at Belmont Pat once again argued about civil rights—this time in *support* of Eisenhower's decision to send troops to escort nine black students into Little Rock High School in September 1957. "I was on the road to becoming a liberal, arguing against the basic unfairness of discrimination—though I wasn't sure about the protests, boycotts, and Dr. King."

Though he was coming out of the closet politically, Pat's only acknowledgment of his homosexuality was his routine YMCA visits, where he enjoyed nude swimming and the ubiquitous shower scene. "People who knew me thought it was commendable that I was spending what little time I had in these physical activities." Avoiding homosexual relationships and reflecting on homoerotic desires, in 1959, as he was transferring buses at High Point, Pat stumbled across a paperback book, *Giovanni's Room:* "There was a magazine rack with twenty or so paperback books—a veiled description on one cover caught my eye. I bought it and read it avidly on the bus. It hit me like a ton of bricks. As a closeted man, it was the first time I had seen something like this in print." Like the fictional David, Pat denied his homosexuality. At the end of Baldwin's novel David lapses into self-hatred and despair; a different fate awaited Pat.

Soon thereafter Pat visited Chapel Hill. The University of North Carolina (UNC) "looked like a university was supposed to look." The first state university in the United States, UNC had for generations been considered the finest in the South. Located on 1,400 acres of land donated by residents living near New Hope Chapel on the hill, the school bestowed on the town a distinctive charm and character; most of its residents earned their livelihood from the institution, and the university viewed itself as a lighthouse for progress and civility.

Pat transferred that summer and pursued studies in mathematics while working as a custodian at the Student Union. His move to the "chapel on the hill" brought him closer to his rendezvous with Quinton and John. "This was the waning days of the Beat movement. There were some really talented student poets and artists. Even when I had to drop out of school or take only one course, I was reading voraciously: Henry Miller, Jack Kerouac, Simone de Beauvoir, William Burroughs, Jean-Paul Sartre, Allen Ginsberg, Albert Camus."

One of those talented artists was Skye, a blond, blue-eyed student on whom Pat developed a "fierce crush." The two soon became roommates.

> He really unshackled my mind and shifted my moorings. We would read *all* of Henry Miller or *all* of Aldous Huxley while making home brew in the basement. We used to send off for peyote to Smith's Cactus Farm in Laredo for five dollars a box. I was exposed to jazz—Miles Davis's *Sketches of Spain*—as we did reefer for the first time following our reading of Huxley. Skye laid the groundwork for what was about to come.

Pat and Skye hung out at Harry's Grill, a restaurant adjacent to the post office on Franklin Street where "all the subcultures of Chapel Hill would gather." Founded by the Macklins, a Jewish couple who immigrated from Brooklyn, Harry's had booths and tables crowded with writers and beats, activists and actors, homosexuals and communists, poets and painters. Smoke and jazz hung heavily in the air.

As a "free spirit," Pat began to complement his long conversations with Skye with introspective writing. One short story featured a closeted homosexual entranced by a man's man. "I was hoping it would be recognized as the great American short story that I could then present to him." Though nothing came of the story nor of his attraction to Skye, Skye was the first person with whom Pat shared his homoerotic feelings, Catholic sins, and romantic infatuations.

In late August 1962 Pat journeyed to the homosexual mecca, New York City. "I thought if I went there I might have a sexual encounter. But I didn't know how to go about it." After checking into the Chelsea YMCA, he hurried down to the Village. "It was wondrous. I was overwhelmed. Washington Park was filled with beats and artists. There were the coffeehouses on MacDonald Street, like Café Wha? where I listened to poetry and folk music while observing the young men with long, straight hair and tight jeans. But I couldn't get up enough gumption; I didn't know how to start the conversation."

Although he did not bring back any treasured sexual experience, he returned to Chapel Hill with a handful of pamphlets and flyers from the Ban the Bomb movement, including one from the Student Peace Union, a national organization that had formed two years earlier. Pat, Skye, and Skye's girlfriend then drove to the Outer Banks island of Ocracoke in Pat's green Pontiac. After several days of camping, Pat chose to remain on the nearly deserted island while the couple returned. That week "gave me the space to do some thinking and get honest with myself."

As autumn waves cut wide swaths across the nine-mile desolate beach, a collage of images floated through Pat's mind: Grandmother Standifer, the boy on the bicycle, debates at St. Bernard, Michelangelo's statuary, *Giovanni's Room*. Enduring storms of solitude, Pat recognized, in the words of Lillian Smith:

> That burden which our fathers had believed to be the "colored races," was our own past, that the heavy weight that lay on our hearts was our own childhood, that the change we felt unable to make was a change in ourselves. We were beginning to see at last what the white man's false beliefs about sin and sex and segregation had done to the minds and spirits of the most powerful nation on earth.[17]

Pat decided to act on his now radically changed set of values. The issue would be nuclear disarmament.

John and Skye

In January, Pat, now living alone as Skye pursued painting in solitude, wrote a letter to the UNC student newspaper, the *Daily Tar Heel*. The chief goal of the Student Peace Union (SPU), wrote the pseudonymous John B. Justice, was "educating the students to the problems concomitant to the age of overkill. Only secondarily will the chapter urge specific programs toward disarmament and permanent peace."[18] As Pat—who years later was an openly gay delegate for presidential candidate Jesse Jackson—admitted, "It was much easier for me to be against the war in Vietnam and form the Student Peace Union than to get involved in civil rights—I never even considered gay rights!"

Wearing a peace button and armed with Ban the Bomb flyers, he sauntered into Harry's. "The beats and poets weren't interested. Across the street, though, was the Carolina Coffee Shop. I had my peace button on— this was before buttons were everywhere—so people began to ask me, 'What the hell is that?'" One of those was a prominent first-year student attending UNC on a prestigious Moorehead scholarship.

As a Northerner, John had graduated from Choate, a private Connecticut boarding school, where he had been the school's football fullback, voted "the straightest arrow" by his fellow seniors, and awarded the School Seal Prize in recognition of his character, leadership, and scholarship. At the university, Pat recalls, "He was part of a circle of the best and the brightest freshmen. John had one of these personalities that made an impact wherever he went and whatever he tackled." Although John had read the Beat poets, he wasn't a bohemian. He agreed, though, to become the fourth member of what soon would become the first SPU chapter in the South.

Pat and John became quick friends. They engaged in long conversations about disarmament, Vietnam, and civil rights. John's second-floor apartment, tastefully furnished with Picasso and Chinese prints, "was like Giovanni's room." Pat continued: "I had not known anyone who was gay, but it was apparent that John was. A couple of the black people in the movement who, if they weren't gay at least went around the corner once or twice, would hang out there, too. There was an ambiance of civil rights, justice, equality—and homosexuality." John's apartment was the first place where Pat talked at length with other gay men who shared his passion for social justice: "We talked about homosexuality and bisexuality mostly on an intellectual level with a bit of sexual tension. At the forefront, though, were discussions about the peace movement and civil rights."

Another SPU member was nineteen-year-old Harold Foster, editor of the NCC newspaper, *Campus Echo*. The soft-spoken Foster frequently joined Pat and others in conversations at John's apartment. As a Lincoln High School student, Harold had been a civil rights leader during the time of the Greensboro sit-ins.

Unlike Durham or Greensboro, Chapel Hill was composed of only a small percentage of African-Americans. There was no substantial black middle class of shop owners and professionals. Some worked in the service sector for various businesses, but most worked directly or indirectly for the university, often renting homes from whites that did not meet the weak housing codes. The most notable black ministers were the articulate accommodationist Rev. J. R. Manley of the First Baptist Church, elected to the school board in 1958, and the quiet but long-term civil rights supporter Rev. W. R. Foushee, who preached at St. Joseph's Colored Methodist Episcopal Church.

Although he lived in Chapel Hill during the theater picketing, Pat "was there, but not in it. I was off in the beat-reefer-jazz movement." Quinton, actively involved in the movement to desegregate theaters and other businesses in Durham, heard of Foster's efforts through Sadie Hughley, one of Quinton's mentors and the NCC librarian.

The College Café

During the short life of Chapel Hill's Student Peace Union, the group fostered dormitory discussions on issues of world peace, sponsored films such as *Power Among Men,* arranged for guest speakers, including Norman Thomas, and tried to organize chapters at other state campuses. "Most of the wrath we got was from the liberal community," remembers Pat. "John Kennedy was president and 'how can you possibly attack foreign policy?'"

SPU also sponsored the Committee for Non-Violent Action as its members came through Chapel Hill on a Quebec-Guantanamo Walk for Peace. These activists discussed the philosophy of nonviolence. Some members, like Pat and Harold, delved more deeply into it. Pat explains: "The real power of satyagraha is that you make the final commitment first. You decide that your life is over and that you have already given it up. Once that happens, the lesser amounts of violence are easier to take since you have already decided that you will make the ultimate sacrifice."

As SPU expanded to about twenty members, doubts arose in Pat's mind. Foremost among them was, "How could we be talking about all of this peace stuff when locally there was no peace between the races?" Acting locally, the group surveyed local restaurants and bars to determine which were segregated, and they discussed with the owners the need for integration. He recalls, "We thought we would talk to all the restaurant owners. We thought that by talking with them they would see the logic of desegregating. Well, we talked to them and no one saw the logic!"

Having made little headway in approaching the owners, they distributed a list of sixteen segregated businesses to the mayor and ministers (as well as to the businesses themselves), urging a boycott. In a letter to the *Chapel Hill Weekly,* Cusick announced that the group would "take whatever action we deem necessary and within our power, including picketing."[19] The College Café was the chosen target.

Operated by Max Yarborough and Jesse West on the main block of Franklin Street, the College Café had for years served locals and students from six in the morning until two in the afternoon. Before dawn on Friday, April 5, 1963, John and Pat began walking the picket line, careful to maintain the city-ordained eight paces from one another. John's vertically lettered sign read, "1863–1963—How Long Must Americans Wait for a Cup of Coffee?" Pat's, painted with slanted letters, read, "Land of the Free—for Whom?"

"This was a *big* step for me," recollects Pat, as it was for the other white picketers. Margaret Evan Bowers, a student member of the Women's International League for Peace and Freedom, picketed before she went to the high school. So did Lou Calhoun, a former Tennessee Golden Gloves boxing champion and the president of a local Methodist youth organization whose members had pledged their support.

In *The Free Men,* a literary account of the Chapel Hill demonstrations written while Quinton, Pat, and John were incarcerated, John Ehle described one encounter with café regulars:

> Two workmen arrived, stopped on seeing the signs and scowled at them. "Damn them," one of the men said, "damn you all. What are you trying to do, make us eat with the niggers?"
>
> That was the first comment of real anger that Pat and John had heard, and it went through them sharply. There were several other like comments, as the workmen came to realize and to resent that the two pickets wouldn't answer, wouldn't argue. . . . "Long pricks with signs on 'em, that's what they got in their hands. Like to hold them poles, boys?" The men were flushed with anger, their features were contorted with it. It was a revelation to see them, to see in faces the depth of hatred that these men held for white men who would represent Negroes.[20]

The protests met swift reaction: "We certainly weren't successful—the man sold out of food!" Pat continued: "It was the policy of certain fraternities that their pledge classes had to eat there, and NROTC members ate there. The man was making money and at the same time it was not an issue that caught fire in the black community."

The picketing of the College Café, located far from the African-American community, by mostly white college students must have struck long-time Chapel Hill residents—both white and black—as peculiar. "It soon came crashing down on us how naïve we were and why we shouldn't be a white group doing it. At Harry's we decided that we had to get into the black community with our all-white group if we were going to talk about segregation. Only later I came to understand the paternalism involved in our action."

In this discussion, Harold Foster detailed his activities in the high school movement three years earlier. As SPU attempted to turn its ill-fated strategy around, Harold agreed to initiate contacts within the black community. Through Rev. Foushee a rally and organizational meeting for the newly formed Committee for Open Business was set for May 3.

At that meeting Foster told the fifty-seven people in attendance: "We are here tonight to find out what happened to the integration spirit of 1960. . . . The Negro community must let the people of Chapel Hill know they are ready for equality and want a community with equality—in toto."[21] Harold was elected as cochairman of a provisional executive committee of twelve that included Cusick, Calhoun, and Foushee. Its first decision was to take over the College Café picket line.

During this time, John had been in Birmingham accompanied by a student reporter from the *Daily Tar Heel*. Birmingham, the iron and steel center of the South, had long taken a hard-line segregationist position. During the past seven years, Rev. Fred Shuttlesworth, the pastor of the Bethel Baptist Church, had locked horns with the public safety commissioner, Bull Connor. On the heels of the standoff in Albany, Georgia, the movement needed momentum.[22] Connor, who had just lost his bid for mayor, was the perfect foil. Sit-ins quickly escalated to protest marches as Martin Luther King Jr. led the fateful Good Friday march in which he was arrested and wrote his famous "Letter from a Birmingham Jail." The mass resistance increased—including 600 schoolchildren power hosed by Connor's police forces—leading to massive arrests and a desegregation agreement on May 10.

While sitting in jail on charges of loitering and failure to obey a police officer for his actions in helping to locate the arrested children of black parents, John wrote his parents:

> Nearly every adult and child in the movement knows me by name—you can't imagine how glorious it is to step from the street where perhaps 20 policemen are gathered on one corner alone, threatening, scaring, etc., into a church where only love and trusting brotherhood greet you. And it's not the old Uncle Tom type revering of the benevolent white—rather it is the complete acceptance of another man into the fellowship of all men who have let themselves love.[23]

Sentenced to a year in jail and fined $200, John, under bond awaiting appeal, returned to Chapel Hill on May 20, 1963.

Howard Johnson's and the Black Cat

The sparks from Birmingham fell onto Durham as well as other cities. Quinton, now president of the North Carolina College youth chapter of the NAACP, was orchestrating a series of demonstrations in Durham with his mentor, Floyd McKissick. As the mayoral campaign came to an apparent desultory conclusion, civil rights activists prepared to launch "an all-out war against segregation" and planned a massive march for election day, Saturday, May 18. Leaders of the conservative Durham Committee on Negro Affairs, frightened that student militancy might result in a white backlash and the defeat of their only black candidate running for City Council, urged restraint. Arguing that democracy had moved from the polling booth "to the streets," Quinton led his several hundred marchers up Fayetteville Street toward the downtown business district with placards, one of which read: "Vote to Make Democracy More than a Word." After a prayerful vigil in front of City Hall, the demonstrators dispersed, walking into nearby businesses to challenge their segregation practices, which resulted in more than one hundred arrests.

On Sunday another rally was held at St. Joseph's Church. Characteristically, Quinton took a backseat at rallies while others sermonized. That afternoon, Roy Wilkins, the cautious executive director of the NAACP, delivered a solemn speech with a qualified endorsement for the student movement—an imprimatur of sorts from the black bourgeoisie. The rally concluded with a fiery speech, interrupted frequently with alternating Amens and Hallelujahs, by James Farmer of CORE, who urged full participation in the direct-action effort.

In a phalanx of automobiles, more than 1,000 people then drove to the edge of town, headed for a Howard Johnson's restaurant partly owned by Luther Hodges, a former governor and now a Kennedy cabinet member. As the churchgoers-turned-demonstrators arrived at Howard Johnson's, they joined several thousand others who crowded into the parking lot and sprawled over the lawn. Quinton assumed tactical command:

> The decision was that all of the leadership would get arrested except for one; I was the one person who was not going to get arrested. I was to avoid arrest at all costs. There had to be one of us out of jail in order to get everybody else out of jail and also to get another demonstration going. We did not go in the building to sit-in; we filled the parking lot with demonstrators and we would not move for people coming out.

Despite police orders to disperse customers threatening to run over protesters, no one moved unless cued by Quinton. On command, they linked arms and began singing "We Shall Not Be Moved"—concluding with "We're going to eat at Howard Johnson's one of these days." After several hours of arrests, nearly a thousand demonstrators had been transported to the Durham County jail.

Pat, who marched that day in Chapel Hill's Armed Forces Day parade with the Women's International League for Peace and Freedom, remembers seeing news photos of the thousand-plus demonstrators being arrested. He admired those who had organized it. "They had to hire Trailways buses to carry them to jail!"

As the Trailways buses rambled toward the courthouse, Quinton led another group of protesters downtown, where they converged against an angry white mob. Quinton recollects:

> The Durham County jail was so full they were hanging out the windows. On the night that the mayor was elected, there were a thousand people in that jail and a thousand black people outside in front of the jail on the steps and an equal number of whites across the street. They were about to merge at the center of the street. The only thing that was separating the crowds was this white line of police. . . .

Unaware of the organizational mastermind behind the largest demonstration in Durham's history, Pat followed the activities closely. "The town was in a state of siege. The finances for the Durham Movement—the people putting up the bond money—were the black bourgeoisie. The students were very upset, though, because for them there was one criterion: getting arrested. So some of these nineteen-year-olds characterized these bourgeoisie as 'Uncle Toms.'"

The self-described "hungry black cat," writer James Baldwin, had visited Durham earlier that year with a similar concern. Pat had driven from Chapel Hill to listen.

> He explained to a student body that didn't want to hear it that they wouldn't even be sitting in college had it not been for these "Uncle Toms'" scratching their heads before the state legislature and getting money for the schools. I was one of the few whites in the whole place. . . . At the time, I remember thinking that he wasn't good-looking, but the mixture of strength, and at times bitterness, of his views coupled with his incredible gentleness created an aura of magnetism.

Another white man in the audience was the liberal editor of UNC's *Daily Tar Heel,* Jim Clotfelter. He described the activist message of the New York–born and educated writer: "Baldwin spoke with the voice of the young—whether he be picketer or artist, educator or student—when he condemned the elders who say, 'Go slow. If we prefer to be safe.' Baldwin said, 'We've doomed ourselves and all of our children. It is a time to take great risks, because if we don't, I don't believe we have a future. And I'd hate to see so much beauty die. . . . "[24]

Baldwin had a particular appeal to Quinton:

> We were interested in him because of his racial analysis and his analysis of our condition, more so than his writing having sexual undertones. Of course there were always attempts to read materials that talked about homosexuality.
>
> He came down in support of what we were doing. He was just this incredibly beautiful-ugly little man. Physically he was ugly, but there was so much beauty inside of him that just radiated. He was incredibly articulate. He was soft, quiet, and very intellectual, although when he spoke, of course, he could be very moving and fiery as he talked about the way in which the white world viewed us. But when we talked with him he was a very quiet, gentle man. He had the most fascinating mind I had ever experienced.
>
> We would always spend as much time as we could around Baldwin; he made us feel that we were somebody. All of our lives we had been scared of whites; whites had been put up as the symbol of what we were not or what we should be. Baldwin gave us a sense of being black, beautiful, and intelligent.

On the heels of the massive Howard Johnson's arrests, the protesters threatened the city with thirty consecutive days of equally massive and volatile demonstrations. Newly sworn-in Mayor Wense Grabarek held an unprecedented meeting with the student radicals and their black elders that Monday afternoon. Unable to make any commitments, he offered that many of their demands were "negotiable." Unswayed, Quinton summoned his fellow students to the NCC campus for another night of protest.

As the students were joined by local blacks, 3,000 demonstrators marched north on Fayetteville Street and veered west on Main Street, heading for City Hall. After spirited speeches and soulful singing, a nucleus of protesters launched their "suicide missions" to sit-in and picket nearby segregated businesses. Whites, anticipating this demonstration, were armed and began pelting the protesters with eggs and glass-filled apples. A few blacks responded by tossing rocks at the white youths and nearby car windshields.

The next day, May 21, as John and Pat prepared to travel to Durham for the Tuesday night rally at St. Joseph's Church, Mayor Grabarek met again with the protest leaders. There he traded his request to the Howard Johnson's corporate leaders to "encourage" the desegregation of its local franchise for a promise from the demonstrators to suspend their planned thirty days of turmoil. He also accepted their invitation to speak at the church that evening. There he would announce that three restaurants had agreed voluntarily to desegregate.

The Fateful Encounter

As Mayor Grabarek praised the decision of the black leadership to suspend the demonstrations, proving "to me that you deserve the rank of first-class citizens,"[25] Pat and John sat attentively in a church pew toward the front. It was here that the two first met Quinton, the tactical genius of the Durham movement. Pat's first impression of Quinton at the rally was when he saw him "walking down a church aisle. He struck me at the time as very aggressive." Quinton recalled:

> I was just simply sitting in the audience. There was a woman I knew, Helen Hammond, a tall, imposing, and gorgeous black woman who had been at North Carolina Central and was then working at the YWCA. At their request, she introduced me to John and Pat, who happened to be sitting in the row next to me.
>
> I was indifferent. The only reason I spent any time with them was that Helen wanted me to. Of course, John immediately homed in on the fact that I was gay and used his flirtatious sexual manners. That whole evening he attended to me. He invited me to come back to Chapel Hill.

For John, personal attraction and political necessity were married in meeting Quinton. As Pat noted: "John genuinely cared for Quinton. It wasn't that he came on to him simply to get him to Chapel Hill. But, for John, it was an affair; for Quinton, it was love." A decade after John's death, Quinton expresses a more detached assessment of their relationship:

"John had an incredible impact on my life. He was very brilliant and we would spend hours upon hours talking about issues. He was the kind of person who tried to anticipate questions you were going to ask and give you answers to your questions before you asked them."

Quinton agreed to help with the Chapel Hill movement. "They asked for some technical assistance so I did some nonviolent workshops in the black community and helped organize some rallies. But I would *not* have been as much time in Chapel Hill nor would have been willing to spend as much time as I did without John." His first official visit to Chapel Hill was to attend the mass meeting at St. Joseph's Colored Methodist Episcopal Church under the pastorship of Rev. J. R. Foushee.

Assuming Tactical Command in Chapel Hill

Quinton immediately brought to the Chapel Hill movement his experience, skills, and credibility. He recognized the potential strengths and liabilities that an alliance with these radicalized students and liberal professors might bring. The Committee for Open Business (COB) began ostensibly as a coalition of black high school students, white professors, and college students. Strains were apparent, Pat recalled:

> There was cultural clash. The professors would make motions while others would amend motions in the best professorial manners and parliamentary procedures. The kids weren't interested in that shit. They wanted to march; they wanted to be militant. There were differences even in the music. The kids wanted to sing, and they had elaborate hand clapping; the professors couldn't quite do the hand clapping, and they didn't particularly like the music.

The presence of the white liberals, long the custodians of the liberal legacy of gradualism, accommodation, and progress, was particularly problematic for the veteran organizer. Quinton noted, "This made it a very difficult community to deal with, because it had prided itself on being liberal and it had made so many great advances. . . . But that did not lead me to believe that Chapel Hill was not basically a racist community with the same problem of other communities."

The perfect answer to them was King's letter, written while he was in the Birmingham jail, as Pat illuminates: "Dr. King forcefully took on the 'white moderates.' He eloquently argued that the greatest stumbling block to black freedom was not the Klan but white liberals 'more devoted to order than justice,' who believed they could 'set the timetable for another man's freedom.' The letter was passed like wildfire throughout the Movement."

Quinton, too, was aware of the absence of credibility between white organizers and the black community. "I wouldn't say that John and Pat were plugged into the black community. When we began the more massive drive, it was necessary to . . . get plugged in to the point that the black community *really* trusted and believed in what we were trying to do."

Though Quinton acknowledged the contributions of the older black generation such as Pastors Foushee and Manley, Quinton was most interested in Harold Foster. "He was key in a number of ways, not necessarily because of his power in the black community but because he was a very intelligent, politically aware young man who we felt was crucial to have involved in what we were doing."

With Baker and the Chapel Hill black teens involved, tactics changed from picketing to sit-ins and marches. He recollects, "We had found at that moment in the movement that picketing was no longer effective. . . . It would have been very difficult for them to convince me that we ought to go out and walk the picket line." A march was set for Saturday, May 25.

Three days earlier, there was an open COB meeting for final march preparations. The old brick church was far from crowded. Among the fifty or so in attendance, some questioned whether the timing was good given that a group of nearly a dozen ministers had just met with the mayor, Sandy McLamroch. He had agreed to form a committee to work toward desegregation of the city's public facilities, and the Merchants Association was about to announce its support of "equal treatment of ALL customers."[26]

Quinton rose and spoke extemporaneously, saying, as he recalls, that "I was very much excited about what we were doing in Durham and inspired to see other black communities respond to the racial segregation. I talked about what was happening: the feelings, the ideologies." The editor of a local newspaper later described his speech as one that "set the house on fire." It was agreed to proceed with the march.

The next day the Merchants Association resolved to call upon all segregated businesses to *voluntarily* change their policies. At the Board of Aldermen meeting that Thursday evening, a member of the Mayor's Human Relations Committee recommended the adoption of a public accommodations ordinance that would compel integration. On Friday Mayor McLamroch formed an Integration Committee—absent any civil rights activists. These events led the *Chapel Hill Weekly* to editorialize: "If demonstrations are coming to Chapel Hill, they will come. But the men of good will in this community have done what they could to make demonstrations unnecessary. . . . "[27] Quinton was more realistic in his assessment of the likelihood of progress in Chapel Hill and the utility of the mayor's promises, noting that McLamroch was "an aristocrat who refused to use any of his influence or jeopardize his position. . . . Sandy wasn't a bad person, but he was a Southerner and had grown up with a particular cultural perspective. His commitment to that was much greater than his commitment to my being able to eat at Leo's Restaurant."

As planned, the marchers assembled at St. Joseph's that Saturday. More than 300 black and white marchers walked down the main thoroughfare of

Franklin Street, filling the spring afternoon air with song—"We Shall Overcome," "Give Me the Old Freedom Spirit," and "Oh Freedom." After the march the Mayor's Committee on Integration released a list of more than 160 desegregated retail businesses and nearly as many other services, noting that fewer than a dozen segregated businesses remained.

However, a survey taken later by the more objective *Daily Tar Heel* that included only those businesses affected by the public accommodations ordinance found that one-quarter practiced some type of discrimination.[28] This included one-third of the restaurants, eight of the nine barbershops, and three of the five motels. Token integration had come to the town's schools, only one African-American was in a supervisory role in town government, and most blacks held service jobs at the university, working for wages lower than those paid to whites for comparable duties.

Hard-line owners of businesses such as Colonial Drug Store, Brady's Restaurant, the Pines Restaurant, and Carlton's Rock Pile grocery were resistant to appeals by the committee for voluntary integration. And a few, like the television repairman James Botsford, reversed business practices, imposing a white-only policy: "Maybe then they will realize they are losing rather than gaining ground. . . . The Negro is looking for freedom and he wants to enforce restrictions and regulations on the merchants."[29]

Quinton's role was to harness this momentum through tactical planning and military-style organizing. As the summer of 1963 officially began, "I was very clear in the decisionmaking as to who we hit and why we ought to hit them and what we ought to do." There were three marches each week. On Sunday afternoon the marchers walked to Colonial Drug Store, and every Wednesday and Saturday they marched downtown. Regular meetings were held with the mayor, whose office was located at the town's only commercial radio station, which he owned, while picketing continued at a variety of businesses.

The business at Colonial Drug Store was cut in half. Each week a team would visit with owner John Carswell to see if he was willing to negotiate. With equal predictability, Carswell would take out his camera to photograph the picketers and place his pistol on the fountain's countertop for "cleaning." Harold Foster, in renewing his picketing of this longtime segregationist, echoed Gandhian philosophy: What "we hope to change—is the man's policies, his stereotyped idea of the Negro . . . he has mentioned that Negroes are barbaric. We hope to change the man morally."[30]

The Merchants Association and the Aga Language

Chapel Hill, characterized by illustrator William Meade Prince as "the southern part of heaven," is largely removed from the typical Southern life of mills and mines, crackers and klaverns, fundamentalists and farmers. Liberal members of the Committee for Open Business, like most in the town, favored civility over confrontation. Quinton observes: "There were a lot of people in Chapel Hill who believed that peaceful negotiations were the way and that Chapel Hill was not a community where they should have demonstrations, because it would ruin its lovely image of a paradise. Their 1,500 blacks were happy on the other end of town and they knew the liberal whites were doing all kinds of wonderful things for them. . . . "

In mid-June the Committee on Integration recommended the adoption of a public accommodations ordinance. Quickly the Merchants Association voiced its opposition to state-enforced integration. The proposed ordinance came before the Board of Aldermen on June 25. Two hundred citizens crowded into the town hall, overflowing into the outside stairwells. The seven board members, including its one African-American member, listened attentively. Various opinions were expressed by Chapel Hillians: "Let's solve these problems as rational people, not as Mussolini did by passing a law to make the trains run on time"; "You have the authority to help in this further extension of human rights over property rights"; "I believe a man has a constitutional right to discriminate."[31] In the end the board voted four to two for tabling it indefinitely.

Had Chapel Hill passed the ordinance, it would have been the first Southern city to have outlawed discrimination in restaurants, theaters, hotels, and other "public accommodations." The larger significance of the Chapel Hill movement began to become apparent to leaders like Foster, Baker, and Cusick.

Political pressure in the form of demonstrations and picketing continued. So, too, did the interminable negotiations and meetings. At the massive Fourth of July march, Pat, wearing baggy blue jeans, carried a sign that read, "Chapel Hill, Southern Part of Heaven: Home of Candy-Coated Racism." During meetings, liberals bickered with activists over goals and tactics while city leaders sought accommodation with skittish merchants and conservative blacks.

But this agenda of civility and routinized confrontation was soon disrupted. During the second week of July, Quinton and Pat prepared youthful protesters for a new phase of activism. Occasionally some of the twenty-odd members of Chief William Blake's police force appeared at the Negro recreation center on Roberson Street to peer through the fence enclosing the ball field.

Blake, a towering heavyset man whose police force included two blacks, had been an officer during the 1947 demonstration when Bayard Rustin and his fellow travelers were run out of town. Now, at forty-five, he was balding and taking on weight. Quinton described Blake as "a decent man who tried to maintain what he needed to maintain in his community but tried to do it in a manner that wouldn't make the situation flare up." Pat agreed:

He looked like the stereotypical sheriff; he was not. The Fellowship of Reconciliation group had made such an impact that he had read up on Gandhi. So he knew when we asked for that first parade permit to march down Franklin Street that we had hoped he wouldn't grant it. But he immediately issued a permit. It would have helped us better had he not. He anticipated every step we made. We used to talk about how it would have been much better, for our purposes, had he been like Bull Connor.

Fortunately, his deputies were not so astute. As Quinton recollects: "They were doing activities that would counter the passivity of the demonstrators. In the Gandhian philosophy, if you had no negative reaction, if you had no violent reaction, then it is very hard to appeal to the moral fiber because the adversaries would be seen as moral also. You needed to have a reaction like you did from the freedom rides."

During those dog days of July, Quinton and Pat taught high school youths nonviolent tactics with a sprinkling of this philosophy. Pat states: "I had learned from Quinton in Durham the nonviolent techniques to pass on to Chapel Hill: how to fall and protect yourself. This created the ire from the Chapel Hill liberals, since we were using nonviolence as a tactic, not a philosophy."

In the early afternoon of July 19, three dozen nonviolent activists assembled at the town center and walked two blocks west along Main Street. Slowly they filed into the Merchants Association's office, sitting down within the six-foot-wide space between the counter and the entrance. As the demonstrators sang, Chief Blake's police arrived. While newsmen photographed and bystanders observed, the protesters declined to leave.

Robert V.N. Brown, whose home was located directly across from the Merchants Association and who was arrested later that day, described the events that followed:

> They stacked the limp bodies up at the curb, which was completely unnecessary. They did it 'cause they were out for Cusick. . . . They laid them out just like you lay out dead bodies. It's like when the decontamination team comes along in trucks. I hadn't seen anything like it since I was in Korea. As the police cars arrived, they would pull bodies off, drag them along the street, throw them into the police cars.[32]

These thirty-four arrests marked a turning point for both the Chapel Hill movement and Pat Cusick. "Like most whites, [for me] a policeman was a friendly image. There is nothing like it for you to get your head whipped, your teeth knocked in, and your ribs kicked. You come to a knowledge that is much different."

Though Pat and Harold were already friends, they got to know one another better over the next ten days, during which they shared a cell in the Hillsborough jail.

Somebody got us a book in there—*Another Country*. We read it and had pro-
longed, in-depth conversations. Of course, I was not Eric, and Harold was not
Rufus, but we used it as a jumping-off place for everything that was happening
to us. We would switch between tactics and relationships between whites and
blacks in the movement. I benefited immensely from sharing the insight of a
young black intellectual, sensitive yet militant, cynical yet hopeful enough to
participate.

In Baldwin's *Another Country*, homophobia and racial prejudice—racial
guilt and sexual attraction—are interwoven. Eric, a white Southerner, travels to New York City, where he meets a toughened Harlem bisexual street
youth, Rufus Scott. Their affair is short-lived. Eric's love for Rufus goes un-
requited, and Rufus's recognition that screwing women and hustling men
were less than satisfying leads to Rufus's suicide. Afterward, Eric wonders:

> But had he ever loved Rufus? Or had it been simply rage and nostalgia and
> guilt and shame? Was it the body of Rufus to which he had clung, or the bod-
> ies of dark men, seen briefly, somewhere, in a garden or a clearing, long ago,
> sweat running down their chocolate chests and shoulders? . . . Certainly he
> had never succeeded in making Rufus believe he loved him. Perhaps Rufus had
> looked into his eye and seen those dark men Eric saw, and hated him for it.

That summer marked a turning point for Pat, as his sexual attractions,
like those of Eric, changed from the blond American type, epitomized in
David of *Giovanni's Room*, to ebony bodies. "While there were some
whites who were attracted to blacks sexually and then came into the movement," Pat admitted readily, "that wasn't the case with me." He recalls one
Saturday afternoon visit to NCC with Quinton. "In the course of thirty
minutes, it seemed to me that everyone on his dorm floor was gay. I could-
n't believe it! They weren't flaming, but their mannerisms weren't all that
straight. Of course, they were very open with Quinton."

As Pat became acquainted with some of Quinton's friends, he learned the
Aga language:

> Like pig Latin, where you take the first letter off the word, in the Aga language
> you would take the first letter off the word, except for configurations like *th* or
> *st*, where you take both, and join to this "aga," assembling both as a suffix:
> Gay would become "aygaga" and man would become "anmaga." They would
> talk real fast so I couldn't understand them. Something like: "I inkthaga
> isthaga anmaga isaga aygaga." (I think this man is gay)—Now, that could be
> very useful.[33]

As the demonstrators were idled in jail, John, living in Ohio for the summer, had earned enough money to pay off his debts. He headed to New
York for work on the upcoming March on Washington. "Quinton and I
were pissed off because we felt that he needed to be in Chapel Hill with
us." Later, Pat confronted his friend.

I wish you would come back here and let somebody else do the March on Washington. We are in real stew here. . . . When we got out, we were told that a two-week moratorium had been arranged so that the town could simmer down. . . . To make matters even more distasteful, the charges against us, in spite of the urging of Chief Blake . . . aren't getting dropped by the town solicitor. Floyd McKissick is so distressed that he is serving as our counsel. . . . We have resumed our civil disobedience workshops . . . indoors so that the police can't watch everything. . . . A front-page editorial said the leaders of COB had "a lust for power, for revenge, or a neurotic need for martyrdom." The executive committee of the COB tried to figure out who among us had the lust for power and against whom we had the desire for revenge. Somebody suggested we cast lots for the privilege of being the first martyr, but I think the pastors on the committee thought this wasn't the way martyrs ought to be chosen.[34]

The Merchants Association arrests also triggered greater division within the city on the hill. As picketing turned to sit-ins and later marches, many of the conservative blacks and white liberals grew increasingly uncomfortable with the tactics engineered by Quinton. In the black community, as Rev. Manley recalls, "Obviously, this was the breaking of the law. . . . This was the kind of thing that some of us couldn't buy."[35] A member of the Human Relations Committee expressed a fear common among Chapel Hill liberals that such "irresponsible action" would jeopardize further progress.[36] Quinton remembers: "We would reply, 'If you agree with my cause, then what you need to do is to act on the fact that you believe in the cause—don't worry about *my* tactics. Don't concentrate on what *I'm* doing. Concentrate on what *you're* doing that supports the cause that we both believe in.'"

Movement activists published a mimeographed newspaper, the *Chapel Hill Conscience*, edited by Bob Brown. In its first issue, they argued:

Over and over we are told by self-styled "Friends of the Negro" that the protests for equal human rights have made their point and that further progress will become more difficult if protests continue. We are told that the protests are going "too far," causing loss of friends, and making negotiations impossible. But what the "moderates" want from negotiations is the opportunity to make a few more token concessions; to buy gratitude for their fatherly kindness; and to put off for a little longer the need to face the fact that a robber cannot buy love and forgiveness by returning stolen property, a little at a time.[37]

As tactics and tensions escalated and tempers and temperatures rose, bickering among members of the COB increased over the "radical" leadership of Harold Foster and the confrontational tactics of Quinton Baker. There was also some ill feeling about the agreed moratorium on demonstrations in consideration for the Merchants Association's declining to press trespassing charges. This was a grave error, according to Pat: "We did not have a real understanding of power. We had power and leverage only at one point of time—the first sit-in during the summer. There was a mistake made when more people of the hard leadership got thrown in jail than we had planned, leaving a weaker group to negotiate, and they made a bad negotiation with the town. Then, the town was almost ready to do anything."

Marching In/Marching Out

In mid-August the momentous March on Washington occurred. "As dawn came, driving through northern Virginia, I will never forget, black folks lined up along the sides of the road waving us on. It was very dramatic," remembers Pat, who was a coordinator responsible for two buses from Orange County.

Before the Washington march, Pat had learned something of its inside politics while visiting the New York office earlier that summer:

> As originally conceived it was going to be an effort of SCLC [Southern Christian Leadership Conference] and SNCC and we were going to take over Washington. But Kennedy got Walter Reuther involved—I was in Rustin's office the day Reuther was sent to town as an emissary. . . . With them involved it became a parade and it hurt the movement in the South. . . . [So] here come the black students from the South wearing blue jeans, singing their songs, and they see the people from the North: older, middle-aged, wearing hard hats with UAW Local something. . . . It was the brushfire movement that very much frightened the establishment. It was not the March on Washington that pressured Kennedy, it was what was happening throughout the South.

Pressure was also put on Bayard Rustin, the tactician for the march. As Quinton tells it:

> Rustin's homosexuality became a big issue in the March on Washington. The leaders did not want to confuse the issue of his sexuality with that of civil rights. I think Dr. King became skeptical. Of course Bayard had been behind the scene for years, and no one raised any question—and it wasn't because they didn't know. But in 1963 the tragedy was that black culture was modifying itself and changing a lot of good values in it in order to appease what was thought to be acceptable hatred to the white community. . . .

Pat fills in some of the behind-the-scenes details:

> On a specific tape from the FBI, according to Taylor Branch in *Parting the Waters,* King said, "Let's hope Bayard doesn't take too many drinks before the march; he will go out and pick up some little brothers." The tape was sent the next day to the White House. Strom Thurmond came out against Bayard. Rustin almost pulled out of the march, but he had to be the coordinator, since logistically he was the only one who could do it.
>
> He told me in the late sixties, knowing that I was still somewhat in the closet, "You should come all the way out. All of my life I ran from getting ex-

posed. I took secondary positions in many activities. But that which I had dreaded all those years came into fruition with Strom Thurmond. Yes, it was on the front page of the *New York Times*: 'Rustin is a pervert.' But the next day, so what else was new? You know, I could have just kicked myself for all of my life being in the closet."

Denounced by Thurmond as a draft dodger, a communist, and a homosexual, Rustin issued a statement to the press on August 12, 1963. After responding to the first two charges directly, the statement ended elliptically: "With regard to Senator Thurmond's attack on my morality, I have no comment. By religious training and fundamental philosophy, I am disinclined to put myself in the position of having to defend my own moral character. Questions in this area should properly be directed to those who have entrusted me with my present responsibilities."[38]

As they returned from the March on Washington, Pat observes, "the Chapel Hill movement started losing steam." Quinton amplified: "The situation in Chapel Hill was always confusing, because you didn't have a strong black community. The students were wanting to go a little more radical—which was *not* what the university people wanted." He continued: "COB was primarily white dominated and white controlled. Harold has always been opposed to that. There were certain types of tactics that Harold wanted to do which certain key people in COB did not want to do. . . . The only thing they could do was to get rid of COB."

Pat recalls the fateful mid-August meeting at Rev. Manley's church:

> Harold was going to resign that night. There were pressures on him to resign—pressures on any young black who was as aggressive as Harold was. When Harold came walking down the aisle of the church wearing overalls— now Harold doesn't wear overalls—he was making a statement about what was happening. The high school kids all started screaming. . . . [Though] the liberals would have liked more "responsible leadership," that did not include someone who . . . was a spokesman for what was happening in 1963 like Harold. . . . They were upset at the direction—it wasn't their agenda.

Describing Harold as "a very complex man," Quinton also noted that "because he was a key person in the black community he could have hurt us. But he quietly walked." Quinton later declared, "He could have been an immense value to the movement, much more so than he was." Pat observes: "People used to characterize Harold as very bitter and sarcastic. Well, he was just speaking the truth! . . . The problem the white community, the liberals, had with Harold was that he was from Chapel Hill and had also been to college—like very few people of the black community in Chapel Hill— and he was articulate."

The Committee on Open Business splintered. The liberal professors and their black counterparts formed the Citizens United for Racial Equality and

Dignity—revealingly known as CURED. The black high school students along with a handful of older activists coalesced eventually as the Chapel Hill Freedom Committee. A beleaguered and exasperated Harold Foster returned to Durham for his studies.

After a summer of earning money painting houses in the Midwest and then working on the march, John surrendered his Moorehead scholarship, dropped out of UNC, and became chairperson of the local chapter of CORE on a salary of twenty-five dollars a week. His duties included a voter registration campaign, which would eventually net 122 new African-American voters. Quinton assumed duties as president of the state NAACP youth chapters while continuing his education at NCC and his responsibilities as an NAACP Commando. Given their overlapping agendas and Pat's departure to another hotbed of civil rights action, Danville, Virginia, to work with King's staff, Quinton and John spent more time together.

Gays and the Civil Rights Movement

"There were more gays than people ever realized in the civil rights movement. But you wouldn't see it from the outside," observed Pat. Those lesbians and gay men working in civil rights recognized the sexual energies just below the surface: "In the midst of a movement that was not directly related to sexual orientation but more involved in day-to-day social justice issues with a common enemy, the movement would bring you closer together. During that period there was not a great deal of conversation about sexual orientation. At some point, that was a given."

Hence Quinton, not surprisingly, assigned himself to Chapel Hill "partly because I was already over there all of the time—it was that relationship with John that kept me in Chapel Hill." Describing the two as "setting up housekeeping," Pat observed with keen interest the relative openness evident in their relationship: "When Quinton and John started going together, it was known to me—this was also known in wider circles." Quinton confirms:

> My relationship with John was not so private. We were always together. We were seen everywhere. We were in the movement together. We appeared together for presentations and meetings. The fact that we were in constant companionship and protecting each other and being there for each other, people started to talk—even if they didn't know for sure. Even when we didn't live together (when I was still in the dorm), I spent most of my time in Chapel Hill and lived in rooms where he was.
>
> During that time for a young black man and a young white man to be constantly together was quite unusual. But any reaction I had in the black community about black-white relationships had to do with the racial issue, not sexual. The times were so different then. I don't remember any negative reactions

to us. No one called us names. If there were negative reactions to us it was because we were civil rights agitators. Everyone in the movement at that time knew that John and I were gay and in a relationship.

Within the movement, black and white romantic relationships were not unusual, however:

There were a lot of interracial *heterosexual* relationships in the movement during that time. There was tension outside of the movement about it; but people inside were much more accepting of it. Of course it would have been very hard to stand up and preach for integration and "freedom now," and then turn around and say, "You guys shouldn't do this."

This is not to imply, though, that racism did not seep into the movement where black and white relationships formed. As in all interracial relationships occurring within a society in which "race matters," Quinton and John struggled with their racism:

There was a lot of incredible dialogue and disagreements in having to think out honestly about the way we were dealing with our relationship. I wasn't so glad to be in a relationship with a white person that I was willing to sacrifice everything. One of the things I tried to do was to get some of those racial things out of the way early: These are the realities of our different perceptions of race.

Quinton also offers:

There were really some good solid white people who came into the movement and got to understand where we were at that time. There, too, were the wine-and-tea liberals who had to have a black person at their social events to indicate their commitment; and then there were the people who were willing to put their lives on the line and be hurt and brutalized. Those white people who got beat up with me, went to jail with me, sat down with me, and got peed on, it is very difficult to question their commitment. Whether they had fought through all of their personal racism is a different story—they were struggling with it.

Quinton and John also confronted racism within the wider circle of friends, acquaintances, and civil rights allies. Quinton recalls a typical affair: "We were invited to dinner at this one good family. The wife came from a very genteel Southern family, but she was an alcoholic. After dinner, she was drunk as a skunk and got to the piano to play 'Old Black Joe' and other favorites. These situations would make John uncomfortable. Afterward John and I would have to talk about how I felt about it."

As John began to better cope with these incidents of veiled racism, he teamed up with Quinton. "We would go to a party and of course someone would corner me and tell me how liberal they were and how some of their best friends were 'colored.' John and I had an agreement that I would call him over and get him in the conversation so I could walk away."

That Quinton and John were involved in a sexual relationship did matter, eventually. As had been the case for Rustin, the personal relationship between Quinton and John became politicized when it served the purposes of others. In this case it was used by the state field secretary for the NAACP as friction between the NAACP and CORE developed. Quinton explains: "McKissick, who had been the state youth adviser for a long time, decided to go with CORE. The field secretary resented what he thought was my loyalty to McKissick and CORE, so he saw the opportunity to raise questions about the nature of my relationship with John and its impact on the state NAACP." Consequently, Quinton was summoned before the executive committee:

> Back then I was rather arrogant and brazen. I said, "My loyalty is to the cause of human rights and justice, not to any organization. If one begins to interfere with the other, you know which one will go. In terms of my personal life, that is *my* business. It has no relevance whatsoever to the NAACP and I refuse to answer any questions regarding it." They discussed it for some time and talked about what was good for the NAACP and that was it. I went back to continue my work in Chapel Hill and my relationship with John.

Ironically, while all the other youthful black Durham leaders who rose under the tutelage of McKissick chose to leave the NAACP for CORE, following their mentor's lead, Quinton chose to remain with the NAACP.

Just as there were few personal or political linkages between Southern gays doing civil rights work and those like Richard Inman and Jack Nichols building a Southern homophile movement, so, too, were there few racial progressives among gay Southerners. Quinton maintains:

> Some of the people who expressed the most overt racism were white gays. The people who have been the least involved were white gays—unless they had been radicalized. So I would have not made any connection with someone being gay and *any* affinity for human rights. Of course I wouldn't say that there were no gays in the movement—there were many—but the gays pretty much wanted to maintain the social structure as it was.

One student, whose column, "View from the Hill," appeared in the *Daily Tar Heel* throughout this period of civil rights activity, was Armistead Maupin Jr. Later known for his journalistic tales of San Francisco gay life, Maupin, raised in North Carolina, was very much a product of his Southern upbringing. An admirer of William F. Buckley, his columns were characterized by their witty, and occasionally weighty, conservatism.

On the newly announced Peace Corps, Maupin penned: "The crystallization of every efficient superstate requires the mobilization of youth. The Nazis were intensely proud of their pick and shovel brigades for young people. The Young Pioneers of the Soviet Union are invaluable to the Communist cause."[39] Like many conservative Southerners, his hatred was particularly directed at Robert Kennedy: "Within the span of a fortnight we have watched the President's little brother try his first case in any court, authorize the Air Force to send reconnaissance planes over the University of Alabama, and treat history like his younger brother, Teddy, treated Harvard exams."[40]

Maupin's attitudes on civil rights were equally strident. Castigating the NAACP and CORE's protest against the planned opening of an Aunt Jemima's Pancake Kitchen in upstate New York, he observed: "The Negro mammy, as thought of today, was a paragon of generosity, loyalty, self-pride and industry. If the NAACP considers these qualities 'negative,' it's high time they reexamine their standards."[41] In a subsequent column, Maupin echoed his complaint about the misdirection of black unrest:

> How many Negro leaders, we wonder, have ever bothered to differentiate between unreasoning prejudice and the honest and fearful concern of the white community? How many have sought positive steps to eliminate the conditions of which the white so often speaks? . . . The Negro illegitimacy rate remains ten times greater than the white. And this tragedy is heightened with the realization that one out of every five Negro fathers ends up deserting his family. Yet the organization that professes to seek "the advancement of colored people" turns its back to these facts and pursues weightier problems (How to get a cup of coffee at Woolworth's—How to get rid of Aunt Jemima).[42]

Though Maupin was perhaps the most well-known campus writer, other students expressed equally conservative views: "All the 'freedom marches' accomplish is to confirm in any wavering minds the image of the Negro as an emotional, empty-headed, shiftless, singing fool. . . . This is not the sort of behavior that is considered becoming to responsible men and women who are demonstrating their capacity for first class citizenship."[43]

Southern gays like Maupin struggled separately in silence. Even the liberal Chapel Hill campus evidenced little acceptance or understanding of the homosexual. Occasional stories and editorials appearing in the *Daily Tar Heel,* for example, championed the liberal homosexuality-as-sickness view: "While we condemn the practice and try to rehabilitate those who are addicted to it, we should make every effort to abrogate the laws which, in North Carolina and elsewhere, still impose criminal penalties."[44]

Interestingly, the author of this editorial, Wade Wellman, two weeks later lamented the "futile picketing of the College Café." Acknowledging that it "is most unfashionable calling oneself a segregationist," he prophesied that "the clamor for race-mixing will lose steam and fade away."[45]

Watts Restaurant and Carlton's Rock Pile

Pat returned from Danville on December 12 for his appeal trial resulting from his August conviction for the Merchants Association sit-in. The county solicitor ignored the amnesty agreement reached during the summer and "singled four of us out to be tried." Sentenced to a fifty-dollar fine and court costs or thirty days, Pat along with three others awaited the appellate ruling. His natural red complexion was more noticeable the day the appeal was denied. They released a statement: "We will not contribute money to support an institution that supports racial injustice. The conscience of the community and the nation must be awakened to the task of eliminating segregation. This is best done through individual sacrifice. . . . "[46]

Although Pat believes that this sacrifice "did inspire the high school students," he now recognizes that "we were very naïve. We thought we would shake the minds and hearts of Chapel Hill by voluntarily serving thirty days over Christmas rather than paying a fine. We couldn't have been more mistaken; they were glad we were put away."

Their imprisonment and the community reaction motivated the formation of the Chapel Hill Freedom Committee, a consortium of different civil rights groups represented in the area, which was housed in office space above a funeral home on the western edge of town. Quinton, described by a newspaper at the time as "a serious young man who has a neat appearance, wears glasses, and speaks in an articulate manner," and John, "a rather handsome, dark-haired fellow with a pleasant voice," were elected cochairmen.[47]

Quinton recognized the need for stronger action:

> Chapel Hill was always a community that prided itself on being open and liberal. It had, as far as it could, the most desegregated community in the South. But that wasn't enough. If we had trusted the liberal civility at the time, we would still be waiting. Chapel Hill was one of the crucial points in the movement where it became clear that the South was *never* going to voluntarily desegregate. But the only way you could really get that point home or draw attention to that was to take action that would cause Chapel Hill to respond in stronger fashion.

Civil disobedience began anew on Friday, December 13, with the denial of the appeal. "We would always strategize on who we were going to hit. We would never hit the same place or do the same thing," recalled Quinton. Sit-ins began at The Pines and Brady's restaurants. Several more were arrested the next afternoon at Leo's Grill, and on Sunday afternoon a group of forty black and thirty white protesters marched silently down Franklin Street with signs reading "Give Freedom for Christmas." On Monday evening, another group, including Quinton and eighty-year-old Father Clarence Parker, returned to The Pines for sit-ins and arrests.[48] "We did not go out and lead a demonstration and go home and say, 'We did a day's work.' I never got to bed before three or four in the morning. We spent long hours hashing over what we did right, what we did wrong, what would be the best tactic for tomorrow, why were we doing this? What people were offering us alternatives and why we should or should not accept them."

The arrests continued. On December 18 sixty-eight protesters were jailed, bringing the five-day total to 104. The next evening there was a public forum attended by more than 200 citizens, including the mayor, the police chief, representatives of the Chapel Hill merchants, liberals, and activists. Not surprisingly, there was no consensus about the desirability of a public accommodations ordinance nor on the extent of racial discrimination in the town. On that same day, more activists were arrested after they refused to leave Brady's, The Tar Heel, and The Pines restaurants.

Though the demonstrations appeared to have little impact on the city, they were affecting some parents of the arrested student protesters. One mother whose white son, Charles, was arrested during the December 19 sit-ins wrote: "Even I am beginning to wonder if there really is some other way. Maybe he is right. I grew up in a little town down next to the South Carolina line and Negroes to my people were always just 'niggers.' But Charles is a generation apart and maybe his mother's attitudes are dead wrong."[49] Black parents of local high school demonstrators often faced tough questions and occasional threats from their white employers who discovered their children's activism.

As the total number charged with trespassing swelled past 200, a Christmas statement was issued by the Chapel Hill Freedom Committee: "We would rather educate than negotiate, rather negotiate than picket, rather picket than be arrested. . . . We are asked to await the outcome of further 'quiet progress,' but see much more quietness than progress, much more civic 'order' than justice."[50]

In late December Pat departed the Durham jail for the Raleigh prison camp. He was introduced to the oppressive system that was marked by "no distinguishing feature between the guards and the inmates" and by "stags and pussy-boys." Resisting the segregated facilities, he immediately launched a two-week fast. Reassigned to Sandy Ridge, he found an integrated facility that masked the racism endemic to the system: "The black convicts all worked at the sewage plant; the whites worked in the tobacco industry."

Meanwhile demonstrations and arrests continued. The most dramatic demonstration occurred at Carlton's Rock Pile grocery located on Durham Road. Quinton was among those who visited Carlton Mize's establishment (a sign hung over the door, "Not open to dogs and niggers") on the first day of the new year:

That night we went in that store and Mr. Myers locked the door. "Oh well, it's time to clean up." He got ammonia and started sprinkling it all through the store and on us. Then he got out Clorox. He poured a combination of pure ammonia and Clorox directly on top of my head. It streamed down. I swallowed some of it. We were determined to stay in there, but people were breaking. . . . I had first-degree burns and some people had second-degree burns from the Clorox. My stomach had to be pumped. It was a nightmare. And to see this man do this as if he was serving tea to the Queen of England was perhaps the most horrendous moment. It was a mixture of the physical pain and the pain of watching this man in his hatred that caused the greatest agony.

When the police arrived, Carlton Mize, with a baseball bat in hand, threatened demonstrators, ordering them not to vomit on the premises.

Thursday night, January 2, 1964, another group visited Watts Restaurant on Pittsboro Road. Describing Mrs. Watts as "a very heavy woman," Quinton narrates the scene as she approached one of the protesters sitting on the floor: "She simply stood over him, pulled up her dress—she had no underpants—squatted, and urinated on him . . . and simply went back to do what she was doing." Later the *Daily Tar Heel* editorialized, "To remove any doubt about the level of her depravity, the next night she directed and aided in the stomping, kicking, beating, and water-hosing of eleven demonstrators."[51]

D Day and Beyond

On returning from prison in January 1964, Pat settled into the black community. Around the corner from the Chapel Hill Freedom Committee's office and to the rear of Chicken Box #2 (a small café on South Graham Street), Pat shared an apartment with Rev. LaVert Taylor, with whom he had become fast friends during his work in Danville the previous fall. "I wasn't trying to be black. I was safe there."

Pat also had returned to a city and activists with changed perspectives. "There had been a whole shift in the tone. There had been a lot of talk the previous summer about 'love' and 'brotherhood,' but around January we really shifted the tone, which also escalated the ire of the liberals."

Quinton articulated the significance this city on the hill may have had for the civil rights movement: "People began strategizing around the fact that Chapel Hill was a model community. By then I had been in Chapel Hill for a long enough time and had convinced McKissick and my other colleagues in Durham that Chapel Hill was an area that we needed to focus our energy."

On January 12 CORE leader James Farmer visited Chapel Hill for the Durham to Chapel Hill freedom march. Bringing well-known speakers to local communities had long been a part of the civil rights strategy, as Quinton explains: "The momentum of the movement was not necessarily built upon an active participation and solid base; it was charisma. We would bring somebody in, a name that would draw massive people." A statement released by organizers read: "The gradual pace of this journey is a reflection of the gradual pace of America toward a true realization of its ideals."[52] Passing Brady's Restaurant and Carlton's Rock Pile grocery, they carried signs like "Don't Burn a Cross, Bear One." After their thirteen-mile walk in sleet and rain, a crowd of 500 gathered at the First Baptist Church to hear John Knowles, the homosexual author of *A Separate Peace,* and CORE national chairman Floyd McKissick address the rally. Then, to a cheering crowd, forty-three-year-old James Farmer declared: "Chapel Hill is a key to the South and the nation." Marking the fourth anniversary of the Greensboro sit-in, he announced a deadline for the city to adopt the long-debated ordinance. "Unless Chapel Hill is an open city by February 1," his voice trumpeted, "it will become the focal point of all our efforts. All our resources, staff funds, and training will be centered here."[53]

The next day, as the worst blizzard in years descended upon Chapel Hill, the Board of Aldermen met. In part resenting these either/or conditions, four of the six members voted against the ordinance amid a packed town hall (forty-five people spent the night there in a protest sit-in). Later one alderman who had consistently opposed an ordinance, Roland Giduz, remarked that Chapel Hill "is not going to be stampeded and coerced. . . . "[54] Along with the majority, he supported the mayor's appointment of yet another committee for mediation between the sides. The all-white committee would report back two weeks later that it could not work against any deadline in its quest to seek voluntary compliance.

On the following Saturday eighty demonstrators marched through the downtown business area carrying signs such as "Black Is Not a Vice; Segregation Is Not a Virtue." A sit-in followed at the entrance to the town hall, where two activists had remained since the aldermen's vote the previous Monday night. Demonstrations, sit-ins, and marches continued unabated.

On "D Day," February 1, several hundred marchers assembled at St. Joseph's Church. According to Pat, "On the first line of the march . . . was every single member of that senior class walking two by two. There had been terrific pressure on those students not to be involved." During that Saturday's protest, seventy-five demonstrators were arrested. The day's activities were followed with a sit-in at Brady's Restaurant and Carlton's Rock Pile grocery. Forty-four protesters were escorted to jail.

This pressure not only lost most of the support from the Chapel Hill liberals but also awakened the sleepy UNC student body. Two hundred students marched from the Upper Quad to Raleigh Street carrying signs such as "Government by Law Not by Threats" and chanting "Down with CORE!" And Armistead Maupin asked, in his column: "Where is the human dignity you speak of? Is it in the screaming hordes of demonstrators who stomp and sway and chant, and sit-in and go limp?"[55]

Meanwhile, the student body president, Michael Lawler, denouncing racial discrimination as "morally indefensible," called for a student boycott of segregated businesses in this "civic drama."[56] A petition, authored by Maupin and a fellow student, quickly circulated, attracting nearly 1,500 signers who agreed that a boycott "would amount to unjustly punishing merchants for exercising their legal rights."[57] These initiatives earned Maupin praise from Raleigh WRAL television editorialist, Jesse Helms.[58] The student legislature, though, endorsed Lawler's boycott. Some students, most notably the Greek houses such as Alpha Tau Omega and Chi Omega, continued to frequent segregated facilities while 150 faculty members signed a statement of support for the boycott.

The height of the demonstrations occurred on February 8, on the heels of the UNC–Wake Forest basketball game. Quinton, who understood the importance of timing, remembers this as the crowning achievement of his tactical efforts. As the game ended, the massive demonstration marched to the center of town. Other demonstrators massed at other key town intersections, including Raleigh Road and Pittsboro Road, with confederates in cars parking diagonally across the roads.

"We decided that we didn't want anyone arrested. Now, how were we going to do that?" A well-trained and hard-core group was required. "We were very selective about who we were going to have block the highways, because there was a very real danger someone was going to get killed. We needed 160 people who were willing to die."

Ten years later, Quinton shared his exuberance with a young generation of student activists:

> It was the most beautiful thing to bring this line of people out into the middle of this intersection, to circle them around, and have them all sit down until the police arrived. There is never an arrest possibility until the police say "Move!" and you don't move. They asked us to move, and I was able to get the group to stand up and simply begin to spiral and file out of there and then to march in such a way that they would block the intersection one block away where the police station and courthouse were. We were able to block both of those intersections with a long line of people and keep them moving around in a circle so that the police could not arrest us.[59]

The demonstrations and arrests continued for another week with little movement on the part of the town aldermen or the mayor. On February 15, after fourteen more arrests in yet another sit-in at The Pines, the Chapel Hill Freedom Committee announced a six-day moratorium, with John refusing to give the city a "blueprint" on how to resolve the conflict.[60] The moratorium was later extended through the end of the month.

Meanwhile support from the conservative adult black community crumbled: "By that point Rev. Manley and others were not with us." Pat continues, "We felt very embattled and frustrated. We were on our way to running up fantastic legal debts; we already owed $50,000 and not one damn thing had happened at Chapel Hill!"

Quinton's strategy, though, required continued mass public involvement: "We had to rely on bodies—the number of people we could amass and put on the streets. . . . Our political power came from our ability to create havoc." In the course of sit-ins and marches, many of the "bodies" were Lincoln High School students along with former students, like James Brittain. Teachers and administrators, under pressure themselves, were increasingly alarmed by these student activities, which jeopardized their learning and complicated their choices for employment.

The Chapel Hill freedom movement again found itself "losing steam"—a phenomenon, Quinton knew, the group could ill afford. "We started out with mass meetings that had ten, fifteen, twenty-five people, and you build up to mass meetings that had five hundred people with a church that is overwhelmingly full that would be rocking with the freedom songs. . . . So you try to always do something that keeps the momentum going."

With some dissension evident in the steering committee, support from liberal whites evaporating, conservative blacks eyeing the long-promised Civil Rights Bill then inching through the Congress, and supporters facing criminal charges and long jail sentences, the movement leaders' ability to mobilize mass demonstrations was impaired. As Quinton acknowledged, "The power we had was to create tensions in communities through protests. It was basically the power of the tactics that we could use and the number of people supporting us and the number of people we could amass at any given time."

Under increased pressure, the issue of Quinton and John's relationship surfaced in the steering committee, as Pat describes:

> Someone from within wanted them to answer questions: Were they homosexual? Were they having a relationship? But the two as well as the rest of the committee stood on the "privacy" principle; it had no business coming before the committee. Now, the two could just as easily have said, "We're lovers," and they would have gotten the backing of the committee. Now my own feeling was that it might be very bad for the movement, but they had the right to have their relationship. What are we in this struggle for if these are the means we use to achieve our ends?

On February 24, 1964, the first set of indictments resulting from the winter protests was presented to the grand jury of Orange County. Among the 450 of what would eventually come to more than 1,200 cases against demonstrators, variously charged with trespass, resisting arrest, assault and battery, obstructing traffic, or blocking the sidewalk, were charges levied against Quinton, Pat, and John. Since the court refused to docket the cases, they and others faced forfeiture of bond and contempt of court charges should their case be called in their absence. Further, most of those charged also confronted school attendance regulations requiring their classroom presence. With the protesters' time and expense being consumed in this way, Chapel Hill quieted. Prodded by Judge Mallard, the grand jury had also returned indictments of "conspiracy to commit a misdemeanor" against Quinton and John arising out of the trespass charges in the now infamous Watts Restaurant sit-in.

Interrupting these proceedings, attorneys for the activists requested the transfer of all pending cases to Federal Court, claiming the defendants' inability to receive a fair trial. In response, Judge Mallard called the move "a false and scurrilous attack upon every court in the state. . . . "[61] Much to the activists' displeasure, trials ensued in Judge Mallard's court in March.

That month Dr. King held his annual meeting of his top staff members at St. Helena, a barrier island off South Carolina. On the heels of that meeting, they met with local SCLC heads for another two days. Pat was invited to attend:

> I drove with LaVert Taylor to South Carolina, headed to what was then known as Frogmore Island. The island had been greatly influenced by the Quakers, who came from Philadelphia after the Civil War to work with the newly freed slaves [Penn Center was cofounded by "spinsters" Ellen Murray and Laura Matilda Towne, who lived together for forty years]. It was one of the few places in South Carolina where a public meeting of blacks and whites could take place.
>
> Driving down, LaVert told me that something had been troubling him—he had seen a reference to Pat being "queer" on a bathroom wall of the Carolina Coffee Shop. "Was it true?" I told him, "I've never had sex with a man, yet. But I hope to someday." I admitted I was attracted to this handsome minister sitting beside me but assured him I wasn't "pressing the issue." LaVert insisted that he was not biased against gays, but that it was best to "guard closely against those tendencies," primarily because of society's ostracism.

During that year's conclave, a decision was made to launch the first economic boycott. Pat also sought counsel from King:

> We walked through the live oaks with Spanish moss draping the ground. I relayed plans of an upcoming fast in Chapel Hill with four of us willing to die, hoping that our deaths would once and for all point out the recalcitrance of the aldermen and the inaction of the town's liberals. But Dr. King argued against it. First of all, it was non-Gandhian and "you don't fast 'against' your opponents but to solidify your supporters. . . . The fast is a bad tactic. It is against the philosophy of nonviolence to only give an ultimatum of 'either/or.' Pat, this gives opponents no opportunity to grow and maneuver." Dr. King convinced LaVert and me to set a certain date to end the fast, suggesting an appropriate time would be Holy Week.

Thus another act of civil disobedience began on Palm Sunday, March 22, when Pat, LaVert, John, and James Foushee (a Lincoln High School student) initiated a one-week fast on the post office grounds on Franklin Street. A flyer distributed to onlookers read in part:

We believe that a fast is the highest form of prayer, and look upon this Holy Week fast as a prayer that the city will live up to its responsibilities. . . . We hope that by fasting publicly, we can remind each person that we have not solved this problem and we hope that each of us, as we observe the final week of Lent, will ask ourselves the question, "Have I honestly and sincerely done all in my power to eliminate racial discrimination in Chapel Hill?"[62]

On the last night of the fast, Holy Saturday, an all-South rally was held on the outskirts of Chapel Hill at the urging of the Grand Kleagle of the Ku Klux Klan. Pat tells the story:

A large contingent from the black community, many nonsubscribers to non-violence, came to the post office to surround us. The Klan passed through in a cavalcade of cars with their hated white robes, masks, and guns. Although they jeered, they didn't stop. It was only later that I learned from Chief Blake that it had been decided to pour a fifty-five-gallon drum of sulfuric acid on us. But the leaders of Klavern No. 9 (Orange County) argued that after the other Klansmen were safely back home, they would bear the brunt of the blame.

After seven days of drinking only water, using umbrellas for shelter, and living in sleeping bags, the fast ended on Easter Sunday with drinking of soup, a mass rally at the First Baptist Church, and a march down Franklin Street.

Mississippi Law Comes to Hillsborough

By April it was apparent that convictions were imminent. In a speech in nearby Chadbourn, Judge Mallard denounced the demonstrators, claiming that many were Northerners paid six dollars a day: "We must not let any-one come along and destroy our minds. . . . "[63] Alerted through back chan-nels that the judge would dismiss most of the cases if the ringleaders admit-ted guilt and accepted punishment, a late-night meeting was held: "In the meeting of the Chapel Hill Freedom Committee where we decided what to do when Judge Mallard sent us the message, I [Pat] served as devil's advo-cate because I didn't think we should make the decision to cut the deal in an emotional atmosphere of singing 'We Shall Overcome.' 'Before people decide to stand in solidarity and take the chance of going on the chain gang,' I pointed out the real horrors of the place."

The "deal with the devil" was accepted.

On the day of sentencing, Pat remembers "a native North Carolinian, James Feldman, who was a member of the '47 bus ride, had come to the courthouse to see us. He also had served a prison sentence." The Hillsbor-ough courthouse was packed as the "ringleaders" sat in front, stared down upon by the magisterial judge. "We knew we were going to prison." The night before, Pat had read the speech Eugene V. Debs had given when he went off to a Southern prison in 1917. Pat felt that he should say something as elegant at his sentencing: "The lawyer told me—being the first to be sentenced to a year at hard labor—'Pat, you can't do it, because he hasn't given sentence to the others. You are going to make him so mad that he will increase the other sentences.' So when Judge Mallard asked: 'Does the defendant have anything to say prior to sentencing?' I said, 'No.'"

Convicted of blocking traffic and resisting arrest, Pat and Quinton were given nearly a year apiece on the prison chain gang. Lamenting that "only two parents have spoken to me" about the fate of their children, Mallard gave forty-seven other demonstrators suspended sentences pending no further civil disobedience.[64] The next day, Judge Mallard sent four more activists, including John, to prison with sentences ranging from six months to one year for their participation in an "international conspiracy that would destroy this country"; another hundred were given suspended sentences.[65]

Coda

As Pat, Quinton, John, and nine others languished in prison, on July 2, 1964, President Lyndon Johnson signed into law the Civil Rights Act that prohibited discrimination in public accommodations. Chapel Hill activists tested the new law immediately:

> Civil rights "testers" were served without incident at Leo's Grill, Brady's Restaurant, the Pines Restaurant, and the Tar Heel Sandwich Shop. . . . When the testers arrived at Watts Grill on Pittsboro Road they were attacked with fists, clubs, and one employee of the restaurant reportedly had a knife. . . . The testers were unrelenting, however, and charges of assault were brought against Austin Watts. . . . The threat of a lawsuit forced Watts to integrate on July 10. . . . In such a manner, the last overt vestiges of racial discrimination in public accommodations in Chapel Hill began to disappear.[66]

At age sixty-five, Pat remembers John, who is now dead, as a person of "commitment and strength" and Quinton, with whom he speaks occasionally by phone, as "the tactician who brought the connection to the statewide movement." As for Pat himself, "I was the genuine article when it came to being a white Southerner. That was what infuriated the crackers who drove the taxicabs in Chapel Hill—the same group that had attacked Rustin years before—they couldn't stand me. My picture hung in every klavern in North Carolina." Charlie Jones, the minister at the liberal Community Church, "called us the 'Father, Son, and Holy Ghost.' We were a very tight trio."

In the early 1960s, Pat, Quinton, and John were homosexually inclined men whose ideals translated into actions and who had an abiding faith in their generation's ability to change the world. Three decades later, Pat reflected: "I had earlier wondered if I would have come out as a gay man if it hadn't been for civil rights. Now, I wonder if I would have gotten as active as I did in civil rights if I hadn't been attracted to a man." As for Quinton, who now lives with his partner of seven years in Hillsborough, the town of his sentencing: "I've asked myself for years, 'Would things have been different were I not different?' I think that the fact that the three of us did have the same sexual orientation made it possible for there to develop a closer relationship for us to work together."

Thirty-five years have passed: the assassinations of Martin Luther King and Malcolm X, the Los Angeles riots of 1967 and 1995, the transformation of George Wallace and the conviction of Brian de la Beckwith, the Civil Rights Acts of 1964 and 1965 affirming equality of opportunity, and California's Proposition 209 eliminating affirmative action. Ever the activist, tactician, and strategist, Quinton observes: "There are some things we gained out of it and some things that we did not. What we were was a group of young, starry-eyed activists who believed if we could eliminate segregation we would develop an open and free society. We *really* believed in 'Freedom Now!' We thought that was what we were going to get."

In the summer of 1974, as the Nixon presidency imploded, the lights were turned out on the last American soldiers remaining in Vietnam, and Martin Luther King's mother lay dead from an assassin's bullet, Quinton spoke to a group of college students about dashed assumptions:

> The assumption that was made was that I . . . was not different. . . . The assumption that if we can integrate all the public accommodations, black people are going to be free. . . . The assumption that racism in this country is not as insidious and destructive as it is and that it had not so completely permeated American society that it was in the marrow of everybody's bones. [The assumption that] what we needed was to be able to go to the restaurant and eat, to be able to buy things downtown. . . . That equal opportunity meant simply opening that door or taking the "For Whites Only" sign down. . . . [67]

Then Quinton returned to those warm feelings he still harbors of the days when he, John, and Pat challenged the city on the hill:

> There was a special song that was created in the Chapel Hill movement. I don't think I've heard it sung anywhere else. We would all be sitting around and making up words. Somebody would start a verse and we would add a verse. . . . We could sing ourselves into a great deal of joy. We could be going someplace to demonstrate and we would just burst into song, or sing all night in jail. It was put to the tune of "When Johnny Come Marching Home Again":

> > *We're marching in the streets again*
> > *Talu, talu*
> > *We're marching in the streets again*
> > *Talu, talu*

We're marching down Freedom's Trail
And we all will go to jail
We'll die before we pay our bail
America, I don't know ya.

They're locking us in the cells again
Talu, Talu
They're locking us in the cells again
Talu, Talu
It's police clubs and blackjacks
Repeatedly beating me on my back
All because my skin is black
America, I don't know ya.

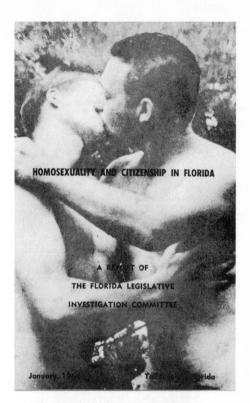

Cover of the "Purple Pamphlet,"
officially known as the Report
of the Florida Legislative
Investigation Committee, 1964.
Courtesy of ONE Institute
International Gay and Lesbian
Archives, Los Angeles, CA.

State Senator Charley E. Johns (center), Dr. B R. Tilley (left),
President of St. Johns College of Palatka, and A. E. Mikell (right),
superintendent of the Levy County schools, discussing plans whereby
homosexuals could be detected before they could "infiltrate" public
jobs (1964). Courtesy of Florida Photographic Collection, Florida
State Archives, Tallahassee, Florida.

Jimmie White's Lounge, a Tampa, Florida lesbian bar circa 1959 where Merril Mushroom would go during her college years in Gainesville, Florida. Courtesy of Merril Mushroom, Dowelltown, Tennessee.

Merril Mushroom (right) with Jimmie's bartender outside the bar (1960). Courtesy of Merril Mushroom, Dowelltown, Tennessee.

Album cover from "It's Me Again . . . Ray Bourbon—
You're Stepping on My Eyelashes," UTC 2, New York,
New York, circa 1960.

Sit-in protest at the Chamber of Commerce building
in Chapel Hill, 1962. Pat Cusick sitting in middle-
center row. Courtesy of North Carolina Collection,
University of North Carolina at Chapel Hill.

Activists outside Judge Mallard's Orange County Court, 1964. From left to right: Pat, Quinton, John, and James. Courtesy of North Carolina Collection, University of North Carolina at Chapel Hill.

Marching down Chapel Hill's Franklin Street, 1963. Courtesy of North Carolina Collection, University of North Carolina at Chapel Hill.

Gordon Hall and Isabel Whitney with Philadelphia Marilyn
(parrot) putting Dutch tiles on a fireplace at the Greenwich
Village home (1959). From the collection of Duke
University, Special Collections, Perkins Library, 90-040,
Simmons, Dawn Pepita, Box 1 of 1. Used by permission of
Duke University and Dawn Simmons.

Dawn Langley
Simmons wedding along
with Matron of Honor
Cousin Rasomanda
Stanton (1969). From
the collection of Dawn
Langley Simmons,
Hudson, New York.
Used by permission.

Jack Nichols cofounded the
Mattachine Society of
Washington D.C. in 1961 and
the Mattachine Society of
Florida, Inc. in 1965. Courtesy
of Jack Nichols.

Richard Inman on
WTVJ Channel 4 FYI
television documentary
"The Homosexual" (19
April 1966). Courtesy
of WTVJ-TV National
Broadcasting Company,
Inc. All rights reserved.

5

Dawn Arises
in Aristocratic
Charleston

The Gordon Langley Hall Affair

SOMEWHERE BENEATH THE NOT-SO-SUBTLE messages of *The Birth of a Nation* and *Song of the South*, the romantic relationships in *Gone with the Wind* and *Fried Green Tomatoes*, and the raw emotionalism of *A Streetcar Named Desire* and *Deliverance* is a scaffolding of race, gender, class, and sexuality that has long contoured Southern culture.

Located at the tip of the peninsula formed by the meeting of the Ashley and Cooper Rivers, Charleston is in many ways the epicenter of Southern culture; its history and architecture occasionally expose this scaffolding. Charles Towne's legacy includes the ill-fated slave revolt led by Denmark Vesey and the notorious abolitionist work of the Grimké sisters a generation later. Spared by Sherman's long march to the sea, a catfish row of brightly colored houses lies near the wharves on East Bay Street where cargoes of indigo and rice were readied for their European journeys; farther along the water's edge south of Broad Street majestically sit the mansions of the Manigaults, Blacklocks, and Draytons, protected by ancient seawalls that form the Battery and overlook Fort Sumter, a not too distant reminder of Northern aggression; on the other end of the city's peninsula lie eighteenth-century suburbs such as Ansonborough, with historic homes purchased for renovation or resale by the Historic Charleston Foundation under the post–World War II leadership of Frances Edmunds. Walking through the cobblestone streets of the "Holy City" takes one past the Dock

Street Theatre, the first opera house in the United States, and Hibernian Hall, built in 1840 and the site of the exclusive St. Cecilia Cotillion, where Citadel cadets escort debutante daughters of the Confederacy—just a stone's throw from the old slave market, where the great-grandchildren of former slaves weave sweet-grass baskets and banter in Gullah. The streets made famous by the fictional black beggar Porgy also lead to the Greek Revival architecture of the College of Charleston, the first municipal institution of higher education, and The Citadel, whose cadets recently struggled in a lost cause to preserve its all-male tradition.

Much as it had been in the decades before, in the early 1960s

> Charleston was a city of thoroughly segregated neighborhoods, transportation systems, public schools, colleges and parks, churches, theaters, restaurants, and even shopping districts. Afro-Americans were expected to shop on King Street north of Calhoun Street, while whites shopped to the south. Even when the city's brown elite occasionally patronized the better stores south of Calhoun, they were not permitted to try on shoes and certain articles of clothing.[1]

By 1962, however, great changes were on the Southern horizon. In the midst of tuning to new episodes of *Gunsmoke, The Defenders,* or *Have Gun, Will Travel* Saturday evenings on Channel 5, viewing first-run movies at the Riviera Theater (such as *Advise and Consent,* a political drama in which a senator with a homosexual past faces blackmail), or listening to Top Ten hits on WTMA 1250 (Elvis Presley's "Return to Sender," Chubby Checkers's "Limbo Rock," and the Four Seasons' "Big Girls Don't Cry"), Charlestonians faced a challenge to long-held social mores and cultural values.

The city's *News and Courier* juxtaposed state and national civil rights stories: the impending integration of Charleston lunch counters, with Southern senators blocking rules limiting filibusters; violence at Ol' Miss as it integrated, and threatened violence as Harvey Gantt registered at Clemson University. Despite the polemics of die-hard segregationists like Tom Waring, who editorialized against "the apostles of race mongrelization and socialism"[2] in the *News and Courier,* by 1962 peaceful segregation had occurred in many public accommodations, although few blacks availed themselves of their new freedoms to shop, eat, and play in previously segregated areas.

1962 also marked the arrival of British-born Gordon Langley Hall.

The Early Years

Gordon was born to the aristocratic Marjorie Hall Ticehurst in Sussex, England, in 1937; his father, Jack Copper, was the chauffeur for Vita Sackville-West, the noted "transvestite" author depicted in Virginia Woolf's *Orlando,* a tale of a man transformed into a lovely woman. Becoming "a real live Orlando" is how Hall remembers his life:

I was the family black sheep in more ways than one: Marjorie, still unwed, had borne me when she was sixteen. . . . Shunned by most of her family . . . Marjorie locked herself in a darkened room for most of the nine months. One close and sadistic relative saw fit to kick her in the stomach. . . . When I was eventually born at home with only a midwife in attendance, the clitoris was so swollen that the startled woman did not know whether I was a boy or a girl.

One of Hall's earliest memories is of Vita reading him stories at Sissinghurst Castle; Hall credits her with encouraging his writing. Effeminate in appearance, he enjoyed dolls during his adolescence and reported occasional bleedings in his genital area.

Fearing embarrassment for himself and disgrace upon his family, Gordon soon fled his native England.

I had been told by my doctor in England that a mistake had been made when I was born (I should have been twins), so I always took assignments that were very masculine (cut my hair short) because I thought it was something that could not be put right. . . . I lived a life of deception. As a child I never went to the bathroom with the other children, I would always run home. When I was in the choir my voice never broke like the other children. . . . I really lived in my own world.

At nineteen, Gordon journeyed to an obscure Ojibway Indian reservation in Gull Bay, Canada. Here he taught, wrote, and served as a midwife. He wrote *Me Papoose Sitter,* a humorous adult story based on those experiences, during his subsequent years as an out-of-work writer living in New York City, following a brief stint as society editor for the *Nevada Daily Mail* in Missouri.

During his first New York summer, while living in a small apartment on West 103rd Street, he also wrote a modern morality play. An Episcopal rector at the nearby St. Martin's Church in Harlem encouraged Hall to write *Saraband for a Saint.* Acknowledging an autobiographical component, the play concerned the relationship and personal problems between two soldiers, an educated African-American and a "talkative" Englishman, who seek shelter in a bombed-out church during World War II. Bishop James Pike described the play: "Here, a broken, wronged, and wrong man is met . . . by one outside his life who makes himself part of his life. The unacceptable is accepted and thus is able to accept himself and become more acceptable."[3]

After the play was performed, Gordon fell ill. A "distant cousin"—Isabel Lydia Whitney, a member of the elite Pen and Brush Club in Greenwich Village—visited him in the hospital. A noted artist and heiress to her branch of the Whitney fortune, Miss Whitney was also a collateral descendant of William Penn, a relative of John Hay Whitney, then U.S. ambassador to the Court of St. James, and Gertrude Vanderbilt Whitney, one of the founders of the New York Museum of Modern Art. Isabel and Gordon became quick friends; they were, in effect, "kindred spirits."

Then in her seventies, Isabel invited young Gordon to live in her forty-room mansion at 12 West 10th Street, "where we could be company for each other and yet retain our individual independence." Like the characters in his morality play, Isabel and Gordon found strength in one another's company: "Although my frustrating affliction was still with me, she had taught me how to live with it. No longer was I running away. . . . There was no need to prove I was strong and masculine when I really wasn't. As she had learned to live with her crippled leg, so she taught me to accept with resignation something that we thought could never be righted."

During those six years that he lived on the top floor of the Whitney mansion, Gordon wrote several other books and articles, including a feature on Princess Margaret published in *Look*. He quickly entered New York society, befriending the likes of Joan Crawford, Bette Davis, and Dame Margaret Rutherford, stage star and Oscar-winning actress. According to Hall, Dame Margaret was so taken by *Me Papoose Sitter* and heartsick over his "affliction" that she invited him to "join their family" during her New York visit in the fall of 1960: "Having no children of their own, Margaret and Stringer Davis [her husband] had picked out several young people whom they liked for their adopted children . . . and made me one of them."

Diagnosed with leukemia and advised to move south during the winters, Isabel Whitney encouraged Gordon to tour the region to seek a fitting residence. Detailed letters and photographs followed his visits to such cities as Nashville, New Orleans, and Charleston. Independently, both Gordon and Isabel chose a pink stucco mansion on Society Street in the Ansonborough restoration area of Charleston. Gordon purchased the home for $13,500 from his book club proceeds of *Golden Boats from Burma*.

Built between 1835 and 1840, the run-down mansion had been residence to one of the South's finest medical scientists and an American patriot, Dr. Joseph Johnson. This typical period house had a large dining room with a drawing room opposite on the first floor, a second floor with an upper drawing room and a Victorian bedroom, and a third floor with several bedrooms. A grand staircase joined the floors. Apart from the main house were the former slave quarters and the kitchen. Hall recalls: "The room that would be my bedroom was full of hay. The yard had old, broken motor cars and rubbish. The beautiful iron gates were lying in pieces. It reminded me of Sissinghurst Castle, where my mentor, Vita Sackville-West, first found it and said, 'I think we could be very happy here.'"

Restoration quickly commenced, with the renovation cost rising to $46,000, not including the cost for mantels, hardware, lighting fixtures, and marble washstands that Isabel brought from New York.[4] Isabel worked from photographs and drawings to direct the work (her bedroom, for example, was decorated with an antebellum yellow rose-flecked wallpaper). Gordon traveled back and forth to Charleston to see it through.

The Grand Arrival

After Isabel's untimely death in February 1962, Gordon Langley Hall arrived in Charleston on September 2—right after a hurricane. In his British accent, Gordon greeted new friends with frequent references to his well-placed connections (Whitney's cousin, Rutherford's adopted son, Crawford's close friend). Using money inherited from Whitney's estate (estimated at $3 million, with Hall named as the alternate executor) and earnings from his books, he continued the restoration project. "It was the first house that I restored to the specifications that had been taught me by my great-uncle and aunt in England, who restored big mansions and smaller houses to perfection. We even brought one mantelpiece that came from President Chester Arthur's White House."

Frances Edmunds, longtime director of the Historic Charleston Foundation, which had sold Gordon the Johnson mansion, was invited to select suitable furnishings. An acquaintance of Gordon's recalls that the home "was absolutely a showplace! These were museum pieces": an antique French harp; George Washington mirrors (Gordon claimed that Jackie Onassis had wanted these); a Joshua Lockwood tall clock; a gilded palmetto mirror; one of the original knife boxes from Washington's Mount Vernon; a painting by Samuel B. Morse completed while he was in Charleston; chairs once owned by Robert E. Lee. When it was finished, the Johnson House joined the select group of Charleston homes open for public viewing each spring under the sponsorship of the Foundation.

Quickly accepted by the "South-of-Broad" society because of his pedigree, accent, and money, Gordon Langley Hall was one of Charleston's most eligible bachelors. As Hall tells it:

> The invitations from would-be matchmakers kept pouring in. One poor soul who would never see forty again, whose only asset was her family name and her illustrious forebear's sword, delighted in arriving at the Dr. Joseph Johnson House clad in white tennis shorts. . . . The Jewish society also seemed to like me. One of their leading hostesses gave suppers that I really dreaded. Always some poor husbandless girl was purposely placed beside me at the table. . . . When I showed no particular interest in the feminine sex, there were those who decided that I must be a homosexual. After more than one party I was driven home by the husband and practically had to fight for my "honor" at the doorstep.

Frances Edmunds was also responsible for introducing Gordon to the accomplished architect Read Barnes, who completed the restoration project.

Barnes, as Hall remembers, "was born a generation before his time because of his visionary views of modern architecture so detested in Charleston. He told me that every new owner of an old house should leave behind something of themselves in it. So we placed French doors in the dining room that opened onto the garden steps."

Barnes's relationship with Gordon extended eventually into the Barnes's family life as Gordon became godparent to the first child born to Read's wife, Ann—who always had a strained relationship with Gordon. Years later, Ann claimed, "My husband never seemed to get all the money he was owed. But people just fell all over Hall." Hall denies the accusation. Later, after Read's suicide, Ann married Jack Leland, a reporter for the *News and Courier*.

Ann Leland also remembers that Peter Manigault, whose family owned the *News and Courier*, befriended Gordon. Soon stories about Gordon Langley Hall began appearing in the newspaper. One of the first, printed in the "women's section," highlighted a tour of England by several prominent Charlestonians. A photograph chronicled their visit to the garden "on the country estate of author Gordon Langley Hall . . . an official biographer of the British royal family."[5] Another article, published in 1964, stated: "Years of planning and five months of actual preparation will be culminated Sunday with the opening of the Isabel Lydia Whitney Memorial Garden Gallery . . . housing the permanent collection of America's first woman fresco painter. . . . British-born author Gordon Langley Hall . . . will guide visitors through the historic house he restored in memory of his cousin."

The newspaper also published features about Gordon displaying pictures at the Gibbes Art Gallery (his art collection was valued at $250,000) as well as praiseworthy reviews of his books.[6] Other stories, like one on a "coming out" gala at the Denver Hilton for his two Chihuahuas, Miss Annabel and Miss Nelly (one black, one white), outfitted in dresses, were covered in *other* papers.[7] In fact, according to Ann Leland, reporters from Charleston's newspaper did not publish anything about Hall for fear of losing their jobs.

Gordon also contributed to the *News and Courier* as well as other publications. In "'Twas the Night Before Christmas," he described the origins of the famous poem and the reluctance of its author, an eighteenth-century professor of divinity, to claim credit. An essay, "Gleaning from the Confederate Museum: The Ladies Do It," described Civil War clothing on display, noting: "During the Confederate days, the men seemed to have been as handy with a needle as the ladies."[8] In another article Gordon described his experiences on the Ojibway reservation with an aging matriarch. This writing also reveals his fondness for matriarchs and inner social circles:

> Standing on the landing stage in front of the warehouse clutching her home-made bouquet of red paper roses, she greeted me upon arrival with a large Margaret Rutherford grin. . . . What I did not know then about this amazing

woman was the fact that she was a great believer in protocol and that her heroine was none other than vivacious Princess Margaret. As I had come all the way from England to be their teacher, in Poor Old Grandmother's estimation I was Queen Elizabeth's own representative. . . . The Gull Bay Social Register was kept at the back of the school attendance chart on my desk. It made very interesting reading. Poor Old Grandmother was second in importance among the ladies of Gull Bay. . . . [9]

Rumors

During his years in Charleston rumors circulated about Gordon's interest in animals, young black men, and a prominent aristocrat. Gordon, so the stories went, allowed animals to live in his house. Few faulted him for keeping his parrot Marilyn, his German shepherd Jacqueline, or his guinea pig Simon housebound. Ann Leland, however, vividly retold stories of a pig and other barnyard animals residing on the third floor. In a letter to his father, Jack Copper, Gordon wrote: "Our pig Frances is growing enormous. She is house trained to paper and she dances . . . and she bangs the toilet seat when she wants water. She thinks she is a dog. . . . She is the cleanest animal I ever had."

More serious rumors abounded regarding his fondness for Negro men. Ann Leland recalls the first significant event that called into question Hall's "most eligible bachelor" status: "The first hint was from Kessler's grocery store on Anson and Society Streets. The store used black delivery boys, so when Hall called to place an order, the owner would tell him the boy would have to stay on the sidewalk to deliver the groceries."[10]

Years later, Hall characterized such stories as "typical jealous gossip" and, politely responding to each of these rumors, wrote:

No barnyard animals lived on the third floor. I told John-Paul [whom he was dating] . . . that my sister and I had a pet pig as children in England. . . . I told him that they were wonderful watchdogs, and the next thing I knew he brought a piglet to me as a gift. His name was Bono. As it was against the law to keep a pig or other barnyard animals within the confines of the city, I had to quickly find Bono a home. He stayed overnight in the old slave quarters, which had a brick floor—and then went to live on John's Island with the agreement that he could be used for breeding but never killed.

The Kessler grocery store incident first appeared in Stephen Birmingham's book, *America's Secret Aristocracy*, as told to the author by none other than Ann Leland's husband. . . . I did take counsel . . . who advised me that I had a clear case to sue Birmingham, his two publishers, and Leland for libel. A staff of five or six people, including the gardener, worked at 56 Society Street. Don't you think the housekeeper or butler would have dealt with Kessler's? . . . I had nothing to do with running the house, buying food supplies . . .

Also rumored was a relationship with another male friend, Joe, who arrived in Charleston about the same time as Gordon. Dr. Leber, an aging gay
man and longtime Charleston resident, describes Joe, who had "a raspy
voice," as a "very kind man who used to cook for everyone." Alleging that
"there was some connection between the two of them," the doctor expressed some resentment: "Well, when Joe finally died he was to leave antiques for his many friends, but the will was held up because Gordon contested it—well, no one ever got anything."

Hall acknowledges the connection with Joe but describes a relationship
far different from that rumored:

> Joe came into Isabel's life when he worked for Coleman's Auction Gallery. She
> bought a tapestry. Joe came to deliver and hang the tapestry, and she decided
> he should work for us. He more or less took over. Joe did all of the cooking; he
> got rid of the cook and the janitor. He really worked himself right in. He
> thought he was our bodyguard!
>
> But he was the bane of my life! One of the reasons I moved to Charleston was
> to make a completely new start. . . . Well, Joe turned up on my doorstep in
> Charleston. . . . In the end, to get him off my hands I set him up in business, rent-
> ing an antique shop and giving him a great deal of stuff to sell. . . . When I wed
> . . . he spat in my face on King Street and painted my name off the antique shop.
>
> I did not contest Joe's will. Before he died, he, in a macabre move, tagged all
> of his possessions—some of which were mine and Isabel's—with prices.
> . . . Not much sold, since Joe's prices were too high. I did request that a table
> and four chairs that had belonged to Isabel's great-aunt, Lydia Wooster Harris,
> the Hudson River painter, be returned or for me to even buy them back. I
> heard no more.

Unaware of or discounting Hall's perspective, these and other rumors circulated among the homosexuals frequenting Charleston's 49 Club or Camden's Tavern, where gossip ran more freely than liquor. But given Hall's
background, wealth, and demeanor, the rumors were overlooked by the
well-heeled Charlestonian aristocracy.

"Queensborough"

Billy Camden moved to Charleston in 1947 from a small South Carolina
town and lived with Heyward, his longtime companion. "The gay couples
really restored Ansonborough. I was on the Board of Directors for the Ansonborough Historic Foundation—it was made up of 80 percent gay men!
There was a gay couple or gay person in almost every home." Pausing, Billy
laughs: "They should have called it 'Queensborough' instead. . . . Now,
they have all moved away or died."

At the time, there was Russell, a former composer for the New York
Metropolitan Opera, and his lover, Tool, a Texas teenager. They moved to

Charleston together in 1959 and lived there until the composer's death twenty years later. And there were Nicky and Tom, who had returned after World War II. Nearby was Joe, whose knowledge of antiques, culinary talents, and kindly demeanor endeared him to many in this close-knit community. Jeremy Morrow was another longtime homosexual resident living near Gordon's home. He occasionally frequented the bars but preferred to attend small dinner parties among Charleston's gay elite or to steal away for a few weeks in Europe or northern Africa to indulge his sexual fantasies.

Now in his mid-eighties, Nicky, widowed after living with Tom for forty-nine years, recalls those pre-Stonewall years:

> We lived as "out" as possible for that time period. We were active socially—visiting other gay couples for dinner, going to one of the town's bars. We were also active in the larger Charleston community. We were always invited as a couple to Charleston's social events. Now, did other people know we were "gay"? Sure. Did we ever declare ourselves gay? No. Some younger people might look back at that time and ask, "How could you live in such a closeted world?" Well, as far as I am concerned it was the best of times! Back then you didn't have to carry that terrible label; you could be free to be yourself, enjoy your company of friends. . . .

Billy remembers the social scene similarly:

> One thing that was very nice about the sixties was our group of twelve couples—all professional people—who formed the "couples club." Each couple entertained once a month in their home. You could invite whoever you wanted; it could be a formal dinner or a cocktail party.

There was also an active bar life. Camden reminisces:

> There were always gay bars in Charleston. The first one I went to was Ratskellars on Court House Square. Some of the bars were mixed, like the Anchor. It was not openly gay, but a lot of bachelors would meet. Then there was the 49 Club, where the front was gay, the back was mixed with couples, and the upstairs was gambling.

For singles there were other diversions, too. Navy and air force men could be readily picked up along the Battery, in the town square, or at the Meeting Street bus stop. African-American homosexuals could also be found walking down Meeting Street. "Cruising was easy," Billy recalls. "Sex was easy in the fifties and sixties! They were just horny soldiers. If they had had a choice—a man or a woman—most would have taken the woman; but the choice, at the moment, was a man—so they took it! Of course, some of these men would want money before or after, and a lot of gay people got into trouble."

Traveling the Seamy Side

As in all cities during the homophile era, the life of the homosexual posed dangers. Unlike cities such as Miami, where police ruthlessly raided bars and patrons' names appeared in the morning newspaper, Charleston was more refined. Care and discretion though, as Billy Camden pointed out, were paramount:

> For people who were in the military, teachers, government and state workers— if they found out you were gay, then they would lose their jobs. So these people were very careful not to be seen in a place known as a "gay bar," which is why a lot of the bars were mixed. Those are the places where people went. Even if you were a civilian working for a private company but were hanging around military or government employees, the navy would investigate you. They'd go in and question you and your employers trying to get people fired.

He vividly recalls one visit from naval intelligence officers:

> They came in with a whole photo book of marines, navy, and air force men they suspected of being homosexuals. They wanted to see if I could identify any. Well, I wouldn't let them interview me at my business. I made them come to my house, making it as inconvenient as possible for them. But I was cordial, and of course I did not recognize any as homosexuals. [Laughs] "Sure are some good-looking men," I commented to one of the investigators, "but I don't know any of them."

During this time Billy owned a gay bar, Camden's Tavern, located in the heart of the town. Despite these and other "terror tactics" used by the government, he fondly remembers Charleston gay life.

> Back then people all dressed. You never saw someone in those bars without a coat-and-tail or a tuxedo. It was a very nice time! Today, you have people wearing cutoffs; they look so grungy. To go out on a date you would put on a shirt, tie, and sports coat, visiting restaurants like Henry's or the Cavalier Club. I go to the bars now, and you might see one or two young men and women dressed appropriately; the rest seem to be having a contest on who can look the worst. It's terrible!

Other dangers also confronted homosexuals during this era. Jack Dobbins was bludgeoned to death by a youth brandishing a silver candlestick from the fireplace mantel. In the fall of 1956 this infamous "candlestick murder" sent a long-remembered message to Charleston's homosexual community. Billy, with whom Jack had stayed when he first came to town, tells the story:

> The guy that killed him got off scot-free because he said Jack had proposi-tioned him for sex. Now, this kid had been in the gay bars; he knew what was

going on! Yet he robbed and killed Jack, then turned himself in to a strong Catholic lawyer. "The boy was protecting his virginity," his counsel argued in court. Well, the boy got off with a slap on the wrist and a trip out of town. Dobbins's mother . . . didn't pursue it because she was embarrassed and hurt. She just wanted it swept under the rug and forgotten about. I'll never forget my mamma saying at the time, "If that would have been you, I would have been there fightin' like a wet hen for justice." But, you know, back then the gay community didn't get justice; we didn't expect it. Then, gay people were often robbed and too embarrassed to report it. If they did report it, the person who was robbed was victimized again by the system.

Gordon was received politely and with interest into Charleston's gay community. "When he first came, everyone accepted him," Camden remembers. Yet this initial enchantment and hospitality quickly turned to disgust and social ostracism. Camden, who had lived around the corner from Gordon, recalls:

We saw him often, but he was *not* in our group. He was at my house several times, but I don't think I ever entertained him. When he first moved here, Joe brought him along to our beach house. He was a small-framed, very effeminate guy with a very thick English accent. At the beginning, the people connected with historic Ansonborough included him. But as soon as it got out what was going on—with all the blacks he entertained—that was the end of it! He would always be with a group of black, screaming queens. Charleston people would have nothing to do with him. He was an insult to the gay community; we were *never* friends.

Nicky first met him at the bookstore where Gordon was promoting one of his biographies. He says that Gordon "patrolled Meeting Street at night. He loved black men almost as much as he liked old ladies with money"—to which Hall retorts: "Sheer poppycock! I didn't even promote a book in Charleston until 1993."

While Hall has long resented those who wrongly labeled him homosexual or spread rumors, he has no animosity toward homosexuals and has long had "homosexual friends." When Gordon was a child, "my mother had a lesbian cousin. We never ever rejected persons like that. In England we just accepted that part of her." In Charleston, as Hall acknowledged, "there were so many gay people that it was hard not to know them. In the arts you're always going to come across gay people and they have a perfect right to their way of life." He also observed other relationships: "On the surface you would know a man and his wife, but you would also know about the other attachment. . . . In England, I grew up in that atmosphere with Vita Sackville-West and her husband, Harold Nicolson—two people who couldn't be more in love—going their separate ways with their sexual preference."

Jeremy Morrow first met Gordon through a man from a prominent Charleston family who "spoke big, but wasn't moneyed." (Jeremy was quick to add: "Gordon did both.") For Jeremy, Gordon Langley Hall was a titillating embarrassment yet, unlike Nicky and Billy, he longed to enter Gordon's social circle. With a barely disguised voice of bitterness, Jeremy snaps, "I wasn't a celebrity! That was important for Gordon. He loved to boast of his friendship with famous or well-connected people."

Jeremy contented himself with eyeing the Society Street residence from a distance and gossiping with "a black male (maybe mixed)—funny, feminine, flaming—who worked for Gordon." Jeremy learned "about Gordon falling down stairs, wearing strange clothes, talking in a feminine voice, menstruating, and just being out-and-out flamboyant."

From Hall's perspective it was his respect for blacks that underlay the antipathy of his Ansonborough neighbors:

> In certain matters I was, perhaps, too liberal for Charleston. For instance, I got into trouble when I wanted to pay my cook her Social Security and went up to the Federal Building with her and arranged it. Some of my neighbors said I should have left "well enough alone, because you are creating a precedent." I just thought I was obeying the law! In the gay community, Joe hated black people! The stories told about me are vicious with no foundation in fact: The black male referred to by Jeremy never worked for me; I never cruised King Street . . . and I had friends who were not well-to-do or famous, such as the poor old cobbler on King Street.

Though the nature of Gordon's relationship with local blacks is contested, no one disputes that these relationships were often on an equal footing. Carson McCullers and her sister, Rita Smith, once visited the Joseph Johnson House. Smith later described how "a young Negro man met them at the door, invited them in, mixed drinks, served them." The man then "took his own off the tray and sat down to join in the conversation. . . . Carson loved the story and delighted in hearing further evidence that fact is often much better than fantasy, but seldom believed unless cloaked in fiction."[11]

McCullers's biographer, Virginia Carr, continued the story:

> Always more of an observer than a participant, Carson had little to say to Hall throughout the evening. But just as [she and her escort] were about to leave, she turned suddenly toward the young man and said, "I want to talk to the *child* (referring to Hall). Please leave us together for a few minutes." Alone with the shy, rather diffident man who now sat beside her, Carson studied him closely without speaking. Then, with a bit of a smile, she said gently, "You're really a little girl." Hall looked at her, then nodded.[12]

Changing Times, Changing Bodies

By 1966 Gordon was tiring of social life and "decided to retire from Charleston society. . . . Being an author I could always say that when I worked I liked to shut myself away from the world." As he began his newest biography of Lady Bird Johnson, Gordon began to feel physically different: "A sort of lethargy had crept into my life. Both body and mind seemed tired; they craved for rest. To add to my discomfort there were strange sensations in my breasts, as if, deep down, some seed long dormant was stirring." Then, early one morning, Gordon woke up in a pool of blood. His housekeeper "panicked and called an ambulance that rushed me to the hospital. My secret was out! The gynecologist came in and said, 'I guess you know what I am going to tell you. There is a vaginal tract that is blocked and if it is not put right, you will not live out the year.' So, you see, I really had no choice."

Gordon visited a local physician, social activist, and friend, Dr. Duncan Pringle. Her family had long been prominent in Charleston society. Her grandfather owned the South Carolina and Pacific Railroad and a cotton mill; her father was a local banker; her mother was called a "communist" and a "nigger lover." Duncan's sister, Margarita Childs, praises Duncan's efforts in providing medical care to Charleston blacks: "Back then, the white doctors would always say that the white patients wouldn't like it if they had blacks in the same waiting room and they couldn't afford two rooms." Duncan encouraged Gordon to meet Margarita, who would remember Gordon as a "nonstop talker."

Contrary to the rumors circulating within the homosexual community, Hall discloses, "even after the age of puberty I was like a vegetable . . . I felt no sensual sensations at all in the sex organs as they were." On Duncan's recommendation, Gordon visited the Medical College of Charleston, where a physician

> Told me that I was a "transsexual." I can honestly say that I had never heard the word. Of course I had heard of sex changes. The Christine Jorgenson story was universal. . . . I asked [him] exactly what a transsexual was. He explained that although I was not normal in the sense that other men or women might be normal, neither was I "a homosexual." This latter was interesting, for although I had never felt at ease with so-called normal people, neither had I been happy in the company of the other kind.

Through the medical college, he learned of the newly established Gender Identity Clinic staffed by a team of doctors at Johns Hopkins University. Formed in 1966, the clinic used surgical techniques developed during the world wars and the clinical procedures employed by the endocrinologist Harry Benjamin.[13]

Though themselves sexual outsiders, Charleston homosexuals exuded the self-hatred and inferiority epitomized in maimed Southern homosexual characters like John Singer, the deaf-mute in *The Heart Is a Lonely Hunter,* or Cousin Lymon, the hunchback in *The Ballad of the Sad Café.* Within this culture, the maimed image of the "transvestite" was that of either a latent homosexual or a person "trapped in the wrong body." The taunts and torments that Gordon endured reflected the confusion of transsexuality with repressed homosexual tendencies and the internalized homophobia endemic to the times.[14]

At the age of thirty, having had no opportunity for corrective surgery when he was growing up, Gordon traveled to Baltimore for a first consultation. A week-long session of physical examinations followed two months later, in December 1967. During this second visit, he met with prominent doctors, including psychiatrist John Money. Revealing that he had never engaged in sexual intercourse, Gordon quoted his long-admired acquaintance Bette Davis: "The romance when mind meets mind—is quite as exciting as when boy meets girl."

Gordon began growing his hair long (showing off his tight, natural curls well before such a style had become fashionable in the South), taking prescribed hormone tablets, and dressing as a woman. When Jeremy Morrow asked about it, Gordon matter-of-factly replied, "I'm having a sex change." Morrow remembers: "Well, we all but fainted. We had never heard of such a thing! He said it was a 'medical necessity'; that was bullshit!"

Not surprisingly, Gordon secluded himself. Walled behind the well-manicured green and white garden dedicated to the memory of Vita Sackville-West, he was attended to by Mr. James, the butler, Viola, the housekeeper, and Irene, the cook. Ignoring the gossip among the well-heeled Charleston elite as well as the homosexual community, Gordon found himself thinking about men and, in particular, one prominent gentleman. "My doctors were glad to know that, where the now opposite sex was concerned, I was having normal reactions. Unmarried, he would have been a marvelous catch. As his wife I would one day have been chatelaine of one of the most famed historic mansions in the city. I might even have made the exclusive St. Cecilia's Ball."

Finally, in the fall of 1968, Gordon took the final step—gender reassignment surgery. Waiting for the bandages to be removed, he/she patiently edited a manuscript on Mary Todd Lincoln and sewed.

Returning to Charleston in October as a 102-pound brunette, Dawn Pepita Hall "knew now that Gordon was truly dead. What he had tried to do, all the years of frustration and worry, and fighting to prove that he was something that he was not, were over. To the new Dawn, Gordon was at peace."

Love at First Sight

Hall was welcomed back into the bosom of the ladies of the Confederacy as Dawn. "It really didn't faze Charleston all that much. I had a lot of money then and a very good family background. They were more worried about who they would marry me off to."

Hall remained the object of humor, innuendo, and gossip, however. There were rumors, which she now confirms, of an affair with one prominent man in Charleston society who jumped the fence for nocturnal visits. Such rumors—according to Ann Leland spread by Hall herself—later found their way into a national weekly tabloid: "Before Dawn married . . . she was the mistress of one of Charleston's leading white aristocrats, a married man with children. This guy was like the study in the old Hathaway shirt ads—tall, dignified, dashing, gray-of-temple, the quintessence of courtly grooviness, Southern style."[15]

There was also a rumor that Dawn was to marry a Mr. Simmons, whom Gordon had met at a party held at one of the Battery mansions. South-of-Broad attitudes quickly changed, however, as Dawn announced her engagement to another Mr. Simmons—a local mechanic, sometime shrimper, amateur sculptor, and, by that time, her "chauffeur," John-Paul Simmons—who also happened to be "a Negro."

> She is rich, he is poor. She is an intellectual and introvert. He is a boisterous and exuberant extrovert. He lives by his body, she by her mind. He is young, she is almost ten years his senior. He is a healthy heterosexual, she until their marriage had been sexually totally inexperienced.[16]

Dawn's biographer, Dena Crane, elaborated:

> Dawn taught John-Paul about art and ideas, antiques and life. . . . John-Paul taught Dawn about affection, spontaneity, adventure and uninhibited perception. Dawn saw John-Paul as an equal and encouraged his creativity. John-Paul saw Dawn as a woman with charm and grace and an uncanny humor.[17]

Dawn—a name chosen by her beau—first met John-Paul midway through the sex reassignment process. He knocked at Gordon's door one evening to escort Irene, the cook, on a date; she had already departed. Within a matter of days, John-Paul had "forced entry into the house dressed in dirty old overalls, with his mechanic's cap over his eyes and his arms full of flowers. He had bought every flower he could find. He told me, 'I'll never leave you again.' "[18]

With both characterizing the meeting as "love at first sight," their relationship progressed. John-Paul "became an integral part" of Hall's path toward womanhood. Describing John-Paul to her father, Jack Copper, Dawn later wrote, "You will like John-Paul as he is very clever with cars and is a natural born mechanic like yourself. . . . He is a rough diamond but his heart is in the right place and he is very good to me."[19]

It was not an easy relationship, however, as evidenced by the letter penned to John-Paul from his older brother, Alex:

> Why is it Johnnie that [you're] still under the impression that you are sixteen years old? . . . The objective of this letter my bro is to bring to your attention the damage you are doing to yourself and to those who love you very much.

...If you hang around those places that's quite all right. ...If you love her [Dawn], man, show more concern and consideration for her safety and well being. ...Those people (your so called friends) are all parasites exploiting you. ...They see that you've got a little something that's why they befriend you. ...You're not even married yet and already you've violated one of the major codes by dealing in promiscuity. Listen, if [that] is all you have to offer this sweet girl, you'd be doing yourself and the family and her a great favor by just leaving her. ... [20]

During Dawn's recovery, she received her first love letter from John-Paul, which read in part, "I love you even though I may not act like I do sometimes. I didn't realize it until you left me. I miss you very much and hope that you will be coming home to me soon."

Wedding Bell Blues

As word of the engagement spread among the Charleston elite, a group of concerned ladies of the Confederacy visited the Johnson mansion. One brought an apple pie for Dawn and a watermelon for John-Paul. Another warned Dawn that if the marriage took place, she would find herself on the "cooling couch" (a bed or table on which the deceased is laid to air out). A third asked Dawn to consider the example of another local socialite with a fondness for the other color: "She fell in love with a nigger, but she married one of her own kind and they've all lived together for years in the old family mansion."[21] To which Dawn replied, "A man worth lying down with is worth standing up with."

Those within the homosexual community acquainted with Gordon were equally upset with Dawn's open relationship. "Back then," Morrow states, "gay men did not *date* blacks, and we certainly didn't 'marry' them. Sex between black and white men was *always* behind closed doors."

Not surprisingly, as the entire affair occurred in the midst of the civil rights movement, it attracted media attention.[22] Stories and photographs appeared in national and international magazines, tabloids, and newspapers ranging from *News of the World* to the *National Insider*. A *Time* article read: "Last week ... Hall, who claims to be 31 (other sources suggest he is 39), revealed an idiosyncrasy that Charleston could hardly ignore ... she was going to marry a 22-year-old Negro garage mechanic."[23]

According to Hall these stories were instigated by a spurned lover, seeking revenge, and Jack Leland, who served as his "henchman ... whose persecution lasted for years": "My engagement photograph was stolen from my living room at 56 Society on the Tuesday and appeared on the front page of London's *News of the World* on the following Sunday. Only someone with access to the media news services could have promoted it so quickly with the headline, 'Royal Biographer Marries Her Butler.'"

Such unwelcome publicity stirred others to action: "Mail arrived by the sackful at the mansion on Society Street, some letters kind and some vicious. I had fifteen Bibles from born-again Christians and a rather nice leather-bound copy of the Koran from Saudi Arabia. . . . 'Her Majesty, the Queen, was sympathetic,' wrote Mother [Dame Rutherford]. Joan Crawford spoke up for me. 'The heart knows why,' she told Mother, at the same time sending me a bunch of yellow roses. . . . "

Quickly dropped from Charleston's party lists and social registry, Dawn was abandoned by her "friends";[24] her enemies threatened to bomb the Shiloh African Methodist Episcopal (A.M.E.) Church, where the ceremony was scheduled to take place. On January 22, 1969, South Carolina's first mixed marriage occurred—the *News and Courier* placed the wedding announcement in the obituary section.

Because of the threats against the A.M.E. Church, the wedding ceremony was held in the lower drawing room at the Joseph Johnson House. After the area was checked for bombs, a group of twenty-five guests and journalists crowded into a small Victorian parlor to view the historic ceremony. ("The street was packed," reminisced Dawn, "their bodies rippling like waves.") Dawn descended the huge staircase wearing silver earrings, two ropes of pearls, a white gown of candlelight lace with a twelve-foot train held by two children, escorted by her father-in-law. The voice of Andy Williams sang the "Battle Hymn of the Republic" in the background as three black bridesmaids led the procession. During the ceremony Dawn's veil slipped several times (her mother-in-law fiddled with it repeatedly) as the black minister stumbled over his words, repeating entire paragraphs of the vows. The reception was held at the Brooks Hotel—which burned to the ground shortly afterward.

Jeremy Morrow was not invited to the wedding. Although Jack Leland attended, Ann later recalled, "Jack couldn't write about it for the *News and Courier* but he sold many stories to other papers"—articles that Dawn would later denounce.

Upon learning that Dawn Simmons had been denied a proper church wedding, Dame Rutherford spoke with the archbishop of Canterbury to arrange a Church of England ceremony. At the twelfth-century St. Clements Church in Hastings, Dawn wore "a gold brocade with leg of mutton sleeves and an enormous train of gold velvet. The veil was kept in place by Mother's [Dame Rutherford] real diamond tiara, which had been skillfully 'woven' into my hair by Princess Margaret's own hairdresser. . . . " As she entered the church, the congregation rose to sing "O Perfect Love."

Harassment intensified during the months following the marriage. Windows of their mansion were smashed. Three shots were fired at John-Paul. Dawn was run down by an unknown driver on Anson Street and her left shoulder was injured. The telephone rang incessantly with crank calls: One caller vowed, "Dawn, I'll kill you"; another warned Dawn that John-Paul was "consorting with other women"; several callers sought Dawn for a 1960s version of phone sex. Dawn's Doberman pinscher, Charley, was poisoned, and their basset hound, Samantha, became a hit-and-run victim. These and other incidents led Dawn to query, "Am I in the middle of one of those Tennessee Williams plays where the innocent young man is literally destroyed by a parody of Southern justice?"

Foreclosure, Delivery, and Departure

Dawn's struggle occurred within a larger conflict over civil rights, known in South Carolina as the "Charleston Movement." Although race relations were considered good by Southern standards, the underlying racial tension erupted during this time. March 1969 marked what the *New York Times* characterized as "the country's tensest civil rights struggle": the beginning of a 100-day-plus strike of 400 predominantly black female hospital workers. As days turned into weeks, Governor Robert McNair ordered 5,000 armed National Guard troops to Charleston, where they remained to enforce curfew until the midsummer settlement.[25]

During the height of the conflict, the A.M.E. Emanuel Church hosted a meeting at which Rev. Ralph Abernathy, Andrew Young, and Coretta Scott King addressed the crowd. In violation of curfew, a night march was held during which hundreds of demonstrators—led by Rev. Abernathy—were arrested and detained.

> The strike had divided the white community. There had been fear abroad in Charleston during the dark nights of the curfew. Some were reminded of a much earlier era. The Charleston poetess Alice Cabiness wrote: "merchants lounging in doorways cursing ease, grouping angrily . . . patrolling windows, counting guardsmen going by / Denmark Vesey smiles with pleasure from another country / black shadows on the empty streets undo the handshakes of my friends."[26]

Dawn and John-Paul ventured out into the city on that fateful evening:

> I had a craving for pigs' feet and chocolate. But you could only get it in the colored's quarter of Charleston. There was a nine o'clock curfew. We were on the way back when the National Guard appeared not quite at nine o'clock. They chased us right up to our property at 56 Society Street and arrested us at bayonet. They took us to the city jail, where they beat us. The last time I saw John-Paul they were taking him upstairs with his hands and face all bloody. They took me into a cell—I can see the roaches crawling up the wall even now—where they kept my shoes. I had to stand on the bed to get away from all of the things crawling on the floor. But I pulled myself together and got my lawyer, who bailed us out. We appeared in court the next morning. Several black men

were in their best Sunday churchgoing jackets. The judge dismissed our case because there was no case. Well, those men threw down their jackets for us to walk on—a very rare experience.

In the midst of all of these controversies, Richia Atkinson Barloga, one of the few local aristocrats who had not abandoned Dawn, was selling her home on Gibbes Street, located South-of-Broad. She arranged for her real estate agent to put a clause in the agreement that allowed Dawn first choice on the property. The thought that Dawn and her Negro husband would take up residence at the epicenter of Charleston society drove one Southern gentleman to offer the couple $5,000 *not* to move into the Gibbes Street home.

About this time, according to Hall, a group of wealthy Charlestonians conspired to remove Dawn from Charleston. With Dawn unable to receive money from Britain because of a mail strike, the local bank foreclosed on the mortgage secured by the house held for the former kitchen quarters (now a gallery) adjacent to the main house. As Dawn recollects: "My lawyer told me that he had never known so rushed a foreclosure. At the last minute, an old friend [Richia] stepped in to say she would pay off the mortgage in full. . . . Unfortunately, she literally disappeared. . . . She had been drugged and taken by a man to a motel . . . emerging ten days later when our home had been sold for a pittance . . . on the steps of the courthouse where so many of my husband's ancestors had also been." With less than twelve hours to leave the mansion, furniture and artwork set on the porch, John-Paul returned to his mother, and Dawn left with Jackie, her German shepherd, for a nearby hotel.

After they resettled in a house on Thomas Street, in one of the poorest areas of Charleston, Dawn's "pregnancy" became the next much-talked-about affair in the long saga of Gordon Langley Hall. The skepticism felt in 1970 was expressed twenty years later by several people who questioned Mrs. Simmons's authenticity as a "real woman": One reader of the black-owned *Charleston Chronicle* wrote to the paper's editor:

> The late Anna Montgomery, who worked at a baby store on King Street, said that he [Gordon] came into the store to make a purchase, and that the women were all laughing, because while looking like a pregnant woman, he forgot to tie down the strings of a pillow case stuffed with cotton. . . . Two months later Gordon or Dawn was seen pushing a baby carriage around town. There was a baby in the carriage, but, isn't Mrs. Simmons supposed to be white or British? The baby that several people saw was as black as ten midnights, not saying that dark skin children are not beautiful gifts from God, but . . .[27]

Characterizing the skin comment as "wicked," Dawn graciously observes: "I can only smile at the pillow stories. I did use cotton wool pads at one point because of the burning in the breasts."

On October 16, 1971, their daughter, Natasha Marginell Manigault Simmons, was born in a Philadelphia hospital that Dawn entered under an assumed name. After returning to Charleston, Dawn often strolled along Charleston's streets with Natasha in an "old-fashioned British baby carriage (pram) just like the one that the Queen had for Prince Charles." Yet Dawn and John-Paul's presence in Charleston was no less explosive in the years following the birth. John-Paul was hung in effigy on Society Street. Anthony Dawson, British actor, longtime friend, and Natasha's godfather, strongly urged Dawn to "consider moving out of that atmosphere in Charleston. It is not a good atmosphere to bring up a child. Now that you are getting so much publicity moving to a 'more civilised part of the United States' can do a lot to make look ridiculous and shameful and uncivilised the behaviour of those people."[28]

Dawn and John-Paul's explosive relationship behind the Society Street walls was less public. His frequent bouts with alcohol and related psychological problems were sometimes too much for even Dawn to bear. Finally she departed for England with her daughter Natasha. Her letters to John-Paul from Europe reveal a dark, turbulent relationship, which, a generation later, is recognized as battered-wife syndrome:

> I am not upset with you as I know you were not yourself the other night. . . . For weeks you have known that you could continue with the house, that the payment only worked out to 25 dollars a week. I have no money left. You know that and you destroyed all of my work when I couldn't give you $30. . . . The British Consul sent you papers six weeks ago so that you could work in England. You are a good mechanic and you know that Cousin Peter has a garage. . . . I shall never stop you from seeing Baby as I love you and have always loved you. Nobody would love a man who had tried to kill them several times, gave them 45 stitches in their face, broke their nose and cheekbone and ruined the eyesight . . . but I never ever shut the door against you. . . . [29]

A few of Dawn's Charleston friends were aware that the strain in the relationship was largely a result of John-Paul's illness. In one letter to Dawn during her stay in England, Robert Holmes relayed that "the grocery store was visited last week by JPS, your husband and the father of your child, accompanied by several dogs. Nurse Mary was shocked by his appearance: nothing but skin and bone with great pouches beneath his eyes."[30]

As disturbing as these stories and John-Paul's treatment of Dawn had been, she remained faithful and hopeful. Her unflagging love and his deteriorating condition brought Dawn back across the ocean the following autumn into the sometimes loving and often hurtful arms of John-Paul.

A Charleston Footnote

During the summer of 1974 John-Paul, Dawn, and Natasha moved north of the Mason-Dixon line and rented a run-down, ten-room, eighteenth-century brown stuccoed mansion in the Catskills. With their promises to re-store the home (it was the site of President Martin Van Buren's marriage ceremony), the community of 8,000 embraced them. The *New York Times* published a story under the title, "Transsexual Starting New Life in Catskills," and a controversial follow-up story summarized the chain of events from summer to winter:

> Today, the house is an empty wreck. The owner has sued for $800 in rent. As of last week, the Simonses [*sic*] were on welfare, living in a local motel. . . . [A] Catskill realty man who was handling the sale of the house, says the couple put down a $200 binder. Cash from the book that Mrs. Simmons was reported to be writing did not materialize. With no money for fuel, the family moved out "in the dead of winter" . . . and the pipes froze and burst, flooding the premises.[31]

Once again, Dawn's version is different. "The man who gave the *New York Times* the 'welfare' news was later jailed for stealing from Social Services."

Shortly thereafter, John-Paul abandoned Dawn for the fifth time. Living in a run-down Catskills motel, she contemplated divorce.[32] Though she de-parted from the motel, she would not divorce John-Paul. In Hudson, New York, Dawn taught art at the Catholic school, became secretary and histo-rian of the Presbyterian Women's Association, and served as secretary of the local Mental Health Association. In the words of Dawn's biographer: "Her writing career was reduced to writing for *The National Enquirer*. She spent seven years in hunger, isolation, and poverty but never thought of herself as poor. She would collect broken objects and flowers and decorate her room with character and style. She devoted her life to Natasha and to giving her everything that money couldn't buy."[33]

Celebrating their twenty-fifth wedding anniversary, she remains faithful to the rugged shrimper whose fateful knock on her Society Street door changed her life. Dawn speaks frequently with John-Paul by telephone and makes occasional visits to the mental health complex at which he resided throughout much of their marriage. "I would never desert him," empha-sizes Dawn. "I always see that he has clothes, pocket money, and every-thing he needs."

Dawn's thoughts, though, often return to the Holy City. "When I am lonely I dream of Charleston, of the congregation at Shiloh A.M.E., of a winter wind whistling through the palmettos, and of Rosabelle Waite's good collard greens." Dawn is now a grandmother. Natasha, named after the heroine in *War and Peace,* has two children, Damian and Tamara Miquel. Reflecting on her life, Dawn says: "It has not been an easy life. . . . I came from a small village in England where no black people lived. I was caught up in something I really didn't understand. . . . Sometimes I think it would have been best had John-Paul never met or wanted me. He probably would have lived out his life in his cabin on Johns Island with his pig, Frances, fishing and hunting. It was so sad what happened."

But a moment later Dawn's hopefulness returns when she recalls how the new owners of her old Society Street house had "taken me out to the garden and offered to give me back the animals' tombstones, which had all been cleaned. That was a great healing. If you wait long enough, it all comes out all right in the end."

6

The Blue Fairy and the Making of a New Activist Generation

JACK WAS BORN DURING THE YEAR OF THE TIGER, 1938. Mary Haliday Finlayson and John Richard Nichols were high school sweethearts. "Mom was a Scottish-American beauty and Dad was a top-notch high school athlete. At the time of my birth he was in training with the Chicago White Sox, but he returned to Washington to get a 'responsible' job as a special agent for the FBI."

Jack remembers the Washington of the 1940s and 1950s as "a genteel place where even a child of twelve could get on the bus, go downtown, walk about, and feel safe. It was clean, beautiful, tree-lined streets with wide avenues and the architecture to go with it. It was full of Southerners. Back then Washington was as Southern as Atlanta is now—if not more so. It attracted all of the people from the South who saw it as the first big city they could go to."

When Jack was three years old his parents separated and he went to live with his immigrant maternal grandparents (Nana and Poppop) in nearby Chevy Chase, Maryland. "Poppop was a Highlander; Nana, a Lowlander. Poppop had learned to read plans and began building." Jack's grandmother, Euphemia Renwick, and her sister, Agnes, married Jack's grandfather, Murdoch Graham Finlayson, and his brother, John Finlayson, in a 1914 double wedding. They raised their families side by side as they prospered as builders.

Nana and Poppop had created a happy fireside clime, a place where reason-
ableness triumphed over petty force, where poetry was a monarch, and where
two glamorous sisters (Mom and her sister Jean) as well as their handsome
brother (Uncle Graham) brought home the zest of the 1940s. Uncle Graham
practiced jitterbugging at the living room mirror. I sat in a chair and watched,
being introduced to Glenn Miller, Helen O'Connell, Bob Eberly, Tommy
Dorsey, Benny Goodman, Harry James, Red Nichols, and, of course, the Andrews Sisters.

Jack's value system, like his grandfather's, was rooted in poetry. Murdoch was for many years president of the St. Andrew Society, a Scottish fra-
ternal order. Jack reminisced:

It was through Robert Burns that Poppop tenderly gave me the best of the
Scotland he loved. . . . He wielded Burns like some unobtrusive patriarch who
was satisfied to leave advice-giving to others if only he could first quote the
poet aloud. Burns's portrait hung above our dining room sideboard. Sitting in
my dining room chair, I faced the great poet daily. Poppop was never more
bliss-filled than when giving a Burns recitation, something he did at the conclusion of every family discussion.

He was six feet tall and still sported tufts of those blond curls which had
once covered his entire head. His eyes were light blue, his voice deep. He'd
stand and wave his arms about with the proud, dramatic flair of a nineteenth-
century orator, zapping me unaware with attitudes delivered in a gentle
brogue.

From Poppop I learned that the constant repetition of themes laden with
values turns those values into one's marrow. One becomes what one absorbs.
From his love for Burns I absorbed a disdain for hierarchy and status. Burns's
songs laughed at lords and nobles, celebrating instead the life of the common
person. The poet had believed, and Poppop tirelessly communicated, that an
honest man is far preferable to a rich one. Burns was extraordinarily conscious
of universal welfare, worrying even about the plight of a field mouse.

As a four-year-old, Jack, already tall for his age, was inflicted with
whooping cough. The family doctor recommended a stay in Florida. He
and his mother traveled on the train, the Silver Meteor: "Miami Beach in
those days was exquisite. We lived in a large guest house with Spanish, red-
tiled roof and beautiful gardens. I remember the exotica of Florida, like the
coconuts that you could break open and actually drink coconut milk from
the shell."

When they returned to Washington, Jack's fondness for exotica began to
extend beyond plants:

I took first to Dorothy Lamour, draped in her South Sea island sarong. I listened to a song called "Moonlight and Shadows," recalling the palm trees and
coconuts I'd found so interesting when I was four. I purchased recordings with
dramatic Latin tempos, starting with the campy "Temptation" and graduating

to "Bolero" and "Malagueña," the latter which I learned to play by ear on the piano. Other exotic women to whom I took a shine included Hedy Lamarr (*Strange Woman*) and Helen Gahagan (*She*). Then I began to dote on Arabian Nights films, listening to Oriental themes, thinking them wonderfully distinctive. The art of the belly dancer caught my eye. I was turned into an incorrigible romantic by the great black-and-white film dramas. I swooned over their musical scores, taking quickly to Bette Davis, Joan Crawford, Ruth Roman, Ida Lupino, Barbara Stanwyck, Vivian Leigh, and Jennifer Jones.

But for Jack the most influential icon of popular culture was from the film *Pinocchio*, the songs of which would complement the poems of Burns, "who lifted a lawless leg upon Meg"—and later Whitman, who "shared the midnight orgies of young men." An exotic cartoon fantasy character easily outdistanced flesh-and-blood actresses:

My goddess was the Blue Fairy. She explained to Pinocchio the essentials of what it means to be a "real boy": to be kind, to be truthful, to be honest, and to help others. Although the film premiered in 1941, it was 1944, when I was six, that I first saw it. I was just old enough to be captivated by her beauty. Electrified, in fact. She was to become a long-lasting childhood obsession. I got the record album and took it home. Fantasizing about Fairyland, which, I supposed, must be something like the Chevy Chase Country Club golf course, I traced her breasts over and over again on tracing paper. Identifying with the Blue Fairy, a stick for my wand, I traversed the golf course, aflame with magic.

The songs on the 78-rpm *Pinocchio* album served as the foundation for my first self-chosen attitudes. I listened to the Blue Fairy's theme, "When You Wish upon a Star." It was essentially my hymn:

> *If your heart is in your dream*
> *no request is too extreme. . . .*

After World War II, Jack's parents' separation was finalized into a divorce:

It didn't occur to me to ask why they weren't living together after Dad's homecoming from New Guinea. The atmosphere of calm and civility in my grandparents' house never made me think of anywhere else as home, and I accepted Dad's Sunday visits as within the natural order. He took me to the movies in downtown Washington. We went often to the Capitol Theatre on F Street, a cinema which featured colorful Saturday afternoon stage shows.

His father moved to New Jersey, working out of the FBI's Philadelphia office, and married again in 1948. This was a time of transition for Jack and his feelings toward his father:

He'd felt unnecessarily guilty at having divorced Mom and, as a strict Methodist, he was sure God's wrath would descend if he should even contemplate such a "sin" again. I began to realize that Dad was a country bumpkin, an athlete whose body was much better coordinated than his brain. He thought too highly of persons in authority and, in fact, was cowed by the lunatic ravings of his local Methodist parson.

Meanwhile Jack's mother (who had been working for IBM as its Washington, D.C., personnel director and later as a systems analyst) was enjoying a long-distance romance with a Philadelphia gentleman.

> Photographs taken of me around this time show me as introspective but determined. Mom, who'd always believed in the power of positive dressing, sometimes made me put aside my play clothes to don my "Sunday-go-to-meeting" duds in order to please her camera's eye. She captured me, usually with my dog, Cinder, looking every inch like a child of privilege, which, of course, I was.

After his dad's marriage, father and son saw less of each other. When they met it was more often for lectures and lessons than fun and frivolity:

> When I went on outings with Dad, he spent time trying to impose his awkward concepts of masculine deportment on me, giving me "butch" lessons: how to walk like a real man, how to talk like a real man, and how to be, if possible, as much like him as nature would allow. His concern was extreme. He feared I might become one of the *unthinkables*, which, not surprisingly, I did.

As Jack was being warned about the "unthinkables," a thirty-eight-year-old Californian union organizer and Communist Party member was supporting Progressive candidate Henry Wallace. At an August beer bust hosted by gay men at the University of Southern California, discussion turned to politics and the 1948 presidential campaign. Youthful idealism and alcohol sparked the speculative chatter: "Would the Progressive platform include a sexual privacy plank in return for homosexual support?" "Could homosexuals be organized politically?" Though "Bachelors for Wallace" never materialized, the prospect of organizing homosexuals galvanized Harry Hay. Under the Scottish pseudonym Eann MacDonald, Hay drafted the first of three proposals for "Bachelors Anonymous" and allied organizations of the "International Spinsters' Orders" and "Well-Wishers Auxiliaries." Though rudimentary in outline, these proposals became the basis for the unthinkable: a homosexual organization whose purposes were to unify, educate, and lead "the whole mass of social deviates."[1]

Mona Lisa

At the age of twelve, Jack's fascination for exotica found a new expression when on a sunny afternoon he met Feredoon:

His father, a diplomat, was in the service of the Shah of Iran. I felt no physical attraction to Feredoon, but he beguiled me in a way I'd never thought possible. He was the first male of my age to show me how two boys can experience a passionate platonic love. He was more emotional than any of my American friends.

He would kiss me full on the lips right in front of his mother and father saying "I love you." Hugging me close, he would whisper in my ear: "I never want to be apart from you. I wish you could come to live with me in Iran forever as my brother, which you will always be even if we're apart."

Feredoon introduced me to the children of other Iranian diplomats, and suddenly I had for my friends the aunts, uncles, nephews, nieces, and cousins of the Shah. In their homes I ate Persian sweets, listened to Persian poetry, and lay dreaming on luxurious Persian carpets, imagining how they might take me across the skylines of the Orient. On these same carpets I was free to collapse with male friends and they'd kiss me tenderly about my face, whispering their allegiances.

Upon returning from a two-week Florida vacation, Jack was stunned to learn that the Iranian government had ordered Feredoon's family to return to Tehran. With only a month before the departure of Feredoon and his sister, Banoo, Jack tried to keep up the threesome's spirits:

On the radio a new song, "Mona Lisa," played and replayed, becoming representative to me of that brief, happy season when we frolicked through the best of times before the long miles would come forever between us. It was a time of calm and simplicity in America, which, though the Korean War had begun, seemed mesmerized by Nat King Cole's velvet voice. I bought a copy of "Mona Lisa" and gave it to Banoo. We had a tearful good-bye. Feredoon held me, kissing my face, telling me to hide in his trunk and return to Iran with him. Banoo promised to write, a promise she kept. As they drove away, my heart sank.

As Jack faced this new emptiness in his life, his mother longed to shorten the miles between her and her longtime fiancé. In 1951 she moved with Jack to Ardmore, a Philadelphia suburb on the Main Line:

In the mornings Mom took the Paoli local to her downtown Philadelphia office while I walked a block and a half to school. Ardmore offered an abundance of superpatriotism, conservatism, and devotion to duty. While Senator Joseph McCarthy fumed in Washington about perverts and commies, Ardmore goose-stepped accordingly.

Ardmore's junior high was managed, at every level, by a highly respected principal, Mr. Edward G. Snow. Mr. Snow, who had snow-white hair, came equipped with a booming voice and was the proudest evangelist I ever knew when it came to crass worship of the Stars and Stripes. He was the Billy Sunday of war glory, frightening every male child with grim prophecies of their coming places in combat, explaining that only a love of country would carry them through hell.

As Jack struggled at Ardmore, a group of seven men—the "Fifth Order"—was initiating the first group of guild leaders at a Los Angeles home. In a room bathed in candlelight, the group, ringed together with hands clasped, pledged: "We are sworn that no boy or girl, approaching the maelstrom of deviation, need make that crossing alone, afraid and in the dark ever again."[2]

It had been three years since Harry Hay had first envisioned such an organization. A year earlier, in August 1950, Hay, accompanied by a gay man he had recently met at the Lester Horton Dance Theatre, began cruising the gay beach near Los Angeles seeking recruits. During the next few months they collected 500 signatures on a petition opposing the outbreak of hostilities in Korea. In the process of explaining the petition, the two organizers discussed the government's crackdown on homosexuals and the importance of banding together. In November Hay shared his now thrice-revised proposal for "Bachelors Anonymous" with two students from his labor school class. The following weekend one of them telephoned Hay; five men soon gathered at Hay's home ready to implement his proposal.

From the list of 500 signatures, those who had expressed an interest in organizing were soon contacted, and the first semipublic discussion groups were formed. While few attended and fewer returned, the core group of five was soon expanded to seven, becoming the Fifth Order. During the winter of 1951 the organizational structure emerged.

The organization's name was suggested by James Gruber, an ex-serviceman attending Occidental College. He remembered listening in awe to a discussion of the *Société Mattachine* during one of the Fifth Order's semipublic meetings. Hay later described to historian Jonathan Katz the purpose of these French medieval groups:

> These societies, lifelong secret fraternities of unmarried townsmen who never performed in public unmasked, were dedicated to going out into the countryside and conducting dances and rituals during the Feast of Fools, at the Vernal Equinox. Sometimes these dance rituals, or masques, were peasant protests against oppression—with the maskers, in the people's name, receiving the brunt of a given lord's vicious retaliation.[3]

In Harry Hay's biography, Hay amplified on the society's origin and purpose: "The Mattachine troupes conveyed vital information to the oppressed in the countryside of 13th–15th century France. . . . I hoped that such a society of modern homosexual men, living in disguise in 20th century America, could do similarly. . . . "[4]

Ratified in April 1951, the Mattachine Society borrowed from the secretive structures of the Freemasons and the communists. With the organization steeped in Marxism, social analysis triumphed over psychoanalysis. Group discussion leaders (referred to as the First Order) were organized into guilds that met together in sessions led by a Fifth Order member who discussed how to foster critical consciousness, the nature of a "homosexual culture," and appropriate collective actions. First Order members led discussion groups that allowed members to remain anonymous while forming a honeycombed structure in which few identities were known outside a particular guild.

Victories

Nineteen fifty-two was a year of growth for both the yearling Jack Nichols and the fledgling Mattachine Society.

Dale Jennings, a writer and civil liberties activist with Southern roots, was a member of the Fifth Order. In the spring of 1952 he was entrapped in Los Angeles's notorious Westlake Park by a plainclothes police officer. Jennings's defense was undertaken by the Mattachine Foundation, which publicized his plight through leaflets distributed on gay beaches and in West Hollywood bars. He admitted that he was homosexual but denied the charge of "lewd and dissolute conduct," and the jury was deadlocked despite forty hours of deliberation. The district attorney declined to retry the case. The Mattachine Society claimed "a GREAT VICTORY for the homosexual minority."[5] Soon new members overwhelmed the Society as discussion groups and guilds mushroomed.

Meanwhile Jack Nichols languished at Ardmore, frequently finding himself sitting in the office, with Principal Snow serving as prosecutor, judge, and jury:

> I wanted to go back home to be with my grandparents and my Iranian friends. At school I became deliberately testy. When [the teacher] noticed I was silent during the flag pledge, she took me to Principal Snow for "correction." Whisked past two scandalized secretaries into Mr. Snow's inner sanctum, I met the ogre on his own ground. He eyed me carefully, smiling slyly, as if to warn, "I intend to browbeat you into submission."
>
> This time, probably to rattle him, I announced: "I am a homosexual." If shocking him was my intent, I succeeded. His eyes narrowed. He walked me out of his office in silence, later calling my best friend's mother and recommending our separation.

Jack begged to leave Ardmore. That November a victorious fourteen-year-old Jack went to live with his uncle and aunt in Florida.

While Jack confronted Principal Snow and even contemplated suicide, the discussion groups and guilds of the Mattachine Society proliferated across the state as mostly gay men gathered at the homes and apartments of First Order guild members. The Society pressed on with its activist agenda by sending candidates for the Los Angeles Board of Education a questionnaire. Would they support a "nonpartisan" presentation of homosexuality in the senior high school students' unit on personal hygiene? Would they favor broadening the guidance services to assist those students who "manifest subconscious aspects of social variance"?[6]

As the new year began, IBM transferred Jack's mother to Miami, where she and Jack lived in an old mansion facing Biscayne Bay. There Jack often sat on the seawall and read.

> Our front window looked out on a lawn that sloped to the water. My favorite spot, Bayfront Park, was the site of a spectacular library. There, browsing among books on comparative religion, I discovered several tomes on the Baha'i World Faith, a religion born in nineteenth-century Iran. Baha'i teachings emphasized planetary and racial unity as well as the equality of the sexes.
>
> The library books contained a Miami address where I could contact Baha'i converts. My initial interest in meeting these people stemmed from the fact that Baha'ism had had a Persian origin. The progressive principles seized my imagination.
>
> The first Baha'i meeting I attended was a "fireside" (Baha'i terminology for gatherings in the homes of the believers). It was conducted in a mansion on Star Island, a rich locale in the middle of Biscayne Bay. The speaker, later to become a mentor, was Ali-Kuli Khan Nabil, Iran's first envoy to America and the first translator of the Baha'i writings into English.
>
> One night after a fireside meeting I got a ride home from an American Baha'i who struck me as effeminate. I decided he was gay. As we sat talking in front of my guest house, I told him about my homosexuality. He reciprocated, telling me that we were to be very secretive. Both of us decided that being gay was a real quandary. Explaining that he'd seen nothing in the Baha'i writings on the subject, he assured me that he was attempting to live a "moral life" and practiced celibacy.

During this era, however, most homosexual men chose not to practice celibacy. More than a few, like Dale Jennings, found themselves in compromising situations, losing their money, jobs, reputations—and sometimes their lives. Mattachine, on the heels of the Jennings victory and an explosion of discussion groups, recognized the need to communicate with a growing and increasingly diverse membership that often lacked the Fifth Order's political consciousness or legal prowess. As Don Slater, a founder, later explained to journalist Rodger Streitmatter: "A social movement has to have a voice beyond its own members. . . . Before this time homosexuals just spoke to themselves. They just talked—whispered really—to each other."[7]

The Mattachine Society thus founded a monthly magazine, in which the editors stressed equality for homosexuals—a radical concept in tepid times. The title of this magazine, in fact, was a tribute to Thomas Carlyle's aphorism, "A mystic bond of brotherhood makes all men ONE." The premiere issue of ONE, published the month Jack journeyed to Miami, spotlighted the Jennings case, noting its importance for this new civil rights movement and recommending actions that a homosexual entrapped by a police officer should follow.

Bertie Backus and Old Walt

In March 1953 Jack received a letter from the Shah's relatives inviting him to live with them in Washington. Convincing his mother that he should move from Miami to D.C. was not difficult. Returning to Washington as the cherry blossoms came into bloom, Jack renewed his love for the capital and spent happy days with his Iranian friends. Attending Alice Deal Junior High School, though, was a loathsome chore. Now, however, Jack brandished a "weapon":

> Remembering how I'd made myself unwelcome in Ardmore's junior high, I asked for an audience with the principal of Alice Deal. Miss Bertie Backus was a sixty-five-year-old woman from West Virginia who looked exactly like Eleanor Roosevelt. Like Eleanor, she was a liberal who was already planning a citywide parade to be held during the centennial of the freeing of the slaves. Miss Backus's warm smile stood in marked contrast to the smug paternalism I'd noticed in Mr. Snow.
>
> Well, I walked into her office and told her "I'm going to tell you what I told the other school principal: I am homosexual. You know, I would really like not having to come to school."
>
> She asked me for a few days to think over the implications of what I'd said, especially with regard to feeling uncomfortable in my classes. When I visited with her again, she asked me to do my best at remaining in class, but if I felt unable, to make her aware of my comings and goings.
>
> Well, that is what I did. I stayed out of class literally all the time. At the same time she invited me to dinner at her home. Over our first meal together I told her about my religious development, and she recommended that I read a poet, Walt Whitman, who, she said, had a universal outlook. In Whitman I stumbled upon the *Calamus* poems celebrating passionate love among men. I was startled.

Shortly thereafter Ali-Kuli Khan Nabil and his niece, Touran, moved from Miami to Washington. Jack introduced him to Miss Backus; the two became good friends. "On Sundays she took me, along with Khan and Touran, on long rides in the country. We'd stop at quaint restaurants or sit on the rocks at the Great Falls of the Potomac. Khan and my school principal both recited, for my edification, verses from Whitman and epigrams from the essays of Emerson."

Jack also began cruising Lafayette Park, located directly in front of the White House. "An older man came by and he realized that I was kind of dense. He fondled his genitals through his pants as he passed by the bench where I was sitting. Nothing happened." Like most gay teens, Jack was not yet reconciled with his same-sex feelings:

> The weight of the social stigma making homosexual feelings *the worst thing that could happen to anybody* bore down on me. I thought, a stunted life, one of self-denial, of turning away from a kind of love that seemed possible to only one lonely teen: me. I could envision always hiding my deepest longings to avoid those who saw homosexuals as ghouls or sickly vampires who wanted only to prey on them, to change them into sickly vampires. Queers were ugly night bats who'd suck the spiritual lifeblood from any careless male.

Only when reading the English poet and scholar Edward Carpenter during that summer of 1953 and the pseudonymous Daniel Cory a short time later did Jack "discover that I had ground to stand on." Jack recalls:

> I rummaged through the basement of an old bookstore and found a rare, mildewed copy of *Love's Coming of Age* by Edward Carpenter. In 1896 it had been the foremost sex-liberation tome of its day. Turning the yellowed pages, I found myself mesmerized by the exquisite spiritual intonations of its author. His gentle sophistication was, for me, my first communion with a great gay thinker.
>
> I was later to discover that this was fitting, since Carpenter had been, in fact, a kind of great-grandfather of the gay liberation movement. He was among the first such thinkers who acted to join his personal life, including his sexual/emotional leanings, with the world as he saw it, becoming a prophet of the perspective that one's personal life is a political statement. He saw far beyond the view that politics is only about elections, economics, and parliaments. He looked to women, gay men, and artists everywhere to plant the seeds of a new age he foresaw, a universal age that would celebrate the underlying unity of earth's peoples—and he had elucidated this in the last century, as did Walt Whitman. Carpenter, in fact, described himself as "the moon reflecting the sun," Old Walt.

Later, in another bookstore, Jack stumbled across the classic *The Homosexual in America*. Written under the pen name Donald Webster Cory, Edward Sagarin's book had an enormous impact on Jack, as it did on a generation of lesbians and gay men.

> I studied this book at great length, memorizing many of its paragraphs, and focusing on parts which seemed to speak directly to my predicament. The "From Handicap to Strength" chapter gave me a very different viewpoint. Until then everyone around me had gone, "Oh! Poor Jack he's handicapped by being gay." Suddenly I had a strength! It was the "great democratic strength" inherent in the homosexual community.
>
> Cory made a powerful case for self-esteem under the most grueling circumstances. He helped me to see poor self-images not as a product of homosexuality, but as the result of the prejudices internalized. At that moment, I was de-

termined to stand outside the condemning culture and, with the healthy pride of a teen, to claim my rightful place as an individual.

Jack shared his newfound book and his nascent enthusiasm with Miss Backus.

"What do you think of it?" he asked, hoping for her approval.
"It makes sense," she admitted.

Jack was "overjoyed!"

Having Ms. Backus's approval of Cory's book was important to Jack, and the revelations from this book led to him challenging his other mentor, Khan:

> I read and reread it, marking sentences that lit up new avenues to self-acceptance. While this was happening, I began questioning Baha'i thinkers about the homosexual question. None had a satisfactory answer, and, I noticed, some looked warily at me thereafter. Khan seemed to brush off my questions as if they were of no account. I put his ambivalence down to his age, inasmuch as he seemed as fond of me as ever.

Unmasking the Fifth Order

In March 1953 a *Los Angeles Daily Mirror* columnist alerted his readers to "a strange new pressure group." Noting that the Mattachine Society's legal adviser had refused to testify when summoned before the infamous House Un-American Activities Committee, Paul Coates warned that homosexuals might soon "swing tremendous political power. A well trained subversive could move in and forge that power into a dangerous political weapon."[8]

Elated by the publicity, the Fifth Order duplicated 20,000 copies and distributed them to its members and those on various mailing lists. Amid growing concern voiced within some of the more mainstream guilds, a convention of Mattachine members was held at the First Universalist Church in Los Angeles on two weekends in April and May. Hay, who had been dropped by the Communist Party as a result of his gay activities, warned the hundred or so delegates, each representing several guild members, of their similarly vulnerable status in a speech entitled, "Are You Now or Have You Ever Been a Homosexual?" That same day, Chuck Rowland, another founder, scandalized the audience by imagining a near future "when we will march arm in arm, ten abreast down Hollywood Boulevard proclaiming our pride in our homosexuality."[9]

By the second day of the April conference it was clear that the Fifth Order no longer enjoyed control over the convention nor the confidence of its membership. Conservative members such as the gruff and outspoken San Franciscan Hal Call and the Brooks Brothers–clad Angelino Kenneth Burns moved swiftly to repudiate the opening day's speeches and to consolidate their views. Determined to rid the organization of "commies," Call shouted down Rowland, "The Society is not big enough for the two of us—there's no room for Russian agents."[10]

On the first morning of the May convention it was clear to the founders that the Society required restructuring, with an open democratic structure replacing secret guilds. The members of the Fifth Order unceremoniously walked to the stage, disclosing their identities to the astonished delegates. By the final day of the May session, the Fifth Order no longer existed, and conservatives, led by Kenneth Burns, were at the helm.

Decades later, both Hay and Hall attested to the differences that still marked the homophile movement in the early 1960s.

> HAY: The original society was based upon this feeling of idealism, a great transcendent dream of what being Gay was all about. . . . The Mattachine after 1953 was primarily concerned with legal change, with being seen as respectable—rather than self-respecting. They wanted to be dignified by professional "authorities" and prestigious people, rather than by the more compelling dignity of group worth.[11]
>
> HALL: They were sort of pie in the sky, erudite, and artistically inclined. . . . We saw Mattachine as a here-and-now, practical. . . . Public protests were not part of our program. Not at all. We wanted to see changes come about by holding conferences and discussions and becoming subjects for research. . . . We knew that if we were going to get along in society, we were going to have to stay in step with the existing and predominant mores and customs. . . . [12]

After the Fifth Order had been unmasked, Mattachine no longer carried the mystique of an organization led by a powerful and secretive group. As the conservatives rejected the concept of a sexual minority culture in favor of individual psychological adjustment within a heterosexual culture, Mattachine's missionary fervor waned. As consciousness-raising guilds were transformed into dutiful task-groups, membership dwindled and enthusiasm withered. A year later, in May 1954, fewer than fifty delegates attended the conference.

"Somewhere Along the Way"

Attending Bethesda–Chevy Chase High School in the fall of 1954, Jack "cultivated" the comradeship of several classmates whom he suspected of being gay. Within a few months he had come out to all of them, presenting each with a copy of *The Homosexual in America*.

> Several indicated that they, too, were gay and the rest, fence-sitters and tagalongs, found the company of admitted homosexuals too interesting to disparage. One, however, reacted with alarm.

His name was Ted. Not only was he attractive, but Ted has remained one of the more intelligent people I've known. I was sure he was gay, and he knew I knew, but still he didn't want to admit it. One day I approached him to talk. He drew away from me and ran to the first landing on the stairs.

"Stay away from me," he shrieked, "I'll have none of you and your perversions!"

I saw in him a fear of the same horrors I'd faced when I was thirteen. "Don't be afraid," I counseled him gently, "It's okay to be the way you are, and I won't tell anyone. I'd like to be your friend." He rushed to the top of the stairs and disappeared.

Shortly thereafter, however, he sought me out. We had friends in common and his curiosity about his own nature got the better of him. I gave him a copy of Donald Webster Cory's book. In no time he came out and made an announcement to his horrified parents.

In the evenings, Ted and I talked endlessly on the phone. We enjoyed intellectual feasts, reading aloud to each other from books critical of organized religion and of the prevailing culture. We discussed our suspicions about teachers and other students.

In addition to proselytizing among his high school comrades, Jack explored Washington's gay bars. Despite his age, most who spotted the 6'3" framed figure with short, curly, dark hair assumed—or chose to believe—that he was an adult.

From boys I'd met at Dupont Circle I learned about The Chicken Hut, a quaint two-story restaurant/bar on H Street, three blocks from the White House and Lafayette Park. Upstairs sat Howard (affectionately nicknamed Aunt Hattie), who played the organ and the piano, sometimes simultaneously. He'd held court in The Hut for over three decades. When I made my first entrance he was playing a Nat King Cole song "Somewhere Along the Way":

> *I used to walk with you*
> *Along the avenue*
> *Our hearts were carefree and gay*

The Hut had the atmosphere of a college hangout. I could sit and watch the faces of young and old, as yet unsure it was alright to be gay, singing happily as Howard's nimble fingers lit up the little bar. He had a theme song for regulars who came in. One of my friends got played "Ten Cents a Dance"; mine was Dietrich's "Falling in Love Again."

In many ways, the Washington of Jack's youth had changed little since the last generation of youthful homosexual Southerners, "Jeb," "Dash," "Max," and "Little Nicky," aptly portrayed in Jeb Alexander's diary and eventually published in abbreviated form with character composites as *Jeb and Dash: A Diary of Gay Life, 1918–1945*. These gay men shared an apartment house above the semi-cruisey Lido Restaurant on Connecticut Avenue during the late 1930s. Frequent cruising in Lafayette Park, excessive drinking at several of the local bars, fervent prattling about essays in the *American Mercury* or *The Nation,* and dining at Peoples, Vick's, or the Candlestick were the norm. But small house parties among this gay circle of men and their friends were the quintessence of gay social life:

In February 1938 Randall gave a birthday party for Nicky, his boyfriend, who later returned to Charleston. Jeb wrote in his diary:

> The punch was good and one might help oneself in the kitchen instead of wait-ing to be served. The punch was rather weak, though, so I had any number of them in the kitchen. . . . There was dancing to music by radio and Victrola. I danced with Randall and Max and others. Had a good time. It was way after midnight that Dash finally appeared. I was somewhat tight by then.[13]

A month later, a party was held in Dash's apartment. After the last guest had departed, listening to the Victrola and finishing off several unfinished drinks, Dash scribbled:

> A drinking party seems no place for serious music, although I was quite willing to have it for the others. I served bourbon, with soda for all except Joe and me. Nicky provided the ice from his Frigidaire. I made the drinks good and strong for I like to see people get gay and lose their self-consciousness and inhibitions. . . . When Max came in things were getting gay and I gave him a strong drink to help him catch up. . . . After Toscanini music we had dance music on the ra-dio. . . . At two all radio programs went off. . . . Bo played the Victrola. . . . The evening seemed so short that I was reluctant for the good time to come to an end. . . . [14]

Little had changed two decades later. Washington gay life remained "staid," as Jack describes:

> There was a stilted bourgeois mentality. In those days, people were pretty proper, enjoying drinking feasts peppered with dancing and inconsequential conversations. Those who ignored "proper" behavior were, if not openly scorned, at least privately criticized. In the bedroom oral sex predominated and anal sex was a subject for petty gossip. Not only was dancing in gay bars disallowed, but a peck on the cheek between men brought hysterical lectures from bar owners about endangered liquor licenses that couldn't survive such "lascivious" behavior.

Though Jack's social life improved, his schoolwork did not. In the spring of 1955 he enrolled in a correspondence course from the University of Ne-braska.

> Miss Backus, who had become a great mentor to me, oversaw my enrollment. Among the courses I took was one in English composition. An assignment re-quired that I write the story of the Three Little Pigs in Shakespearean style. I sat with Miss Backus one evening, going over the assignment, returning home

forthwith to complete it. No sooner had I done so than I called her to report my success and to read my composition aloud.

Her "roommate," Miss Mary Louise, Dean of Women at The American University, answered the phone in tears. "Is Miss Backus there?"

"She's dead, Jack," replied the Dean. "She's had a heart attack."

Bertie Backus was the first friend I ever had who died. I ran to my room and burst into tears. Later, I attended her memorial service, my entire family in tow. I knew she'd loved me with platonic passion and that she'd lived just long enough to give me a push toward some better future. I knew too that she'd carried, for reasons of her own, confidence that I was to be an active contributor to that future. How would I fulfill her dream? I wondered.

A Fateful Encounter

It was the summer of 1960. Robert Stack accepted an Emmy for his role in the television series *The Untouchables,* John Kennedy selected arch rival Lyndon Johnson as his vice president during the Democratic Convention in Chicago, and Brenda Lee's "I Want to Be Wanted" floated on the airwaves. Informal after-the-bar parties remained the norm in Washington's gay nightlife.

At one such party, Jack was sitting alone listening to the fashionable though less than fascinating conversations swirling around him. Preparing to bid farewell to his host with accolades of Southern gratitude, suddenly:

I overheard a firm voice saying, "Donald Webster Cory, who wrote *The Homosexual in America,* has made an excellent case for our rights." I rose from the sofa and walked toward a group of five who were standing by the window, searching for the voice I'd heard. The man who spoke was animated by a peculiar intensity, each of his words clipped, authoritative and academic in tone. As I approached he looked at me appreciatively, stepping back to make room in the semicircle.

"I've read *The Homosexual in America,*" I told him. His eyebrows did a little dance.

"And what did you think of it?" he asked.

"I think every gay person should read it," I replied, "and that's why I came over to speak with you because I've never before met anyone discussing it in public. I wanted to say hello. My name is Jack Nichols."

"I'm Frank Kameny," he said.

Suddenly the men surrounding us melted away and Kameny and I were alone, eagerly sharing our impressions of Cory's book.

"Ideas by themselves are fun," I told him, "but what good are they if we don't put them into some sort of action?"

"That's exactly what I'm doing," he said.

"How so?"

Kameny explained how he'd graduated from Harvard as a Ph.D. in astronomy. He'd been born twelve years before me, had been reared in Queens, New York, and, though an atheist, was of Jewish extraction. Astronomers, he said, must have security clearances, especially because of the new space programs, both Soviet and American, and he had lost his as a result of government suspicions labeling him a homosexual.

Kameny took my phone number. "I don't have a phone right now," he said, "because I haven't been able to afford one since beginning this struggle to get the government to reinstate me. I've been writing a brief to present to the Supreme Court about my case. It'll be the first time a homosexual has approached the Court to get his government job back. I'll call you, if you like, and you can come over to visit. We'll discuss these matters."

Clearly, the times were changing. The idea that a homosexual might successfully challenge the government's antigay policies in court was no longer a far-fetched hope. Two years earlier, *ONE* had successfully fought the "obscenity" charge by postal officials in the U.S. Supreme Court.[15] News of that favorable decision had elevated the stature of the magazine and opened the way for other homosexual publications. At *ONE*'s height, 5,000 subscribers read the often provocative essays targeted to the homosexual on issues ranging from bisexuality and police harassment to gay marriage and adoption.

By the mid-1950s two less radical movement publications were also distributed nationally: *The Mattachine Review* and *The Ladder*. The *Review*'s first issue was published at the beginning of 1955. Emphasizing assimilation, accommodation, and acceptance within the majority sexual culture, its editor, Hal Call, stressed "evolution rather than revolution."[16] Like its parent organization, the Mattachine Society, the target reader was the "homophile"—citizens who supported the homosexual or the study of homosexuality—not the homosexual. The *Review*, whose circulation numbered around a thousand, preached conciliation and communication as the "sexual variant" quietly integrated into heterosexual society: "The homosexual adjusts best who can make the greatest compromises with his own social and sexual needs, and the best adjusted individuals are those with the fewest contacts in the homosexual world."[17] On those few occasions when the *Review* did speak against heterosexual oppression, the arguments put forth were assimilationist in substance and self-deprecatory in tone. Hal Call, for example, condemned the routine harassment of homosexuals in gay bars because their closure would increase the visibility of homosexuals in "more elite bistros," whereas the presence of gay bars afforded "offending the least number of non-homosexuals."[18]

The Ladder conveyed the means by which the lesbian could ascend from her "well of loneliness." Founded in 1955, it was sponsored by the Daughters of Bilitis, honoring the fictional heroine of Pierre Louÿs's *Songs of Bili-*

tis, who, as Sappho's contemporary, lived as a lesbian. Both the magazine and the organization, under the leadership of Del Martin and Phyllis Lyon, redressed the male dominance and bias found in the other two publications and in the Mattachine Society. Stressing toleration, the unique problems confronting the lesbian, and women in literature, *The Ladder's* small subscription base of around 700 masked its larger readership among women who passed copies from one to another or who held "Ladder parties" to read and discuss the monthly essays.

All of these publications covered Frank Kameny's case as it tunneled through the bureaucratic labyrinth and edged into the courts. Eventually turned down by the U.S. Court of Appeals in 1960 and abandoned by his attorney, Frank assumed the arduous task of penning a petition for review by the Supreme Court.

Frank telephoned Jack a few days after their fateful encounter. Jack climbed the stairway to Frank's cramped, dingy apartment on Columbia Road; he recalled: "A bathtub sat in the room's center, and his nearby bed was ruffled. In spite of these dreary surroundings, our conversation sparkled." After a long discussion, the two decided to begin grassroots action. Their first order of business was to request copies of *ONE, Mattachine Review*, and *The Ladder* at local newsstands.

As Jack met regularly with Frank throughout the fall and winter of 1960, Frank continued to develop and polish his written arguments for the Court. In January 1961 he submitted his case; three months later, his petition for certiorari was denied. His efforts, however, were far from futile. The process streamlined his thinking and politicized his agenda. As he explained in an interview with Eric Marcus thirty years later:

> It forced me to sit down and think through and formulate my entire ideology on this whole issue. My ideology has not changed one iota in all the years. At that time, the government put its disqualification of gays under the rubric of immoral conduct, which I objected to because under our system, morality is a matter of personal opinion and individual belief on which any American citizen may hold any view he wishes and upon which the government has no power or authority to have any view at all. Besides which, in my view, homosexuality is not only not immoral, but is affirmatively moral.[19]

During the same month that Frank received notification about the Court's decision, the Mattachine Society was disbanding. Since Hall and the other conservatives had taken over the organization eight years earlier, there had been a slow but steady growth in society chapters, following the first two years when it nearly collapsed. Of course new members learned nothing about the organization's radical roots or the contributions of the founders. By 1960 there were chapters of Mattachine in several major cities outside of California, including New York, Boston, Denver, Detroit,

Philadelphia, and Chicago; its membership hovered at around 200. "By 1960," wrote historian John D'Emilio in his groundbreaking history of the early homosexual rights movement:

> The New York group had surpassed San Francisco as the largest of the society's chapters. The New Yorkers resented the fact that their membership dues disappeared into the national office, and frustration led them to accuse officers Hal Call and Don Lucas of fiscal irregularities. . . . Finally, in March 1961, an exasperated Call persuaded a majority of the national board to dissolve the organization, leaving each chapter to fend for itself, with the San Francisco group in charge of the *Review*. . . . The New York Mattachine, ignoring demands from San Francisco that it change its name, went its own way as an independent organization.[20]

A few days after receiving notification of the Court's decision, Frank organized. He contacted the leaders of New York Mattachine, Curtis Dewees and his lover, Al de Dion. "At the time, they were right at the center of deeply divided politics," Frank remembered. "Curtis and Al saw an opportunity to get a Washington Mattachine group going as a way to add to their power within the Mattachine structure. They figured they would have no trouble controlling us. . . . "[21] With names provided by New York, Frank and Jack sought people willing to join.

A Footnote in History

By the spring of 1961, Jack was becoming impatient with his white-collar day job as well as the day-to-day political minutiae of organizing. He was also tiring of his "Ozzie and Harriet homosexual lifestyle" of domestic suburban bliss with his live-in boyfriend, Tom—a Brandoesque young man from the Alabama flatlands.

It had been four years since Jack first met Tom at The Chicken Hut on a Sunday afternoon. Over the years, eros had been supplanted by the friendship of comrades: "While Tom went to mixed bars where sailors, soldiers, and marines were numerous, I went to the gay bars. I was able to understand Tom's reluctance to join me. He was eager for lusty sex but found too many gay men of the time restrained by hypocrisy and strict social fashions."

Seeking a "second adolescence," Jack embarked on a two-week Florida vacation, staying with his grandparents.

> Nana had set up special rules. I had to be home for dinner at six and, of course, there was no barhopping. When my grandmother served meals and then sat regally at the end of the table, I summoned up memories from childhood. Poppop, recapitulating essences of our conversations, still stood at the end of the table and recited Robert Burns's poems.

My first day wandering at the ocean's edge found me thinking of Tom at home, working himself to the bone and loving every minute of it, cruising at night. We were different, he and I. The resuscitation of passionate romance was now hopeless.

Near the boardwalk a few vacationing bodies sprawled on the sand. Climbing wooden stairs, I turned and surveyed the beach, noticing a lusty dark-haired youth. He looked back at me, but I pretended only a mild interest. When I looked again he smiled. It was a come-on smile saying, "Come join me on my blanket."

"I'm Warren," said the youth with olive skin, dark brown eyes, and a mysterious drawl. He was nineteen and he told me proudly, "I'm a hillbilly." He had a small nose and a chipped front tooth. His eyes were large, his face elastic, blessed with an ease that knew nothing of city jitters. He punctuated his statements with pointed expressions.

"What brings you to the beach?"

"My tan," answered Warren slyly, "I'm workin' on my tan."

They spent the rest of the day together, and Jack prepared to return to his grandparents' house for dinner. He bade his newfound friend good-bye. The next afternoon they met in a motel room.

The remainder of our time together found me lying at Warren's side or walking with him long miles on the sands. He talked ceaselessly about the little mountain town. His pride at being a hillbilly seemed unbounded, while I, a city boy, fell spellbound at his simple stories about relatives and friends. He grinned, telling me excitedly about the West Virginia town where he lived and about its singular gay bar where 3.2 beer was served and where Red Eyes—beer and tomato juice—were the house specialty. "Maybe we'll have one there someday," he said.

Warren told Jack about his lesbian sister, Donna, who lived across the river in Ohio. After their two-week beach interlude, Jack boarded the train bound for Washington's Union Station; Warren returned to his beloved West Virginia hills. Both promised to meet again.

During the next few weeks Warren telephoned Jack several times while Jack was out "philandering"; he did not leave his phone number, and Jack yearned for his hillbilly buddy. Impulsively, he boarded an all-night Greyhound bus headed for West Virginia:

As I emerged from the station at nine o'clock in the morning, I saw, on the corner, a lone man who struck me as cruising. I strode up to him and asked, "Where's The Pad?"—the town's gay bar. "Well, you've come to the right person! It's the gayest bar in town, and you just happen to be talking to the gayest person in town. I'm John."

John twittered as I told him about my search for Warren. "You must be in love," he said. He led me to a cheap hotel where I slept 'til evening, promising to see him at the bar.

Bartending at The Pad that night was Bruce, Warren's on-again, off-again boyfriend. Mixing a Red Eye, he winced at Jack's intimate reference to Warren, who he claimed was out of town for the weekend. Sipping his drink, Jack sat somberly at the wood-hewn bar deciding how to spend his West Virginia holiday without his beach friend. As he readied to order another Red Eye, Warren arrived with girls in tow.

He saw me instantly. We were transfixed. As I stood, the astonishment on his face turned into a broad smile. Bruce placed another Red Eye in front of me and beckoned to Warren. They argued, but I couldn't hear. Warren told me that he would meet me in an hour at the hotel.

Before their love was consummated, the hotel phone rang.

I answered to a hysterical Bruce. He'd discovered our whereabouts, no doubt from gay John. "You tell that whore to get his ass down here in two minutes," he screamed, "or I'll tell his brother here all about him and we'll be up to get him." As I replaced the receiver, I repeated what Bruce had said.

Slipping down the rear stairway, the two would-be lovers hurried through the alleys to Warren's garage, where they lay on an old sofa. Once again wrapped in a lover's embrace, there was a sudden commotion from his grandmother's house:

We looked through the window to see lights turning on and off. "My brother's lookin' for us," gasped Warren. We decided I should return to the hotel and that he'd meet me the next day. I told him my bus left at 6:00 P.M., and he promised we'd be together by 2:00. In the meantime, he said, he'd try to calm his brother's fury.

Two o'clock found me waiting in vain for Warren's call. As the hours passed, I sank into gloom, boarding the bus at six for the return trip to Washington, hoping there'd be a message from him there. But there wasn't.

Back again at the nation's capital, Jack dreamed longingly about Warren, blending memories with dreams. Crestfallen and in desperation, he telephoned Donna:

I reached her at the Kismet bar. Her tone, mixing with the noisy chorus of bar chatter, was warm and friendly. "No, Hun," she said. "I don't know where Warren is right now, but I'll sure let him know you called when I see him. He told me about meeting you. He hasn't forgotten you."

I got on an airplane and went to Ohio to meet Donna. When I returned, I wrote and asked Donna to live with me in the most luxurious apartment house in Washington—it even had Chanel Number 5 in the fountain! Inviting her to live with me in luxury was, I admit, a weird ploy. I justified it thinking how Warren's gay sister would give—when he stopped being lost—persuasive testimony on my behalf. Her call, accepting my invitation, astounded me.

Excursions

On August 1, 1961, the leaders of the New York Mattachine, Dewees and de Dion, met in Washington to discuss organizational strategies with Frank and company. "By the standards of the day," Jack recalls, "both were somewhat conservative and macho. Curtis was a quiet, dark-haired man, and Al was brown-haired and assertive." Meeting that evening in room 120 at the Hay-Adams Hotel, most memorable for Jack was the "identification and ejection of Detective Fouchette, an uninvited D.C. vice-squad goon."

In actuality, the detective had been invited because the mailing list provided by New York Mattachine included the D.C. chief of the moral division—using an alias. The chief directed one of his minions, Sergeant Louis Fouchette, to attend the meeting. After Fouchette had been recognized by another participant, Frank studied the plainclothes officer, spotting his gun holster hidden by his suit jacket. Confronted by Frank, Fouchette slunk away to file his report.

The following month, Jack met Donna's plane at National Airport. Soon Jack and his new "sister" Donna "threw caution to the wind and invited in chaos." Jack quit his day job. Living with an unemployed Donna in their upscale apartment, Jack assisted Frank in operationalizing strategies and crafting the purpose statement for the Washington Mattachine. Jack argued forcefully for the inclusion of a statement of cooperation among allied civil rights groups with parallel interests. While Frank was initially troubled by "mixing causes," he eventually acquiesced and later embraced the position.

On November 15, 1961, a group of a dozen or so women and men met to form the Mattachine Society of Washington, electing Frank as president; Bruce Scott, another victim of government security clearances, was chosen as secretary. Jack, sidetracked by Donna's arrival, was later to be elected secretary and then vice president. Though Frank spoke forcefully against adopting the Mattachine name, desiring something "more expressive" and perhaps with less political baggage, the group thought otherwise. At the time, Jack favored the Mattachine name, if only because it would "make us more identifiable to the gay community."

Regardless of its name, Mattachine-Washington had the imprint of Frank Kameny. It quickly assumed an aggressive stance. Within a year, Frank had written letters demanding meetings with governmental officials from all three branches of the federal government (two meetings with congressional staffers from the offices of Representatives William Fitts Ryan [D–N.Y.] and Robert Nix [D–Penn.] materialized).

During the next sixteen months Jack bounced from job to job and traveled to Pittsburgh, Detroit, Chicago, West Virginia, New York, Cocoa Beach, and Miami. Living on the fringe, he and Donna met and discarded boyfriends and girlfriends along the way.

During the early months of 1962, though, they were still living in Washington, where Jack sometimes joined Tom on "his cruising rounds, hanging out in those locales where servicemen, hustlers, and other assorted yokels mingled with gay men who preferred rough trade." One spring night, in front of The Post House, a restaurant adjacent to the Greyhound station, Jack spotted "a young golden stallion dressed from his collar to his boots wholly in black, his biceps bulging against short-rolled sleeves."

Experiencing the "great democratic strength" of male camaraderie, Jack bonded with George, an eighteen-year-old Southerner, AWOL from the army, who bragged that "Hank Williams is the greatest composer who ever lived." The two soon decided to hitchhike to Detroit and would return by way of West Virginia, meeting up again with Donna. Lines from Whitman's *Leaves of Grass* sprang to Jack's mind:

> *We two boys together clinging,*
> *One the other never leaving,*
> *Up and down the roads going, North and South*
> *excursions making. . . .*

Jack knew that Frank would not be happy to learn that he was departing yet again from Washington and his responsibilities to the Society. Visiting Frank at his new residence, an upper-middle-class home in the Palisades area, Jack recollected:

> I related to Kameny as a mentor, if not something of a father figure. He'd often lay down the law to me, always in his authoritative and precise tones. During the many hours we'd spent discussing liberation strategy, I'd grown to admire him. Telling him I was leaving was no easy task, and he wasn't about to let me off the hook without a lecture.
>
> "Why Michigan?" he asked sternly. "We have important work for the Society to do right here in Washington." Kameny had little patience with anything that might impede the work to which he devoted all his waking energies.

After trekking from Washington to Michigan, the pair journeyed farther west to Chicago before heading back briefly to Washington and then to New York City to live with Donna and her girlfriend. George and Jack hustled on Times Square.

> When I ran into George at one locale or the other we'd stop and swap stories in a coffee shop. I missed him and as the days wore on I began to regret the unhappy effect our chosen profession had on him. His smile was on the wane, and there was traffic smog, irregular meals, and needed clothing changes.
>
> The johns we met were varied in their approaches. Some were accustomed to picking up hustlers regularly, their self-assurance giving them away. But there were many more who seemed utterly inexperienced. Closet cases from Long Island and New Jersey, they were shy men with little knowledge of sex.

The going rate for hustlers was ten dollars. Fifteen or twenty was considered good fortune. On a lucky day we got picked up three or four times, but I lacked the business sense that demanded a rapid turnover.

After a month or so of plying their trade, George tired of street life. He announced that he was giving himself up to the military police. Telling them he was gay, George was quickly and quietly discharged, and he returned to his beloved West Virginia hills.[22] In the late summer of 1962 Jack headed south.

Googie's

Grandfather Murdoch and his brother had long retired, moving with their wives to a large oceanfront dwelling on Florida's Neptune Beach. Jack's mother now worked with General Dynamics as the first woman manager at the space center in Cape Canaveral.

The trip to Florida lasted twenty-four hours. I disembarked and traveled across the causeway to stay with Mom, who'd bought a house on Cocoa Beach. She'd asked me on several occasions to consider living at the beach, but there was a scarcity of gay nightlife, and I saw my visit with her as a temporary rest stop where I'd catch my breath.

I landed a job as night auditor at The Ko Ko Motel, spending part of each day tanning and swimming. Cape Canaveral was gearing up for its fourth manned space flight. Though spirit in the area was high, I missed having a larger supply of gay friends. The only men cruising were closet military types from Patrick Air Force Base, but their furtiveness raised evasion to new levels.

It was then that Donna, her affair at an end, called and announced she wanted to join me. "Come on," I encouraged, and in no time she stepped off the Greyhound, smiling broadly. Again, silly romantic that I was, I allowed the long-lost image of her brother to propel me. Mom welcomed Donna warmly, but hardly a month had passed before Donna began insisting we should move to Miami.

The couple soon relocated to an inexpensive 28th Street garage apartment along Biscayne Bay. Wasting little time to unpack, they walked across the street from the bus station to the Carnival Club:

I met a small, well-chiseled blond in his late twenties whose actual name escapes me but whom we soon took to calling—behind his back—Schmuckski. He quickly became exactly what we needed, a faithful servant who catered to our every whim.

I liked Schmuckski the first night. But his abandonment of his own wants while he catered exclusively to mine destroyed the initial attraction I might otherwise have encouraged. It soon became a very one-sided affair; I'd put my hands behind my head with my consciousness dulled to his presence by too much beer. This arrangement seemed perfectly natural to him.

Among those I'd hustled or those who'd thrown themselves at me while trampling personal pride under their own feet, there was present, no doubt, an unexplained masochism. Anybody who has done any hustling realizes that those who are easily hustled are also easily told what to do. As usual, I explained these people to myself by citing Donald Webster Cory's references to the self-damaging effects of discrimination. That I wasn't attracted to them didn't matter. They hadn't expected me to be, inasmuch as they usually reflected society and disliked themselves. Disregarding their feelings seemed somehow to enhance their attraction to me.

Jack and his entourage soon began to hang out at Googie's, a garish shack named after and managed by an elderly vaudevillian with huge rouge cheeks. Jason, a handsome street hustler from Baltimore, soon joined Jack's circle of friends.

> Googie would arrive as patrons greeted her with applause, and the bartender would lift her frail little body over the bar. On Fridays and Saturdays when her bar was filled to overflowing, the juke would play "The Stripper" and Jason, a few beers under his belt, would saunter to the middle of the dance floor dropping his clothes on the way in front of a hundred frenzied, applauding customers. I was always amazed at Googie's cool. Normally we worried about the savagery of Miami police, who were eager to harass queers. But Googie worried not at all about police harassment. She applauded the gutsy hustler, too, taking a cowbell from the shelf, ringing it with startling energy, and then, not satisfied by the noise she'd created, hurling tin trays across the barroom while a nude Jason did bumps and grinds to the roar of a hundred customers.

Donna and Jack moved into Coconut Grove and later into a twenty-five-dollar-a-week efficiency in Miami Springs, complete with a swimming pool. Despite his Mattachine background and the heavy-handed role then played by the Johns Committee, Jack paid little attention to the gay political scene in Florida. "I was vaguely aware of what was going on in Florida from the references in ONE magazine. But I really didn't make connections. It's important for us as gay people to recognize that many political and social things can be going on around us and we can be living right in the middle of it and not be tuned into it!"

Jack was, however, tuned into male beauty. Around Halloween he met Steve, a "shapely blond" Miami resident:

> He was just coming out and it happened that I was the first person he studied in earnest. I took him everywhere to show him the ropes: how to cruise, where to go cruising. At Googie's and other favorite spots, Steve and Donna danced happily whenever "Breaking Up Is Hard to Do" would play.
>
> When Googie's closed at one o'clock, we headed for the bars on Miami Beach: The Coral Room for Donna and Polly and Billie Lee's for Steve, Jason, and me, directly across from the Coral Room. Crossing the moonlit causeway in Steve's

car with the radio blaring, we were always nervous about Miami Beach cops. Police were everywhere; they were like flies and perpetually on the lookout for gays and for youthful rowdies. Sometimes we stayed in Miami, driving down NW 27th Avenue about five miles south of Googie's to The Deluxe Club, a mixed all-nighter filled with Mafia molls, racetrack enthusiasts, gay men, lesbians, and other diehards who refused to stop drinking before five in the morning.

The Prodigal Son Returns

In mid-January 1963 Jack persuaded Donna and Steve to return with him to Washington. As they packed up Steve's Rambler, Jack's excursion into chaos was nearing a close: "My experiment with irresponsibility and my flirtation with irrationality were at an end. A steady job, decent housing, and those free choices which only financial independence could bring now held special promise."

Quickly, Jack caught up to the activities of friends and family:

Tom expressed his relief I'd lived through my long spree without injuries. "Mae," he said, "you just better settle down now. It's time for you to grow up." I called Dad at the FBI to say I'd returned, and he hurried to meet with me. But when I told him about my activism, he was deeply disturbed. I was a junior, after all, bearing his name. He begged me to use a pseudonym until he retired in two years. I agreed to do so, choosing the name of Warren D. Adkins, keeping my promise to myself that Warren would become a footnote in history. I telephoned George, too, finding him at home in the hills. Within two days he stepped off the bus and we hugged. Our last days together had been somber, but now his happy spirits had returned.

Jack then called on Frank Kameny. Looking for a roommate, Frank acquiesced to his returning starry-eyed comrade's request that Jack and Steve live with him.

Kameny's house was brick, two-storied, and surrounded by lawns which were more ample in the back. The interior was mostly bare. He used the smaller of his upstairs bedrooms as an office, leaving a sofa bed in the living room for me to share with Steve.

As a scientist Kameny was vehemently committed to the scientific method. He was a rationalist and was contemptuous of supernaturalism, mysticism, and of any occult "sciences," especially astrology. As a roommate he was fair and agreeable. His scientism was evident even in the kitchen, where he showed us carefully how he kept foods belonging in one category with their kind, while others were separated by variety with equal exactness.

Kameny seldom went to movies and had no interest in spectator sports. His knowledge of popular music was nil, inasmuch as his radio remained tuned to a classical station. Petty gossip bored him, and even the negative personal characteristics of those who opposed him failed to excite his interest. His focus in such situations always remained on the merits of an argument, not on personality.

While rooming with Frank, Jack met Randolfe Wicker. A graduate of the University of Texas, where he had been a campus and civil rights activist, Wicker had stayed in New York City five years earlier during the summer of 1958, when he helped to publicize Mattachine lectures on the West Side, attracting large crowds. In 1961 Wicker emigrated to Manhattan. Living on the lower East Side, he edited several magazines for Countrywide Publications. Wicker quickly became reinvolved in the city's homophile movement. As he distributed Mattachine literature in various gay bars, he was struck by the apathy of New York's homosexual patrons as well as the political conservatism of homophile leaders Dewees and de Dion. He formed the Homosexual League of New York in 1962 and organized a groundbreaking call-in radio program on WBAI in which several homosexuals described their reasonably well-adjusted lives. Coverage from this program led to increasing media coverage, including stories in *Newsweek*, the *New York Times*, and the *Village Voice*.

Randy Wicker, like Frank Kameny, emerged as a new-generation spokesperson for a more politicized and public homophile movement. Though the two shared a displeasure with the accommodationist policies articulated by the old Mattachine, their personal styles could not have been more dissimilar. Jack recalls his first meeting with Wicker, who was then engaged in a spirited conversation with Kameny:

> I walked into the house one morning to find Kameny and Wicker engaged in a ferocious but friendly war of words. Knowing how to tweak Kameny, Wicker good-naturedly argued with him over the "proper" color of a slogan button he intended to make, one that would read "Equality for Homosexuals." He suggested that the button be lavender, but Kameny saw in this an outrageousness that could not be tolerated and insisted, therefore, on black and white.

As Jack recentered himself, pouring his energies into Mattachine, he became an able and dependable colleague for Frank, who continued to mentor the young stallion:

> Perhaps the word "precise" describes Kameny's speaking patterns better than any other. He excelled as an *original repetitive,* which is to say that he originated responses to questions about homosexuality with scientific precision, made lengthy paragraphs of them, and then repeated these carefully honed statements in debate. He was eager that I should grasp these statements so that I, too, could use them in public situations, avoiding thereby any speculative meandering that could easily lead me into unscientific briar patches.

Assuming a full-time job as a registrar for a technical college, Jack worked closely with Frank, who had convinced leaders of New York Mattachine and the Daughters of Bilitis along with the Janus Society of Philadelphia to join with Washington Mattachine in a loose coalition. The East Coast Homophile Organizations (ECHO) first met in January 1963 and continued with monthly meetings over the next two years.

Jack collaborated with Frank in strategizing ways of breaking down anti-gay prejudices. "Kameny and I agreed we must plan challenges to the psychiatric establishment. This singular aspect of our cause united the two of us, perhaps, more than did any other issue." Doggedly, Jack assembled medical opinions and scientific research challenging the commonly held belief that homosexuality was an illness:

> As I helped develop such ideas, part of my passion, I knew, had been fueled by my early adolescent experiences. When my aunt-in-law had called me "sick," and my depression over this circumstance had led me at age fourteen to attempt suicide, I emerged from that depression inwardly furious that I'd been so deluded by the quackery around me. My disdain for organized religion, including Baha'ism, had, in part, similar roots. But it was psychiatric nonsense that infuriated me most. Kameny knew this and encouraged my anger. In autumn he suggested that I approach the executive board of the Washington Mattachine, presenting my viewpoint.

Jack's letter, dated October 14, 1963, represented a watershed for the fledgling East Coast movement as it contested the medical establishment's authority. Cogently and clearly, Jack argued that homosexuality was not a disease, concluding in Coryesque language:

> It is often all too easy for us to sit in the comfort of a 20th Century apartment among certain enlightened heterosexuals and to imagine that after all our situation is not so bad. It is BAD. . . . The mental attitude of our own people toward themselves—that they are not well—that they are not whole, that they are LESS THAN COMPLETELY HEALTHY—is *responsible* for UNTOLD NUMBERS OF PERSONAL TRAGEDIES AND WARPED LIVES, and for poor self images. . . . By failing to take a definite stand—a strong stand—that is scientifically open, I believe that you will not only weaken the Movement 10-fold, but that you will fail in your duty to homosexuals who need more than anything else to see themselves in a better light. The question "Am I Sick?" is not an academic, drawing-room inquiry. It is an agonizing cry—and before you dare to give a drawing-room answer, I hope that you will give just a little more thought to the subject.[23]

Doubt, disgust, and indifference greeted Jack's open letter. Movement conservatives of the past generation like Call and Dewees gave little thought to it. Clearly, if change was to occur in the manner envisioned by Kameny, Wicker, and Nichols, then a new generation of activists would need to be recruited and educated.

In 1964 two such men entered Jack's life; one would stir his spirit, the other sharpen his strategies.

7

The Mississippi of the Homosexual and the Politics of Dialectics

"**D**o the homosexuals, like the Communists, intend to bury us?"

With this lead, *Life* magazine reported on the "secret world" of homosexuality. Describing homosexual life as "sad and often sordid," the June 1964 issue of this widely read periodical identified Miami as one of six "major" cities with huge homosexual populations. Accompanying silhouetted photos of men in leather bars and at cruising areas were portraits of Hal Call of the Mattachine Society and Don Slater of *ONE* along with a shot of a balding Santa Monica Boulevard tavern owner leaning against his bar. A sign behind him read, "Faggots: Stay Out." *Life* conveyed a somber message to the nation: "Today, especially in big cities, homosexuals are discarding their furtive ways and openly admitting, even flaunting, their deviation. . . . This social disorder, which society tries to suppress, has forced itself into the public eye. . . . "[1]

The story gave prominent coverage to the Florida Legislative Investigation Committee's report—particularly its recommendations and "inflammatory" photographs. It also contrasted Florida's efforts with those of Illinois, whose 1961 Model Penal Code (modeled after American Law Institute recommendations and partly based on the British Wolfenden Report) decriminalized homosexual behavior between consenting adults.

Florida homosexuals were newsworthy throughout the Mississippi summer. Interspersed with stories of church burnings, murders of civil rights workers, and the Mississippi Freedom Party were occasional articles on the perils of "homosexualism." Typical was a *Miami Herald* Sunday feature entitled "The Life of a Homosexual: It's Sad, Not Gay." Mirroring *Life*, it described the Dade County gay scene as "a shadowy world within a world." The story raised suggestive questions like: "Is Dade's homo population growing fast? Do they pose an increasing threat to children? Are they infiltrating government, schools, and other positions of high responsibility more than ever?" Its captions reflected the story's tone and content: "More Deviates Among Young"; "Salacious Ads Aimed at Young"; "Medics Differ on Legal Point"; "A Sadism Club at Dade School"; "Action Hinted on Some Bars."

State Attorney Richard Gerstein, "primarily concerned with this recruitment of youth," announced a countywide crackdown. "It's a growing problem and anyone who says it isn't is just ignoring the obvious." Stressing the transmission of venereal disease, he reminded citizens that homosexuality "inevitably leads to serious criminal activity including blackmail and extortion. . . . "[2] Meanwhile, in a West Coast homophile publication, George Arents, an affluent Coconut Grove homosexual resident, repeated a quip from the lips of a local politician: "Sure, you can force all the fancy boys out of Coconut Grove, but if you do, you will turn the whole beautiful area into a slum. . . . "[3]

In the midst of yet another wave of police harassment, *ONE* editorialized:

> After watching the Florida situation since 1955 we at One begin to believe that the whole mess there may continue for a long time if the only weapons used against the Committee are words. . . . If the homosexuals in Florida had given $1.00 each to ONE rather than the thousands of dollars they have given to lawyers and psychiatrists and blackmailers how much different things would be today![4]

Armed with more than words, Richard A. Inman, a thirty-seven-year-old Tampa-born entrepreneur-turned-taxi-driver, stepped forward. In response to "nine years of oppression from the Florida Legislative Investigation Committee," the trial of Billie Lee, the *Life* exposé, and Gerstein's planned crackdown, he formed a state-chartered corporation, the Atheneum Society of America.

The Society's objective was "to combat . . . gross injustices affecting homosexual citizens which are perpetuated by certain heterosexuals who masquerade behind the guise of 'justice' and 'decency.'"[5] At the Atheneum Society's first annual board meeting in July 1964, Richard assumed the presidency, Marty Lemlich, a heterosexual Dade County attorney who had known Richard for seventeen years, became secretary, and Lea Surette, the barmaid at the Mermaid Room, was elected vice president. The Society was dedicated to cooperating with local branches of the American Civil Liberties Union (ACLU) and bar associations, monitoring left- or right-wing groups that "would impede the progress of the homophile movement," and working for legislative and religious reforms. Within six months Richard claimed more than 4,000 subscribers to the Society's publications in nineteen states. However inflated the claim may have been, *Viewpoint,* the Society's newsletter, was certainly read by influential Florida politicians, members of the media, and law enforcement officers.

Richard's first political actions were to threaten the county with a lawsuit and the Miami Beach City Council with the prospect that "continued harassment will lead to ... a parade." He further taunted his nemesis, the Coral Gables *Times:* "And I will be at the head of [the parade], with hair-ribbons flying and 'bells-a-ringing.' Again we'll see how the national press enjoys that one, at the height of the tourist season."[6] Behind the scenes, he penned a confidential letter to John Pennekamp, the influential associate editor of the *Miami Herald,* in which "I made various charges against State Attorney Gerstein's office, the Miami Police Department, and the Sheriff's office."[7]

> He [Gerstein] took the word of an article in *Life* magazine that Miami was one of *six* cities with a major population of homosexuals. But not one word out of him when the Valachi hearings disclosed that Miami was one of *two* "open cities" for the Cosa Nostra. Not one word out of him when Mayor High disclosed that 67 Cosa Nostra people live in this area. Has there been any "crackdown" against them? Your headlines haven't yet begun to tell the WHOLE story about what's going on in South Florida.[8]

East Coast Movement Politics

As public awareness grew, activists as diverse as Hal Call and Frank Kameny recognized a shift in movement politics. For Call, who reveled in his coverage by *Life,* this change soon rendered quaint the Mattachine approach:

> One of the biggest public relations successes came more than ten years after I took over the Mattachine, in 1964. In January of that year, people from *Life* magazine contacted us and wondered if we could help them get a photographic representation of the homosexual community in the San Francisco area. It had to be authentic news, not staged. ... That was the first time a national magazine had ever treated the subject of homosexuality with any sensitivity or understanding. My photograph was in it. ...
>
> [But Mattachine] went downhill from the time the Society for Individual Rights [SIR] came into being in 1964. A lot of the people who worked with Mattachine in the early days became involved in SIR because it was more strongly a membership-participation and volunteer service-type group.[9]

The month Richard was elected president of the Atheneum Society, Frank delivered the 100th lecture before the New York Mattachine Society. Articulating the need to address forthright the "sickness issue," Frank dissected the "circular reasoning" of mental health professionals, concluding, as Jack Nichols had penned earlier, that "until and unless valid positive evidence shows otherwise, homosexuality per se is neither a sickness, a defect, a disturbance, a neurosis, a psychosis, nor a malfunction of any sort."[10]

Frank argued for an activist approach whereby homosexual organizations would employ political strategies, already in use by the civil rights movement, to redress discrimination and harassment. His logic and zeal won over a number of Mattachine members. Two such men were Julian Hodges, a son of an outstanding North Carolina family, and Dick Leitsch, a former Louisville library employee and public school teacher. Like other gay Southerners, they had crossed the Mason-Dixon line searching for sexual freedom.[11] Within the year, these Southern recruits to Northern militancy would run for office in the Mattachine–New York chapter on a social protest, antisickness platform against the old-guard slate, including Curtis Dewees and Edward Sagarin (aka Donald Webster Cory), who opposed political activism and urged deference to the medical experts.

Another Northern émigré and a post-Stonewall gay activist was Perry Brass, a Savannah poet born in 1947. Eventually leaving the University of Georgia, he worked in New York City. In "When I Was Twelve Years Old," he wrote:

> Lying in bed with another man,
> I wonder sometimes how we are able
> to step out of the brutalizing process
> long enough to express any feelings
> for one another. . . .
> The doctors
> say that there must be something wrong
> to want to lie here instead of killing
> each other. . . . [12]

This anger and angst would soon be unleashed by a Southern band of youthful radicals under the antisickness, civil rights banner hoisted by Frank.

Talk of the Nation

Like Hodges, Leitsch, and Nichols, Richard Inman was not new to the "secret" and "sordid" world of gay life. He frequented many of the bars and parties in Miami, and his two long-term gay relationships were spliced between a couple of failed heterosexual marriages. Richard's checkered past included one arrest during a 1954 raid at Vick's Bar and another in 1960 at the Rendezvous as well as an unrelated conviction for failing to have proper attire, resisting arrest, and drunkenness. There were also dark rumors of a deeply closeted, covert past.

Arriving in Miami in the 1940s, Richard worked for two years for Cauley & Martin Mortgage before he and a business partner bought out the company in 1951, changing the name to Guardian Mortgage. An entrepreneur, Richard owned dozens of Miami properties during the 1950s, including a ninety-unit apartment complex, the Dorn Hotel, and several bars, including the Melody Lounge at the Dorn, the Huddle Bar in Coral Gables, and the Record Bar, located on North Miami Avenue and catering to motorcyclists.

In 1960 he bought out his business partner. He reorganized and consolidated, and his operations became collectively known as Richard A. Inman, Inc. He involved himself in politics, serving as a co–campaign manager for Representative and later Senator George Hollahan, a former city judge from south Miami. Four years later Richard filed for bankruptcy, with liabilities of $123,000.

For Richard, his financial tragedy was the homophile movement's political gain:

> I had never before been a member of a homophile organization. Such organizations were entirely to be found only in the major cities of the North and in California. . . . I knew nothing about the history, aims, or goals of the homophile civil rights movement. . . . In the past, homosexuals had meekly accepted their arrests, paid their fines to the court, and then run for cover. Never before had anyone stood up to the Legislative Investigation Committee, the State Attorney, or the police departments when confronted by their harassment tactics.[13]

As news of the Society's existence surfaced, State Attorney Gerstein subpoenaed Richard requesting information, including Atheneum's membership list. The gangly 6'2" Richard, with receding hair and an earnest face, appeared at Gerstein's Miami office to recite a U.S. Supreme Court decision (357 U.S. 449) that found Alabama's demand for the NAACP membership list to be a constitutional violation. Acknowledging the similarity, Gerstein reluctantly dismissed Richard, who quickly gained statewide attention from the media, law enforcement organizations, and the Johns Committee.

Joining New York Mattachine in 1964—the same month as the *Life* magazine exposé—Richard wrote Julian Hodges two months later describing the power of Gerstein and the probable reason for his announced "crackdown":

> Gerstein personally has Grand Jury powers . . . [which] is awesome and a weapon of great fear if capriciously used. This power is used daily here. Any time of the day or night he can drag you out of your house, bodily if necessary, take you to his office, where without benefit of legal counsel being present, he can interrogate you, transcribe your testimony, use the testimony against you, and refuse you a copy of the transcript. . . . He has the power to investigate (or

not), to prosecute (or not), and through . . . scores of ex-assistants . . . who have been appointed or elected to judgeships and other high positions, he is almost to the point of being able to influence the judicial processes of this county. . . . He now employs almost 70 Assistant State Attorneys in his office. All these men formerly had law practices and many have held high civic positions, or positions with civic organizations. . . . So you can see he has more tentacles than an octopus. . . . Only Dan Sullivan could make him jump. . . .

As of this moment, I am beginning to suspect that Gerstein is *not* the man behind this whole thing. I think he is having pressure put upon him by someone (not in any *official* position) who he is either afraid of or from whom a word could ruin *him*. Such a man in such a position could be Dan Sullivan, the director of the Greater Miami Crime Commission.[14]

Pursuing the Society's objective, Richard confronted and cajoled, threatened and flattered, distorted and fabricated. When the Miami Beach police entered several gay bars taking photos in a December 1964 raid, for example, Richard moved into action:

I knew that the next night the Miami Beach police chief was going to be on a panel show debating homosexuality. . . . I attended the panel meeting and sat at the back of the room in the middle. When it came for audience participation time, I stood many times and asked questions. . . . The spotlight was finally kept on me and before long the . . . whole thing became a sort of pro-homosexual meeting. . . . When most everyone was gone . . . I went up to the chief and others and introduced myself. . . .

I'm sure if I'd attacked or made the chief look bad with a single question, I'd have gotten noplace with him. But I did take him aside and asked, "What do you want with those pictures you took in the bars?" The chief invited me to come to his office the next morning where he showed me the pics. . . . He said he took the pics at the demand of the vice mayor and mayor to show the city council "what went on in the bars." . . .

I did tell the chief that I was there representing many whose pictures were taken and about forty wanted to sue. I said several bars wanted to do so also, but that I was going to recommend "no action this time." But "There better hadn't be another time because I can't keep them out of court a second time."[15]

Despite his gravel voice and sometimes inarticulate style, Richard quickly became the lightning rod for Florida's nonexistent homophile movement. Featured in newspaper stories and op-ed pieces (one municipal paper, the Miami Beach *Sun*, endorsed the repeal of the state's sodomy and related statutes), he appeared at public speaking engagements such as the Florida Bar Association and was a guest on radio talk shows such as Larry King's, where on December 23, 1964, he "first publicly admitted to being a homosexual."[16]

At such occasions Richard outlined the aims of the "homophile movement": ending job discrimination within government employment; halting police harassment; removing laws that prohibit consensual and private adult homosexual behavior; and allowing free assembly of lesbians and gay men in the bars. Richard was also one of the first homophile leaders to value attacks from right-wing groups:

> They are giving us marvelous publicity and are getting so riled up and making such utterly fantastic charges that the majority of the public will soon be saying "ridiculous, isn't it?" The right-wing can make homosexuality the talk of the nation like we could almost never do. Then, when people like Pomeroy, Gebhard [of the Kinsey Institute] and others are interviewed they will be listened to with even greater interest.[17]

Publicly tossing out the startling figure of 200,000 Florida homosexuals, Richard privately engaged in correspondence and conversations with political leaders and kingmakers. He also engaged in a long-term battle with two powerful politicians: Charley Johns and Richard Gerstein.

Developing Relationships

In 1964 a new gay bar opened across from Hoover's FBI headquarters, aptly named The Hideaway. Jack Nichols together with a heterosexual couple visited the bar in July. As they sat in the corner of the bar facing the doorway drinking their beers, the couple asked Jack what he hoped to find.

"A liaison with an enchanting spirit," he laughed, "and a body beautiful to house it, of course."

Later, as the couple conversed between themselves, Jack glanced around. He saw "an apparition":

> He wore a blue shirt that showed his absolute definition. His face had classic symmetry, his cheekbones high, his jaw strong, his eyes hazel with lips full. He was blonde, his hair styled in a civilian mode, a handsome wave directly above his forehead. I'd never seen anyone like him. The description penned by Old Walt in his *Leaves* came to mind: "Dress does not hide him, / The strong sweet quality he has strikes through."
>
> It was clear that he was new to Washington, or at least to the bars. My first thought, perhaps, was that I'd better make his acquaintance pronto or I'd lose him in the crowd, a crowd that hadn't yet discovered him. He ordered a beer from the waitress. I waited 'til she disappeared and, without hesitation, stood and went directly to his tableside. I smiled and he did, too, a voluptuous welcoming beaming ear to ear.

Born Elijah H. Clarke in Hindman, a small town in the hills of southeastern Kentucky, "Lige" was working at the Pentagon office of the army chief of staff, editing secret messages from the CIA and other governmental agencies. Stumbling into The Hideaway the night before with two army buddies, he returned the next evening motivated by more than curiosity. Lige remembers: "I was a little nervous, but before I could even order a beer, a guy came over to me and invited me to join him and some friends for a drink. . . . I said, 'Sure!' Later he asked me to dance, so we did and I loved it. Everything seemed so simple, so natural."[18]

Before the week was over, the two had enjoyed a Friday night date and by Sunday afternoon Jack, who was vice president of Mattachine-Washington, invited Lige to Frank Kameny's house for the printing of the Society's newsletter. Soon the couple leased a one-bedroom apartment in Arlington's Wakefield Manor—the army brass assumed Lige was living at Fort Myer, a few blocks distant. Later, in the first nonfiction book penned by a male couple, they wrote: "Those first few months we enjoyed long nights, dragging ourselves to work early each morning. We laughed, played, and touched. On weekends we drove to the beach in the borrowed convertible, listening between Beatles records to LBJ's cornball election promises."[19]

While Jack and Lige engaged in a summer courtship, Richard organized the Atheneum Society. During that summer he received a few responses from his lengthy letters to Frank Kameny and Julian Hodges. He had originally sought to affiliate his organization with the Mattachine Society, but, hearing nothing from Hal Call, he formed the Atheneum Society and began publishing a newsletter and magazine, *The Atheneum*. First published in August 1964, the mimeographed, two-page publication was sprinkled with homophile notes from around the country and some news of local interest.[20]

Throughout that summer and fall, Frank's energies were directed elsewhere. Together with Jack, he cajoled other leaders to join their regional organizations with Mattachine-Washington, forming an umbrella organization—East Coast Homophile Organizations (ECHO). Richard's activities, though, were not going unnoticed. In an August 23 letter to Hodges, for example, Frank scribbled a postscript: "Have just seen 'Atheneum.' Am much impressed. I quite agree with you that they need both support and advice—also that, if it is not too late, they are logical candidates for including in ECHO."[21] Hodges, who had already responded to an earlier letter from Richard, quickly exchanged a brief series of letters with Richard.

Round One: Charley Johns

Richard Inman, like Charley Johns, had an agenda. In the autumn of 1964, the now disgraced Florida Legislative Investigation Committee proposed to codify and update the variety of sex laws described in the ill-received *Homosexuality and Citizenship in Florida*. The Florida Sexual Behavior Act would make it easier to convict someone on the misdemeanor charge of "deviant sexual conduct" by including same-sex kissing and dancing and would tighten laws related to sex with minors. Other recommendations included fingerprinting all state employees and checking arrest records for sexual or related offenses, hiring additional school personnel to investigate suspected homosexual teachers, and revoking state contributions to retirement benefits for any employee convicted of a sex offense.

A political insider, Richard sought to outmaneuver Johns, the veteran "pork-chop" politician. If the state was reconsidering the revision of criminal codes, reasoned Richard, why not consider the adoption of an entirely new Unified Penal Code? Such an approach would promise something for everyone, ranging from a streamlined judicial system to a quiet revocation of the state's sodomy statute.

> I have been invited to go to Tallahassee (at the Committee's expense) to testify in a public hearing, regarding my suggestions and my reasons for wanting the Model Penal Code as it applies to sex offenses. I started throwing everything in the book at them: legal prostitution, legal gambling, clinics for dispensing narcotics, etc. They are reeling from the effects. I am hoping that they will give me the Code in return for shutting my mouth. . . .

Practicing the politics of dialectics, Richard also saw this maneuver as an opportunity for alliance with other organizations by "drawing certain parallels between . . . [such] organizations and ours . . . difficulties with government, churches, law, police."[22]

Mostly, though, Richard emphasized progressive legal reform that would garner support from more sensible politicians who were nevertheless weary of any association with homosexuality.

> On the subject of homosexuality, NO politician wants to be approached directly, or have it known that he has even talked to you about such matters. All politicians know that the laws (sex laws) are ancient and should be changed, but NONE WOULD *DARE* CHANGE A LAW TO *BENEFIT* HOMOSEXU-ALS. . . . They do not want any publicity connecting them with homosexual legislation that would give homosexuals a break.[23]

The adoption of the Model Penal Code, thought Richard, provided such cover. Behind the scenes he lobbied state legislators—many of whom he knew on a first-name basis—including the sixteen-member Dade County delegation. The Atheneum Society sent copies of the Sex Offenses Sections of the code along with the most recent issue of the *Atheneum Review* to all 155 Florida legislators in December and January. Recognizing that it would be politically difficult for a single legislator to propose such changes, Richard recognized the value of the committee structure as a shield of anonymity. Believing that "were they to abolish this one, there would not be such a committee formed again for many years," the Atheneum Society advocated *expanding* the proposed Sexual Behavior Act: "In this new act they have conceded that those crimes which were formerly against nature are no longer (illegal) for legally married couples. It is now a simple matter of same sex, or the fact that the participants are not married that makes these sexual acts illegal."[24]

Agreeing with the legislative goals of reducing adult-minor sexual relationships and getting homosexuals off the streets and out of the parks, Richard argued that adults should be allowed to "gather in bars of their own choosing, solicit one another if they wish, and then depart. . . . "[25] Further, he characterized the committee's pending legislation as "so full of loopholes that it could generate a tremendous increase in the crime of blackmail."[26]

Johns and his supporters marshaled their own forces. In March 1965 the Decent Literature Council informed the press that a "secret bill," based on the Illinois Model Code and sponsored by the Atheneum Society, "a homosexual lobbying group," would be introduced by an unnamed Boca Raton state representative when the Florida legislature convened on April 6. In a meeting of over 200 Coral Gables residents, the council's president warned that this bill would allow homosexuals to marry and adopt children.

Rarely caught off guard, Richard hastily responded to these assertions: "In the first place, we aren't proposing any legislation. In the second place, 'marriage' is utterly ridiculous, adoption of children is completely objectionable. . . . "[27] Privately, Richard was furious. It was disastrous: "This representative, according to my talk with him this morning, will not now introduce the bill to establish a "commission" to adapt the Model Code. . . . He will be quite busy fighting for his political life. This is a shame because I have no one else ready to gamble on introducing it."[28]

Given the tactical error of the Society's public association with proposed legislative reform, Richard now engaged in full-fledged "covert activities."

Jack's Writing Project

Lige and Jack returned to Washington from a Manhattan Christmas holiday. Frank was waiting. At the time, Jack remembers, "there were hardly more than fifteen gay organizations nationwide, most of them one-man operations. I listened eagerly as he gave me impressions of people with whom he'd corresponded, comparing their approaches to those we were formulating." One of these was Richard Inman.

Among homophile activists, a disproportionate number of whom had Southern roots, Florida was known as "the Mississippi of the homosexual." Richard's initiative was seen as having strategic value for both the movement and the Washington Mattachine. Given Jack's Southern background and his familiarity with south Florida, Frank considered Jack the ideal point man for a new project. He asked Jack to initiate contact with Richard.

Writing to Richard under his alias, Warren D. Adkins—a tribute to Jack's West Virginia love—Jack apologized for Frank's failure to correspond, promising to be a "faithful correspondent."[29] Praising Richard, he wrote:

"Your work will be remembered when those people [who now ridicule you] have been long forgotten."[30] Although Jack kept his word on answering Richard's almost daily letters, his prediction about Richard's legacy was less prophetic.

While engaged with Richard, Jack and Lige joined Frank in a struggle to convince the conservative membership of Mattachine-Washington to adopt an antisickness policy. Jack recalls:

> We set out among the membership to cajole and convince. Lige and I began one of our first diplomatic blitzes, a task for which Frank had little taste and, being too serious and short on compromise, only a minimal ability. Part of our strength, we knew, lay in our looks, as well as in the fact that we were beginning to be perceived by the membership as symbols of wholesomeness, an all-American male duo. We consciously used our appeal to help our militant perspectives succeed.

In March 1965 the Washington Mattachine membership overwhelmingly approved the militants' position on the "sickness question." Late that spring, spurred by news of the Cuban crackdown on its homosexual citizens, Jack and others picketed the United Nations and the White House. Lige lettered the placards with slogans such as: "Castro Persecutes Homosexuals—Is the U.S. Much Better?" Dropping off Jack and the signs near the White House, Lige sped away to his afternoon shift at the Pentagon.

A new spirit of militancy was enveloping the East Coast. Cultural change supplanted individual adjustment. In May the New York militants, led by Julian Hodges, were victorious in their Mattachine chapter election. That same month ECHO endorsed summer demonstrations at the State Department, the Pentagon, the White House, the Civil Service Commission, and at Philadelphia's Independence Hall. Here the men were joined by several women of the New York chapter of the Daughters of Bilitis, founded in 1958 by Barbara Gittings, who was now the "militant" editor of *The Ladder*. Meanwhile several members of the Janus Society, led by Clark Polak, were arrested for conducting a sit-in at a Philadelphia restaurant that refused to serve homosexuals.

Deeply immersed in Mattachine politics, Jack emphasized to Richard the importance of giving "careful thought to tactics—for we are engaged, whether we like it or not, in a Movement that calls for real political strategy."[31]

Round Two: Richard Inman

Richard Inman, a political veteran and realist, hardly needed advice from the youthful Nichols. Encouraged to submit material for publication in the *Eastern Mattachine Magazine,* Richard believed that premature publicity would create problems. "Please, for now, NO MENTION of us in Florida or anything about Florida. I'm trying to let things cool here for awhile. Everything is fine with the members of the legislature. The Johns Committee will be done away with and their proposed Sex Act will be bottled up in the Mental Health Committee."[32] Richard went on to communicate his optimism on another committee's forming to study the adoption of a Model Penal Code for Florida.

Unfortunately, the Mental Health Committee, which included several Johns Committee members, approved the Sexual Behavior bill. Worse yet, another legislative committee voted out a Criminal Sexual Psychopath bill crafted and supported by the Florida Psychiatric Association's president and south Florida's state attorney. House Bill 124 allowed a trial judge, on a motion by the prosecuting attorney, to certify a person for a psychiatric hearing. Should the person be found "suffering from a mental disorder . . . coupled with criminal propensities to the commission of sex offenses," he would be declared a criminal sexual psychopath. Classified, tried, and committed—though not indicted for any crime—he would be remanded into the custody of the Division of Corrections until "cured" or for a period not to exceed twenty-five years at his or his family's expense. At the time of his commitment, a trustee would be appointed by the court to oversee the psychopath's property. The trustee could petition the court to sell the person's estate to satisfy expenses for treatment and hospitalization. This bill passed the Florida House of Representatives overwhelmingly (96–3).

The battle then went to the Senate, which was controlled by another group of pork-chop legislators. Richard as well as members of allied organizations such as the Florida ACLU, the Criminal Defense Attorneys' Association, and the Hollywood (Florida) Democratic Club immediately turned to the telephone and the typewriter: "Guess I've written somewhere around 200 letters and made at least that number of calls in the last week."[33] Some of his telephone calls were cut short by those who believed that their phones were tapped ("Most of them are their own worst enemies," lamented Richard).

By the end of May 1965 Richard—an activist with heart problems—was tenuously holding onto his Diamond Cab job as the sixty-day legislative session neared adjournment. In an open letter to the chair of the Johns Committee, he petitioned Representative Richard O. Mitchell to withdraw the proposed legislation, which "will be even more ineffective and unenforceable than that which we now have." Copies of this letter were sent to state legislators and newspaper editors.

Richard's understanding of the intricacies of Florida politics, coupled with his diverse network of contacts, was apparent in a letter to Jack the following week:

Got a call from Tallahassee at 8 A.M. that sex legislation was topic #2 at the lobbyists' regular morning breakfast (at 5:15 A.M.) for the legislators. Every morning about half to two-thirds of the legislators have breakfast (at the lob-byists' expense) together in the Duval Hotel dining room (private) and discuss the coming events of the day. . . . He said that Sen. Johns and Rep. Mitchell and about 14 other present and former members of the Johns Committee . . . were planning to introduce legislation that would be extremely bad for our county, causing our delegation and their friends to have to trade votes to de-feat it and they would be forced to trade "no" votes on the various bits of sex legislation and thereby vote "yes" on the sex legislation. . . .

Johns is a devil that must be watched every second. He won't stop trying 'til the final bell at midnight this Friday. As I predicted, by concentrating on the Senate, we have so far been able to block all legislation in Senate committees, but if any get to the floor for a vote, we'll probably be dead, as I think we only have 20 or 21 votes there and 22 is necessary to control a floor vote. In return for the support of our friendly senators, the president of the Senate has been willing to refer these bills to the committees where we hold a majority control (our senators gave him a new six million dollar hospital for his little county of 10,000 people). . . . [34]

The key, however, as Richard elaborated a month later, was four sup-portive members on the Rules Committee: "Senator Johns and Rep. Mitchell were aware of the feelings of the four . . . and didn't dare publicly utter a word about it. They had their own legislative programs to take care of and if they had started hurling charges publicly the entire session could have turned into chaos."[35]

During this legislative session, Richard also had to contend with several dozen Dade County homosexuals who sent critical, anonymous letters about him to various lawmakers. Through his networks of contacts, these, too, were passed back to him:

The letters are just awful. They accuse me of every vile sex act in the book (children yet) and scream that Atheneum doesn't represent the thinking of ho-mosexuals in Florida. . . . Several are ones that have been saying the sugariest things to my face. All I can say is that they just don't realize what they are do-ing. Apparently they feel that none of this legislation . . . would have been in-troduced if I hadn't formed Atheneum.[36]

Later, as Richard predicted, the legislature quietly and unceremoniously failed to continue funding for the Johns Committee, killing both the Sexual Behavior and the Criminal Sexual Psychopath bills.

Candlelight Energies

In June Lige's Aunt Monte, living near Bird Road in Miami, invited her nephew for a visit. Lige asked Jack to accompany him. Jack explained to Lige the importance of contacting Richard: "Right now he's the only per-son in Florida spearheading Movement concerns. . . . Maybe we could even try to talk him into starting a Mattachine in Florida."

Jack wrote Richard to inform him of their pending visit to "an interesting hot spot to those of us who live safely in the North." Jack offers: "Frank had told me I should meet with him. So we went down with an agenda." Frank's suggestion for the meeting, however, did not mean he assumed the role of puppetmaster in Jack's relationship with Richard:

> After that initial contact with Inman my contact with him was strictly on my own. Frank was not influencing me, here. I became my "own man." While Frank was a great mentor to me, I had my own ideas. In fact, it was kind of a mystery to Frank exactly what was going on since he knew nothing about the amount of correspondence.
>
> Richard was taxi driving during the day and, being the celibate he was, would hole himself up in a hotel room and type these long, lengthy, full-of-energy letters. Almost without fail there was a letter from Richard in my P.O. box in Arlington every other day, if not every day. That was a shitload of correspondence to answer! Frank couldn't have kept up with that even if he had wanted to. I may have discussed certain critical things with Frank, but I was the one writing practically every other night and spending a couple of hours trying to figure out how to answer Richard.

Jack and Lige's visit came at a good time for Richard. Waiting for the court to act on reapportionment and awaiting word on the composition of the Criminal Law Revision Committee, Richard had time to reflect.

The couple met Richard at the Candlelight Restaurant in the Grove:

> The night was filled with the glow of tropical romance. Lige had an aura of fresh magnetism. By instinct, I suppose, Richard Inman recognized us as we entered the restaurant. He rose from his seat at the bar and took us to a booth, where we ordered supper.
>
> Inman was tall and skinny. His complexion was bad, his ears protruding, and he had a terribly earnest but raspy voice. But he was dead serious about gay rights. . . . Outside of Washington this was the first time Lige and I had put our talents as diplomats to work. Lige's handsome form, his engaging smile, and his easy humor were great boons. As he joined me in an attempt to persuade Inman to streamline his gay rights agenda, he was well-nigh irresistible. By urging Inman to change the name of his fledgling organization so that it reflected, along with other Mattachine groups, a party line that emphasized gay equality, we argued that he could become part of a national trend, one that might ease the isolation he was experiencing as he struggled alone.
>
> Inman wasn't difficult to persuade. He'd worked in a vacuum. . . . There in the Candlelight, new energies were born.

The Scene Behind the Scene

Richard Inman was the Gordon Liddy of pre-Stonewall gay politics. His unconventional tactics, web of contacts, and philosophy of "political dialectics" differentiated him from other homophile leaders. In his legislative struggle he adeptly used the media both openly and surreptitiously (e.g., backgrounders to Herb Rau, an influential political columnist whom Richard characterized as the "local Walter Winchell"). Richard used his closely guarded connections with those in the "rackets" (including the Mafia's top Florida man, Santo Trafficante), federal agencies, and anti-Castro fronts who provided protection. He also relied on wealthy but closeted homosexuals like George Arents who supported Atheneum financially, on friendly capitol reporters who kept his lobbying efforts outside prying public eyes, on a cadre of gay politicos as well as state politicians who delivered key votes, and on longtime political insiders such as the chief clerk of the Florida House and former secretary of the Johns Committee, Mrs. Lamar Bledsoe (to whom he even sent a vase of red roses).

In a letter to Julian Hodges, he declared: "The mastery of political dialectics is obviously necessary to survive in this type of work." Richard continued:

> I am on a friendly (yes, believe it or not) "let's talk" basis with John Evans, the Staff Director of the Florida Legislative Investigation Committee . . . and am expecting him in town this coming week for a meeting to discuss the Model Penal Code and the Miami "situation." I have requested that he bring investigators from the State Attorney General's office with him and he has agreed. I am not sure whether Mr. Gerstein is aware of this but I would prefer to assume that he has found out. I would prefer to plan as if I were walking on thin ice so I will be prepared.[37]

A year later, in a letter to Mark Forrester, the secretary for the Society for Individual Rights, Richard detailed other "behind-the-scenes" activities:

> Rep. Richard Pettigrew was the greatest help to us. Long ago I had singled him out for several reasons and as time has gone by my choice proved its value. . . . [He] was voted "most valuable freshman representative." . . . He is from possibly the biggest law firm in Florida, one of the partners is the new president of the Young Demo Clubs, another is the president of the Dade County Bar Association, another is chief legal counsel to the Catholic diocese here . . . another is chief lobbyist for the race tracks and a former congressman. . . .
>
> Robert Delaney, chief of the Capitol Bureau of the *Orlando Sentinel,* was trapped by the Johns Committee. Delaney is the man who labeled the report . . . the "purple pamphlet" and nicknamed the Committee, the Johns Committee. He was always very critical of them. . . . He was convicted and faced a 20-year sentence for committing an "unnatural act" (he got probation—finally).
>
> He was well-liked by most all the legislators and they were quite embarrassed when this happened. I never let them forget the incident. I sent the legislators (individually) letters saying that such things shouldn't be allowed to happen. It's a case of using a little used law for the purpose of getting even with a political opponent. I pointed out that this is the identical same law used against homosexuals and most of the time it is used only for a shakedown.

This was powerful ammunition. . . . I wrote to other Capitol reporters, mentioning Delaney and our fight against the laws and asking . . . for no publicity for us that would stir up the public as we only wanted to get rid of the laws that hurt their buddy, Bob Delaney. Therefore, when the session came, I was able to send two complete general mailings to all the legislators, write and call many and in spite of all the activity not one reporter in the Capitol mentioned anything about Atheneum or what we were up to. . . . 38

Although picketing as well as sit-ins and other forms of civil disobedience had been used by gay civil rights activists like Quinton Baker and Pat Cusick, it was just beginning to be appropriated by homophile leaders like Frank Kameny and Jack Nichols. Richard publicly adopted an antipicketing position but kept an eye to how this and other political tactics might best be exploited in the future. Writing in the February issue of *Viewpoint*—whose intended audience was mainstream politicians and media types—Richard "pleaded" with the Atheneum "members" who advocated more confrontational tactics such as opposing members of the Johns Committee, exposing members of the Committee's investigating staff by "dragging skeletons out of the closets," picketing government agencies, or filing their own slate of candidates:

If we are to make friends with the lawmakers, justify their faith in our integrity, and find ways of being able to sit at the conference table (in private) with them to discuss our differences and desires, then however provoked . . . we must not panic and strike back at them blindly. . . . Picketing and other mild forms of civil disobedience could result in physical violence and do irreparable harm to the homophile movement.39

Of course, privately, Richard supported such tactics. For example, he wholeheartedly endorsed Mattachine-Washington's April 17 picket on the White House, led by Jack, with signs lettered by Lige that included: "Gov. Wallace Met with Negroes—Our Gov't Won't Meet with Us." Richard wrote to the seemingly more militant Jack: "Believe me, this just thrilled me to hear such things. With this bunch of closet queens I have to contend with down here, I'd have to be a picket line of one and such would be silly. I'd have done such things long ago if I had been able to get others to go along."40

Richard's strategy proved effective. After some months of negotiation, the president of the Dade County Bar Association and the chairman of its legislative committee endorsed updating Florida's penal code and influenced the Florida Bar Association to support the creation of the Criminal Law Revision Committee. Richard continued to meet behind closed doors throughout the summer of 1965 with key legislators in order to influence the composition of the committee, which would report its recommendations at the 1967 legislative session.

Becoming a Mattachine

In their first letter to Richard after their June 1965 visit, Jack and Lige were full of praise, telling him that "we are spreading the word to everyone we meet about what an indispensable man you are to the Movement."[41] Richard invited Jack to serve as a director and vice president of the Atheneum Society. Jack accepted, though he initially declined the vice presidency.

As a member of the Atheneum board, Jack quickly moved on his agenda to bring Richard into the Mattachine-Washington fold. Writing in mid-July, Jack pushed Richard for several changes: a statement of purpose for the Society ("I think that Atheneum would do well to orient itself in an activist direction . . . "); a constitution ("What I would like to see disappearing is the mystery which surrounds Atheneum"); restricting the Society's scope to Florida ("This would set a good example . . . 'Of America' . . . puts homophile organizations in competition with each other unless . . . [it] offers services to its members that no others do . . . "); and changing the organization's name to Mattachine. Although this last change was Jack's primary interest, he proposed it diplomatically:

> I have a personal preference for Mattachine but I have also developed a fondness for the word "Atheneum" . . . probably "Atheneum" is too well known in Florida now to even consider a name change, but there are a good number of homosexuals coming to Florida from other parts of the country who would recognize "Mattachine" and not "Atheneum" . . . which is sort of a brand name now.[42]

Jerome Stevens, an old-guard homophile running the League for Social Understanding, pleaded with Richard not to affiliate with Mattachine:

> Mattachine has a reputation which is as pink as you can imagine in many circles in California. The reason is not quite certain. ONE does not have this reputation. I respect you as an intelligent, practical and probably the most intelligent Civil Rights leader the movement has. Why you want to belittle yourself by becoming subservient to other leaders I do not understand.[43]

Nevertheless, Richard agreed to the change, recalling that when he first thought of forming Atheneum in May 1964 it was to be christened Mattachine.

Atheneum's transformation into Mattachine was more an alliance between Florida and Washington than a change in Richard's fundamental philosophical views or strategic aims. Richard did, however, become a useful lever for Jack and, indirectly, Frank to exercise greater influence in homophile politics. In turn Mattachine became a useful organizational umbrella for Richard's political dialectics. As Jack told Richard: "You and I, agreeing as we do, important policies could be ground out and presented to the rest of the Homophile Movement, setting standards and important ideas. . . . Who needs to know that the policies agreed upon by membership are the products of just a few minds?"[44]

Richard began confiding in Jack, giving him an "inside view of Atheneum work." Years later Jack remembers with amusement:

> Trudging to the post office each day where I would almost without fail find a five- or ten-page letter from Richard. He really did like Lige and me and truly needed someone to whom to express his inside thoughts about Movement politics and tactics. He was open to advice from us. He was also quick to say what he thought and did so in his voluminous correspondence. There was not a person in the Movement that Richard was not in correspondence with (he sent me copies of it all). But he corresponded with me most frequently. What went on between us was mostly the up-close, cards to your face, intimate contact. His letters were sincere in tone, honest in content, and direct in style.

Political Dialectics and Movement Politics

This extensive correspondence between Jack and Richard was, as Jack notes, "some of the most remarkable letters of the Movement during that era." These documents detail Richard's behind-the-scenes maneuvering and political thinking within the context of Southern politics and the homophile movement. Providing a candid assessment of their effectiveness, they reveal a stark portraiture of Richard A. Inman.

"In the beginning," Richard wrote:

> I was subpoenaed by Gerstein and was under great pressure from the press and law enforcement agencies and the Johns Committee. I have frequently had to use deceptive actions and statements with these people to get them off my back, even if only temporarily. . . . I have been devious almost to an extreme on many occasions. But that's politics. . . . Dialectics MUST be used and I'll use them whenever necessary to gain our point. This is a major point that has apparently been long lost to the other organizations. . . . If I find it necessary to agree with some legislator today that Black is White, I will do so, even if the next day I have to agree with another that White is Black. The MOMENT is the thing. . . . There is only one yardstick in politics: performance. . . . [45]

In a confidential letter, which Jack later told Richard was "the most complete description of you and your work I've seen. . . . [It] lays a kind of groundwork . . . [for] the truly active leaders here in the North,"[46] Richard defined dialectics:

> We all need to master *political dialectics*. In some ways, this could be described as the way a politician will say one thing in his platform then do the opposite once elected and then get away with it without anyone calling his cards. It could

be described as disagreeing with someone, but agreeing with them to their face so strongly that they don't hear you put words into their mouth and then before they know it, they are doing what you wanted them to do in the first place.[47]

Believing that "we will not have equality or understanding . . . until the laws are changed," Richard confided in Hodges: "I am not above playing the dirtiest kind of politics. I think more of it is needed in behalf of all of us. It is the old thing that will get us what we want NOW. I am right in line with the Negroes in that I want equality NOW, not tomorrow."[48]

Richard's letter to the Dade County legislative liaison, Richard Pettigrew—one of three legislators to have voted against the sexual psychopath law—illustrates this tactic:

> You will remember that last February [1965] I mentioned that many from our Society and affiliated organizations were in favor of picketing. . . . On April 17th, our affiliate in Washington picketed the White House and on the 18th, our affiliate in New York picketed the United Nations. [When votes on the various sex bills were occurring in May] many members of our clubs in Miami, Ft. Lauderdale, Tampa, St. Pete, Orlando and Jacksonville began openly defying me and challenged my leadership of the Society. They began making preparations to converge upon Tallahassee. . . . Plans for picketing were proceeding against my wishes and I successfully pleaded for them to stop and wait to see if another general mailing would have any effect. The result was my "Open Letter" to Rep. Mitchell. . . . The final result, of course, justified my plea and I'm pleased to say that my position is more firmly cemented than at any time since the founding of this Society.[49]

Inman implored Pettigrew to help him:

> It must be stopped and not allowed to spread down here. Picketing is like a fever. The kids in Florida see the kids in Washington getting huge amounts of publicity for the cause from the picketing and so the kids down here want to picket. . . . You must help me quiet this whole thing down. We must all act rationally. . . . Let's pass the Model Code and stop this thing right in its tracks before *sex* becomes a huge political issue here in Florida. Let's stop this thing before every political campaign is dirtied by this whole matter.[50]

This, of course, was quite different from the reality of the situation. Richard was bluffing. "While Florida's Mattachine had subscribers, supporters, and contributors," Jack confesses, "it had no active membership other than Inman himself. . . . Inman had threatened Florida politicians with something which—in 1965—could never have materialized, a picket line around the Capitol Building in Tallahassee." However, during Mattachine-Washington's picketing of the State Department, "Lige constructed a sign that read 'This demonstration is sponsored by the Mattachine Society of Florida, Inc' as part of a specific strategy we'd worked out. . . . We took a photo of the phony sponsorship sign. . . . "[51]

As Richard divulged his strategy of political dialectics to other movement organizations such as San Francisco's Society for Individual Rights, Jack expressed concern. Repeating the worry of Bill Beardemphl, then president of SIR, "that someday certain people were going to 'call your bluff,'"[52] Jack told Richard:

> Much of the political moves and pulls which you make—while very important—are difficult for outsiders to grasp or appreciate unless they are really involved. Therefore, I think other areas—more conventional—should be stressed to outsiders, including homophile leaders in other states. . . . Your orientation is in what Frank once called "smoke-filled back room politics" which is necessary and excellent. BUT most average people are NOT AWARE that these exist and when you take certain chances, they probably tend to get queasy and to wonder. . . . [53]

Jack went on to suggest "no more involved explanations to other homophile leaders about your involved and sometimes risky political moves" and to try to "give a more conventional front to MSF."

Reluctantly agreeing, Richard nevertheless found himself at odds with both the more conservative approach of those long-established homophile organizations like ONE Institute as well as the more radical street politics emerging in New York.

Like Jack,[54] Richard's position was to the left of that of the West Coast leadership such as Jerome Stevens, the curmudgeonly founder of the L.A.-based National League for Social Understanding, and Don Slater and Dorr Legg, longtime leaders of ONE Institute. This older generation of activists favored an educational approach over civil rights activism, bickered over precise use of language such as "homophile," and relied on mental health professionals and social researchers rather than on gay activists and sympathetic politicians. Writing Jerome, Richard asked: "What the hell else are we if we're not fighting for Civil Rights? Are we a university where someone goes to get an education? Hell no! Furthermore, if it is 'radical' to push test cases in court and attempt to influence legislation then I gladly plead 'guilty as charged.'"[55]

Jerome firmly replied: "Civil Rights without education is impractical. Without educational material . . . civil rights material is prejudiced and emotional. Giving lectures helps the individual and it builds professional support for the Civil Rights stands necessary for the improvement of society. . . . "[56]

Richard shared little of Jerome's conservatism: "Laws are on the books here in Florida that make it a crime for two or more homosexuals to assemble in a public place (a bar, etc.) and one makes it a crime for a homosexual to own a bar or be employed in a bar. These are obviously unconstitutional and must be removed from the law books. It is from such laws that anti-homosexual feelings of the general public stem."[57]

Richard did share Jerome's disdain for communist activists and leftist organizations. He steadfastly opposed those seeking to model the homophile

movement along the lines of the Vietnam, free speech, or civil rights struggles. Richard's concern, though, was primarily tactical. "Civil disobedience
like sit-ins . . . DEFINITELY NO! We start that and then we'll be classed
right along with the Vietnam and Berkeley crowds. Why in hell do some of
us think we must ape others? Can't we be original? Don't we have an original and unique problem?"[58]

In another letter to Jack, Richard underscored the differences between
the homophile and the civil rights movements:

> Too many of us have looked upon the Negro civil rights movement, seen what
> they have done that has created their success and then gotten the idea that if
> these ideas worked for the Negro, they will work for the homosexual. NOT
> NECESSARILY SO AT ALL. The Negro problems are of a totally different na-
> ture than that of the homosexual. We CAN look upon their efforts to see what
> they have done that has produced good and bad effects, but then we . . . must
> formulate our own strategy.[59]

In a characteristically lengthy letter to the Society for Individual Rights,
Richard lambasted those who sought to emulate the civil rights movement:
"As long as the majority of homosexuals cannot be identified upon sight,
and as long as they continue to live in apathy and fear of exposure, they
will not join in a mass demand for their Constitutional rights. . . . "[60] After
the Watts riots he declared: "We should be referring to it as the Homophile
Constitutional Rights Movement. Particularly since the recent LA riots, the
words 'civil rights' are acquiring a bad taste in many mouths."[61]

Richard was also leery of the more radical element represented by the
new generation of gay activists. He seldom saw eye to eye with Mattachine–New York strategies and proposals advanced by the "reckless"
Wicker, the "too-gutsy" Leitsch, or the "Caesar-like" Hodges. "I believe all
the wrong tactics are being used in New York, but there is no sense in
telling Randy or any of them."[62] Influenced by Jack and Frank, Richard
was concerned about "anarchists" like Dick Leitsch and Randy Wicker
who opposed the "corporate image" of the pickets. Echoing Frank,
Richard believed proper attire was a must: "Whether you call it a 'corporate' or a 'professional' image, I see nothing wrong with either. Both are
better than a bunch of painted fairys mincing around the block."[63]

Not surprisingly, Richard found himself attacked by other leaders in
their private correspondence. Dick Leitsch, for example, wrote to fellow activist Elver Barker, thanking him for sending copies of Barker's correspondence with Richard and Jack:

> I am very happy you said what you did. Unfortunately, the so-called "ho-
> mophile movement" is not an effective movement, but too often an albatross
> around the necks of those who are trying to be effective in the cause for which
> we are all supposedly working. Richard Inman, Clark Polak, Hal Call, and

Shirley Willer are the obstructionists, who frequently have to be worked against more diligently than the recognized opposition![64]

Richard, too, was troubled by the liberationist positions of Polak, whose *Drum* magazine included physique photography and articles such as "Beginner's Guide to Cruising" and advocated gay marriage or adoption of children. These objections, again, were rooted in tactical considerations, not personal preference. For example, publicly Richard dismissed gay marriage and adoption as "absurd"; privately, he supported them as a long-term goal:

> Laws and society must first have an entirely different viewpoint with respect to homosexuals than they do now. Therefore, though marriage and adoptions (and I'd just love to have a little kid of my own) are important, they are not of most importance right now. Right now, laws need changing and until they are changed, law enforcement officers and general society will not change their opinions of homosexuals.[65]

In another letter, he wrote:

> Diversions such as marriage, adoption and an unnecessary preoccupation with the subject of pornography all tend to create enormous resistance in the minds of the public and lawmakers against the homophile movement. These major and minor items should be listed and separated and the entire emphasis of the movement put upon the first category [model legal code, nondiscrimination in government and private employment, honorable discharges, freedom to assemble in bars]. Shove the others to the back, at least for now, until we get the items in the first group accomplished.[66]

For Richard few issues generated deep-felt emotional reaction. One, though, was communism. Among the many people with whom Richard corresponded was Chicago's Bob Basker, of Mattachine-Midwest. Though more allied with Frank Kameny's position, Basker astonished Richard when he defended the right of "commies" to assume leadership in the homophile movement. Richard viewed himself as a "patriot." Supporting—like most Americans—the blockade of Cuba and lamenting the Bay of Pigs fiasco, he exploded: "Do you realize that with the letters I have in my files from politicos and others of prominence what a target our files would be for communists to get their hands on? What a setup homophile organizations are for communist infiltration, takeover, blackmail. . . . "[67]

Paradoxically, Richard shared Lenin's philosophy that the end justified the means. In practice, Richard had little genuine interest in fostering a grassroots, democratically based homophile organization. Jack, though, was quick to point out that having the *image* of one was critical: "Whenever you give a little freedom you also gain. Can't afford to look too centralized, as it leads to revolt rather than cooperation. A voice gives the membership a spirit, a morale, a feeling of significance."[68] Richard agreed but lectured Jack about the Zen of leadership: "The Movement has a natural momentum of its own. If you want to sit it out, it will roll over you. If you want to race ahead, you'll outstrip it and you'll be lost anyway."[69]

Forming the National

Richard's politics of dialectics was most apparent in the fight over the formation of a national homophile organization. Jack ardently opposed Frank's efforts to centralize ECHO. Writing Richard, he bemoaned: "Kameny is out (come hell or high water) to create a National Organization and I am going to do whatever I can to block such a step."[70] He warned Richard, "If he were to be on the Board of a national organization he would have faith in himself to sway it and get it to do what he thought best. I just do not have that much faith in Frank."[71] Similarly, Richard respected Frank's intellect and accomplishments. But he, too, opposed Frank—and was backed by Hodges and Leitsch—on the creation of a "super homophile organization."

Characteristic of his Republican Party, states' rights leanings, Richard envisioned a national organization that would "keep its paws off of any form of local administration and stick strictly to helping to formulate an agreeable national policy and a listing of major national goals."[72] Later he articulated the design for a now familiar model: "The national should . . . keep them informed of all latest developments re the Movement and re research and re fact. The national would have a nationwide list of attorneys, doctors, ministers, psychiatrists, and others who are sympathetic. . . . "[73]

Despite Jack's repeated invitations, Richard refused to attend the fall 1965 ECHO Conference held in New York City. Richard felt that his presence might be interpreted as an endorsement of a centralized organization. He, along with Jack, pushed hard for a national gathering "to which the leaders of ALL U.S. homophile organizations have been invited"—including West Coast conservatives in the League for Social Understanding, the entrepreneurial sexual freedom advocates like Philadelphia's Clark Polak of the Janus Society, the Society for Individual Rights, the largest and most active membership organization, based in San Francisco, as well as the New York militants—and to which "all can contribute something."[74]

Richard expressed optimism to Mark Forrester of SIR: "Certainly there are many, many important points on which we can all agree such as abolishing discrimination by private employers and government, revision of sex laws, freedom of assembly, picketing regulations and the need for a clearinghouse. . . . "[75]

Immediately after the October ECHO Conference, the largest gathering of homophile organizations to date, Jack wrote Richard telling him to "hold onto your hat." Ecstatic, Jack explained that agreement had been reached for a Kansas City planning conference in February in which each organization would have one vote, with the purpose much along the lines that Richard, Jack, and others had been advocating. "I do not believe a super organization will be the outcome," a "much heartened" Jack wrote.[76] Richard agreed to come.

Kansas City

In addition to collaborating on "the national" during the fall and winter of 1965, once the new charter for the Mattachine Society of Florida was filed and approved,[77] Jack and Richard entered into a publishing venture between Mattachine-Florida and Washington.[78] In the December issue of the Florida Mattachine *Viewpoint*, it was announced that the two Mattachines would "jointly publish . . . a new magazine entitled *The Homosexual Citizen*." Replacing the subscription for the *Eastern Mattachine Magazine*, the *Citizen* would include "news of civil rights and social rights for homosexuals." Its title would remind readers "by combining the words 'homosexual' and 'citizen' of a truth that is too often forgotten."[79]

The first issue of *The Homosexual Citizen* came out at the beginning of 1966. The twenty-page booklet included contributions from members of Mattachine-Washington and Florida highlighting the ECHO Conference, articles on picketing, and an essay from a college student. Richard penned a review of Benson's *In Defense of Homosexuality*, which he praised for the absence of "apologetic remarks" and for its forceful "philosophical argument for social application." Warren D. Adkins and Robert C. Hayden (Jack and Lige) wrote about the "unwholesome conformism" and the "distorted sexual concepts of that twisted society" among those who choose marriage because of notions of "duty" or "obligation" or to avoid suspicion of being "queer."

In subsequent issues, the "Florida Section" was edited by Lige. In the May issue, Jack critiqued the "sickness theory," detailing its abuse by psychiatrists and politicians and the necessity that homosexuals refute it. His argument went well beyond the "abuse" of psychology in the hands of homophobic psychiatrists and reactionary politicians. Articulating a sentiment that would become the hallmark of Gay Liberation a few years later, Jack declared: "Homosexuality is not a psychological issue. It is a social issue which, unfortunately, has psychological effects."[80]

Not surprisingly, this position was met with skepticism, if not hostility, by some homophile leaders. Elver Barker, for example, after reading this essay in an otherwise "outstanding" issue of the *Citizen*, wrote to Jack and Richard:

> In our movement it is of the utmost importance that we not overlook the existence and nature of the unconscious, either with reference to the individual or

to the social group. There is very real evidence that in many cases psychosexual development can and should be guided through controlled parent-child relationships during the formative pre-pubertal years, and at least exclusive homosexual development prevented. For those of us who would prefer a complete life with children, to be exclusively homosexual is a definite handicap, even in a culture where homosexuality is accepted.[81]

Despite such criticisms, in the *Citizen* Richard railed against petty internecine bickering. Anticipating the Kansas City summit between East Coast and West Coast homophile leaders buffeted by representatives of three Midwestern groups, he hoped that the gathering "will deal only with issues and ideas and will not make personal attacks upon the individuals espousing them."[82]

Held in the Crystal Room of the State Hotel, the National Planning Conference was attended by fifteen organizations ranging from ONE Institute and the Daughters of Bilitis to the Janus Society and Mattachine–New York. Richard reported: "Arriving Friday night prior to the conference, many leaders, though they had corresponded for several years, met for the first time. Representatives from the East Coast and the West Coast, of organizations both old and new, large and small, activist-oriented and social-service oriented . . . analyzed the ideology of the movement, its strategy and methodology."[83]

With more than forty people participating, Richard addressed the group at the first morning session. Preaching the politics of dialectics, he lectured the assembly:

> The strength of our Movement lies NOT in great numbers of members, but in the use of covert influence of a few well placed persons. We must realize that most homosexuals who are potentially our greatest assets do not go to gay bars, will not attend meetings of homophile organizations, nor will they become members. They are the gay politicians, government administrators, law enforcement officials, advertising and public relations men and newspapermen.

Three decades later, Jack recalls Richard's presence and impact:

> Certainly Frank Kameny and Barbara Gittings as well as others were glad that Inman was in Florida—even though they may not have been quite sure *what* was going on. There was nothing like that in Georgia or anyplace else in the South. And, at that time, Florida was the *worst* place in the Union.
>
> In Kansas City, he met up with people with whom he'd long corresponded. Neither of us was particularly wild about Hal Call, and I was less than impressed by jovial Guy Straight, though Inman struck up a laugh-filled friendship with him in the coffee shop. This association with Straight and his materials was, I think, later part of his bookstore's "obscenity" problems.

Rev. Clarence Colwell, minister of the metropolitan mission of the United Church of Christ in northern California and president of the Council on Religion and the Homosexual, served as the conference moderator. Heated and lengthy debates characterized the sessions, particularly on the issue regarding the nature of homosexuality and its classification as a sickness. Jack recalls:

> Bill Beardemphl of SIR denounced aspects of our East Coast militancy. On the floor Kameny and Beardemphl traded—in bombastic tones—the disagreements. Ideologically, Richard was much closer to us on the sickness question whereas much of the rest of the movement was not. The rest were far behind us in terms of strategy and ideology. I remember Kay Tobin Lauhusen collaring me in an aside and whispering, "The West Coast people are methodological and the East Coast groups are ideological."

The delegates gave near unanimous approval (44–1) for a resolution demanding an end to discrimination in the workplace and the military as well as the cessation of police harassment and "Gestapo-like 'purges.'" From Jack's vantage point, however, it lacked substance. "We spent hours in an ideological battle . . . which resulted in a mediocre statement that meant nothing. The Conference statement on pathology was hopelessly watered down. We went home with dimmed hopes." The sickness issue was tabled for the fall conference in San Francisco.

During the conference, Jack resigned his office of vice president of the Florida Mattachine. "I was overwhelmed by Washington-Mattachine. I turned the vice presidency over to Foster Gunnison Jr., who we were all meeting for the first time." A forty-one-year-old bow-tied Connecticut aristocrat with two master's degrees, Gunnison had recently come across Donald Webster Cory's classic and had become involved in Mattachine–New York. He amiably agreed to succeed Jack Nichols as Florida's vice president. "Though Inman very much liked Gunnison, I think he'd have preferred it if I'd stayed on. He didn't argue, though, and the transition was smooth."

Although Foster shared Jack's distaste for "fringe elements" like beatniks and Vietnam protesters, he, like Frank, favored a centralized national organization. Describing Richard as a "lone wolf," Foster, like Jack, supported a place for social activities such as those sponsored by SIR.[84] He did not share Richard's penchant for secretive maneuvering or belief in the strategic value of closeted homosexuals. However, he shared Richard's Republican leanings.[85]

In his first Florida Section essay appearing in *The Homosexual Citizen*, "The Agony of the Mask," Foster first cautioned against the "unabashed homosexual who throws it in your face. . . . The exhibitionist seeking one more way to attract attention, the rebel seeking one more way to strike a blow. . . . " He then thoughtfully outlined the problems of remaining in the closet:

Secrecy retards the growth of the homophile movement . . . deprives the homophile movement of institutional support . . . distorts research . . . and the public image . . . supports cruel, self-defeating or unenforceable laws . . . encourages persecution . . . corrupts the public morality . . . and personal morality . . . damages self-image . . . destroys self-identity . . . fosters loneliness and isolation.[86]

Characterizing Foster as "less forceful than myself," Jack found that his absence meant that there was no one to encourage Richard to retain his Mattachine affiliation. "My giving up the position was one of the things that made Richard feel bereft of any kind of anchor to the movement." Within a year the Mattachine Society of Florida (MSF) was officially disbanded. Foster, who later credited his correspondence with Richard with "sharpening" his thinking about movement strategy and championed Richard as "an unsung hero of the movement,"[87] served as an officer for the Florida League for Good Government. In the newsletter, Richard informed his readership that this organization "will continue with a much broader program than MSF ever undertook."[88]

Richard continued to seek the abolition of the city of Miami's antihomosexual ordinances and to battle his nemesis, Richard Gerstein. He no longer believed, however, that a national organization or a collection of regional homophile fiefdoms would have an impact on the homosexual's day-to-day life.[89] Impatient with the progress of the homophile movement and skeptical of its leaders' motives, Richard redirected his energies to south Florida.

Patience

Since Jack had first met Lige at The Hideaway and quickly employed him to assist in the printing of the Mattachine newsletter, their two-year romance had been saturated with movement politics: picketing, meetings, printing, canvassing, organizing. As Jack worked late hours answering Richard's letters or speaking with Frank by telephone, Lige immersed himself in painting. One of his paintings "showed a small Disney-esque village with a stone bridge and an orange sky, inspired by thoughts of his never-forgotten birthplace in the hills. Lige was very patient with me and, consequently, I call that painting Patience."

But even Lige's mystical patience had limits. Jack arrived in Kansas City hoping to "ease my way out" of Florida:

My life had become a series of MSW board and committee meetings and late-night hours at the typewriter. It was my idea that since Gunnison had shown such continuing interest in our viewpoints and projects, there seemed an immediate opportunity for him, one that would give him status in the newly developing movement and take the heavy workload off my back, especially the correspondence—a daily fix that Inman required.

While Foster Gunnison picked up the brunt of correspondence with Richard, there was a growing divide between Lige's yearning for lover's companionship and Jack's ideal of movement comradeship.

> One evening as we sat listening to Mattachine speeches, hearing once more the familiar rhetoric and trying to laugh at old movement "jokes," Lige realized that our lives had succumbed to a routine. If this was gay liberation, there was little joy. . . . We were spending ourselves—feverishly—for others. . . . Somehow, Lige thought, we must get back to more basic things. But Jack was too involved, too preoccupied. . . . He didn't understand Lige's wishes. Abruptly, Lige called a halt to our habit-ridden existence and insisted that we separate— at least for a while. . . . [90]

Timidity, Audacity, and Uncertainty

From the founding of the Atheneum Society in 1964 through the dissolution of Mattachine of Florida in 1967 and the eventual demise of the Florida League of Good Government in 1969, Richard Inman was a center of controversy and an object of admiration, jealousy, and harassment.[91] Despite his commitment to act locally, as the founder of the first state-chartered homosexual organization in the South and the first Southerner to openly challenge legalized discrimination of gay men and lesbians, Richard struggled against those hiding in their Coconut Grove closets as well as politicians prescribing prejudice and police enforcing homophobia.

In 1965, he recalled the early struggles in establishing and presiding over Atheneum:

> Such pressure was put on her [Lea Surette, the bartender and Atheneum vice president] and her employer by Miami Police that she resigned last October 1st. For months, the pressure has been building up against Marty [the heterosexual lawyer and fellow Atheneum officer]. Yesterday, his office phone was completely tied up with protest calls and this morning he informed me that I would have to get a new Secretary and legal counsel. . . .
>
> On March 1st a "watch" was placed on my PO box. In a letter dated March 9th to Sen. Eastland [a Mississippi Democrat] and the Senate Internal Security Sub-Committee (with copies to the Miami Postmaster, the FBI in Miami and the Florida Civil Liberties Union) I protested the "watch." . . . They [The Johns Committee and Duane Baker], Gerstein, the Miami police and others continue to harass me. They attempted to use a 20-year-old boy to trap me. . . .
>
> After failing twice to persuade my employer to fire me, the Miami police have started giving me tickets. . . . Since October (and it has been many years since I had received a ticket), I have been given four tickets. The last one comes up in court this March 19th. I may lose my job for one month and this will take all of what little I have saved in the past. Prior to that EVERY PENNY I have earned since last July (above a very nominal living expense) has gone into Atheneum. They are quite determined (since they can't shut me up or stop me politically) to run me out of town, or better yet, out of Florida. . . .

> Everyone is hiding and are afraid that somehow they will be connected and exposed. Everyone now says "count me out." Last night, two bars asked me politely "don't come around here anymore." . . . So now without a lawyer, advisors, staff, or money I WILL have to reduce operations somewhat. But I WILL CONTINUE ALONE IF NECESSARY. . . . [92]

While a few like George Arents, "a collector of classic Dusenbergs and handsome beach boys,"[93] supported Inman's effort financially, little political activism was forthcoming from the Coral Gables–Coconut Grove gay community. Rose Levinson, by then a successful attorney, recalls:

> While we were cheering in the stands, we believed it would not be possible, it would not work out. It was just about as silly as believing that by looking at a tree you could make it grow. We never dreamed there would be a world like we have today. We just figured this is it! Did we want Inman to be successful? Yes! Were we ready to risk anything? No! It was too absurd. Most of us never dreamed of such a future—we wanted to be personally successful, that was all. But, at the time, wasn't that enough?

Richard also recalled an incident at one gay bar where he "got into a debate with one of the guys of the Coconut Grove crowd about the relative merits of the homophile movement." Richard lamented: "He wouldn't give a donation because 'I don't believe you'll ever be able to do any good for anybody and for that matter, you'll probably wind up causing us to all get hanged in the long run.' THEN, this doll of a trick walked in and up to him. He handed the kid three $100 bills if he'd go home with him. He and the kid departed while I nearly cried into my drink."[94]

At both the state and municipal levels, the invisible gay presence was both an impediment and an asset:

> In any government, large newspaper, court system or so forth there are officials who are gay. They are also usually the biggest bunch of clannish closet queens that exist. We were lucky enough to know who many were and have access to information as to who else was in a position of influence. Such closet types just *hate* to get mail from a homophile organization. I wrote them all regardless of how high their position was. I made no reference to knowing they were gay, but said that they should use their influence to help us get certain things defeated, and the Model Code passed. I must admit that some of the highest officials nearly became raving savages, they were so furious that I would dare write about such a subject. I followed the letters with another saying that I certainly hoped I would find no evidence that they had not done their part. In spite of their fury, they did.[95]

Gays were also found among the local political campaign managers and advance men where, to Richard's dismay, they sometimes did great damage to the movement: "Various power plays are being pulled by many of them."[96] Richard went on to describe reports in Herb Rau's political column, "Miami Confidential," that several supporters of Miami Mayor

Robert King High, who was running for governor, suddenly abandoned him. Farther down in the column, according to Inman, there was a note warning readers not to invite "the Admiral" and Attorney General Earl Faircloth to the next "political shindig," since Faircloth had just learned that the Admiral served on his opponent's finance committee. Continuing, Richard described the lavender-and-lace side of Florida politics:

> "The Admiral" is the president of the Tiger Bay Political Club here (the most powerful political organization in the state). . . . Both items are related, though I do not believe the columnist knows it. Both incidents were triggered by a private investigative report ordered by a state official (gay) from a Miami private detective. When the detective started digging he sold out his client and others and went where the green was greener.[97]

As Richard continued to meet political difficulties throughout the summer of 1965, he continued to fill Jack in on south Florida's seamy side:

> The meeting at George's house for tonight is off. To my everlasting humiliation, these SOBs down here are still hearing stories about the possibility or probability of me being some kind of informer or undercover agent and they are wary of a meeting being a set-up for a raid. . . . None will come right out and accuse ME, but say such things as "so many people's phones are probably tapped, including yours, that it would be almost impossible to hold a meeting without the cops knowing and raiding it." Few will even listen to my arguments in rebuttal and if I make my arguments too strong, then they start saying (as one guy told me another had told him) "something smells, or he wouldn't be wanting to get us all together in one place at the same time."
>
> These fools down here who are the (gay) professional political campaign managers are all now fighting each other and cutting each other's and my throats. All are actually acting as if all heterosexual candidates and/or managers have resigned from the forthcoming re-apportionment elections and have left the field wide open to them. Therefore, their attitude is not whether a candidate wins who is pro- or anti-homosexual, but (assuming ALL candidates will be pro-homosexual) which gay manager or group of managers will get HIS candidates into office. . . .
>
> The "Admiral" and one of his cronies, a top political reporter . . . and one other . . . are at the root of all the trouble here. None of the three have ever backed or managed a loser in a campaign. That's quite a record, but now with them fighting each other and others and me, they are riding for a terrible fall. I just pray it doesn't somehow break into the open. . . .
>
> So, there you have it. No trust at all. Just suspicion, guilt, hatred, and avariciousness. It's a pity and a crime, but that's screaming bitches for you.[98]

Shakedowns and Shibboleths in Local Politics

The ability to influence local politicians was critical in Richard's strategy for rescinding local city ordinances and ending police harassment and shakedowns. Mulling over Miami's liquor laws in mid-July 1965, he added a handwritten note to his usual error-ridden, typed letter to Jack: "I've been trying to make up my mind to get on [Mayor] Bob High's back about the city liquor laws. They prohibit homos from holding a job in a bar or a license. He'd be *furious* if I made a big *public* issue about it and he's not in a position to suggest or approve that it be taken out. It'll cause much bad feeling between him and I, if I do anything."[99]

Jack advised caution: "You might wait until you can REALLY make a big public stink about it—and concentrate on more fundamental issues at the present time (UNLESS you feel that this might win MSF favor with the bars). . . . I can't see making Bob High mad at you if he is presently amiable."[100] After thinking about it, Richard agreed: "I'll just leave well enough alone for now 'til the state criminal code has been changed. Then I'll quietly go see Bob High and ask for an all new code here that simply omits mention of the assembly or employment in the bars, etc."[101]

Richard recognized that the adoption of the Code would simplify these efforts: "We shouldn't attempt to tackle all the city government to get anti-homosexual measures removed from the books of each. Instead the Unified Code would mean that all courts of the 27 cities would be abolished and the one Metro court would try all criminal cases. . . . Once all law was under one roof, then it would be easy to get the Metro Commission to adopt an entirely new Penal Code. . . . "[102]

As a political pragmatist, Richard created and abandoned organizations as the need arose. That July he chartered the Florida League for Good Government (FLGG) to "use that organization as a wedge" in the forthcoming debate on the Model Penal Code.[103] According to Richard, "FLGG will (to all outward appearances) be a heterosexually politically oriented organization (slogan will be "Government is your business—know your business") while MSF will be strictly a civil rights oriented homophile organization." Disbanding Atheneum, he believed, would hasten the Code's adoption: "We became too closely identified with pushing for the Model Penal Code. We must get away from that, otherwise (since that is what we want passed) people, and mostly the legislators, are going to develop resistance. . . . "[104]

The formation of a new chartered corporation promised other benefits:

Under Florida law it is necessary for a non-profit corporation to be at least two years old in order to get a private club liquor license. FLGG will qualify by the time of the 1967 session of the Legislature. I have told certain legislators that "my price" for keeping sex out of politics in Florida is (1) that they pass the Model Code, and (2) that we be given a private club liquor license with a special proviso written into our bill that exempts our club from having to make the membership list or membership records available for inspection by the State Beverage Dept. or by any governmental organization.

I believe you will agree that such a license should be highly prized and we'll get it! Private club licenses even now sell for as much as $25,000 to $35,000 just for the piece of paper. Control of such will give Mattachine of Florida quite a unique asset . . . it could become a highly profitable source of income to sustain Mattachine of Florida.[105]

In early August, a dismayed Richard learned that Mayor High had killed a proposal for an expanded metropolitan government and supported a city stop-and-frisk ordinance. Richard phoned John Pennekamp of the *Herald* to express his outrage about "High's lack of leadership and double-cross of Metro." Behind the scenes, Richard convinced several of High's major campaign workers to resign and a few major supporters to withdraw. Later that day Rep. Pettigrew contacted Richard, warning him "to let up" on the mayor and stop tossing his "weight around" if he wanted things to keep on track in the legislature. High, according to Richard, "was so furious that he's blowing fire," all the more infuriated by Richard's threat to "increase Civil Rights activities including picketing at City Hall."

Richard was in a political dilemma, however: "I can't MOVE without being accused of rocking the boat. . . . This means that now if I'm to do nothing but be a good quiet boy for the next two years, the 1967 Legislature may, or may NOT approve the Penal Code. If I'm to remain so quiet, I can't make ANY further local moves at all. All I can do is sit in a rocking chair and wait out the two years. . . . What in hell to do?"[106]

After consulting with Frank Kameny, Jack wrote back a week later: "Nothing should tie your hands behind your back—nothing should make you sit in a rocking chair for two years. Sit tight for a little while and see what reaction you get to your threat to High about picketing."[107]

On September 5, 1965, the *Herald* began a series on lawlessness in south Florida focusing on mob-controlled narcotics and prostitution. Richard confided to Jack the names of several Miami police officers "in charge of the shakedown of the bars and gay kids. They're grossing several million a year . . . and have always made the 'queers' the patsy for their cover-ups each time they got a little unfavorable publicity about something else. I'm NOW just waiting any moment for them to attempt something as a smoke screen for this big exposé."[108]

Richard penned an "open letter" to the mayor a month later. "If I don't hear (a promise) from him . . . copies will go to everyone from the Governor on down."[109] His letter was a land mine:

> Certain laws on the books are almost totally useless and unenforceable, but are sometimes used to entrap various persons who may be unpopular with certain police officers, politicians, and others. . . . You have done a magnificent job helping to scuttle Metro and especially their Unified Penal Code. . . . But what of the tens of millions of dollars of illegal betting and prostitution that has been uncovered by the *Herald*? If you are the man who has the ability to be Governor, where's your leadership now? It is my belief that corruption can-

not exist on such a gigantic scale without some form of "official" sanction.
There is little question in my mind that these same "officials" who give sanction to such lawlessness are the same ones who constantly harass, shakedown,
and blackmail homosexuals. . . . They will welcome your "stop-and-frisk" law
as a weapon to use against "independent" gamblers so that in quick time the
"syndicate" will have full charge of the County.[110]

Mayor High telephoned Inman. "He screamed. Got totally out of hand
and I hung up on him and called Dick Knight [of the *Herald*]. . . . He said,
'Hold off 'til I call Bob.'" According to Richard, Knight called back asking
him to wait for a few days, when

He'd have definite word for us. I've [Inman] demanded the whole vice squad
be assigned to the city stockade (I'm serious) and I've demanded a promise
that High will work FOR Metro and the Code and in some way kill the stop-
and-frisk when it comes to the final reading. That's a big order. Doubt if I'll get
it. I'm walking a thin ice because of a possible charge of blackmail of the
Mayor.[111]

Three days later, Richard informed Jack:

I'm going to give Bob the list of names of the cops that have been shaking
down the kids and the names of the attorneys that work with them. . . . The
Grand Jury has started an investigation of what has been revealed in the *Herald*. Most every issue now carries front page headlines of new "exposés."
. . . The Grand Jury had "directed" Gerstein (HA!) to request help in the investigation from the Attorney General (Earl Faircloth). WHAT a slap in the face
to Gerstein. Of course, Gerstein is in up over his head anyway. . . .
   Several of the local gay bars are mob owned, including the old "Billie Lee's"
(now the Mayflower). . . . I think I told you I have a friend in the FBI didn't I?
Well, he sent me the enclosed pics on August 25th. The guy is the boss man of
the syndicate's homo shakedown detail for the whole U.S. He's in Miami one
day, New York the next, and LA the next. Did you know the syndicate has a list
of wealthy gay guys who they regularly shakedown? . . . I was able to find out
that [he] was the silent partner with [Nat] the owner of The Spot (semi gay).
. . . I've known [Nat] for 12 years. Remember the "E Club?" [Nat] owned it,
too. Guess who's [Nat's] other partner? GERSTEIN! Has been for years.[112]

Richard, of course, had little use for the owner of The Spot, at the time
the largest gay club in the county, whose owner "and his bartenders (all
hoods, but GAY hoods yet), are telling the gay kids here in Dade that *I AM*
an informer for Gerstein."[113]
   The next day, Mayor High called Richard to apologize for "blowing my
stack." According to Richard, if "enough facts" were given to the mayor
and Knight, then both the city's Internal Security Division and the *Herald*
would "run it down" with the paper devoting one of its series articles to
"Official Shakedowns of Homosexuals." Richard went on to tell Jack:

That's exactly what I want, of course. I have the "dope" on the Chief, a captain, two lieutenants, two sergeants, three detectives and five plainclothesmen. . . . [The chief] started as a patrolman and today drives a new Lincoln Continental, lives in a $200,000 home, has a yacht (53 footer). . . . Bob . . . said for me to come to his office Wed. morning at 9:30 (groan—I don't know how I'll get out of bed so early) and he'll set the rest of the entire morning aside for me. I told him I have 34 separate items to discuss and that I have four kids who will call while I am there to talk to him and testify anonymously on the phone as to what policemen shook them down, how much, when, and so forth. Bob was VERY pleased with this. . . . [114]

As might have been predicted, the all-morning session at the mayor's private law office became truncated into a forty-five-minute affair: "He kept saying 'you've REALLY GOT something here.' I knew it was good evidence, too, to get the 'queerbait' squad disbanded. High quickly agreed to a full investigation and the *Herald* has indicated that they may make 'Official Shakedowns of Homosexuals' a topic of their crime series."[115]

In a letter to his friend Dick Knight of the *Herald,* a close associate of the mayor, Richard expressed his regrets about the abbreviated morning meeting: "Bob didn't want to hear any of my arguments about why the bars should be left alone and why, as a proper alternate, enforcement should be confined to the parks, playgrounds, public toilets, etc. But then, he was pressed for time. I was able to only mention the attorneys . . . and [the vice] squad and their methods."[116]

There was also "no time" to talk about the chief, the Sheriff's Department's "funneling" information to private investigators associated with the John Birch Society, and related matters. Richard did, however, levy his allegations about the state attorney:

With the frequent praise I see of him in the *Miami Herald,* I sometimes wonder how the *Herald* could have the wool pulled over its eyes so consistently and for so long. CERTAINLY, Gerstein is the ONE MAN WITH THE POWER TO HAVE CLEANED UP THIS COUNTY LONG AGO, IF HE'D WANTED TO DO SO . . . he'll create a veritable reign of terror for all the gay kids in Dade (especially those with money and/or position). I believe that up to now he has left me alone, thinking that due to his initial subpoena of me (a first round that I clearly won hands down) he probably thinks I'm going to leave him alone. I'LL NEVER LEAVE HIM ALONE. Nor will I leave anyone else alone who I believe is responsible in any way for shakedowns, blackmail, and harassment of the gay community here.[117]

Richard also used his carefully cultivated network of other media contacts. Three weeks later columnist Herb Rau penned cryptically: "Insiders claim that payoffs to keep bolita and vice running rampant in Miami are peanuts compared to payoffs along the homosexual front. Recent plans for an official crackdown in this respect were suddenly called off. A high-

placed attorney gets most of this legal business."[118] Richard outlined how
the shakedown worked:

> Whenever a gay kid is picked up by the squad the detective books them and
> (confidentially) recommends [this particular] attorney who, he says, "can
> probably get you out of all this and who can get you out of here without bond,
> arrange a private hearing, no publicity. You'd like all that wouldn't you?" You
> can guess the rest. The [detective] calls [the attorney] who comes down and
> gets the victim out of jail. The legal fees vary from $500 (for a single man who
> does menial work) to $5,000 (for a married man with children who owns his
> own business) for the defense of a charge of "being a disorderly person." Then
> the court clerk assigns the case to this judge who dismisses it for lack of suffi-
> cient evidence or on a technicality. This is over a million dollar annual business
> just in this one court.[119]

In a letter to Mayor High, Richard linked these shakedowns to the city's
antigay ordinances:

> You have three ordinances on your books that cause most of the shakedowns
> of "gay bars." One is an ordinance that prohibits homosexuals from owning
> or being employed in a bar. Another is one that prohibits more than two ho-
> mosexuals from gathering in a bar. And the third is one that prohibits the
> wearing of clothes of the opposite sex (prohibiting "drag shows").
>   I hold no illusions about coming into one of your Commission meetings, rais-
> ing hell and demanding that these ordinances be removed. I would not embar-
> rass you in such a way and furthermore, I know where I'd get: nowhere. But
> clearly these ordinances ARE unconstitutional. They have just never been tested.
>   But rather than go through all the court fights, expenses, etc., in fighting all
> the cities and Metro, I supported the Unified Penal Code in hopes that once
> "unified" it could be revised and updated and in doing so, possibly it could be
> arranged for these objectionable items to be left out of the new code. If it
> couldn't then I'd only have to fight ONE court fight to change or remove these
> laws. Sooner or later I do intend to do it. . . . I have patience, but I also won't
> wait forever. . . . I'm only 38 now and I expect to be around for a long time to
> come. If I'm not, others will use my files and carry on in my stead. (I HAVE
> made provision for duplicate files in case I have some unwelcome visitors.)[120]

In pursuing the shakedown story, the *Herald* faced a problem when it tried
to trace the arrests with the attorney and the local judge. The name of the
representing attorney in the suspect court cases was absent from all the
records. Though the mayor did secure from the Miami City Commission a
revision in procedure, no proposals were forthcoming to amend or delete
the three ordinances.
    Even this small triumph proved costly. In response to the political heat
generated by the *Herald* exposé, gay bars as well as the independent rackets
were raided. Richard explained:

The *Herald* has accused the police of allowing the "Syndicate" to take over South Florida. . . . Momentarily I'm expecting the *Herald* to include in their series an article about how the cops shake down the gay kids. The appearance of that article will be a great victory for us. But in the meantime, there is a backlash. . . . The cops, being caught in the middle, can't raid those who have been paying off for fear they'll testify against them, so to improve their arrest records, the cops are harassing the hell out of the other bars. . . . 121

In early October Richard wrote Jack: "It was pretty bad for the bars this weekend. Saturday night at the Mermaid, the cops hit the place five times in two hours and kept one or two squad cars parked outside for about five hours (no arrests anywhere)."122 He gave more detail to Dick Knight of the *Herald*:

The entrapment and harassment has increased tremendously in the past week. The barmaid, Olga, at the Roman Room has been busted twice in the past week. Both for minors. The one had ID that showed he was 21, but when the cops came in, strangely they went directly to him and he admitted he was under 21. . . . Internal Security is trying to get around to the bars to ask the owners to cooperate in testifying if they have ever been shaken down by certain officers, such owners tell me they don't DARE to cooperate. . . . 123

In the midst of these weekend raids and series of police entrapments, Richard decided to write an "open letter" to the media and politicians "that should effectively counter that, but it will direct MUCH heat upon me."124 Though the letter was originally dated October 5, Dick Knight persuaded Richard to postpone its "immediate mailing"125 to two hundred people until the *Herald* had made a decision on running the homosexual shakedown story. When the story did not run, Richard released a slightly toned down letter on October 14, which read in part:

Certain laws give rise to graft and "official" shakedowns. Such laws are, in the most part, unnecessary and almost unenforceable, but are enforced to build impressive arrest statistics or for shakedown purposes. It would seem that whenever official corruption is attacked, corrupt officials resort to "smoke screen" tactics. Among the first of those to feel the "heat" of such tactics are homosexuals and bars that cater to them. . . . Harassment tactics against homosexuals have been tremendously increased in the past two weeks and will no longer be tolerated by the homosexuals in this community. We, our friends, our investigators and attorneys are standing by, prepared to meet further abuses of official authority with full exposés and court action.126

The police, as Richard had predicted, struck back:

Yesterday six guys were charged by the sheriff's office with offenses ranging from "lewd and lascivious conduct" to "indecent assault." Their names and addresses were in the paper. I immediately sent all six copies of . . . our *Viewpoint*. One called this morning to say that after being arrested and while they

were interrogating him, the detectives went into the other room (without clos-
ing the door and while pretending to talk quietly) and one asked another, "Is
this guy on that list we got from Richard Inman at the Mattachine Society?"
He said their remarks didn't fool him but were made to each of the defendants.
. . . [127]

Richard also began to receive harassing phone calls:

> Each time they would disguise their voices differently and talk real sissyfied
> and say such things as "There's a bad man over here that I want you to come
> take care of for me," and "You said you would help people and I need help.
> I've got this little doll who's got a HUGE piece of meat that I can't possibly
> handle and I thought you might be able to give him a hand."[128]

Despite the intimidation and harassment, Richard maintained his struggle,
employing the politics of dialectics. He confided in Jack:

> I want to make it appear that ANYONE who raids a bar or entraps a homo-
> sexual is doing it for shakedown purposes. . . . Also I want it to become appar-
> ent to all the SOLE REASON for passing laws or maintaining them on the
> books, whereby they restrict the freedom of assembly for homosexuals, is for
> the sole purpose of making it easy to shake the bar operators down. . . . I want
> to make criminal law revision something that the lawmakers, honest police-
> men, and the public WANTS.[129]

The Trials of Richard Inman

Throughout the fall and winter of 1965 little progress was forthcoming in
influencing Mayor High or the city of Miami to rescind the ordinances.
Hopes for a stronger metropolitan government and its adoption of a uni-
fied set of criminal codes went unrealized. As Richard prepared for his
Kansas City trip in February 1966, he sued the city of Miami in Circuit
Court with representation by Tobias Simon and Maurice Rosen of the
ACLU. Asking for an injunction and a declamatory decree, he asserted that
the set of laws "arbitrarily denies to certain and various persons their rights
to the equal opportunities upon which this great country was founded."
Judge Grady Crawford, who had sentenced the Simpson murderers to
twenty years' imprisonment a decade earlier, presided over this first civil
rights legal action brought in the South by an admitted homosexual.

Richard was also busy following the formation of the new Criminal Law
Revision Committee approved by the 1965 legislature. Immediately he began to prepare a "brief" for the Committee, proposing to bring noted experts from the Kinsey Institute and the American Law Institute to testify before the Committee in behalf of the Model Penal Code. He also announced
a "wait and see" plan on the progress of the Committee, "temporarily"
abandoning ideas to subpoena some government officials and for the

League for Good Government to push for statutes requiring all candidates to release complete financial statements and for grand juries to hire their own counsel.

As publicity of the trial heated up, Richard appeared more frequently in public, ranging from WKAT radio "Talk of Miami" to speeches at Florida State University in Tallahassee and the local Unitarian Church. He was now on the board of the Florida ACLU's publication, *The Torch,* where he sifted through news articles and provided analysis and commentary. His article for the *National Insider,* entitled "Stop Harassing Homosexuals: It's Unconstitutional and Degrading," laid out his arguments for peaceful assembly of lesbians and gay men in bars against the backdrop of the history of homosexuality.

Countering Inman, Detectives John Sorenson and David Narrow of Dade County Sheriff's Department Morals and Juvenile Squad hit the late-night radio rounds and circuit of clubs and churches, school assemblies, and PTA meetings.[130] The detectives criticized the Mattachine Society and warned about the "recruitment of juveniles into homosexuality." Estimating a county homosexual population between 35,000 and 50,000, Sorenson lectured that "60 percent of them are recruiting," using delinquent "hustlers" as "procurers" of fellow classmates who at two, five, and ten dollars a trick run the risk of "turning queer": "One out of three hustlers become homosexual. . . . One out of fifteen commits suicide because he becomes so involved. It becomes worse than dope addiction once a boy goes beyond the point of no return."[131]

During the first three months of 1966 the detective duo had spoken to fifteen of the forty-seven county junior high schools. Included in their lecture program were two films, *Boys Beware* and *Girls Beware* ("emphasis is placed on the male because of the mobility and recruitment factors"[132]), occasionally accompanied by a booklet for distribution entitled *Hope for Homosexuals.* In discussing a "cure" for homosexuals, this "pink booklet" recommended: "Then you must learn to hate, despise, crucify and mortify your flesh. You must learn to look into a mirror and honestly say, 'My body, my flesh is worthless, worm-eaten, and full of decay and death!' Cultivate a shame of your nakedness. Go to the throne of God in prayer and ask for a divorce from the love of flesh that has enslaved you."[133]

Perhaps most notable, however, was their joint appearance on WTVJ's "FYI" broadcast on April 19 at ten in the evening. Ralph Renick "hosted" Florida's first in-depth television report, billed as a "documentary," on "The Homosexual." After a brief introduction the documentary showed film footage in its negative form of silhouetted lesbians and gay men gathering on the 22nd Street Beach. Promising to show "both sides," the documentary featured extensive commentary by Detective Sorenson as well as confessional exploits of a rehabilitated hustler and testimony from two mothers whose sons' lives were "ruined" through their involvement with homosexuality.

Toward the end of the documentary, Richard Inman appeared. Practicing the politics of dialectics, he played off the documentary's theme of juvenile recruitment by linking it with law enforcement methods: "Suppose these homosexuals . . . are made to fear that each adult they encountered might be a policeman. What's the outcome? Only juveniles who might tend to give them a greater measure of safety and freedom from entrapment. . . . "

Viewing this program years later, Jack Nichols observed:

> You also need to understand that Inman was a political creature. He was attempting to work within the context of this negative program and turn it around. . . . He even goes so far in the program to deny that he is a "practicing homosexual," even though he was from age fourteen onward. While that may be infuriating to a gay activist today, Inman probably saw it as a strategy of talking from the closet: "I'm not really one of those, but I want to make sure you are not unfair with those who are."

In a follow-up editorial, Channel 4 reported that the sheriff's office had received tips about homosexual molestation (leading to one arrest) as well as "several instances of divorced or widowed mothers bringing their adolescent sons to police for instruction on the 'facts of life.'"[134] The following evening, Detective Sorenson appeared with Renick on another Channel 4 editorial announcing "just today we had approximately twenty calls. . . . I would say we could make ten cases."[135] Because of the "overwhelmingly favorable" viewer reaction, the show was repeated the following month in an earlier time slot.

As the Circuit Court proceeding dragged on, the Florida League for Good Government developed a political action program for the May primary and November elections. In June Judge Grady Crawford refused to dismiss Inman's suit despite the claim of the city attorney's office that his admission that he was "no longer a practicing homosexual" on FYI gave him no "bona fide, actual present need" for such an injunction. This victory was short-lived, however. Ten days later Judge Crawford announced that the ordinance was legal, since it showed a "rational relationship to a specific situation . . . public health, morals, safety and general welfare."[136]

Undaunted, Richard, assisted by the ACLU, appealed to the Third District Court. Through the remainder of 1966 and into 1967, Richard's adversaries counterattacked. Meanwhile Miami was rife with news of scandal, with a grand jury investigation of the municipal court system (nearby Broward County was conducting its own one-year grand jury investigation of the "homosexual problem" and subpoenaed Inman), the ouster of Dade County Sheriff Tal Buchanan following evidence of corruption, gangland-style killings, and murder-robberies of "bachelors."

Reunion

As Richard was withdrawing from Mattachine, Jack was seeking a reconciliation with Lige. Jack had quit his long-term job at the technical college, bouncing from job to job, impatient to regain the romance that he had mistakenly taken for granted. While the two were no longer living together, they saw one another at Mattachine meetings and occasionally for dates on long weekends together. Lige recalls: "It was the most passionate period of our relationship, that stormy year we were separated. . . . We were dating, then cutting off, then seeing each other again. Jack broke my door down once. . . . He wrote nearly fifty poems for me. . . . "[137]

During their separation, Jack continued his Mattachine work, appearing with Frank Kameny on a three-hour Washington television show and, in late 1966, in a CBS documentary, "The Homosexuals." Agreeing to appear "full face," he prepared for his interview with Mike Wallace by "being grilled by Kameny so that I wouldn't wander, during the interview, into speculative and possibly unscientific briar patches." During his one-hour grilling by Wallace, "I spoke pointedly about how my family had always treated me as a person and not as some sort of monster, and when he asked the proverbial 'What caused your homosexuality?' I replied that I'd given little thought to such origins, just as, I supposed, most blondes, or left-handed persons think little about the origins of their characteristics."

Jack soon escaped to Florida to sort out his life. Throughout 1967 he and Lige wrote to one another. Finally, in midsummer 1968, Lige wrote his final letter to Jack: Yes, he would join Jack in Florida, where they would reunite as a couple.

> Mom sold me her Cadillac, and when Lige arrived we packed the car and headed north by way of Kentucky. . . . Finding an apartment in New York wasn't easy. We walked the streets for two weeks, following ads we'd marked in the *Village Voice*. Finally we settled into a ninety-dollar-a-month efficiency in hippieville, around the corner from Tompkins Square Park, a few blocks from Randy Wicker's button store.

With Wicker's help, Jack secured a position at Countrywide Publications, where he was responsible for editing six magazines, including *Companion* and *Strange Unknown*. "Working at Countrywide, Lige and I met a most peculiar editor, a pudgy, animated man who sat near my desk. He told of plans to create a new newspaper unlike any other on earth. The man was Al Goldstein. His paper would be called *Screw.*"

In the first issue appeared the first homosexual column written by two gay men, aptly entitled "The Homosexual Citizen." Buoyed by the success of that column and the eruption of Stonewall, Goldstein later financed the first national weekly news magazine, *Gay,* edited by two gay Southerners—Jack and Lige.

Calling the Bluff

In April 1967, a month after the disbanding of Mattachine-Florida and fourteen months after the original ruling, the three-judge panel upheld Crawford's decision, reasoning that such ordinances "prevent the congregation . . . of persons likely to prey upon the public by attempting to recruit other persons for acts which have been declared illegal by the Legislature of the State of Florida." Judge Tillman Pearson added that selling liquor is "a public concern and may be limited and regulated by the state as a privilege." The court, however, grudgingly acknowledged that "it may be that the ordinance is inartfully drawn and that enforcement of one or more provisions may prove difficult or impossible."[138] Richard appealed to Florida's Supreme Court and received notice three months later that it refused review.

With little hope on the horizon, Richard—who had already abandoned Mattachine—now disbanded his eleventh commandment never to speak ill of a politician in public. In the summer and fall of 1967, he attacked, slashed, and burned. Appearing before the Miami City Commission, Richard charged their police department with "gross nonfeasance of duty" for failing to properly investigate the attack, robbery, and murder of a gay man. Speaking at Miami's Columbus Hotel, Richard claimed that police were using the city's antihomosexual ordinance to "shake down bars that cater to homosexuals."[139] *Viewpoint,* now of the Florida League for Good Government, widened its attacks, publicizing much of the information that Richard had threatened city officials with for years. The once-restrained newsletter was cluttered with Richard's commentaries and related news articles. State Attorney Roger Harper was tagged an "overt hypocrite," and Richard Gerstein's ex-assistants were identified as "the backbone for the criminal defense of the Mob." In the wake of the Coral Gables ordinance, Inman sent an "open letter" to that city commission. He charged Gerstein with permitting "personal friends" to operate a local gay bar and police with accepting payoffs for gay bar protection.[140] Gerstein responded by stating that Inman's accusations were "complete fabrication of facts."[141] No charges were ever brought against Gerstein on the basis of Richard's allegations.

Richard's efforts also had little impact on the bars, as they continued to be raided, or on politicians, as ordinances passed and those accused of wrongdoing retained power. In October 1967, through the efforts of the ACLU, Richard appealed the ruling upholding Miami's antihomosexual ordinances to the U.S. Supreme Court, which later refused a hearing.

His trials continued. That same month the Atheneum Book Shop, which he managed on Southwest 1st Street, was raided by the Miami vice squad.

Confiscating 1,265 magazines, thirteen packets of photographs, and a twelve-minute film, the police charged Richard with possessing obscene literature. Deploring "smut traffic" and describing all of the films, photographs, and magazines seized as "obscene," Miami Judge Gerald Tobin "reluctantly dismissed" the charges the following month on the "technicality" of lack of a warrant. "On the basis of the U.S. Supreme Court decisions and state laws, this court has no alternative but to . . . find you not guilty." Directing a steely look at Inman, Tobin paused and then punctured the silent courtroom: "But this court is unhappy with the decision."[142]

The man who had rebuked Clark Polak's male physique photography in *Drum* and who had proclaimed four years earlier, "I totally REJECT any form of T-ROOM literature . . . homosexuals look bad enough in the eyes of heterosexual society as it is,"[143] was now in the pornography business.

A year later, Richard sued the city of Miami and its Sheriff's Department for illegally seizing books as pornographic. On the cusp of the great watershed where the homophile movement was transformed into gay power, a federal judge dismissed Richard's suit during his second obscenity trial. Richard Inman soon vanished.

Two months after Stonewall erupted in Greenwich Village, a feature Sunday news story in the *Miami Herald*'s "Tropic Magazine" fleetingly mentioned Richard Inman, observing: "The Miami [gay] subculture shows few signs of the minority group syndrome. Since the demise of the Mattachine Society of Florida . . . Miami has had neither homosexual organizations nor militants. A politically docile, socially invisible subculture, it attracts little attention, and less support."[144]

That would soon change. The seeds of change had been sown in Miami.

Coda

When Richard first met Jack and Lige at the Candlelight in the summer of 1965, Jerome Stevens prophesied: "My predictions for the future of Richard Inman? He will hand over his mailing list, become disillusioned because his opinions count for nothing more than one of many votes of Mattachine officials and thus he will leave the movement and all of his startling work will be credited to the Mattachine local branch."[145] At the time, Richard humbly responded:

> I aspire to no such glory. If I can build an organization of sufficient strength to rid the state of Florida of its existing unjust antihomosexual statutes, laws, bills, and ordinances, and then be able to concentrate on re-education of the public and as a result, see happiness be found and enjoyed by the homosexuals of Florida (a type of happiness they have never before known), I'll be fully content and be ready to go meet my "Maker." Of course, if we are not successful

here, others will follow our lead. They will attempt to emulate our successes
and avoid our failures. . . . [146]

What of Richard A. Inman's place in gay history? Was his politics of dialectics an effective (or an ethical) approach for the Southern gay struggle
in the shadows of Charley Johns? Does he deserve more than a historian's
footnote? What did years of practicing the art of political dialectics really
accomplish?

For Rose Levinson, nearing the end of her illustrious legal career,
"Richard Inman was a rainmaker. Not everyone is. People like Richard Inman or a decade later, Jack Campbell, come around so rarely; they changed
a lot of things." During the 1970s a new generation of gay activists, like
Jack Campbell and Bob Kunst, would transform the political landscape:
Miami's ordinances would be rescinded; bar raids and police shakedowns
would end; a Dade County nondiscrimination law would be passed; gay-
owned businesses and gay political organizations would emerge; and the
state's sodomy statute would be overturned. In the 1960s, though, to believe that this would happen was "about as silly as believing that by looking at a tree you could make it grow."

Richard Inman's actions did not lead immediately to these changes but
they certainly laid the groundwork at a time, as Rose underscores, that was
far from hospitable to homosexuals and when few lesbians and gay men
provided support: "Of course we talked about Inman's suit, but what could
we do? We were afraid to become a party to it. We wanted to keep our jobs
and if we had our own business we were afraid of losing clients. Richard
could do it because he was 'out.' We were glad he was doing it as long as
we didn't have to get involved."

Inman's impact, though now forgotten, was apparent. In 1971 Municipal
Judge Donald Barmack heard the case against four bartenders at the Bachelor II Lounge on Coral Way arrested during a November undercover police
raid for serving drinks to homosexuals. Two weeks before Christmas he
acted on the motion for dismissal on constitutional grounds by the attorney
of the four bartenders—Rose Levinson. "You cannot label a person a homosexual or a lesbian or a pervert and refuse to serve him or her a drink."
Noting that neither Plato nor Oscar Wilde could legally visit a Miami bar,
the judge continued, "You pass a law like this and pretty soon you can
refuse to serve somebody because he's a Democrat or a Republican or blue-
eyed."[147] The judge ruled the 1954 ordinance unconstitutional. The ordinance was quietly repealed by the city following recommendations of a
committee reviewing Miami's criminal code.

During that same month, the Florida Supreme Court struck down the
state's 103-year-old "crimes against nature" sodomy statute for its "vague-
ness and uncertainty in language." The Florida legislature declined to write

more appropriately worded legislation, quietly deleting the sodomy statute in its 1972 overall reform of the penal code.

In June 1972 the American Civil Liberties Union represented the newly formed Gay Activist Alliance of Miami and its president, Robert Barry, a lighting engineer, and Charles Lamont, a former Methodist minister. After a two-hour hearing in which the ACLU presented its case to U.S. District Court Judge William O. Mehrtens for a permanent injunction against two Miami Beach ordinances prohibiting female impersonation, the judge struck down both ordinances as "over-broad" and having a "chilling effect on the parties' First Amendment rights." Barry yelled outside, on the courthouse lawn: "Bring out the gowns!" while another activist asked his friend, "You mean you're not in your drag yet, honey?"[148]

So what of Richard Inman? Jack Nichols, now living in Cocoa Beach and completing his memoirs, eulogizes:

> Richard Inman, like a bright comet, soared through skies, lighting up America's early gay and lesbian liberation cause. Unique in our movement's history, he was committed to what he called "constitutional rights" and his brave willingness to step forward in a benighted area where savage antigay persecution had become standard government fare was, to me, a foremost inspiration in those heady times. I made Richard Inman my confidant and comrade-in-arms because I knew he was working virtually alone, sometimes despairing. I embrace the memory of him still. He serves our history as a shining example of what a single, committed, energetic individual can do—even though suffering setbacks himself—in the ongoing struggle to right the lot of the wrongly persecuted.

But Richard Inman was a complex character—neither hero nor victim. Though viewed by some homophile activists as a "loose canon," he never came out of his covert closet—until now:

> I have worked for years to build a wall around myself so as to be immune from attack from ANY SIDE. . . . I should explain something to you now. I lived in Cuba for two years and traveled back and forth there much. . . . Dr. Justo Carillo, a member of the five-man "Revolutionary Council" . . . is an old friend. . . . After buying this hotel in 1960, I invited Dr. Carillo to quarter his leaders of his [anti-Castro] "Montecristi Movement" here. I donated ten hotel rooms and one apartment to them. . . . The bar jumped. All the Cuban leaders came here and drank in the bar and met in the rooms. Naturally, Police Intelligence squad and others, FBI and others (including Dept. of Justice) asked me to cooperate with them as they were sure there were MANY pro-Castro agents among the group. I did.
>
> The records of who lived here were always open to them and there was always a government agent on the premises at all times. I gave them the use of my docks free and one night (months before the Bay of Pigs) two Army trucks pulled up to the side of the hotel and about 30 men unloaded several hundred cases of sub-machine guns and ammo and put them on four small boats that

left the dock at 4 A.M. .... All that Miami preparation work centered around this hotel. ...

These things DID endear me to the FBI here and for that reason (I know at least 20 of their local agents) I do feel that they have been much responsible in not letting anything happen to me as [far as] Gerstein and the Miami police are concerned. ... In the beginning, I told Bill and several others of the agents that I wanted them and ALL law agencies to stay off my back. They've kept their part of their word and helped me that time Gerstein and a sergeant tried to trap me with the 20-year-old sailor. ...

I did have words with Bill one day when I said that if Gerstein tried any funny stuff with me and put me in court as any kind of defendant, I'd be forced to subpoena all Bill's boys and others to show the court what I'd done in the past. That didn't set too well with him and he accused me of blackmail. ... I agreed with him ... but I told him "one hand washes the other." ...

While operating the bar and hotel, the FBI brought the assistant agent in charge of the Miami office of the Bureau of Narcotics to meet me. ... Young, blond, and a doll. They said they had evidence that possibly three of the 183 so-called "anti-Castro fronts" were communist fronts that were selling dope here to finance their work. The FBI Bureau of Narcotics wanted me to work with him to help them uncover these pro-Castro agents. I said OK (like a fool).

He and I devised a perfect "cover story." He was to be my old long lost lover returned. Who would dream that a government agent would use that kind of cover? One day soon I'm sitting in the bar with the bar full of Cubans (they ALL knew I was gay) talking to one of the suspect Cubans when "Jimmy" came in the door behind me and stood looking at me and grinning. I did a double take, grinned, asked him to take the glasses off, yelled "Jimmy" and practically jumped all over him in my excitement. I introduced him to the "suspect" (whispering into his ear about Jimmy being my old lover) and invited Jimmy to sit and I bought him drinks for the rest of the night. ... But from that moment on Jimmy was IN. ...

You remember that I said when I lost my hotel, I went "South" to the Caribbean until things cooled off. I spent five months in Grand Cayman Island. ... When I got back and just asked them [narcotics feds] for some cash to reimburse myself in seeing that I had gone bankrupt while trying to help them, they refused. Then when they heard that I was starting Atheneum, I was called into the office. The assistant had been the same agent that had caught and arrested Billie Lee (remember?). They were afraid that I'd now (since Atheneum and yelling for protection of the gay bars) possibly play tricks on the Narcotics Bureau. ... [They] threatened me and said that if I ever did such a thing, that my resulting death would be just one of those "unsolved mysteries." ...

He is right and I know it. Gerstein, Headley, High, the "mob" and even the FBI and the Narcotics Bureau wouldn't be the least upset. The gay bars and most of the gay kids won't either (since they don't know the whole real story). ... [149]

By 1969, the rays of hope cast by Camelot's sword were mere reflections of an eternal flame, the dreams of the visionary on the mountaintop were shadowed by an assassin's bullet, the decade of youthful idealism was shattered by Altamont and Watergate. As the light at the proverbial end of the Vietnam tunnel dimmed, *Life* magazine had suspended publication, Jack Kerouac was dead, the New York Mets had won the World Series, and Richard Inman had vanished from the homophile movement and from gay history.

Afterword:
A Conversation
with Barbara Gittings

JS: During this era there appeared to be fewer lesbians politically involved than gay men.

BG: There were fewer women—nobody can deny that. And while we try hard to play up the involvement of women during those early movement years, the fact is that the majority of the participants were men. You must remember that men were raised to be more venturesome than women. We simply don't know how venturesome women would have been if they didn't have these constraints. During this era, women politicians were few; women lawyers like Rose were few; women movers and shakers of *any* kind were few. And lesbians generally were closeted *everywhere* except, to a very small degree, in major metropolitan areas.

JS: That was particularly true in the South.

BG: Southern communities seemed to be very close-knit. Although you could lose yourself in San Francisco or New York City and find other gay people, if you left your Southern town and journeyed one hundred miles to Atlanta you still couldn't be assured of anonymity! Family ties and connections followed you.

JS: Even today one of the first questions often asked when meeting someone new in the South is "Are you related to so-and-so?"

BG: North or South, lesbians were inhibited by our situation, and many women were simply not temperamentally inclined to be activists. Also it takes a long time to make activism popular—particularly if your family will reject you, your peers may be uncomfortable (and may make *you* uncomfortable), and your job will be at risk. Facing these consequences yet feeling that something ought to be done puts a person in a difficult dilemma. So, we had to encourage women who came into the movement without any streak of activism in them. I was not an activist when I joined the movement; my motivation was personal—I wanted to find my people and learn about homosexuality. But, as I began to see that *I* could make a difference, then activism began to appeal to me.

JS: Was there similar networking among lesbian leaders as is documented here among the men who corresponded with one another so extensively?

BG: I was too busy running the New York chapter of Daughters of Bilitis and later putting out *The Ladder* to engage in heavy correspondence. I was three thousand miles apart from Del Martin and Phyllis Lyon and we didn't carry on heavy ideological discussions; I prepared the material for each issue and then sent it out to San Francisco where they cut the stencils, printed it, and mailed it out. The magazine let me reveal my views to many others, and that was more important for me than one-on-one correspondence.

JS: To what degree are the lesbians' stories portrayed in this volume comparable to those of other women you knew during this era?

BG: Rose is a wonderful illustration of the thinking of the time. She became a lawyer and helped gay people when they got into trouble, but she assumed that she couldn't do anything about stopping the harassment and arrests in the first place.

JS: One of the revelations in this volume is the paradoxical nature of gay life. On the one hand, most gay people faced rampant homophobia with police harassment in those few places where they could congregate. However, many of the stories, like those of Rose and Merril, also reveal a life of "normality" and "gayness" which someone coming out of the Stonewall Generation, like myself, finds startling.

BG: Some of this may be the haze of recall, but there is a lot of the "don't rock my boat, I've worked so hard to float it" attitude also. Lesbians and gay men back then put a lot of effort into building their secret, good lives. They lived in their small secret compartments which may have been fun inside, but they couldn't go beyond them. Exposing themselves put their world at risk. And look at the price they paid! *Lonely Hunters* is rife with the problems that these people faced and had to deal with over and over again. They had to conceal; they had to pretend. If they were harassed or arrested—like Rose, Merril, or Arlen—they had to talk or bargain their way out. Even if they were never arrested or harassed, they were living like criminals—living in an underworld.

JS: For some of the youthful gay people profiled in *Lonely Hunters* that very secrecy—clandestine rendezvous, coded language—lent to the adventure.

BG: I felt somewhat that way myself. You realize that you do not belong to this big heterosexual world and then you find *your* people. You now belong. You're special; you're separate. The problem, though, was not only in the price paid for this secrecy but that you didn't leave a good legacy for the next generation of gay people. Every generation had to experience the same problems and misery and isolation in growing up and searching for other gay people. Sure, some, perhaps most, finally trickled through all of the barriers and found themselves living a good—though closeted—social life, but what had they done for the next generation? This is what our movement should be trying to change. We ought to leave a legacy of different circumstances.

JS: Was there a sense of leaving a generational legacy among lesbian and gay activists during this era?

BG: The big questions for my generation were: "Are we normal?" "Are we sick?" "Are we sinful?" "Are we criminal?" We didn't ask "What legacy are we leaving for the next generation?" Although we certainly assumed that what we were doing would result in a better world.

JS: What is the legacy of homophile activists chronicled in *Lonely Hunters*?

BG: Organizing is our first legacy. One of the major problems that we have had in the gay community has been our invisibility—how can you organize a people you can't see? We put much effort into trying to reach and organize these secretive people. We produced magazines and formed organizations in the face of this invisibility and inertia. Our second legacy was that we crystallized some of our specific problems and showed what could be done about them. Getting rid of the albatross of the sickness label was a *major* accomplishment of our generation—but it wasn't done without an internal struggle.

JS: Social movements, like personal lives, never occur outside a historical and cultural vacuum. While one could write a history of the gay South divorced from the politics of McCarthyism, the rabidness of conservative Christianity, and the pervasiveness of Jim Crow, it would be a very different history. From your experience, to what extent were homosexuality and homosexuals targets and to what degree were they pawns?

BG: We certainly have been pawns because we were easy targets. Most homosexuals back then couldn't or wouldn't fight back. And, in most cases, we couldn't get anyone else to stand up with us; we were everybody's pariah. The whole Johns Committee and all that went before and after is a very good illustration. Politicians used us for cheap publicity; the police used us for easy money. Occasionally, the police used us just as a show of their power.

JS: How was the South seen as a region for organizing?

BG: Quite frankly, we didn't think a whole lot about the South. We had our hands full. We couldn't even organize gay people in Greenwich Village. You must understand that the Daughters of Bilitis was founded initially to provide a better place for women to meet than the bars. Many women joined DOB because they were isolated; they hoped to meet someone "special." And, they probably put up with a lot of organizational stuff that really wasn't of much interest to them.

Those early gay periodicals—*Mattachine Review, ONE Magazine, The Ladder*—were crucial in overcoming this isolation but our outreach was limited. At first the magazines couldn't be sold anywhere and most people were afraid to have their names on gay subscription lists. We had to build our circulation largely by the magazine being passed hand-to-hand. Kay and I tried to get *The Ladder* for sale in public places for the first time. At our peak in 1966, we were selling a hundred copies each month at a Greenwich Village bookstore and fewer copies at three bookstores in Philadelphia. That was a tremendous breakthrough!

JS: What were your views about other social movements, or in the parlance of the day "mixing causes," chronicled in this book?

BG: I wanted to see us concentrate on gay issues because the narrower your platform the easier it is to get support from a wide variety of people. Besides, the National Organization for Women and the various civil rights groups didn't want to have anything to do with us early on! The pressures for us to be active in other causes really didn't emerge until the leftists swarmed into the movement after Stonewall.

I also viewed our movement as being different. Most other social change movements don't have to contend with invisibility. So we had two major purposes. One was to get the bigots off our backs—change laws, change attitudes, change practices. The second was to provide pleasant and safe ways for lesbians and gay men to meet. I can't think of any other social change movement that has had to provide a social base to that extent. Organizations like DOB and the Society for Individual Rights grew because they brought people together who were interested in meeting others. Even the lectures, debates, and other high-minded activities we held often served as a way for people just to come and meet one another.

JS: Were there no important lessons garnered by homophile activists from those working in the civil rights movement?

BG: We benefited enormously from the Black civil rights movement since we could see that people had gone out and done something that wasn't too popular and had succeeded. It was also educational for us to see how we could adopt some of their tactics, particularly the use of confrontation and how not to distract attention from your message by controversial dress and behavior.

JS: Throughout this era there were divisions about tactics, strategies, and goals among movement leaders. Perhaps progress would have been more rapid had there been greater unity and centralization.

BG: When you have a movement like ours it is a problem to try to subsume all of the different talents and tactics under one umbrella; it will *never* work. But, that has been a saving grace of our movement. We do not have a single goal, no single agenda, no charismatic leader. Outsiders who have tried to take over our movement because they thought we were a nice army of soldiers ready to take marching orders have been unsuccessful. And it really works much better when you let people just erupt into whatever it is they do best. So, as you chronicle in *Lonely Hunters*, Richard Inman was best at rattling cages, Rose Levinson helped gay men in the courts, Jack Nichols pushed for public protest. Some of the best work of subsequent generations were efforts by an individual or a handful of people. For example, the launching of the AIDS quilt—surely one of the most inspired ideas of the twentieth century; those who organized in their hometowns to fight Anita Bryant or to set up alternative proms for gay teens. For our opponents, it's like punching pillows; they knock gay people down here but we just bubble up somewhere else.

JS: What can gay activists of today learn from their forebears?

BG: Tactics and strategies are right for their times. It isn't that one is always right or wrong. During the homophile era it was right for us to dress conservatively when we protested although soon after Stonewall the dress code was abandoned. Earlier it was useful to let straight people in law, religion, and the behavioral sciences speak for us. People now say how benighted that was, that we hid behind the ministers, psychiatrists, and lawyers. But this was needed for us to gain legitimacy and to lessen the stigma attached to us at the time.

Also, Stonewall was a major turning point of the movement, but it was *not* the beginning of the movement. Stonewall was not planned, it simply happened. It is yet another example of how people and issues bubble up. This is the beauty of our movement. We are truly free spirits. Today's activists should resist the temptation to try to centralize or regiment gay efforts. I encourage young gay people to do whatever they can do to make a difference in their own lives. This, in turn, will make a difference in all of our lives and leave a legacy for future generations of better conditions for our living and loving.

Barbara Gittings was a founder in 1958 of the New York chapter of Daughters of Bilitis and served as its first president. In 1963 she became editor of the *The Ladder: A Lesbian Review,* assisted by her long time companion, Kay Tobin Lahusen, who later co-authored *The Gay Crusaders* (1972). The two live together in Wilmington, Delaware.

Notes

Introduction

1. These range from oral histories (e.g., Fellows, 1996; Marcus, 1992; Nardi, Sanders, and Marmor, 1994; Nestle, 1993; Power, 1996) to detailed studies of specific communities (e.g., Chauncey, 1994; Kennedy and Davis, 1993; McKay, 1993; Newton, 1993; Quinn, 1996) and events (e.g., Bérubé, 1990; Duberman, 1993) as well as more sweeping historical studies (e.g., Adam, 1987; D'Emilio, 1983; Deitcher, 1995; Faderman, 1991; Weiss and Schiller, 1988) and historical documentation (e.g., Blasius and Phelan, 1997; Cant and Hemmings, 1988; Duberman, 1991; Duberman, Vicinus, and Chauncey, 1989; Katz, 1992). Excellent resources for the general reader include Marcus, 1992; and Witt, Thomas, and Marcus, 1995.

2. The local histories of lesbians and gay men are only now being documented. With few exceptions, though, the South has not been the focus, and currently, no book recounts the oral histories of gay and lesbian Southerners. There are, however, a number of other excellent books, such as the semiautobiographical *My Mama's Dead Squirrel: Lesbian Essays on Southern Culture* (Segrest, 1985) and *Memoirs of a Race Traitor* (1995); the edited letters of Lillian Smith, entitled *How Am I to Be Heard?* (Gladney, 1993); the historical essays in *Carryin' On* (Howard, forthcoming); and the edited diary in *Jeb and Dash* (Russell, 1993). There are also profiles of Southerners ranging from contemporary fiction found in short stories of rural gay men in *Restless Rednecks* (Wood, 1985) or the coming-of-age novel *Rubyfruit Jungle* (Brown, 1973), the contemporary ethnographic narratives of young people found in *Growing Up Gay in the South* (Sears, 1991), or journalistic profiles appearing in *Heartlands* (Rist, 1993). A variety of articles have also appeared in scholarly journals (e.g., Atkinson and Boyles, 1985; Birchard, 1977; Duggan, 1993; Sears, 1989; Taub and Leger, 1984) and in lesbian/gay periodicals on one or more aspects of lesbian/gay Southern life (e.g., Carby, 1986; Norse, 1984; Patron, 1994; Real, 1983) and have been the subject of theses or dissertations (e.g., Duggan, 1992; Remington, 1983). A few books dealing more generally with Southern culture or history contain extended references to homosexuality (e.g., Daniel, 1980; King, 1975) as do the gay travelogues of *In Search of Gay America* (Miller, 1989), *Hometowns* (Preston, 1991), and *States of Desire* (White, 1983) and several edited literary and academic collections (e.g., Butters, Clum, and Moon, 1989). The majority of written work on homosexuality and Southern culture is found in literary works such as the plays of Tennessee Williams or Lillian Hellman, the prose of Jean Toomer, Carson McCullers, Alice Walker, and Truman Capote, or in biographies and autobiographies, including *Craig Claibourne's Feast Made for Laughter* (Clai-

bourne, 1982), *The Lonely Hunter: A Biography of Carson McCullers* (Carr, 1975), and *Bessie* (Albertson, 1972).

3. The homophile era, spanning two critical important events of gay history—World War II and Stonewall—falls in the middle of the five Southern generations that I plan to chronicle. Several of the central characters in this book represent different generations and cross at this temporal juncture.

4. Blackwood, 1986; Conner, 1993; Herdt, 1984; Murray, 1992; Nanda, 1990; Roscoe, 1991; Wafer, 1991; Williams, 1986; Faderman, 1981.

5. Duggan, 1993; Senelick, 1982.

6. Katz, 1992; Duberman, 1980/1981.

7. Katz, 1992, p. 346.

8. *Alyson Almanac*, 1991, p. 17.

9. For example, see Esler, 1982; Huntington, 1974, 1977; Kriegel, 1978; Mannheim, 1952; Marías, 1970; Riley, 1978; Spitzer, 1973; Strauss and Howe, 1991.

10. Ortega y Gasset, 1923, pp. 146–148; Mannheim, 1952. Here I chronicle Southern gay cultural and historical life (in Ortega y Gasset's [1923] term, the "ontological location") through *dramatis personae*—the life stories of lesbian, gay, and bisexual Southerners. In selecting particular life stories, I have found particularly useful the work of the eminent sociologist Karl Mannheim (1952, pp. 288–289, 303–304), who differentiates among *generationslagerung* (a generation located within a common stream of culture and history), *generationszusammenhang* (an actualized generation self-consciously connected to a "common destiny" and whose members participate in "the characteristic social and intellectual currents of their society and period,") and *generationseinheit* (a unit within an actualized generation characterized by "an identity of responses, a certain affinity in the way in which all move with and are formed by their common experiences." Thus within the homophile era there were homosexuals unaffected by social and political events such as McCarthyism or the civil rights movement, and there were others of the same generation who were deeply affected by and contributed to such events. Some, such as Barbara Deming, Bayard Rustin, and Lillian Smith, worked in the civil rights movement, and others, such as Jim Kepner, Richard Inman, and Barbara Gittings, struggled independently for gay rights. Finally, there were homosexual contemporaries such as Roy Cohn and Frank Kameny, who represented "polar forms" of the political and intellectual response to McCarthyism and civil rights. Like all applications of the theory of generations, my chronicle of five generations of homosexual Southerners is imperfectly bounded by the "zones of dates," ranging from fifteen to thirty years. Here, several individuals, epitomizing that particular era, are selected as illustrative of the *generationslagerung, generationszusammenhang,* and *generationseinheit.* Their thoughts and deeds provide insight into the sexual understandings best characterized by that generation. These zones of dates also have been defined around epochal historical moments (e.g., the 1964 March on Washington), which I have embroidered into these individual life stories, since, as Julián Marías (1970, p. 101) notes, "determining the generation to which a man belongs requires much more than a knowledge of when he was born: we must also know the *structure* of the world at that time. . . . "

11. Although I have begun the generational count with the colonization of North America by the Europeans, I certainly acknowledge the existence of sexually variant

native men and women, now known as "two-spirited" persons (Blackwood, 1986; Roscoe, 1991; Williams, 1986). One also comes across stories of astonishment recorded by Spanish explorers encountering cross-gender behavior and admonishment by missionaries condemning homosexuality among Native Americans. In 1595, for example, one Franciscan missionary raised the confessional question: "Mujer con mujer; has tenido acto, como si fuera hombre?" (Woman with woman; have you acted as if you were a man?). Evidence of European homosexual relations can be found in the same-sex relationships among colonists such as Captain Richard Cornish of Jamestown, executed in 1624 for sodomizing his indentured servant. Florida, though, has the honor of being the site of the earliest known homosexual execution fifty years earlier (Katz, 1992).

12. Carhart, 1895. The folk ballad, as reported by Duggan (1992, p. 324), goes: "You have heard of Freda Ward / Who lived many miles from town / As she went down the stone-paved walk / Alice Mitchell cut her down."

13. These overlapping stories, or, to use Ortega y Gasset's analogy, generational lives that overlap like tiles of roof slate, offer insight into how different age groups of Southerners constructed their sexual identities and made sense of historical realities. As Ortega aptly pointed out, "It is idle to try to find out what really happened at such and such a date if one does not ascertain to which generation it happened, that is, within which form of human existence it occurred. The same event happening to two different generations is a vital and hence historical reality which is completely different in each case" (quoted in Marías, 1970, p. 102). Thus, in this book I include three coterminous generations of Southerners.

14. Here Mannheim's concept of *generationseinheit* is most helpful. "Those groups within the same actual generation which work up the material of their common experiences in different specific ways, constitute separate generational units. . . . Thus within any generation there can exist a number of differentiated, antagonistic generation-units. Together they constitute an 'actual' generation precisely because they are oriented toward each other, even though only in the sense of fighting one another" (Mannheim, 1952, pp. 304, 306–307).

15. Photographs, audio recordings, and narratives not included in this book as well as materials from the entire Generations Project can be found on the World Wide Web at http://www.jtsears.com.

Chapter One

1. The Miami Homosexual Problem, 17 January 1955.

2. Collier, 8 August 1954.

3. Fortman, 10 August 1954.

4. Smith, 31 October 1954.

5. The latter article, typical of these stories, included the following: "Hypnotism was offered Monday as a possible cure for homosexuals . . . by Miami's most celebrated amateur hypnotist, City Commissioner H. Leslie Quigg. 'I think I can help some of these people . . . if they will come to me.'"

6. Fortman, 10 August 1954.

7. Smith, 5 November 1954.

8. Rundell, 8 November 1954.

9. Youths Get 20 Years, November 1954.

10. This 1955 Idaho homosexual male prostitute scandal involving prominent citizens was later chronicled by John Gerassi in *The Boys from Boise: Furor, Vice, and Folly in an American City* (New York: Macmillan, 1966).

11. Pedersen, 1954, Miami Hurricane, p. 5.

12. Ibid., p. 7.

13. Voltz, 1 September 1954; Lasting War on Perverts, *Miami Daily News,* 27 February 1956.

14. Voltz, 4 September 1954.

15. Voltz, 31 August 1954.

16. Voltz, 1 September 1954.

17. Miami Homosexual Problem, 17 January 1955, p. 60.

18. Pedersen, 1956, Miami's New Type of Witchhunt, p. 9; Pedersen, 1954, *Miami Hurricane,* p. 6.

19. Miami Homosexual Problem, 17 January 1955, p. 60.

20. Sheriff Kelly's future political opponent, Ruebin Clein, publisher of *Miami Life,* would later print a pamphlet alleging Kelly's homosexual leanings. *ONE* editor Jim Kepner quipped, "It does go to show how hard it is to tell the witches from the witch hunters" (Pedersen, 1956, Miami's New Type of Witchhunt, p. 11).

21. Six Suspected Perverts, 13 August 1954; Flynn, 13 August 1954.

22. Miller, 13 August 1954.

23. Tounsley, 24 September 1954.

24. Harris, 1969, pp. 165–166.

25. Johns Names Aide, 7 September 1954.

26. Pedersen, 1954, Miami Hurricane, p. 7.

27. Dade Open to Maniacs, 21 November 1953; Unit Urges Crackdown, November 1953.

28. Patron, 1994, p. 10.

29. Filing an injunction, Kelly won a court decision that required the county manager either to leave the law enforcement agency as it was or to place him in charge of the new department. In May 1959 Thomas Kelly assumed his new appointive position as director.

30. Hardin and Bonafede, 27 February 1956, pp. 1A, 6A.

31. Hardin and Bonafede, 29 February 1956.

32. Hardin and Bonafede, 1 March 1956.

33. Experts at Odds, 7 March 1956.

Chapter Two

1. Statement of Facts, R. J. Strickland, 14 August 1958, 2-74. Florida Historical Archives, Series 1486 (hereafter cited as FHA), Carton 1.

2. Professors' and students' names appearing in this chapter, with the exception of those interviewed for this project who chose to use their own names and one professor who has publicly discussed this event, are pseudonyms. The names of state employees directly involved in the investigation, however, are a matter of public record.

3. About one-fifth of Florida's population was African-American, compared to nearly one-third in Alabama and one-half in Mississippi. Further, nearly one-third of Florida blacks eligible to vote were registered (a proportion 50 percent higher than in any other Southern state), with prohibitive measures such as the poll tax repealed. Nevertheless, throughout the first half of the century, Florida—particularly its central and northern regions—was part of the Old South: It led the nation in lynchings in 1937, with six Southern states recording fewer lynchings during the peak years of 1889–1918; the 1949 Lake County conviction of three Groveland blacks tried for the rape of a white woman rivaled the publicity of the famed Scottsboro Boys a generation earlier; the Christmas night bombing of NAACP head Harry Moore of Brevard County marked the first assassination of a civil rights leader in the United States; and the Ku Klux Klan remained a potent force, ignored by civil authorities and feared by local blacks.

4. See, for example, Reports 8-4, 8-60, 11-456, and Memo to Strickland dated 30 October 1960, all located at the FHA, Carton 1.

5. Although the Committee continued for eight years, it was in actuality a series of two-year special committees renewed biannually by the legislature. Though investigations included bolita operations and wholesale bootlegging, the Committee's primary interest was on civil rights activists, communists, and homosexuals. In 1961 the legislature formally extended the Committee's charge in this area (Ch. 61–62 Laws). Following "numerous complaints about alleged homosexual activities," the legislature authorized the Committee's probe into "the extent of infiltration into agencies supported by state funds by practicing homosexuals. . . . " In actual practice the Committee had assumed that charge several years earlier.

6. In only one case did a file link both activities to one person. That was the case of political science professor Dr. Haines, whose file was filled with letters of commendation and complaints (including one from the American Legion), with a note accompanying the materials: "There is a question as to whether or not this man is a homosexual. His associations and activities which [he] condones puts him in the above stated position. It is definitely known throughout the Gainesville area that he is one of the worst pinks if not actually a member of the Communist Party in the University of Florida." Fact Sheet 13-417, FHA, Carton 13.

7. Fact Sheets 13-427, 13-420, 13-426, FHA, Carton 13.

8. Fact Sheets 13-408 and 13-418, FHA, Carton 13.

9. Statement of Facts, R. J. Strickland, 12 August 1958, 2-72. FHA, Carton 1.

10. Statement of Facts, R. J. Strickland, 19 August 1958, 2-53. FHA, Carton 1.

11. Progress Report of Chief Investigator R. J. Strickland in re University of Florida Investigation, for the Week of September 29 Thru October 16, 1958, 3-159. FHA, Carton 1. Also, Statement of Facts, R. J. Strickland, 2 October 1958, 4-69. FHA, Carton 1.

12. Statement of Facts, R. J. Strickland, 20 November 1958, 4-94. FHA, Carton 1.

13. Investigation of Homosexual Activities at the University of Florida. Sworn Testimony of Witnesses, 16 January 1959, 2-76, p. 1248. FHA, Carton 7.

14. Statement of Facts, R. J. Strickland, 21 November 1958, 4-72. FHA, Carton 1.

15. Progress Report of Chief Investigator R. J. Strickland in re University of Florida Investigation, for the Week of September 29 Thru October 16, 1958, 3-159. FHA, Carton 1.

16. Investigation of Homosexual Activities at the University of Florida. Sworn Testimony of Witnesses, 6 January 1959, 4-44, pp. 310–312. FHA, Carton 7.

17. Statement of Facts, R. J. Strickland, 5 December 1958, 3-160. FHA, Carton 1.

18. Ibid.

19. Deposition taken by John Tileston, 15 December 1958, 3-153, p. 11, FHA, Carton 6.

20. Ibid., pp. 12, 15.

21. Statement of Facts, R. J. Strickland, 18 November 1958, 4-67. FHA, Carton 1.

22. Investigation of Homosexual Activities at the University of Florida. Sworn Testimony of Witnesses, 6 January 1959, 4-44, pp. 432–434. FHA, Carton 7.

23. Hesser, 13 January 1959. See also Hesser, 12 January 1959; and Students Morals Questioned, 13 January 1959.

24. Investigation of Homosexual Activities at the University of Florida. Sworn Testimony of Witnesses, 5 January 1959, 4-43, p. 11. FHA, Carton 6.

25. Statement of Facts, R. J. Strickland, 21 November 1958, 4-72. FHA, Carton 1; Statement of Facts, R. J. Strickland, 12 August 1958, 2-71. FHA, Carton 1.

26. Investigation of Homosexual Activities at the University of Florida. Sworn Testimony of Witnesses, 6 January 1959, 4-44, pp. 392–393. FHA, Carton 7.

27. Ibid., pp. 398–401.

28. Ibid., pp. 403–407.

29. Investigation of Homosexual Activities at the University of Florida. Sworn Testimony of Witnesses, 5 January 1959, 4-43, p. 7. FHA, Carton 6.

30. Ibid., pp. 10–11.

31. Investigation of Homosexual Activities at the University of Florida. Sworn Testimony of Witnesses, 7 January 1959, 4-8, pp. 692–693. FHA, Carton 7.

32. Ibid., p. 693.

33. Ibid., pp. 742–744.

34. Statement of Facts, R. J. Strickland, 12 August 1958, 2-68. FHA, Carton 1.

35. Investigation of Homosexual Activities at the University of Florida. Sworn Testimony of Witnesses, 5 January 1959, 4-43, pp. 62–64, 67. FHA, Carton 6.

36. Ibid., pp. 200–202.

37. Typical procedure used to secure these depositions as outlined here can be found in 4-44 and 4-17, FHA, Carton 7.

38. Typical procedure used to secure these depositions as outlined here can be found in 4-44 and 4-17, FHA, Carton 7.

39. Investigation of Homosexual Activities at the University of Florida. Sworn Testimony of Witnesses, 5 January 1959, 4-43, pp. 85–87. FHA, Carton 6.

40. Typical procedure used to secure these depositions as outlined here can be found in 4-44 and 4-17, FHA, Carton 7.

41. Investigation of Homosexual Activities at the University of Florida. Sworn Testimony of Witnesses, 5 January 1959, 4-43, pp. 88–89. FHA, Carton 6.

42. Ibid., pp. 89–90.

43. Ibid., pp. 90–92.

44. Ibid., pp. 97–98.

45. Ibid., pp. 101–102.

46. Ibid., pp. 110–113.

47. Investigation of Homosexual Activities at the University of Florida. Sworn Testimony of Witnesses, 6 January 1959, 4-44, p. 265. FHA, Carton 7.

48. Ibid., pp. 269–270.

49. Ibid., p. 493.

50. Ibid., pp. 491–492.

51. Investigation of Homosexual Activities at the University of Florida. Sworn Testimony of Witnesses, 7 January 1959, 4-8, p. 666. FHA, Carton 7.

52. Investigation of Homosexual Activities at the University of Florida. Sworn Testimony of Witnesses, 8 January 1959, 2-77, p. 812. FHA, Carton 7.

53. Ibid., pp. 815–823, 826–830.

54. Ibid., p. 867.

55. Ibid., p. 871.

56. Investigation of Homosexual Activities at the University of Florida. Sworn Testimony of Witnesses, 7 January 1959, 4-8, pp. 575–576. FHA, Carton 7.

57. Investigation of Homosexual Activities at the University of Florida. Sworn Testimony of Witnesses, 9 January 1959, 4-3, pp. 976–977. FHA, Carton 7.

58. Ibid., pp. 979, 982, 1000.

59. Ibid., pp. 1014–1015, 1020.

60. Ibid., p. 1025.

61. Investigation of Homosexual Activities at the University of Florida. Sworn Testimony of Witnesses, 22 January 1959, 2-75, p. 1506. FHA, Carton 7.

62. Investigation of Homosexual Activities at the University of Florida. Sworn Testimony of Witnesses, 6 January 1959, 4-44, pp. 247–250. FHA, Carton 7.

63. Ibid., p. 304.

64. Investigation of Homosexual Activities at the University of Florida. Sworn Testimony of Witnesses, 16 January 1959, 2-76, pp. 1192–1197. FHA, Carton 7.

65. Investigation of Homosexual Activities at the University of Florida. Sworn Testimony of Witnesses, 22 January 1959, 2-75, p. 1612. FHA, Carton 7.

66. Investigation of Homosexual Activities at the University of Florida. Sworn Testimony of Witnesses, 6 January 1959, 4-44, pp. 329, 340–341. FHA, Carton 7.

67. Ibid., p. 446.

68. Investigation of Homosexual Activities at the University of Florida. Sworn Testimony of Witnesses, 7 January 1959, 4-8, p. 656. FHA, Carton 7.

69. Investigation of Homosexual Activities at the University of Florida. Sworn Testimony of Witnesses, 9 January 1959, 4-11, pp. 1424–1425. FHA, Carton 7.

70. Florida U. Dismisses 14, 4 April 1959.

71. Stowe did have a file, which noted that he "is known in and around Gainesville area to be a homosexual although it is in a stage of investigation at this point to develop the facts concerning same"; the investigation never got beyond this "stage" (Fact Sheet 13-421, FHA, Carton 13). He was also named by one admitted gay student (whose first campus homosexual experience was with the president of the hot rod club) who described Stowe's parties, where, as at Davies's parties, "we would discuss something about what was playing on Broadway in New York and who has a new record out and about what, and certain new books or certain groups at the University or the different professors . . . we didn't go out there and discuss who was blowing who, when. . . . Everybody was fully clothed. . . . Nobody ever

got drunk. That was sort of taboo" (Investigation of Homosexual Activities at the University of Florida. Sworn Testimony of Witnesses, 6 January 1959, 4-8, pp. 604, 606–607. FHA, Carton 7). Similarly, only one female faculty member was under investigation; a note was attached to her file stating, "This person's name is being retained in Gainesville Po. Dept. file due to observations made upon her and her associations with other women" (Fact Sheet 13-422, FHA, Carton 13).

72. Report to the Florida Legislative Investigation Committee from Mark R. Hawes, Chief Counsel, Re Investigation of Homosexual Activities in State Institutions, 13 February 1960. FHA, Carton 1.

73. McGarrahan, 1991, pp. 10–12.

74. Fact Sheets 13-410, 13-409, 13-423, 13-421. FHA, Carton 13.

Chapter Three

1. Personal correspondence from Julia Penelope to James T. Sears, 24 September 1996. It was only recently that Penelope's mother, shortly before her death, corrected Penelope's original understanding of her father's absence, which was that he had simply disappeared into the Bermuda Triangle (see Stanley, 1980, p. 195).

2. Professors' and students' names appearing in this chapter, with the exception of those interviewed for this project who chose to use their own names and state employees directly involved in the investigation and whose names are a matter of public record, are pseudonyms.

3. Dydo, 1993, pp. 257–258.

4. Brandle, 1960.

5. These and related violations of academic freedom later earned the university a censure by the American Association of University Professors. Committee for Academic Freedom in Tampa, July 1961. In J. B. Matthews Papers, Box 107, Committee for Academic Freedom, 1960–1961, New York Public Library Archives; Brandle, 1960; Denley, 1961.

6. Probers Used, 15 April 1963.

7. Florida Legislative Investigation Committee, 1964, p. 3.

8. Ibid., pp. 2, 4.

9. Ibid., pp. 6–8.

10. Ibid., pp. 7–8.

11. Ibid., p. 8.

12. Ibid., p. 9.

13. Ibid., p. 31.

14. Ibid., pp. 21–28.

15. Sosin, 1964.

16. Ibid.

17. "John" Like Report, 1964, p. 11.

18. Ibid.

19. WJXT News Editorial, 20 March 1964.

20. Official Obscenity, 20 March 1964.

21. Back up State Charges, 17 April 1964.

22. Sherrill, 1964.

23. A New Look, 23 September 1964.

24. Atlanta Lesbian Feminist Alliance Papers, Box 16, 94-040. Special Collections Library, Duke University.

Chapter Four

1. All quotations cited in Wolff, 1970.

2. Ibid., pp. 152, 161.

3. Lee, 1960, p. 10.

4. Smith, 1949, p. 111.

5. Ryan, 1883, p. 187.

6. Details of the lesbian relationship between these two women may be found in her letters (Gladney, 1993).

7. Smith, 1949, pp. 77–78, 81–83, 84–85.

8. Frazier, 1957, pp. 124–125.

9. The Ten Richest Negroes in America, 1949.

10. Address delivered at the Atlanta Cotton Exposition and quoted in Cox, 1951, p. 95.

11. Du Bois, 1994, p. 80.

12. Ibid., p. 41.

13. Frazier, 1957, p. 126.

14. Rustin, 1971, p. 17.

15. Truman signed two executive orders on July 26, 1948, one forbidding discrimination in the federal civil service and the other in the armed services. These actions, taken in the midst of the presidential campaign, were in response to a series of recommendations from the President's Committee on Civil Rights, which had issued its controversial report, "To Secure These Rights," the previous October. One Jacksonville minister wrote Truman, "[I]f that report is carried out, you won't be elected dog-catcher in 1948. The South today is the South of 1861" (Leuchtenburg, 1991, p. 60).

16. Smith, 1954, p. 10.

17. Smith, 1949, p. 234.

18. Justice, 15 January 1963.

19. Cusick, 3 April 1963.

20. Ehle, 1965, p. 12.

21. Hicks, 5 May 1963.

22. Known for its amiable race relations, this southwest Georgian town of 60,000 was the site of demonstrations and sit-ins throughout 1961 and 1962. After initiating a voter registration campaign, SNCC quickly expanded its goal toward total desegregation of the tightly knit town. Absent federal intervention and confronted by an amiable police chief, Laurie Pritchett, who had read up on the philosophy and tactics of nonviolence, SNCC efforts resulted in a stalemate with only token integration.

23. Ehle, 1965, p. 29.

24. Clotfelter, 6 February 1963.

25. Davidson, 1996, p. 146.

26. Barksdale, 1977, p. 225.

27. Ibid., p. 227.

28. Sterling, 12 January 1964.

29. Whiteleather, 16 July 1963.

30. Barksdale, 1977, p. 234.

31. Ehle, 1965, p. 73.

32. Ibid., pp. 84–85.

33. According to Pat, "Straight inmates at the Raleigh penitentiary were quite proficient and, as recently as three years ago [1993], this language was used by young black gays in D.C."

34. Ehle, 1965, pp. 87–88. According to Cusick, this "August 2 letter," reported by Ehle, was actually a journalistic invention: "John Ehle talked me into using this fabricated letter to John so that he could carry some of the story. Didn't like it then and less now as I actually told John over the phone and in the March office what I thought about his absence from Chapel Hill. . . . " (Letter to James T. Sears from Pat Cusick, 31 December 1996).

35. Interview with Rev. J. R. Manley by A. Harrison and K. Hamilton, 11 June 1974, Tape No. 19, Duke University Oral History Project.

36. Barksdale, 1977, pp. 240, 242.

37. *Chapel Hill Conscience,* 31 July, 1963, pp. 2–3. Quoted in ibid., p. 243.

38. Rustin, 1971, p. 110.

39. Maupin, 14 December 1962.

40. Maupin, 15 February 1963.

41. Maupin, 7 March 1963.

42. Maupin, 25 April 1963. Two weeks later, the chairman of the Chapel Hill Progressive Labor Club lambasted Maupin: "We ask Mr. Maupin: If you lived in a rat infested slum; if your children were undernourished; if you were constantly spit upon and discriminated against; if you were chronically unemployed or underemployed; if whenever you found a temporary job, the boss kicked you around and paid you Lenoir Hall–type wages—don't you think you would also be inclined towards violence?" (Phelps, 5 May 1963). Another letter, though chastising Maupin for his "rather unenlightened racial views," assailed Phelps for "the usual Marxist intermingling of truths, half-truth, and outright lies" (Neely, 8 May 1963). Finally, Maupin quipped: "[O]ne must learn to bear the burden of public disgrace as best one can and to carry on with a stiff upper lip." Noting correctly that the word "inferiority" never appeared in his column, Maupin nevertheless opined, "Many Negro leaders, we felt and still feel, ignore the shortcomings of their race and foster an irresponsibility that only increases racial antagonisms" (Maupin, 10 May 1963).

43. Wilson, 5 November 1963.

44. Wellman, 16 March 1963. See also McInnis, 22 April 1964; Harkness, 13 May 1964.

45. Wellman, 2 April 1963.

46. Why Four People, December 1963.

47. Harkness, 18 December 1963.

48. 3 More Arrested, 15 December 1963; Bulkley, 17 December 1963.

49. Thompson, 7 January 1964.

50. Open Letter, Christmas 1963.

51. Chapel Hill—North Carolina or Alabama? 7 January 1964.

52. Bulkley, 11 January 1964.

53. Bulkley, 14 January 1964; Chapel Hill Gets, 15 January 1964.

54. Giduz, 19 January 1964.

55. Maupin, 6 February 1964.

56. Wales, 8 February 1964.

57. Greenbacker, 11 February 1964.

58. Himes, 26 February 1964.

59. Interview with Quinton Baker, 2 June 1974, Tape No. 67, Duke University Oral History Project.

60. Dick, 16 February 1964.

61. Dick, 2 March 1964.

62. Why We Are Fasting, 1964.

63. Wales, 30 April 1964.

64. Seely, 24 April 1964.

65. Mallard Sends, 25 April 1964.

66. Barksdale, 1977, pp. 272–273.

67. Interview with Quinton Baker, 2 June 1974, Tape No. 67, Duke University Oral History Project.

Chapter Five

1. Fraser, 1989, pp. 412–413.

2. Ibid., p. 412.

3. This passage is quoted from Hall's *Man into Woman* (Simmons, 1971, pp. 62–63). Published by a friend of Rutherford, the original book title was changed and "sensational passages" inserted without Hall's consent.

4. Letter to Irac C. Moore Jr. from Gordon Hall, 5 April 1963.

5. Patlas Plant Tree, 1962.

6. Leland, 1962; Ripley, 1964; Johnson House, 1964.

7. According to Hall, these are evidence of further distortion by Leland: The trip "was to launch *Dear Vagabonds*, a book I had written for [a] Denver socialite, Mrs. Brownie Adams, at which the Governor of Colorado attended" (Personal correspondence from Dawn Langley Simmons to James T. Sears, 12 January 1995). Hall also received some money following the death of Mrs. Adams. In a letter sent to Hall after Adams's death, Mrs. Hugh March Andrews of New York City wrote: "She must have been a charming and interesting lady. Hope you are as far off on my age as you were on hers! Do you mean she left you *money* as well as things? How does it feel to be *left* something?" (Letter to Gordon Hall from Mrs. Hugh March Andrews, 31 March 1968).

8. 'Twas the Night Before, 1963, p. 6.

9. Poor Old, 1964.

10. See also Birmingham, 1990, p. 149.

11. Carr, 1975, p. 520. Years later, Hall elaborated: "The young man was probably Gussie, our under butler who later joined the Marines. . . . Gussie loved celebrities . . . he acted more like family" (Personal correspondence from Dawn Langley Simmons to James T. Sears, 27 February 1995).

12. Ibid., p. 519.

13. As MacKenzie (1994) points out, isolated efforts to transform males into females surgically can be found as far back as the 1920s in Denmark and into the 1930s in Germany. It was not until the end of World War II that homosexuality, transsexuality, and sex-change procedures entered public awareness with the publication of the two Kinsey Reports and extensive news coverage of Christine Jorgenson's "sex-change" surgery in 1953. Now there are about forty clinics specializing in sex-reassignment surgery in the United States, most adhering to Benjamin's step-by-step procedures of living the role of the other gender, participating in psychological tests, ingesting hormones, and enduring a series of progressive surgeries.

14. An early exception to this confused association was the work of the pioneer sexual researcher Magnus Hirschfeld, whose *Die Transvetiten* (1910, 1991) was one of the first works to challenge this long-held stereotype. Another turn-of-the-century pioneer, Havelock Ellis, first distinguished between two types of "aesthetic inverts." One simply wore the other gender's clothing (the "transvestite"), and the other "so identified himself with those of his physical and psychic traits which recall the opposite sex that he feels really to belong to that sex although he has no delusion regarding his anatomical conformation" (1906, p. 36). Hall, however, did not fall into either the category of "cross-dresser" or the "transsexual" in that his "anatomical conformation" was, itself, blurred. Though Gordon's gender identity was male, he never considered himself a man. Until midadulthood, however, he accepted the "peculiar condition" that fate had assigned him. Individuals like Hall are intersexed persons "usually born sexually ambiguous at birth due to hormonal, gonadal, chromosomal, and/or genital contradictions. Some intersexed persons develop secondary sex characteristics of the 'opposite' sex during puberty" (MacKenzie, 1994, pp. 45–46).

15. Riley, 1970, p. 11.

16. Parkin, 1971.

17. Personal correspondence from Dena Crane to James T. Sears, 31 October 1994.

18. Dawn's New Day, 1968, p. 34.

19. Letter to Jack Copper from Dawn Simmons, 22 September 1969.

20. Letter to John-Paul Simmons from Alex Simmons, 24 June 1968.

21. New Book, 1993, p. 2; Riley, 1970, p. 11.

22. Hall had already signed a contract on a "'crash' schedule" with Doubleday "to take advantage of the publicity when the wedding takes place. . . . " This letter to Dawn from a senior editor continued: "[It] is especially reassuring to me that we have exactly the same book in mind and if we continue to think of the book as a medical documentary we will come up with something that will be so much more than a sensational flash-in-the-pan" (Letter to Dawn Simmons from Lawrence P. Ashmead, 23 December 1968).

23. Dawn's New Day, 1968, p. 34.

24. Years later, an unsigned letter writer to the African-American Charleston paper, the *Charleston Chronicle*, apologized for their treatment: "What is disturbing to me and many of the old-timers who were around at the time of their wedding, was that we refused to speak out at the mistreatment of two people obviously in love." (Letters to the Editor, 1989, p. 5).

25. Fraser, 1991.

26. Ibid., pp. 422–423.

27. Letters to the Editor, 1989, p. 5.

28. Letter to Dawn Simmons from Anthony Dawson, 14 September 1972.

29. Letter to John-Paul Simmons from Dawn Simmons, Summer 1972.

30. Letter to Dawn Simmons from Robert Holmes, 18 September 1972.

31. Follow-up on the News, 1975.

32. Siegelbaum, 1975.

33. Personal correspondence from Dena Crane to James T. Sears, 31 October 1994.

Chapter Six

1. For a description of these embryonic efforts, see Jonathan Katz's (1976) interview with Hay and related documentation, pp. 406–420.

2. D'Emilio, 1983, pp. 68–69.

3. Katz, 1976, pp. 412–413.

4. Timmons, 1990, p. 130.

5. Ibid., pp. 163–168.

6. Katz, 1976, p. 416.

7. Streitmatter, 1995, p. 18.

8. Katz, 1976, p. 416.

9. Marcus, 1992, p. 34.

10. As reported by Jim Kepner in Timmons, 1990, p. 178. Later Kepner elaborated on these events: "Harry had been involved in Freemason-type secret societies in high school, and brought this complex romanticism into the impossible structure of Mattachine—which the newcomers rebelled against in 1952 and which Chuck realized was an impediment before the April 1953 convention. Far more anathema to the newcomers were ideas of homosexuals as a minority and the concept of a minority culture. They clung desperately to the gut belief that 'we are just like everybody else except for what we do in bed' and couldn't dare accept any suggestion that homosexuals were *different* per se. . . . Hal Call's shouting match with Chuck Rowland occurred during a recess in the lobby of the church. I was involved in this conversation when Hal's usually mottled and boiled complexion turned beet red, but I don't recall that he used the term Russian Agents—more like subversives. The need for an open democratic structure and some accommodation with the newcomers had been strongly argued by Chuck *before* the April convention, but imperiously rejected by Harry." Personal correspondence from Jim Kepner to James T. Sears, 2 February 1997.

11. Katz, 1976, pp. 419–420.

12. Marcus, 1992, pp. 62–63.

13. Diary of Jeb Alexander, 5 February, 1938. I have chosen to use the pseudonyms assigned by Ian Russell (1993).

14. Diary of Jeb Alexander, 5 March, 1938.

15. The issue termed "obscene" by postal authorities was published in October 1954. It included a satirical poem with the words, "Some peers are seers but some

are queers ... / And some boys WILL be girls," as well as a short story by Jane Dahr, "Sappho Remembered," whose allegedly graphic imagery was: "She touched the delicate pulse beats beneath the light golden hair on the child-like temple." Streitmatter, 1995, p. 35.

16. Ibid., p. 21.

17. Ibid., p. 38. See *Mattachine Review*, "Quote," George W. Henry, March/April, 1955, p. 23. Kepner, however, challenges this meaning of "homophile." The term, he says, which "has a well established usage dating back to about 1902, does *not* mean citizens who supported the homosexual or the study of homosexuality. This was a piece of idiocy in a resolution presented in an ECHO meeting. The term means and had long meant persons whose erotic inclination was toward persons of the same gender—generally but not necessarily implying its expression in genital sexual acts. It is *almost* a synonym for homosexual or gay, but like gay, it puts the focus on inclination, or even on love, rather than on sex activity." Personal correspondence from Jim Kepner to James T. Sears, 2 February 1997.

18. Ibid., pp. 38–39. See *Mattachine Review*, "Why Perpetuate This Barbarism?" June 1960, p. 13.

19. Marcus, 1992, p. 95.

20. D'Emilio, 1983, p. 123. Kepner, who was involved with Mattachine during this transition, elaborated: "It was the 'national' organization, specifically the non–San Francisco chapters, that was dissolved. The New Yorkers, led by Dewees, de Dion, and McCarthy, were, if possible, even more conservative than Call, but they had that unique New York chauvinism that assumed that New Yorkers could do the better job. They retained the Mattachine name on my advice, based on a resolution pushed by Hal Call in 1953 that the new Mattachine Society had no connection with earlier groups using that name—thus surrendering any exclusive claim to the name." Personal correspondence from Jim Kepner to James T. Sears, 2 February 1997.

21. Marcus, 1992, p. 96.

22. During this era, about 2,000 homosexuals were purged from the military each year. Generally an administrative hearing that resulted in the discharge of an "undesirable" was favored over a court-martial proceeding with its inevitable guilty verdict and dishonorable discharge (D'Emilio, 1983; Bérubé, 1990).

23. Letter to the Executive Board of the Mattachine Society of Washington from Warren Adkins, 14 October 1963. From the private collection of Jack Nichols; copy located in Sears papers.

Chapter Seven

1. Welch, 1964, pp. 61, 63.

2. Wickstrom, 1964.

3. George, 1964, p. 16.

4. "John" Like Report, 1964, p. 12.

5. Dear Friend (Open Letter) from Richard Inman, 7 August 1965. Correspondence to Warren D. Adkins (Jack Nichols) from Richard Inman, 15 January 1965–19 October 1965, Manuscript Collection, Stonewall Library and Archives, Ft. Lauderdale, Florida. Cited hereafter as Inman Papers.

6. Labelle, 1965, p. 2.

7. Letter to Guy Straight from Richard Inman, 26 September 1965, Inman Papers.

8. Ibid.

9. Marcus, 1992, pp. 66–68.

10. D'Emilio, 1983, p. 164.

11. Though Mattachine–New York received numerous letters detailing difficulties of growing up gay in the South, no activism was evident. Ronald Mayer, for example, a would-be activist who had just completed his doctorate at Ohio State, was bound for a teaching job at Auburn. He exchanged letters with Curtis Dewees throughout 1958 and 1959, hoping first to establish a Mattachine in Ohio and later to find like-minded Alabama activists. Mayer was disappointed to learn from Dewees that "there is next to nothing in the way of contacts in the South" (Letter to Ron Mayer from Curtis Dewees, 14 June 1958). Other letters received by New York Mattachine during this era included those from a Georgian prison chaplain seeking materials for several of his prerelease inmates, a librarian at a Tennessee psychiatric hospital requesting subscription information to the *Eastern Mattachine Newsletter,* and an aspiring playwright scouting for "various humorous situations that have or could occur" when a heterosexual man inherits a large homosexual magazine. International Gay Information Center Papers, New York Public Library (hereafter cited as IGIC), Box 1, File 12, Mattachine Society of New York, Dick Leitsch Correspondence.

12. Papers of Perry Brass, Box 96, IGIC.

13. Letter to Bernardino del Boca from Richard Inman, 20 August 1965, Inman Papers.

14. Letter to Julian Hodges from Richard Inman, 22 August 1964, IGIC.

15. Letter to Mark Forrester, Secretary, Society for Individual Rights, from Richard Inman, 7 August 1965, Inman Papers.

16. Letter to Mayor Robert King High from Richard Inman, 1 October 1965, Inman Papers. Inman continued, "I did so because I didn't want to be constantly faced with such offers as Barker [a former Johns Committee investigator] made to me."

17. Letter to Mark Forrester, Secretary, Society for Individual Rights, from Richard Inman, 7 August 1965, Inman Papers.

18. Tobin and Wicker, 1972, p. 181.

19. Clarke and Nichols, 1972, p. 2.

20. The publication continued through April 1965 (vol. 2, no. 4).

21. Letter to Julian Hodges from Frank Kameny, 23 August 1964, IGIC.

22. Letter to Julian Hodges from Richard Inman, 12 October 1964, IGIC.

23. Ibid.

24. Giltmier, 1964.

25. Open letter to Legislators from Richard Inman, 11 January 1965, Inman Papers.

26. Ibid.

27. Reynolds, 1965.

28. Letter from Richard Inman to *Citizens News* and others, 12 March 1965, Inman Papers.

29. During the homophile era, the use of aliases among activists was common: Lyn Pedersen or Dale McIntire (Jim Kepner), Gene Damon (Barbara Grier), Ran-

dolfe Wicker (Charles Gervin Hayden Jr.), Kay Tobin (Kay Lahusen), David Free-
man (Chuck Roland), Lily Hansen (Lilli Vincenz), and Ann Ferguson (Phyllis Lyon).
Others, such as Harry Hay, Frank Kameny, Shirley Willer, and Richard Inman, preferred to use their own names. For some, it was a matter of family: Nichols used an
alias until 1968 at the request of his father, Jack Nichols Sr., who was working in
Washington as an FBI agent; Randolfe Wicker legally changed his name at the request of his father. For others, it was a political decision rooted in their experiences
with McCarthyism. Phyllis Lyon "killed off" Ann Ferguson in the fourth issue of
The Ladder in a moving appeal to readers to use their own names when communicating with the magazine. And a few, like Jim Kepner, used pseudonyms as a means
to disguise the relatively small number of people involved in the movement.

30. Letter to Richard Inman from Warren D. Adkins, 24 January 1965, Inman
Papers.

31. Letter to Richard Inman from Warren D. Adkins, 9 February 1965, Inman
Papers.

32. Letter to Warren D. Adkins from Richard Inman, 10 February 1965, Inman
Papers.

33. Letter to Warren D. Adkins from Richard Inman, 30 April 1965, Inman Papers.

34. Letter to Warren D. Adkins from Richard Inman, 1 June 1965, Inman Papers.

35. Letter to Bob King from Richard Inman, 16 July 1965, Inman Papers.

36. Letter to Warren D. Adkins from Richard Inman, 1 June 1965, Inman Papers.

37. Letter to Julian Hodges from Richard Inman, 22 August 1964, IGIC. In
March 1965 Hodges would write about Inman, "I am strengthened and encouraged
by the emergence of one Richard A. Inman as a battler and crusader I'm proud to
have in this movement. . . . "

38. Letter to Mark Forrester from Richard Inman, 7 August 1965, Inman Papers.

39. *Atheneum Viewpoint,* February 1965.

40. Letter to Warren D. Adkins from Richard Inman, 21 April 1965, Inman Papers.

41. Letter to Richard Inman from Warren D. Adkins and Bob King, 24 June
1965, Inman Papers.

42. Letter to Richard Inman from Warren D. Adkins, 10 July 1965, Inman Papers.

43. Letter to Richard Inman from Jerome Stevens, 26 July 1965, Inman Papers.

44. Letter to Richard Inman from Warren D. Adkins, 13 July 1965, Inman Papers. Frank Kameny communicated a similar view to Jack's in response to Inman's
letter asking what Frank was doing in addition to organizing pickets. Reportedly
Frank said: "Tell Inman that I'm running the homophile movement from behind the
scenes." Letter to Richard Inman from Warren D. Adkins, 6 September 1965, Inman Papers.

45. Letter to Warren D. Adkins from Richard Inman, 14 July 1965, Inman Papers.

46. Letter to Richard Inman from Warren D. Adkins, 12 August 1965, Inman Papers.

47. Letter to Mark Forrester, Secretary, Society for Individual Rights, from
Richard Inman, 7 August 1965, Inman Papers.

48. Letter to Julian Hodges from Richard Inman, 10 November 1964, IGIC.

49. Letter to Rep. Richard A. Pettigrew from Richard A. Inman, 28 June 1965, Inman Papers.

50. Letter to Mark Forrester, Secretary, Society for Individual Rights, from Richard Inman, 7 August 1965, Inman Papers.

51. Ibid.

52. Letter to Richard Inman from Warren D. Adkins, 12 October 1965, Inman Papers.

53. Letter to Richard Inman from Warren D. Adkins, 13 October 1965, Inman Papers.

54. Nichols was not, as Duberman (1992, p. 287) concluded, "As late as 1965 . . . writing against those who were demanding civil liberties for homosexuals—and 'who are unbalanced enough to have demonstrations.'" Throughout Nichols's correspondence to Inman, he was an ardent supporter of and participant in such demonstrations. The letter referred to by Duberman, known generally for his careful scholarship, which was penned April 1, 1965, and clearly marked "April Fools Day," satirized members of the older research/education-oriented generation like Stevens.

55. Letter to Jerome Stevens from Richard Inman, 22 July 1965, Inman Papers.

56. Letter to Richard Inman from Jerome Stevens, 26 July 1965, Inman Papers.

57. Letter to Jerome Stevens from Richard Inman, 1 August 1965, Inman Papers.

58. Letter to Warren D. Adkins from Richard Inman, 15 September 1965, Inman Papers.

59. Letter to Warren D. Adkins from Richard Inman, 1 July 1965, Inman Papers.

60. Letter to the Board of Directors, SIR, from Richard Inman, 5 August 1965, Inman Papers.

61. Letter to Warren D. Adkins from Richard Inman, 4 September 1965, Inman Papers.

62. Letter to Warren D. Adkins from Richard Inman, 20 July 1965, Inman Papers.

63. Letter to Warren D. Adkins from Richard Inman, 14 July 1965, Inman Papers.

64. Letter to Elver Barker from Dick Leitsch, 27 May 1966, IGIC.

65. Letter to Jerome Stevens from Richard Inman, 16 July 1965, Inman Papers.

66. Letter to Warren D. Adkins from Richard Inman, 1 July 1965, Inman Papers. Inman was "shocked" to learn that summer that Bob King had agreed to write an article for the *National Insider* in support of gay marriages and adoption. Writing Jack, he warned: "Though I would never let such a thing split us, I don't want . . . anyone playing it up like there WAS a split, and that's just what others who oppose us will do." Letter to Warren D. Adkins from Richard Inman, 1 July 1965, Inman Papers. Writing back, Jack assured Richard that this was wishful thinking on the part of the *National Insider* and that he was penning an antilegalization article (Letter to Richard Inman from Warren D. Adkins, 6 July 1965, Inman Papers).

67. Letter to Richard Inman from Warren D. Adkins, 28 September 1965, Inman Papers.

68. Letter to Richard Inman from Warren D. Adkins, 21 July 1965, Inman Papers.

69. Letter to Warren D. Adkins from Richard Inman, 4 September 1965, Inman Papers.

70. Letter to Richard Inman from Warren D. Adkins, 2 September 1965, Inman Papers.

71. Ibid.

72. Letter to Warren D. Adkins from Richard Inman, 23 August 1965, Inman Papers.

73. Letter to Warren D. Adkins from Richard Inman, 4 September 1965, Inman Papers.

74. Letter to Guy Straight from Richard Inman, 26 September 1965, Inman Papers.

75. Letter to Mark Forrester from Richard Inman, 23 September 1965, Inman Papers.

76. Letter to Warren D. Adkins from Richard Inman, 26 September 1965, Inman Papers.

77. The charter was initially rejected by the secretary of state as advocating goals "against public policy," following a request for an opinion from the attorney general's office. After Inman threatened a mandamus suit through the ACLU, the charter was granted and eventually found its way into Herb Rau's column, who advised readers: "Raise an eyebrow—and limp a wrist." In a related story appearing in the Coral Gables *Times*, Duane Barker, former Johns Committee investigator and more recently investigator for the personnel department of the Broward County School Board, stated, "In spite of hundreds of talks by a handful of us on radio, TV, and before live audiences, we now have the Mattachine Society of Florida, Inc. It's not just a coincidence that only months after the Florida Legislative Investigation Committee folded, that the Mattachine reared its ugly head" (Labelle, 1965).

78. Two thousand copies of the first issue of Florida Mattachine *Viewpoint* were printed. Richard was disappointed to find that more than 300 were returned because of bad addresses and that of the eighteen bars to which copies were sent only two had given them out to patrons. The September issue was also distributed to delegates at the fall ECHO conference, and the October issue was also sent to police and politicians involved in the gay bar shakedowns.

79. *Florida Mattachine Viewpoint,* December 1965.

80. Adkins, 1966, p. 17.

81. Letter to Warren D. Adkins and Richard A. Inman from Elver Barker, 23 May 1966, IGIC.

82. *The Homosexual Citizen,* February 1966, p. 14.

83. Adkins and Marshall, 1966, pp. 8–10.

84. Duberman, 1993, pp. 102–105.

85. In fact, according to Jim Kepner, "Until the time of his death, he was supplying material and rough versions of articles to Bill Buckley and Richard Viguerie. His commitment to gay rights was mixed with an equally strong commitment to landlords' rights, smokers' rights, and a generally far right philosophy." Personal correspondence from Jim Kepner to James T. Sears, 2 February 1997.

86. Gunnison, 1966, pp. 15–18.

87. Duberman, 1993, p. 103.

88. No More Mattachine, 1967, p. 1.

89. Letter from Richard Inman to *Citizens News* and others, 12 March 1965, Inman Papers.

90. Clarke and Nichols, 1972, p. 5.

91. He departed from Mattachine with some ill feeling. After he had received an unsolicited newsletter from Mattachine Society–New York in June 1968, he angrily wrote back: "MSF has not been in existence for over one year. You can thank Mr. Dick Leitsch as one of the contributing causes. An ex-MSNY member (so he claimed) decided (?) to 'go straight' and became a police informer and public speaker for the police, PTAs etc. in the Tampa Bay area. I wrote Dick desperately seeking information regarding the guy and whether he was what he said, an ex-MSNY member. Dick never gave me the courtesy of a reply, though I wrote several letters pleading for information" (Letter to Ed Trust from Richard Inman, 20 June 1968, IGIC).

92. Letter from Richard Inman to *Citizens News* and others, 12 March 1965, Inman Papers.

93. Personal correspondence from Jim Kepner to James T. Sears, 2 February 1997.

94. Letter to Warren D. Adkins from Richard Inman, 19 September 1965, Inman Papers.

95. Letter to Mark Forrester, Secretary, Society for Individual Rights, from Richard Inman, 7 August 1965, Inman Papers.

96. Letter to Robert King from Richard Inman, 28 June 1965, Inman Papers.

97. Letter to Warren D. Adkins from Richard Inman, 3 July 1965, Inman Papers.

98. Letter to Warren D. Adkins from Richard Inman, 7 July 1965, Inman Papers.

99. Letter to Warren D. Adkins from Richard Inman, 24 July 1965, Inman Papers.

100. Letter to Richard Inman from Warren D. Adkins, 30 July 1965, Inman Papers.

101. Letter to Warren D. Adkins and Robert King from Richard Inman, 2 August 1965, Inman Papers.

102. Letter to Warren D. Adkins from Richard Inman, 13 August 1965, Inman Papers.

103. Letter to Warren D. Adkins from Richard Inman, 14 July 1965, Inman Papers.

104. Letter to Jerome Stevens from Richard Inman, 1 August 1965, Inman Papers.

105. Letter to Bob King from Richard Inman, 16 July 1965, Inman Papers.

106. Letter to Warren D. Adkins from Richard Inman, 13 August 1965, Inman Papers.

107. Letter to Richard Inman from Warren D. Adkins, 20 August 1965, Inman Papers.

108. Letter to Warren D. Adkins from Richard Inman, 6 September 1965, Inman Papers. Shakedowns, of course, were not unique to the South. See, for example, the reprint of the 1950 *Esquire* magazine article on a midwestern foreman victimized by the rackets in Duberman, 1991, pp. 173–176.

109. Letter to Richard Inman from Warren D. Adkins, 16 September 1965, Inman Papers.

110. An Open Letter to Mayor Robert King High from Richard Inman, 16 September 1965, Inman Papers.

111. Letter to Warren D. Adkins from Richard Inman, 16 September 1965, Inman Papers.

112. Letter to Warren D. Adkins from Richard Inman, 19 September 1965, Inman Papers.

113. Letter to Warren D. Adkins from Richard Inman, 26 September 1965, Inman Papers.

114. Letter to Warren D. Adkins from Richard Inman, 21 September 1965, Inman Papers.

115. Letter to Guy Straight from Richard Inman, 26 September 1965, Inman Papers.

116. Letter to Dick Knight from Richard Inman, 24 September 1965, Inman Papers.

117. Ibid.

118. Rau, 14 October 1965.

119. Letter to Bill Beardemphl from Richard Inman, 15 October 1965, Inman Papers.

120. Letter to Mayor Robert King High from Richard Inman, 1 October 1965, Inman Papers.

121. Letter to Mark Forrester from Richard Inman, 11 October 1965, Inman Papers.

122. Letter to Warren D. Adkins from Richard Inman, 4 October 1965, Inman Papers.

123. Letter to Dick Knight from Richard Inman, 11 October 1965, Inman Papers.

124. Letter to Warren D. Adkins from Richard Inman, 3 October 1965, Inman Papers.

125. Letter to Dick Knight from Richard Inman, 6 October 1965, Inman Papers.

126. To Whom It May Concern from Richard A. Inman, 4 October 1965, Inman Papers.

127. Letter to Bill Beardemphl from Richard Inman, 16 October 1965, Inman Papers.

128. Letter to Warren D. Adkins from Richard Inman, 16 October 1965, Inman Papers.

129. Letter to Warren D. Adkins from Richard Inman, 10 October 1965, Inman Papers.

130. Several months earlier, Richard had met with Detectives Sorenson and Narrow. After several cancellations on both sides, Richard later described their three-hour meeting as "cordial." At that meeting, both sides agreed on "mutual cooperation."

131. Arvidson, 1966.

132. Lawmen Conduct, 12 April 1966.

133. *Florida Mattachine Viewpoint*, February 1966.

134. Another Look, 29 April 1966.

135. The Homosexual Program, 19 May 1966.

136. Judge OKs Suit, 1 June 1966; Homosexual Law OK, 11 June 1966.

137. Tobin and Wicker, 1972, p. 183.

138. Behrens, 1967.

139. *Florida Mattachine Viewpoint,* July 1967.

140. *Florida Mattachine Viewpoint,* September 1967.

141. State Attorney Denies, 17 August 1967.

142. Man Freed, 1 November 1968.

143. Letter to Julian Hodges from Richard Inman, 22 August 1964, IGIC.

144. Baxter, 1969.

145. Letter to Richard Inman from Jerome Stevens, 20 June 1965, Inman Papers.

146. Letter to Jerome Stevens from Richard Inman, 1 August 1965, Inman Papers.

147. Gay Bar Law, 10 December 1971.

148. Wright, 1972.

149. Letter to Warren D. Adkins from Richard Inman, 30 September 1965, Inman Papers.

Sources

Introduction

Material used for overview of the South

Ayers, E. (1992). *The promise of the New South*. New York: Oxford University Press.

Campbell, D. (1981). *The celluloid South*. Knoxville: University of Tennessee Press.

Cash, W. J. (1941). *The mind of the south*. New York: Knopf.

Clayton, B. (1972). *The savage ideal: Intolerance and intellectual leadership in the South, 1890–1914*. Baltimore: Johns Hopkins University Press.

Davenport, F. (1970). *The myth of Southern history*.

Evans, E. (1976). *The provincials: A personal history of the Jews in the South*. New York: Atheneum.

Franklin, J. (1956). *The militant South*. Boston: Beacon Press.

Key, V. O. (1949). *Southern politics in state and nation*. New York: Knopf.

King, R. (1980). *A Southern renaissance*. New York: Oxford University Press.

Levine, L. (1977). *Black culture and black consciousness*. New York: Oxford University Press.

MacKethan, L. (1990). *Daughters of time*. Athens: University of Georgia Press.

Manning, C. (1993). *The female tradition in Southern literature*. Urbana: University of Illinois Press.

Odum, H. (1936). *Southern regions of the United States*. Chapel Hill: University of North Carolina Press.

Osterweis, R. (1973). *The myth of the lost cause, 1865–1900*. Hamden, CT: Archon Books.

Palmer, R. (1979). *A tale of two cities: Memphis rock and New Orleans roll*. Brooklyn: Institute Studies for American Music, Brooklyn College of the City University of New York.

Reed, J. (1986). *Southern folk, plain and fancy*. Athens: University of Georgia Press.

Rubin, L. (1963). *Writers of the modern South*.

Rubin, L., Jackson, B., Moore, R., Simpson, L., and Young, T. (1985). *The history of Southern literature*. Baton Rouge: Louisiana State University Press.

Simpson, L. (1975). *The dispossessed garden: Pastoral and history in Southern literature*. Athens: University of Georgia Press.

Smith, S. (1985). *Myth, media, and the Southern mind*. Fayetteville: University of Arkansas Press.

Stampp, K. (1965). *Era of Reconstruction, 1865–1877*. New York: Knopf.

Taylor, A. (1976). *Travail and triumph: Black life and culture in the South since the Civil War*. Westport, CT: Greenwood.

Taylor, H. (1989). *Gender, race, and region in the writings of Grace King, Ruth McEnery Stuart, and Kate Chopin*. Baton Rouge: Louisiana University Press.

Tindall, G. (1967). *The emergence of the New South, 1913–1945*. Baton Rouge: Louisiana State University Press.

Vandiver, F. (1964). *The idea of the South*. Chicago: University of Chicago Press.

Woodward, C. V. (1951). *Origins of the New South, 1877–1913*. Baton Rouge: Louisiana University Press.

Woodward, C. V. (1961). *Burden of Southern history*. Baton Rouge: Louisiana University Press.

Wyatt-Brown, B. (1982). *Southern honor*. New York: Oxford University Press.

Zilensky, W. (1973). *The cultural geography of the United States*. Englewood Cliffs, NJ: Prentice-Hall.

Zinn, H. (1964). *The Southern mystique*. New York: Knopf.

Lesbian and gay sources cited in Introduction

Adam, B. (1987). *The rise of the gay liberation movement*. Boston: Twayne.

Albertson, C. (1972). *Bessie*. New York: Stein & Day.

Alyson almanac (1991). Boston: Alyson.

Atkinson, M., and Boyles, J. (1985). The shaky pedestal: Southern ladies yesterday and today. *Southern Studies* 24(4):398–406.

Bérubé, A. (1990). *Coming out under fire: The history of gay men and women in World War Two*. New York: Plume.

Birchard, R. (1977). Metropolitan Community Church: Its development and significance. *Foundations: Baptist Journal of History and Theology* 20(2):127–132.

Blackwood, E., ed. (1986). *Anthropology and homosexual behavior*. New York: Haworth Press.

Blasius, M., and Phelan, S. (1997). *We are everywhere: A historical sourcebook of gay and lesbian politics*. New York: Routledge.

Brown, R. (1973). *Rubyfruit jungle*. Plainfield, VT: Daughters Press.

Butters, R., Clum, J., and Moon, M. (1989). *Displacing homophobia: Gay male perspectives in literature and culture*. Durham, NC: Duke University Press.

Cant, B., and Hemmings, S. (1988). *Radical records: Thirty years of lesbian and gay history, 1957–1987*. New York: Routledge & Kegan Paul.

Carby, H. (1986). It jus be's dat way sometime: The sexual politics of women's blues. *Radical America* 20(4):9–24.

Carhart, J. (1895). *Norma Trist: A story of the inversion of the sexes*. Austin, TX: Boeckman.

Carr, V. (1975). *The lonely hunter: A biography of Carson McCullers*. Garden City, NY: Doubleday.

Chauncey, G. (1994). *Gay New York*. New York: Basic.

Claibourne, C. (1982). *Craig Claibourne's feast made for laughter*. Garden City, NY: Doubleday.

Conner, R. (1993). *Blossom of bone*. San Francisco: HarperCollins.

Daniel, R. (1980). *Fatal flowers: On sin, sex, and suicide in the Deep South.* New York: Holt, Rinehart & Winston.

D'Emilio, J. (1983). *Sexual politics, sexual communities: The making of a homosexual minority in the United States, 1940–1970.* Chicago: University of Chicago Press.

Deitcher, D. (1995). *The question of equality: Lesbian and gay politics in America since Stonewall.* New York: Scribner.

Duberman, M. (1991). *About time: Exploring the gay past.* New York: Meridian.

Duberman, M. (1993). *Stonewall.* New York: Dutton.

Duberman, M., Vicinus, M., and Chauncey, G. Jr., eds. (1989). *Hidden from history: Reclaiming the lesbian and gay past.* New York: New American Library.

Duggan, L. (1992). *The trials of Alice Mitchell: Sensationalism, sexology, and the lesbian subject in turn-of-the-century America.* Ph.D. diss., University of Pennsylvania.

Duggan, L. (1993). The trials of Alice Mitchell: Sensationalism, sexology, and the lesbian subject in turn-of-the-century America. *Signs* 19(4):791–814.

Faderman, K. (1981). *Surpassing the love of men: Romantic friendships and love between women from the Renaissance to the present.* New York: Morrow.

Faderman, L. (1991). *Odd girls: A history of lesbian life in twentieth-century America.* New York: Columbia University Press.

Fellows, W., ed. (1996). *Farm boys: Lives of gay men from the Midwest.* Madison: University of Wisconsin Press.

Gladney, R. (1993). *How am I to be heard? Letters of Lillian Smith.* Chapel Hill: University of North Carolina Press.

Herdt, G. (1984). *Ritualized homosexuality in Melanesia.* Berkeley: University of California Press.

Howard, J., ed. (Forthcoming). *Carryin' on: Essays on the Southern lesbian and gay past.* New York: New York University Press.

Katz, J. (1992). *Gay American history.* 2d ed. New York: Crowell.

Kennedy, E., and Davis, M. (1993). *Boots of leather, slippers of gold: The history of a lesbian community.* New York: Routledge.

King, F. (1975). *Southern ladies and gentlemen.* New York: Stein & Day.

Marcus, E. (1992). *Making history: The struggle for gay and lesbian rights, 1945–1990.* New York: HarperPerennial.

McKay, A. (1993). *Wolf girls at Vassar: Lesbian and gay experiences, 1930–1990.* New York: Times Change Press.

Miller, N. (1989). *In search of gay America.* New York: Atlantic Monthly Press.

Murray, S., ed. (1992). *Oceanic homosexualities.* New York: Garland.

Nanda, S. (1990). *Neither man nor woman.* Belmont, WA: Wadsworth.

Nardi, P., Sanders, D., and Marmor, J. (1994). *Growing up before Stonewall: Life stories of some gay men.* New York: Routledge.

Nestle, J. (1993). Excerpts from the oral history of Mabel Hampton. *Signs* 19(4):925–935.

Newton, E. (1993). *Cherry Grove, Fire Island: Sixty years in America's first gay and lesbian town.* Boston: Beacon Press.

Norse, H. (1984). Of time and Tennessee Williams. *Advocate* 404 (October 2):38–41.

Patron, E. (1994). Jackie Jackson: The life and times of a Dixie belle. *TWN* (October 12):10.

Power, L. (1996). *No bath, but plenty of bubbles: An oral history of the Gay Liberation Front.* London: Cassell.

Preston, J., ed. (1991). *Hometowns: Gay men write about where they belong.* New York: Dutton.

Quinn, D. (1996). *Same-sex dynamics among nineteenth-century Americans, a Mormon example.* Urbana: University of Illinois Press.

Real, J. (1983). Dragtime: "Dressing up" down South. *Advocate* 373 (August 4):46–50.

Remington, B. (1983). *Twelve fighting years: Homosexuals in Houston, 1969–1981.* Master's thesis, University of Houston.

Rist, D. (1993). *Heartlands: A gay man's odyssey across America.* New York: Plume.

Roscoe, W. (1991). *The Zuni man-woman.* Albuquerque: University of New Mexico Press.

Russell, I. (1993). *Jeb and Dash: A diary of gay life, 1918–1945.* Boston: Faber & Faber.

Sears, J. (1989). The impact of gender and race on growing up lesbian and gay in the South. *National Women's Stories Association Journal* 1(3):422–457.

Sears, J. (1991). *Growing up gay in the South: Race, gender, and journeys of the spirit.* New York: Haworth Press.

Segrest, M. (1985). *My mama's dead squirrel: Lesbian essays on southern culture.* Ithaca: Firebrand.

Segrest, M. (1994). *Memoirs of a race traitor.* Boston: South End Press.

Senelick, L. (1982). The evolution of the male impersonator on the nineteenth-century stage. *Essays in Theatre* 1(1):31–46.

Taub, D., and Leger, R. (1984). Argot and the creation of social types in a young gay community. *Human Relations* 37(3):181–189.

Wafer, J. (1991). *Taste of blood.* Philadelphia: University of Pennsylvania Press.

Weiss, A., and Schiller, G. (1988). *Before Stonewall.* Tallahassee: Naiad Press.

White, E. (1983). *States of desire: Travels in gay America.* New York: Dutton.

Williams, W. (1986). *Spirit and the flesh.* Boston: Beacon.

Witt, L., Thomas, S., and Marcus, E. (1995). *Out in all directions.* New York: Warner.

Wood, R. (1985). *Restless rednecks: Gay tales of a changing South.* San Francisco: Grey Fox Press.

Material used in my appropriation of the generations concept

Escoffier, J. (1992). Generations and paradigms. In H. Minton, ed., *Gay and lesbian studies*, pp. 7–26. New York: Haworth Press.

Esler, A. (1982). *Generations in history: An introduction to the concept.*

Huntington, S. (1977). Generations, cycles, and their role in American development. In R. Samuels, ed., *Political generations and political development*, pp. 9–16. Lexington, MA: Lexington Books.

Kriegel, A. (1978). Generational difference. *Daedalus* 107(4):23–38.

Mannheim, K. (1952). The problem of generations. In P. Kechskemeti, ed., *Essays on the sociology of knowledge*, pp. 276–320. London: Routledge & Kegan Paul.

Marías, J. (1970). *Generations: A historical method*. University: University of Alabama Press.

Ortega y Gasset, J. (1923). *El tema de nuestro tiempo* [The Modern Theme]. Madrid: Revista de Occidente.

Riley, M. (1978). Aging, social change, and the power of ideas. *Daedalus* 107(4):39–52.

Spitzer, A. (1973). The historical problem of generations. *American Historical Review* 78(5):1353–1385.

Strauss, E., and Howe, N. (1991). *Generations*. New York: Morrow.

Chapter One

Material used for the reconstruction of the Simpson murder (in chronological order)

Simpson "Nice Boy," His Landlady Says, *Miami Herald*, 4 August 1954.

Donaldson, B. (4 August 1954). Suspect Hunted in Steward Murder, *Miami Herald*.

Southworth, G. (5 August 1954). Two Sought in Murder of Steward, *Miami Herald*.

"I'm a Sad Sack But No Killer," Says Serviceman, *Miami Herald*, 5 August 1954.

Two Bar Companions of Slain Man Sought, *Miami Herald*, 6 August 1954.

Officers Seek New Leads, *Miami Herald*, 7 August 1954.

Collier, B. (8 August 1954). Tip About Pistol Led to Quiz, *Miami Herald*.

Sosin, M. (8 August 1954). 2nd Boy Seized in North Miami, *Miami Daily News*.

2 Brazen Youths Re-enact Murder of Airline Steward in North Miami, *Miami Herald*, 9 August 1954.

Pass Up Hitch-Hikers, Sheriff Tells Drivers, *Miami Herald*, 9 August 1954.

Southworth, G. (10 August 1954). 5,000 Here Perverts, Police Say, *Miami Herald*.

Fortman, P. (10 August 1954). "Why Did It Happen to Us?" *Miami Herald*.

Smith, J. (10 August 1954). Indictments Held Up in 2 Slayings, *Miami Herald*.

Sosin, M. (10 August 1954). Separate Hearings in Killing Sought, *Miami Herald*.

Flynn, S. (11 August 1954). Ginsburg Hearing Set in Triangle Murder, *Miami Herald*.

Clean This Place Up! *Miami Herald*, 11 August 1954.

Grand Jury Will Hear Witnesses in 2 Slayings, *Miami Herald*, 12 August 1954.

Grand Jury Indicts 3 in Killings, *Miami Herald*, 13 August 1954.

Hearing Inquest Held Unnecessary, *Miami Herald*, 14 August 1954.

Slaying Suspects Denied Freedom, *Miami Herald*, 3 September 1954.

Separate Trials Denied for Pair, *Miami Herald*, 22 October 1954.

Smith, D. (31 October 1954). Simpson Murder Case Comes Up This Week, *Miami Herald*.

Smith, D. (4 November 1954). Jury Set in Murder Trial Today, *Miami Herald*.

Smith, D. (5 November 1954). Robbin', Rollin' of Deviates Told, *Miami Herald*.

Smith, D. (6 November 1954). Defense to Ask Dismissal, *Miami Herald*.

Smith, D. (7 November 1954). Jurors Weighing Verdict in Slaying of Air Steward, *Miami Herald*.

Rundell, R. (8 November 1954). Pair Faces 20 Years Maximum, *Miami Herald*.
Rundell, R. (15 November 1954). Do You Wonder What Happened? *Miami Herald*.
Youths Get 20 Years in Slaying, *Miami Herald*, November 1954.
Pedersen, L. (aka Jim Kepner) (1954). Miami Hurricane, *ONE* 2(9):4–8.
Pair Granted Free Appeals, *Miami Herald*, 8 December 1954.
The Miami Homosexual Problem: A Special Report, *Miami Life*, 17 January 1955.
Kepner, J. Miami Hurricane, *NewsWest*, 1–15 April 1977, pp. 26–28.

Material used for the pre-1954 purge and gay life (in chronological order)

Dade Open to Maniacs Chief Says, *Miami Herald*, 21 November 1953.
Turn-About Not Fair Play, Say Beach Police, *Miami Herald*, 21 November 1953.
Beach Plans Bums Rush Off for Perverts, *Miami Herald*, 25 November 1953.
Unit Urges Crackdown on Perverts, *Miami Daily News*, November 1953.
Kepner, J. (1954). Miami Junks the Constitution, *ONE* 2(1):16–21.
Patron, E. (12 October 1994). Jackie Jackson: The Life and Times of a Dixie Belle, *TWN*, pp. 10–11.

Material used for the 1954 description of political actions, bar raids, harassment, violence, and arrests (in chronological order)

Dade Open to Maniacs Chief Says, *Miami Herald*, 21 November 1953.
Unit Urges Crackdown on Perverts, *Miami Daily News*, November 1953.
Pedersen, L. (1954). Miami's New Type Witchhunt, *ONE* 4(4):8–12.
Collier, B. (August 1954). $200,000 Outlay Urged for Center to Treat Deviates, *Miami Herald*.
Clean This Place Up! *Miami Herald*, 11 August 1954.
Six Suspected Perverts Held in Beach Raid, *Miami Daily News*, 13 August 1954.
Flynn, S. (13 August 1954). Beach Police Round up 35 in Pervert Crackdown, *Miami Herald*.
Miller, J. (13 August 1954). Perverts Seized in Bar Raids, *Miami Herald*.
Roberts, J. (15 August 1954). How L.A. Handles Its 150,000 Perverts, *Miami Daily News*.
Hypnotist Offers to Help Deviates, *Miami Herald*, 31 August 1954.
Voltz, L. (31 August 1954). Police to Harass Pervert Hangouts, *Miami Herald*.
Voltz, L. (1 September 1954). Evans Sets Thursday as "D-Day," *Miami Herald*.
Voltz, L. (4 September 1954). Perverts Disperse But Drive Goes On, *Miami Herald*.
Johns Names Aide to Fight Perverts, *Miami Daily News*, 7 September 1954.
Stiff Laws Urged on Perversion, *Miami Herald*, 8 September 1954.
Ordinance Would Kill Pervert Bars' Permits, *Miami Herald*, 10 September 1954.
Tounsley, F. (24 September 1954). Perverts Swarm Here, *Ft. Lauderdale News*.
City Judge Hired in Sex Case, *Miami Herald*, 26 January 1955.
Collier, B., and Thompson, L. (17 November 1955). Deviates, Minors' Drinking Spur Call for Federal Laws, *Miami Daily News*.

Hearing Before the Subcommittee to Investigate Juvenile Delinquency of the Committee on the Judiciary (1955). United States Senate, Eighty-third Congress, Second Session, Pursuant to S. Res. 89, Investigation of Juvenile Delinquency in the United States, 16 December 1954. Washington, DC: U.S. Government Printing Office.

Hearing Before the Subcommittee to Investigate Juvenile Delinquency of the Committee on the Judiciary (1956). United States Senate, Eighty-fourth Congress, First Session, Pursuant to S. Res. 62 as extended, Investigation of Juvenile Delinquency in the United States, 16 November 1955. Washington, DC: U.S. Government Printing Office.

Miami's Whirligig, *Miami Daily News*, March 1956.

Harris, S. (1969). *The puritan jungle.* New York: Putman.

Material used for the description of 1956 crackdown (in chronological order)

Hardin, B., and Bonafede, D. (27 February 1956). Homosexuals Return, Find Heat's Off Again, *Miami Daily News.*

Hardin, B., and Bonafede, D. (28 February 1956). Deviate Hangouts' Owners Prosper, *Miami Daily News.*

Hardin, B., and Bonafede, D. (29 February 1956). Let Deviates Alone, Police View, *Miami Daily News.*

Hardin, B., and Bonafede, D. (1 March 1956). Police Policies on Deviates Hit by Psychiatrist, *Miami Daily News.*

Hardin, B. (5 March 1956). Beach Hits at Deviate Hangouts, *Miami Daily News.*

For Better Policy on Sex Perverts, *Miami Daily News*, 6 March 1956.

Experts at Odds on Deviates Law, *Miami Daily News*, 7 March 1956.

Smith, J. (11 March 1956). Mental Tests Out in Sex Offenses, *Miami Herald.*

Roberts, J. (15 March 1956). Rev. Ed Wall Must Stand Trial, *Miami Daily News.*

Roberts, J. (16 March 1956). Pervert "Prey" Racket Aired, *Miami Daily News.*

Gables Man Ruled Guilty in Sex Case, *Miami Herald*, 20 March 1956.

Gay Death of Teacher Called Suicide by Cops, *Miami Daily News*, March 1956.

Becker, P. (20 July 1956). Wall Acquitted in Moral Charge, *Miami Daily News.*

Smith, J. (20 July 1956). Ed Wall's Story Unfolds at Trial, *Miami Herald.*

Officials Make Sure Child Molester Goes, *Miami Herald*, 19 September 1957.

He Gets 15 Years as Sex Deviate, *Miami Herald*, 29 September 1957.

Material used to amplify Mushroom's description of 1950s Miami, written by her and used with her permission

The true tale of the Tongueston Trio—1959, *Common lives/lesbian lives* 18 (Winter 1985):9–12.

Womonwrites 1988: Memories of the '50s, *Common lives/lesbian lives* 18 (Winter 1985):67–71.

dykeling merril meets dykeling penny. In J. Stanley and S. Valentine, eds., *Finding the lesbians*, pp. 188–190. Freedom, CA: Crossing Press, 1990.

Letter. In S. Wolfe and J. Stanley, eds., *The coming out stories* (1st ed.), pp. 135–138. Watertown, MA: Persephone Press, 1980.

Dear Julia. In S. Wolfe and J. Stanley, eds., *The original coming out stories* (2d ed.), pp. 55–58. Freedom, CA: Crossing Press, 1990.

Gay girls and gay guys. In J. Nestle and J. Preston, eds., *Sister and brother*. San Francisco: Harper San Francisco, 1994.

Other material used in section on 1950s Miami

Feather, L. (31 December 1952). Hippest entertainer in square circles—That's Frances Faye. *Downbeat*, p. 7.

Zeimer, M. If only Eddie could be here now. Unpublished ms. Demorest, GA.

Material on the history of south Florida (in alphabetical order)

Dunn, M., and Stepick, A. (1992). Blacks in Miami. In E. Grenier and A. Stepick, eds., *Miami now*, pp. 41–56. Gainesville: University Press of Florida.

Gannon, M. (1993). *Florida: A short history*. Gainesville: University Press of Florida.

George, P. (1978). Colored town: Miami's black community, 1896–1930. *Florida Historical Quarterly* 56(4):432–447.

George, P. (1979). Policing Miami's black community, 1896–1930. *Florida Historical Quarterly* 57(4):434–450.

George, P. (1986). Brokers, binders, and builders: Greater Miami's boom of the mid-1920s. *Florida Historical Quarterly* 65(1):27–51.

Key, V. O. (1950). *Southern politics*. New York: Knopf.

Kharif, W. (1985). Black reaction to segregation and discrimination in post-Reconstruction Florida. *Florida Historical Quarterly* 54(2):161–173.

Moore, D. (1994). *To the golden cities: Pursuing the American Jewish dream in Miami and L.A.* New York: Free Press.

Portes, A., and Stepick, A. (1993). *City on the edge: The transformation of Miami*. Berkeley: University of California Press.

Railey, H., and Polansky, L. (1994). *Old Miami Beach*. Miami Beach: Miami Design Preservation League.

Redford, P. (1970). *Billion dollar sandbar*. New York: Dutton.

Rothchild, J. (1985) *Up for grabs*. New York: Viking.

Smiley, N. (1974). *Knights of the fourth estate: The story of the Miami Herald*. Miami: Seemann.

Sofen, E. (1961). *A report on politics in Greater Miami*. Cambridge, MA: Joint Center for Urban Studies of the Massachusetts Institute of Technology and Harvard University.

Wilbanks, W. (1984). *Murder in Miami*. Lanham, MD: University Press of America.

Wolff, R. (1960). *Miami metro*. Coral Gables: University of Miami, Area Development Series, No. 9.

Interviews

Jim Kepner, West Hollywood, CA, October 1993.
Rose Levinson (pseudonym), Miami, FL, 16 March 1995.
Merril Mushroom, Dowelltown, TN, 1 October 1995.
Jim Patterson, Columbia, SC, 7 October 1995.

Chapter Two

Primary material for this chapter was secured from the Florida State Archives, Florida Legislative Investigation Committee Records, Tallahassee, FL, which houses forty-five boxes containing 25,000 pages incorporated as 4,399 documents.

Additional sources cited (in chronological order)

Hesser, C. (12 January 1959). Homosexual Probe Hits Florida U., *Miami News*.
Hesser, C. (13 January 1959). Morals Cleanup at U-F Pledged, *Miami News*.
Students Morals Questioned, *Miami Herald*, 13 January 1959.
Florida U. Dismisses 14 for Homosexuality, Associated Press, 4 April 1959.
McGarrahan, E. (8 December 1991). Florida's secret shame, *Tropic*.

Material used on the University of Florida (in alphabetical order)

Kerber, S. (1979). William Edwards and the historical University of Florida campus. *Florida Historical Quarterly* 57(3):327–351.
Prescott, S. (1992). White robes and crosses: Father John Conoley, the Ku Klux Klan, and the University of Florida. *Florida Historical Quarterly* 77(1):18–40.

Material used on race relations and the civil rights movement (in alphabetical order)

Clark, J. (1994). Civil rights leader Harry T. Moore and the Ku Klux Klan in Florida. *Florida Historical Quarterly* 73(2):166–183.
Colburn, D., and Scher, R. (1976). Race relations and Florida gubernatorial politics since the *Brown* decision. *Florida Historical Quarterly* 55(2):153–169.
Hampton, H., and Fayer, S. (1990). *Voices of freedom*. New York: Bantam.
Howard, W. (1988). Vigilante justice and national reaction. *Florida Historical Quarterly* 67(1):32–37.
Lawson, S., Colburn, D., and Paulson, D. (1986). Groveland: Florida's little Scottsboro. *Florida Historical Quarterly* 55(1):1–25.
Mormino, G. (1994). GI Joe meets Jim Crow. *Florida Historical Quarterly* 73(1):23–42.

Tomberlin, J. (1972). Florida whites and the *Brown* decision of 1954. *Florida Historical Quarterly* 51(1):22–36.

Wagy, T. (1979). Governor LeRoy Collins of Florida and the Selma crisis of 1965. *Florida Historical Quarterly* 57(4):403–420.

Interviews

Arlen Davies (pseudonym), Columbia, SC, 8 March 1996; East Texas, 17 June 1996.

Merril Mushroom, Dowelltown, TN, 1 October 1995; 16 June 1996.

Jim Patterson, Columbia, SC, 7 October 1995; 26 July 1996.

Chapter Three

Primary material for this chapter was secured from Florida State Archives, Florida Legislative Investigation Committee Records, Tallahassee; New York Public Library Archives, New York City; ONE Institute International Gay and Lesbian Archives, Los Angeles; Special Collections Library, Duke University, Durham, NC.

Other material for this chapter (in chronological order)

Brandle, L. (22 March 1960). Florida Coalition Criticizes Dr. Hardeman, Tampa Professor, *St. Petersburg Times.*

Ousted in Probe, *Miami Herald*, 5 April 1961.

Denley, B. (May 1961). Outspoken Professor Losing Tampa U. Job, *St. Petersburg Times.*

Fellows, B. (30 June 1961). Tampa Councilman Loss Bid to Probe Professor's Firing, *St. Petersburg Times.*

State Opens Campaign to Combat Problems Created by the Increase of Homosexuals. (April 1962). *Florida's Children* 13(2):1, 6.

Newman, G. (25 April 1962). Metro Has List of Homosexuals, *Miami News.*

McIntire, S. (aka Jim Kepner) (July 1962). No Guts in Florida, *ONE*, p. 11.

Probers Used "Half-Truths," Says University President, *Miami Herald*, 15 April 1963.

Florida Legislative Investigation Committee (1964). *Homosexuality and Citizenship in Florida.* Tallahassee, FL.

Sosin, M. (18 March 1964). Dade Bans State Sex Report, *Miami News.*

WJXT News Editorial Comment, 20 March 1964.

Official Obscenity, TV 9 Editorial, 20 March 1964.

Back up Sex Charges, School Chief Demands: 123 Teachers Accused, *Miami Herald*, 17 April 1964.

Educators to Probe Sex Cases, *Miami Herald*, 20 May 1964.

Williams, R. (23 May 1964). Sex, Tallahassee, *New Republic*, p. 5.

Sherrill, R. (1 June 1964). Teacher Perversion List Called Myth, *Miami Herald.*

"John" Like Report of the Johns Committee. (1964). *ONE*, 12(6):9–13.

Wickstrom, K. (10 August 1964). Only Facts Are Needed in Homosexuality Study, *Miami Herald.*

A New Look for State Laws, *Miami Herald*, 23 September 1964.

Sherrill, R. (8 May 1965). Public's Morals Safeguard Aim of Mitchell Bills, *Miami Herald*.

Johns Group Bills Advance, *Miami Herald*, 26 May 1965.

Strothman, J. (6 September 1965). That "Purple Pamphlet" Still a Saleable Item, *Miami Herald*.

Vinciguierra, T. (26 September 1965). Johns Probe Aide Heads New Inquiry, *Ft. Lauderdale News*.

State's "Purple Pamphlet" Costly in Smut Market, *Miami Herald*, 22 April 1967.

McCarrahan, E. (8 December 1991). Florida's Secret Shame, *Tropic*, pp. 9–12, 16–18.

Florida Opens Records of Anti-subversives Panel, *State Newspaper*, 1 July 1993.

Taylor, R. (1 July 1993). When Florida Spied on People, *Atlanta Constitution*.

Florida Reviews an Era of Fear, *New York Times*, 4 July 1993.

Reporter's Life Shattered by '60s Panel, *Contax*, 11 August 1993.

Other material

In addition to the audiotaped interview, other sources for Penelope's quotations, used with her permission, are "My Life as a Lesbian," in J. Penelope Stanley and S. Wolfe, eds., *The coming out stories* (1st ed.), pp. 195–206 (Watertown, MA: Persephone Press, 1980). This selection can now be found in a second edition entitled *The original coming out stories* published by Crossing Press, 1989; Personal correspondence from her to James T. Sears, 24 September 1996, now archived in the Sears Papers at the Special Collections Library of Duke University, Durham, NC. Also cited in this chapter is U. Dydo, ed., *Stein Reader* (Evanston, IL: Northwestern University Press, 1993).

Interviews

Merril Mushroom, Dowelltown, TN, 1 October 1995; 16 June 1996.

Julia Penelope, Lubbock, TX, 23 June 1996.

Sue Sponnoble, Miami, FL, 11 January 1995; 31 August 1996.

Chapter Four

In addition to my interviews with Quinton Baker and Pat Cusick, additional material quoted from and used with their permission are the Duke University Oral History Project: Tapes 66, 67, and 105a/b of Quinton Baker, 2 June 1974; Tapes 61–65 of Pat Cusick, 10 June 1974. Additionally, Transcript No. 4007, L-43 of Pat Cusick from the Southern Oral History Program, Southern Historical Collection, Library of the University of North Carolina at Chapel Hill. Other quoted material incorporated into this chapter is from the personal correspondence to James T. Sears from Pat Cusick, 31 December 1996, and from Quinton Baker, 6 January 1997. These are now located in the Sears Papers at the Special Collections Library of Duke University, Durham, NC.

Newspaper accounts and pamphlets (in chronological order)

Washington, B. (30 March 1911). Durham, NC, A City of Negro Enterprises, *Independent*, 642–650.

Wanted Pickets [1960 Pamphlet]. North Carolina Collection Clipping File Through 1975, p. 1085. University of North Carolina Library, Chapel Hill.

Smith, L. (September 1960). The South's Moment of Truth, *The Progressive*, 32–35.

Maupin, A. (14 December 1962). View from the Hill, *Daily Tar Heel*.

Justice, J. (15 January 1963). Peace Group Moves South. Letter to the Editor, *Daily Tar Heel*.

Clotfelter, J. (6 February 1963). Lean, Hungry Black Cat: From "Cool" to Cold, *Daily Tar Heel*.

Maupin, A. (15 February 1963). View from the Hill, *Daily Tar Heel*.

Maupin, A. (7 March 1963). View from the Hill, *Daily Tar Heel*.

Wellman, W. (16 March 1963). Homosexuality: Crime or Sickness? *Daily Tar Heel*.

Wellman, W. (2 April 1963). Cafe Pickets Waste Steps, Wellman Says, *Daily Tar Heel*.

Cusick, P. (3 April 1963). Letter to the Editor, *The Weekly*.

Maupin, A. (25 April 1963). View from the Hill, *Daily Tar Heel*.

Hicks, B. (5 May 1963). Integration Group Maps First Plans, *Daily Tar Heel*.

Phelps, L. (5 May 1963). Letter to the Editor, *Daily Tar Heel*.

Neely, C. (8 May 1963). Neely Knocks Phelps as Exploiter of Negro, *Daily Tar Heel*.

Maupin, A. (10 May 1963). View from the Hill, *Daily Tar Heel*.

Whiteleather, A. (16 July 1963). His Reaction to Protests: Business Closed to Negroes, Durham *Morning Herald Tribune*.

Wilson, C. (5 November 1963). Marches Are Self-Defeating, *Daily Tar Heel*.

Why Four People Chose Jail, December [1963 Flyer], Congress of Racial Equality–Chapel Hill. North Carolina Collection Clipping File Through 1975, p. 739. University of North Carolina Library, Chapel Hill.

3 More Arrested as Race Protests Continue Here, *Daily Tar Heel*, 15 December 1963.

Bulkley, J. (17 December 1963). 36 Arrests Made Here in Four Days of Sit-Ins, *Daily Tar Heel*.

Harkness, P. (18 December 1963). CORE Hopes Chapel Hill to Be First in the State, *Daily Tar Heel*.

Open Letter to Fellow Citizens of Chapel Hill from the Chapel Hill Freedom Committee (Christmas 1963). North Carolina Collection Clipping File Through 1975, p. 736. University of North Carolina Library, Chapel Hill.

Why We Are Fasting [1964 Pamphlet], North Carolina Collection Clipping File Through 1975, p. 738. University of North Carolina Library, Chapel Hill.

Bulkley, J. (7 January 1964). New Year Brings Race Violence to Chapel Hill, *Daily Tar Heel*.

Chapel Hill—North Carolina or Alabama? *Daily Tar Heel*, 7 January 1964.

McReynolds, D. (7 January 1964). A New Kind of Christmas in Chapel Hill, *Daily Tar Heel*.

Thompson, F. (7 January 1964). New Generation Offers a Challenge, *Daily Tar Heel.*

Bulkley, J. (11 January 1964). Durham-CH March Planned, *Daily Tar Heel.*

Sterling, S. (12 January 1964). DTH Survey Shows Unequal Service at 25% of 116 Places, *Daily Tar Heel.*

Board Vote Bypasses Accommodations Law, *Daily Tar Heel,* 14 January 1964.

Bulkley, J. (14 January 1964). More Demonstrations on Tap if Law Fails, Farmer Warns, *Daily Tar Heel.*

Bulkley, J. (15 January 1964). Farmer Threatens Big Demonstrations, *Daily Tar Heel.*

Chapel Hill Gets Racial Deadline, *Raleigh News and Observer,* 15 January 1964.

Giduz, R. (19 January 1964). Chapel Hill Story, *News of Orange County.*

Clotfelter, J. (26 January 1964). 4 White Men Tell Why They Are Involved in CR Battle, *Durham Morning Herald.*

Corner, P. (26 January 1964). For Chapel Hill, Disdain Is Rule Instead of Hate, *Durham Morning Herald.*

Maupin, A. (6 February 1964). View from the Hill. *Daily Tar Heel.*

Orange Integrationist Sees "Racial Turmoil," *Raleigh News and Observer,* 7 February 1964.

Harwell, F. (6 February 1964). 200 Protest CORE, *Daily Tar Heel.*

Seely, F. (7 February 1964). SCEF President Says, "Seek Your Rights," *Daily Tar Heel.*

Wales, P. (8 February 1964). Lawler Asks Boycott of "White Only's," Cites Students' Roles, *Daily Tar Heel.*

Wales, P. (9 February 1964). Stepped Up Sit-Downs Block Town's Traffic, *Daily Tar Heel.*

Greenbacker, J. (11 February 1964). Petition Is Circulated Opposing Lawler's Civil Rights Statement, *Daily Tar Heel.*

Dick, J. (16 February 1964). Integration Heads Call Civil Disobedience Halt, *Daily Tar Heel.*

Dick, J. (20 February 1964). Straley: Boycott Mistake, *Daily Tar Heel.*

Grand Jury Gets Sit-Ins Monday, *Daily Tar Heel,* 21 February 1964.

Integration Leaders Extend Moratorium, *Daily Tar Heel,* 22 February 1964.

Court Fails to Docket Sit-In Cases, *Daily Tar Heel,* 25 February 1964.

Himes, S. (26 February 1964). Helms: No! Letter to the Editor, *Daily Tar Heel.*

Dick, J. (2 March 1964). Federal Court Gets Sit-In Cases in Surprise Move, *Daily Tar Heel.*

150 Faculty Agree to Respect Boycott, *Daily Tar Heel,* 8 March 1964.

Dick, J. (10 March 1964). Six Are Charged with Conspiracy, *Daily Tar Heel.*

Integrationists Start 8-Day Fast Today, *Daily Tar Heel,* 22 March 1964.

. . . And the Fast Ended, *Daily Tar Heel,* 1 April 1964.

McInnis, H. (22 April 1964). Homosexuals in Flicks, *Daily Tar Heel.*

Seely, F. (24 April 1964). Local Civil Rightists Draw Jail Sentences, *Daily Tar Heel.*

Mallard Sends 4 More Demonstrators to Jail, *Daily Tar Heel,* 25 April 1964.

Mississippi Law Comes to Hillsboro, *Daily Tar Heel.* 28 April 1964.

Wales, P. (30 April 1964). Odd Events in Hillsboro, *Daily Tar Heel.*

Harkness, P. (13 May 1964). Homosexuality a Disease, Not a Case of Immorality, *Daily Tar Heel.*

Books and other materials directly related to Chapel Hill and Durham used in the development of this chapter (in alphabetical order)

Barksdale, M. (1977). *The indigenous civil rights movement and cultural change in North Carolina.* Ph.D. diss., Duke University.

Barksdale, M. (1986). Civil rights organization and the indigenous movement in Chapel Hill, NC, 1960–1965. *Phylon* 47(1):29–42.

Chafe, W. (1980). *Civilities and civil rights.* New York: Oxford University Press.

Chappell, D. (1994). *Inside agitators: White Southerners in the civil rights movement.* Baltimore: Johns Hopkins University Press.

Davidson, O. (1996). *The best of enemies: Race and redemption in the New South.* New York: Scribner.

Dentler, R., Baltzell, D., and Sullivan, D. (1983). *University on trial: The case of the University of North Carolina.* Cambridge, MA: Abt.

Ehle, J. (1965). *The free men.* New York: Harper & Row.

Lomax, L. (1971). *The Negro revolt.* New York: Harper & Row.

Rustin, B. (1971). *Down the line.* Chicago, IL: Quadrangle.

Stolpen, S. (1978). *Chapel Hill: A pictorial history.* Norfolk, VA: Donning.

Other material cited or drawn from for this chapter (in alphabetical order)

Branch, T. (1988). *Parting the waters: America in the King years, 1954–1963.* New York: Simon & Schuster.

Cox, O. (1951). The leadership of Booker T. Washington. *Social Forces* 30 (October):91–96.

Du Bois, W.E.B. (1994). *Souls of black folk.* New York: Gramercy (originally published 1903).

Frazier, E. F. (1957). *Black bourgeoisie: The rise of a new middle class.* New York: Free Press.

Gladney, R. (1993). *How am I to be heard?* Chapel Hill: University of North Carolina Press.

Hampton, H., and Fayer, S. (1990). *Voices of freedom: An oral history of the civil rights movement from the 1950s through the 1980s.* New York: Bantam.

Lee, H. (1960). *To kill a mockingbird.* New York: Popular Library.

Leuchtenburg, W. (1991). The conversion of Harry Truman. *American Heritage* 42(7):55–68.

Ryan, A. (1883). *Poems: Patriotic, religious, miscellaneous.* Baltimore: Piet.

Smith, L. (1949). *Killers of the dream.* New York: Norton.

Smith, L. (6 June 1954). Letter to the Editor, *New York Times,* p. 10.

The ten richest Negroes in America. *Ebony* 4 (1949).

Wolff, M. (1970). *Lunch at the five and dime: The Greensboro sit-ins.* New York: Stein & Day.
Wynn, L. (1991). The dawning of a new day: The Nashville sit-ins, February 13– May 10, 1960. *Tennessee Historical Quarterly* 50(1):42–54.
Zinn, H. (1964). *The Southern mystique.* New York: Knopf.

Interviews

Quinton Baker, Hillsborough, NC, 25 September 1996; 13 October 1996.
Pat Cusick, Boston, MA, 22 September 1996; 14 October 1996.

Chapter Five

In addition to the audiotaped interviews, other sources for Simmons's quotations come from the following personal correspondence from her to James T. Sears: 1 November 1994; 1 January 1995; 12 January 1995; 30 January 1995; 27 February 1995. Also included is the personal correspondence from Dena Crane to James T. Sears, 31 October 1994. These are now archived in the Generations Collection of the Sears Papers located at the Special Collections Library of Duke University, Durham, NC.

Additional sources of quotations from Simmons, used with her permission (in chronological order)

Hall, Gordon Langley (November 1963). 'Twas the Night Before Christmas. *Charleston News & Courier.*
_____ (20 September 1964). Poor Old Grandmother and the Queen. *Preservation Progress* 8(4).
Simmons, Dawn Langley (1971). *Man into woman.* New York: Macfadden.
_____ (1983). *Margaret Rutherford: A blithe spirit.* New York: McGraw-Hill.
_____ (15 February 1989). Marriage That Shocked. *Charleston Chronicle.*
_____ (22 February 1989). Racism Scars Wedding. *Charleston Chronicle.*
_____ (8 March 1989). To John Paul: 20 Years of Marriage Is Like Yesterday. *Charleston Chronicle.*

Other material used in the development of Simmons's life story (in chronological order)

Patlas Plant Tree of Friendship, *Charleston News & Courier*, 23 November 1962.
Leland, J. (23 December 1962). Gordon Langley Hall Scores with Novel for Juveniles, *Charleston News & Courier.*
Letter to Irac C. Moore Jr., 5 April 1963, from Gordon Hall, in Dawn Pepita Simmons Papers, Correspondence, 1874–1970, Section 20. Special Collections Library, Duke University, Durham, NC (hereafter referred to as Simmons Papers).

Johnson House Works Shown at Art Gallery, 5 November 1964, *Charleston News & Courier*.

Hill, P. (8 November 1964). Author Is Restoring Home in Memory of His Cousin, *Charleston News & Courier*.

Ripley, W. (13 November 1964). Osceola's Story by Local Author, *Charleston News & Courier*.

Letter to Gordon Hall, 31 March 1968, from Mrs. Hugh March Andrews, in Simmons Papers.

Letter to Jack Copper, no date, from Gordon Hall, in Simmons Papers.

Letter to John-Paul Simmons, 24 June 1968, from Alex Simmons, in Simmons Papers.

Dawn's New Day, *Time*, 2 December 1968.

Letter to Dawn Simmons, 23 December 1968, from Lawrence P. Ashmead, in Simmons Papers.

Man Who Changed Sex, Husband on Honeymoon, *Columbia* (SC) *Record*, 23 January 1969.

Dawn Hall Marries Her (His?) Ex-Chauffeur in Private Rites, *Greenville* (SC) *News*, 23 January 1969.

Startling Bride Wants Children, *Raleigh News and Observer*, 23 January 1969.

Letter to Jack Copper, 22 September 1969, from Dawn Simmons, in Simmons Papers.

Riley, B. (20 December 1970). Myra Breckinridge with a Twist, *National Insider*.

Parkin, M. (7 March 1971). The Life and Love of a Trans-Sexual, *The Sunday Times* of London.

Letter to John-Paul Simmons, Sunday [Summer 1972], from Dawn Simmons, in Simmons Papers.

Letter to Dawn Simmons, 14 September 1972, from Anthony Dawson, in Simmons Papers.

Letter to Dawn Simmons, 18 September 1972, from Robert Holmes, in Simmons Papers.

Carr, V. (1975). *The lonely hunter: A biography of Carson McCullers*. New York: Carroll & Graff.

Follow-up on the News: Transsexual Life, *New York Times*, 21 November 1975.

Siegelbaum, D. (14 December 1975). Author, Socialite, Former Man and Now "Mother" Faces Divorce, *Sunday Times-Union* (Albany NY).

Birmingham, S. (1990). *America's secret aristocracy*. New York: Berkeley [orig. publ. 1987, Little, Brown & Co.].

Letters to the Editor, *Charleston Chronicle*, 8 March 1989.

New Book, *Charleston Chronicle*, 6 September 1993.

Material used for description and history of Charleston or transsexuality (in alphabetical order)

Ellis, H. (1906). *Studies in the psychology of sex*. Part 2. New York: Random House.

Fraser, W. (1989). *Charleston! Charleston!* Columbia: University of South Carolina Press.

Hirschfeld, M. (1991). *The transvestites: An investigation of the erotic drive to cross dress*. Transl. M. Lombardi-Nash. Buffalo: Prometheus.
MacKenzie, D. (1994). *Transgender nation*. Bowling Green: Bowling Green State University Popular Press.

Interviews

Billy Camden (pseudonym), Charleston, SC, 26 September 1994.
Margarita Childs, Charleston, SC, 16 August 1994.
Dawn Langley Hall [Simmons], Hudson, NY, 19 October 1994; 6 November 1994.
Dr. Leber (pseudonym), Charleston, SC, 3 August 1994; 15 September 1994.
Ann Leland, Charleston, SC, 1 June 1994; 15 June 1994.
Jeremy Morrow (pseudonym), Charleston, SC, 31 May 1994; 8 August 1994.
Nicky (pseudonym), Charleston, SC, 13 September 1994.

Chapter Six

Primary material for this chapter was secured from the ONE Institute International Gay and Lesbian Archives, Los Angeles; New York Public Library, Manuscript Division; Diary of Jeb Alexander [pseudonym], 1937–1940, from the personal collection of "Nicky," Charleston, SC. Additional material used to amplify Nichols's description and used with his permission are draft notes (1994) of his unpublished memoirs-in-progress as well as *I Have More Fun with You Than Anybody* (with Lige Clark) (New York: St. Martin's Press, 1972). Other sources come from personal correspondence from Nichols to James T. Sears (22 March 1996, 10 June 1996), and from Jim Kepner to James T. Sears (2 February 1997), Sears Papers at the Special Collections Library, Duke University, Durham, NC.

Material used in the description and chronology of the origins of the homophile movement

Bérubé, A. (1990). *Coming out under fire: The history of gay men and women in World War Two*. New York: Plume.
D'Emilio, J. (1983). *Sexual politics, sexual communities*. Chicago: University of Chicago Press.
Katz, J. (1976). *Gay American history*. New York: Harper & Row.
Marcus. E. (1992). *Making history: The struggle for gay and lesbian equal rights*. New York: HarperCollins.
Russell, I. (1993). *Jeb and Dash: A diary of gay life, 1918–1945*. Boston: Faber & Faber.
Streitmatter, R. (1995). *Unspeakable: The rise of the gay and lesbian press in America*. Winchester, MA: Faber & Faber.
Timmons, S. (1990). *The trouble with Harry Hay*. Boston: Alyson.
Tobin [Lahusen], Kay, and Wicker, R. (1975). *The gay crusaders*. New York: Arno Press.

Interviews

Jack Nichols, Cocoa Beach, FL, 13 January 1995.

Chapter Seven

Copies of all correspondence and news articles cited here are located in the Sears Papers at the Special Collections Library of Duke University, Durham, NC.

Material used for the section on the Atheneum Society, Florida Mattachine, and Richard Inman

Stonewall Library and Archives, Ft. Lauderdale, FL: Correspondence to Warren D. Adkins (Jack Nichols) from Richard Inman, 15 January 1965–19 October 1965, Manuscript Collection; *Atheneum Review*.

ONE Institute International Gay and Lesbian Archives, Los Angeles: *Atheneum Review*; *Atheneum Viewpoint*; *Florida Mattachine Viewpoint*; *Florida League for Good Government Viewpoint*; National Planning Conference of Homophile Organizations minutes.

Private Collection of Jack Nichols, Cocoa Beach, FL: "The Homosexual," FYI television documentary; 1 April 1965 letter to Dick Leitsch from Warren Adkins.

International Gay Information Center Papers, Manuscript Division, New York Public Library (in chronological order):

Letter to Ron Mayer from Curtis Dewees, 14 June 1958, Box 1, File 8, in Mattachine Society Inc. of New York Papers, 1957–1968, Curtis Dewees Correspondence.

When I Was 13 Years Old, Papers of Perry Brass, Box 96.

Letters to Julian Hodges from Richard Inman, 22 August 1964 and 12 October 1964, Box 7, File 1, Mattachine Society Inc. of New York Papers, 1957–1968.

Letter to Julian Hodges from Frank Kameny, 23 August 1964, Box 8, File 5, Mattachine Society Inc. of New York Papers, 1957–1968.

Letter to Julian Hodges from Richard Inman, 10 November 1964, Box 1, File 9, Mattachine Society Inc. of New York Papers, 1957–1968.

Letter to Richard Inman from Julian Hodges, March 1965, Box 7, File 1, Mattachine Society Inc. of New York Papers, 1957–1968.

Letters to Warren D. Adkins and Richard A. Inman from Elver Barker, 23 May 1966, and to Elver Barker from Dick Leitsch, 27 May 1966, Box 1, File 13, Mattachine Society Inc. of New York Papers, 1957–1968, Dick Leitsch Correspondence.

Letter to Dick Leitsch from Randy Wicker, 11 February 1968, and Letter to Randy Wicker from Dick Leitsch, 20 February 1968, Box 1, File 17, Mattachine Society Inc. of New York Papers, 1957–1968, Dick Leitsch Correspondence.

Letter to Ed Trust from Richard Inman, 20 June 1968, Box 1, File 17, Mattachine Society Inc. of New York Papers, 1957–1968, Dick Leitsch Correspondence.

Other sources cited in this chapter (in chronological order)

Giltmier, J. (15 December 1964). Homosexual Law Deletions Asked, *Miami Herald*.

"Secret" Bill Easing Sex Laws to Be Exposed by Club, *Coral Gables Times*, March 1965.

Labelle, M. (11 March 1965). Miami Cabbie Leads Drive to Relax State Homo Laws. *Coral Gables Times*.

Reynolds, J. (23 March 1965). Laws on Sexual Behavior Reviewed, *Ft. Lauderdale Sun-Sentinel*.

Inman, R. (17 October 1965). Stop Harassing Homosexuals: It's Unconstitutional and Degrading, *National Insider*.

Rau, H. (16 November 1965). State Charter for Mattachine Society of Fla., Miami Confidential, *Miami News*.

Pro-Pervert Club Wins Charter, *Coral Gables Times*, 25 November 1965.

City Bar Law Is Challenged, *Miami News*, 12 February 1966.

Homosexual Suit Filed, *Miami Herald*, 12 February 1966.

Homosexual Is Group Subject, *Kansas City Times*, 21 February 1966.

Another Look at Miami's Homosexual Problem, WTVJ, Channel 4 editorial, No. 1856, 29 April 1966.

The Homosexual Program Gets Results, WTVJ, Channel 4 editorial, No. 1868, 19 May 1966.

Judge OKs Suit Against Bar Law, *Miami News*, 1 June 1966.

Homosexual Law OK, Court Says, *Miami Herald*, 11 June 1966.

Judge Upholds Homosexual Law, *Miami News*, 30 June 1966.

Behrens, D. (5 April 1967). Anti-homosexual Rule in Miami Code Upheld, *Miami Herald*.

Homosexual Law Upheld, *Miami News*, 21 July 1967.

Homos Barred from Bar Work, *Coral Gables Times*, 7 August 1967.

Homo Leader Blasts New Gables Law, *Coral Gables Times*, 14 August 1967.

Power, M. (16 August 1967). High Court to Decide Liquor Law, *Miami Herald*.

State Attorney Denies Homo Bar Flourishes, *Coral Gables Times*, 17 August 1967.

Homo Law Adopted Unopposed, *Coral Gables Times*, 4 September 1967.

Supreme Court Next in Drink Limit Fuss, *Miami Herald*, 19 October 1967.

Top Court Upholds Miami Law, *Miami Herald*, 16 January 1968.

Defendant Goes Free in Smut Case, *Miami News*, 1 November 1968.

Inman v. City of Miami, Fla. App. 1967, 197 So. 2d 50; cert. den. 1968, 389 U.S. 1048, 19 L. Ed. 2d. 841, 88 S.Ct. 769.

Man Freed in Lewd Film Case, *Miami Herald*, 1 November 1968.

Obscenity Trials Delayed, *Miami Herald*, 10 June 1969.

Ramirez, R. (10 December 1971). Law Upset Forbidding Serving Homosexuals, *Miami Herald*.

Other sources relating to Nichols (in chronological order)

These materials are available in the Sears Papers at the Special Collections Library, Duke University.

Adkins, W., and Marshall, J. (April 1966). Kansas City Results, *The Homosexual Citizen*, pp. 8–10.

Adkins, W. (May 1966). A Homosexual Looks at the "Sickness Theory," *The Homosexual Citizen*, p. 17.

Personal correspondence from Jack Nichols to James T. Sears, 22 March 1996 and 10 June 1996.

Materials on harassment and arrests of homosexuals (in chronological order)

Wilkerson, D. (n.d.). *Hope for homosexuals*. Brooklyn, NY: Teen Challenge.

Wickstrom, K. (9 August 1964). The Life of a Homosexual: It's Sad, Not Gay, *Miami Herald*.

Rau, H. (14 October 1965). Claims Bolita, Vice Payoffs Not the Biggest, Miami Confidential, *Miami News*.

Arvidson, M. (12 April 1966). Moral Squad Takes Homo Issue to Parents, *Miami Herald*.

Lawmen Conduct a Dade Study, *Miami Herald*, 12 April 1966.

Baynes, W. (15 February 1967). Grand Jury Begins Homosexual Hunt, *Miami Herald*.

Wass, G. (13 March 1967). Homosexual Cure Unlikely, *Ft. Lauderdale News*.

Teen Marine Awaits Term in Murder, *Miami News*, 15 June 1967.

Patrus, A. (7 November 1971). Police Start Crackdown on Homosexual Bars: Arrest 6, *Miami Herald*.

Glass, I. (8 November 1971). "Gay" Bar Law Here May Get Test in Court, *Miami News*.

Trial for Violating "Gay" Bar Law Continued, *Miami News*, 10 November 1971.

Gay Bar Law Ruled Invalid, *Miami News*, 10 December 1971.

New Visibility of Homosexuality Merely Hints at Hidden World, *Miami Herald*, 30 April 1972.

Elder, R. (22 June 1972). Gay Activists' Suit Attacks Female Impersonation Law, *Miami Herald*.

Gay Activists Win Beach Suit, *Miami News,* 22 June 1972.

Wright, C. (23 June 1972). Impersonation Laws Killed, *Miami Herald*.

Stulberg, R. (23 June 1972). Gay Activists Call Court Ruling on Impersonation "Great Victory," *Miami News*.

Material on social and cultural life of lesbians and gay men during this era (in chronological order)

"John" Like Report of the Johns Committee. (1964). *ONE* 12(6):9–13.

Welch, P. (26 June 1964). Homosexuality in America, *Life* 56(26):61–64, 70–74.

Havemann, E. (26 June 1964). Why? *Life* 56(26):76–80.

There Are No Police at Sea, So 200 Cruise, *Miami Herald*, 9 August 1964.

George A. (1964). Note from Florida: Good News, *Citizen News*.

Gunnison, F. (April 1966). The Agony of the Mask, *The Homosexual Citizen*, pp. 15–18.

No More Mattachine Society of Florida, Inc. *National Homophile Clearing House Newsletter*, April 1967.

Baxter, M. (24 August 1969). The American Minority, *Tropic* Magazine.

Sex Not Everything in "Gay" Relationship, *Miami News*, 27 August 1970.

Wilcox, B. (19 September 1970). Church for Homosexuals Begins, *Miami News*.

Dangaard, C. (5 December 1970). Homosexuals' Church a Theater, *Miami Herald*.

Wilcox, B. (1 February 1971). Homosexual Church Rolls to Double, Founder Predicts, *Miami News*.

King, T. (20 March 1972). Gay Bars Misunderstood, *Miami News*.

General lesbian/gay historiography

D'Emilio, J. (1983). *Sexual politics, sexual communities.* Chicago: University of Chicago Press.

Duberman, M. (1991). *About time: Exploring the gay past.* 2d ed. New York: Meridian.

Duberman, M. (1992). *Stonewall.* New York: Dutton.

Marcus, E. (1992). *Making history: The struggle for gay and lesbian equal rights.* New York: HarperCollins.

Tobin [Lahusen], Kay, and Wicker, R. (1975). *The gay crusaders.* New York: Arno Press.

Interviews

Rose Levinson (pseudonym), Miami, FL, 16 March 1995.

Jack Nichols, Cocoa Beach, FL, 13 January 1995.

About the Book
and Author

As in his highly acclaimed *Growing Up Gay in the South,* James Sears masterfully blends a symphony of Southern voices to chronicle the era from the baby boom to the dawn of gay rights and the Stonewall riot. Sears weaves a rich historical tapestry through the use of personal reminiscences, private letters, subpoenaed testimony and previously unpublished court and legislative documents, and newspaper stories.

Here you'll dance on the 22nd Street Beach of Miami, suffer at the hands of faceless accusers and angry white mobs, descend into the netherworld of hustlers and murderers, learn about corrupt politicians and covert operatives, and experience the transformation from infatuation to love, from man into woman, and from childhood to old age. In the process, the previously hidden history of gay men and lesbians in the South from the end of World War II to the Stonewall riot slowly unfolds to reveal such landmark events as the formation of the first state-chartered gay organization and the first racially mixed marriage between a white transsexual and an African-American in the South. Here too you will learn of more common yet no less courageous activities such as the contributions of homosexuals to the civil rights movement, growing-up experiences from east Texas and the Carolinas to Washington, D.C., and Alabama, and everyday life at the beach or in the bars.

James T. Sears is a professor at the University of South Carolina, where a course he taught on Christian fundamentalism attracted national attention and the ire of Pat Robertson, who dubbed Sears "Satan in the university." Sears resides on the sea islands near Charleston and in cyberspace at http://www.jtsears.com.

Index